SUPER HANDYMAN'S ENCYCLOPEDIA OF

HOME REPAIR HINTS

AL CARRELL

SUPER HANDYMAN'S ENCYCLOPEDIA OF

HOME

●   ●   ●

BETTER, FASTER, CHEAPER, EASIER IDEAS

FOR HOUSE AND WORKSHOP

REPAIR

HINTS

. . .

Prentice-Hall, Inc., *Englewood Cliffs, N.J.*

Super Handyman's Encyclopedia of Home Repair Hints: Better, Faster, Cheaper,
Easier Ideas for House and Workshop
by Al Carrell
Copyright © 1971 by King Features Syndicate, Inc.
All rights reserved. No part of this book may be
reproduced in any form or by any means, except
for the inclusion of brief quotations in a review,
without permission in writing from the publisher.
ISBN 0-13-875922-7
Library of Congress Catalog Card Number: 70-151664
Printed in the United States of America *T*
Prentice-Hall International, Inc., London
Prentice-Hall of Australia, Pty. Ltd., Sydney
Prentice-Hall of Canada, Ltd., Toronto
Prentice-Hall of India Private Ltd., New Delhi
Prentice-Hall of Japan, Inc., Tokyo

10 9 8 7 6

HOW TO USE THIS BOOK

Whether you own your own home or rent an apartment, the fact that you are looking at this book is proof enough that you want to find easier or better ways to handle the hundreds of home handyman challenges that arise: Do you want to avoid spilling paint when you stir it? Replace a broken light bulb without gashing yourself? Make a foolproof, safe lock for your garage door? Spruce up those wall switch-plates? Or just find a use for some old bleach bottles your wife's about to throw out?

Whatever your problem or project, you'll probably find a helpful hint here. Hundreds of handymen throughout the United States and Canada—and often their wives, too—have passed along their clever ideas on how to do, redo, or undo. This book represents the wisdom accumulated from thousands of hours of trial-and-error and many costly mistakes *you* will never have to make. It's also a treasury of sudden insights—bursts of real genius and inventiveness that can spur you on to similar "breakthroughs." Super Handymen are made, not born.

Also, every effort has been made to make using this encyclopedia as easy as ABC ... and that suggested the bright idea of alphabetizing these handy hints! Ideally, you can look under the task you're doing or the item to be used and find help. For example, if you're going to paint, you'll get lots of help in Chapter "P" under *Paint*. But if you don't find just what you're after, there's a super cross-index—at the back of the book—that will come to your rescue. The cross-index shows you there are other painting tips under *Brushes, Spray Cans*, and several other categories.

And if you've got one of your wife's old stockings lying around, look it up in the cross-index—you'll find out how to use it to strain paint. (As a matter of fact, don't throw *anything* out until you're sure there isn't a use for it somewhere in these pages.) If you're safety-conscious, look up *Safety* in the index, and you'll find everything you ought to check—ladders, gas pipes, stairs, and so on.

To get the very most out of this book, you'll probably want to read all the way through, savoring all the gems various handymen have offered. And whether you're the clumsiest all-thumbs type or a master craftsman, you'll come across hints you'll want to put into practice right away.

After you've finished the book, keep it handy to consult each time you tackle a new project. And remember, if you find a good idea in here, there's no reason you can't improve on it. If you do, let me know, so we can make this book even better!

Use it in good health, and may you enjoy all the satisfaction of a job well done

Al Carrell

SUPER HANDYMAN'S ENCYCLOPEDIA OF

HOME REPAIR HINTS

Abrasives • Accident Prevention • Adhesives • Aerosol
Spray Cans • Air Conditioning Units • Allen Wrenches •
Alligator Clips • Anchors for Posts • Anvils • Apartment
Dwellers • Appliances • Automobiles

A
•

ABRASIVES   Abrasives are a must, not only for the craftsman but for the home handyman. All of the materials and substances used for smoothing, sanding, polishing, and grinding—such as sandpaper, rotten-stone, pumice, rouge, quartz, flint, and emery—fall into the broad category of abrasives.

The selection of the right abrasive is probably even more important than the technique of using it. The accompanying table will help. If it doesn't answer your question, your friendly hardware dealer will.

Choosing the proper abrasive for a particular job usually means the difference between satisfactory and perfect. Most home handyman chores will call for the use of what used to be called *sandpapers*. However, the proper name for these now is *coated abrasives*. Here are a few basics:

In selecting the proper coated abrasives, four primary factors should be considered:

1. *The abrasive mineral*—The *type* of rough stuff on the material.

2. *The grade*—The coarseness or fineness of the mineral.

3. *The backing*—Either paper or cloth. Paper comes in A, C, D, or E weights. A (finishing) is the lightest weight for the lightest work. C and D (cabinet) are for heavier work, while E is for the toughest jobs. Cloth comes in X and J weights. The heavier X is used for machine-sanding jobs.

4. *The coating*—The coverage of the mineral on the surface. *Open-coat* means the grains are spaced to cover only a portion of the surface. *Closed-coat* means the abrasive material covers the entire area. Naturally, closed-coat abrasive will provide maximum cutting, but will clog faster. It should be used for hard wood as well as hard metals. Open-coat is best on gummy or soft woods, soft metals, or paint.

MOST WIDELY USED COATED ABRASIVES

ABRASIVE	BACKING	GRADES (readily available)	BROAD USES
FLINT	Paper (A, C, & D weights)	Extra coarse through extra fine	Small hand-sanding wood. Removing paint. Clogs fast but very cheap. Great for gummy surfaces that would clog any paper used.
GARNET	Paper (A, C, & D weights)	Very coarse through very fine	Hand-shaping and sanding of wood. Also for cork and composition board. Cuts better and lasts longer than flint. Don't use in power sander.
ALUMINUM OXIDE	Paper (A, C, & D weights)	Very coarse through very fine	Hand or power sanding or shaping of wood. Also for metals, paint smoothing, or end-grain sanding.
	Cloth (X)	Very coarse through fine	Mostly used for belt sanders.
SILICON CARBIDE	Waterproof paper (A weight)	Very coarse through super fine	To smooth coats on wood, metal, etc. For sanding floors, glass, or plastics. Used wet with water or oil.
EMERY	Cloth (X & J weights)	Very coarse through fine	General light metal polishing. Removing rust and corrosion from metal. Can be used wet or dry.
CROCUS	Cloth (J weight)	Very fine only	Super high-gloss finishing for metals.

There are three popular ways to grade coated abrasives. The *simplified markings* (fine, very fine, etc.) used in the chart on p. 2 give a general description of the grade. *Grit* actually means the number of grains which, when set end-to-end, would equal one inch. The "0" symbols are more or less arbitrary. The coarsest is 4½, and the finest is 10/0 or 0000000000. The table below compares these three methods of grading and gives general uses for different grades.

COMPARATIVE GRADES AND USES

GRIT	"O" SYMBOLS	SIMPLIFIED MARKINGS	USES
600	none	Super	High satinized finishes—
500	none	fine	wet sanding
400	10/0	Extra	High finish on lacquer,
360	none	fine	varnish, or shellac top
320	9/0		coats—wet sanding.
280	8/0	Very fine	Finishing undercoats or
240	7/0		top paint coats—leaves
220	6/0*		no sanding marks—dry sanding.
180	5/0	Fine	Final sanding of bare
150	4/0*		wood—smoothing a previously painted surface.
120	3/0	Medium	General wood sanding—
100	2/0*		plaster smoothing—preliminary smoothing of previously painted surface.
80	1/0		
60	½*	Coarse	Rough sanding of wood—
50	1		paint removal.
40	1½		
36	2	Very	Rust removal on rough
30	2½	coarse	finished metal. Usually
24	3		requires high speed of heavy machine to cut well.
20	3½	Extra	Primarily for heavy-duty
16	4	coarse	industrial uses only.
12	4½		

* Grades normally supplied when marked Very fine, Fine, Medium, or Coarse.

Other Finishing Abrasives—The best known of the are *pumice, rottenstone, rouge,* and *steel wool*. Pumice is a volcanic abrasive powder used for fine finishing. It is generally lubricated with water or oil, and runs from 0000 down to 0. Rottenstone is a finer powder than pumice and is used to give an even higher sheen. Rouge is a powder used mostly in the polishing of metal. Steel wool has a wider range of uses, as shown in this quick reference table:

GRADE	USES
0000 super fine	Primarily used by the home handyman in rubbing down after the final lacquering, shellacking or varnishing.
000 extra fine	Removes paint spots from woods—cleans polished metals such as stainless steel or chrome.
00 fine	When used with linseed oil will satinize or dull a high-luster finish on wood.
0 medium fine	OK for use in brass finishing—removes stains from kitchen and bathroom tiles and from better cookware.
1 medium	Removes rust from cast iron—cleans heavier cookware—cleans glazed tiles—removes shoe and furniture marks from wood floors.
2 medium coarse	Removes scratches from brass—removes paint from ceramic tiles—used to rub down floors between coats.
3 coarse	OK for use to remove paint spots on linoleum—removes paint from furniture for refinishing.

Here are some hints about using abrasives, sent in by readers.

"Usually the home handyman will find it more economical to buy sheets of sandpaper and cut off a piece that's the right size for the job. Chances are the sheet will have the grit number marked in only one place on the sheet. By transferring the grit number to each piece that is cut off, you'll never have to guess what grade you're picking up."

Sanding rounded surfaces presents a bit of a problem. Most times it can be done more easily by making a series of parallel slits in the sheet of sandpaper. For smaller contours, make the slits closer together. The length of the slits is also governed by the size of the object.

Here's a trick for sanding down inside a narrow slit: "Turn a hacksaw blade upside down and wrap the sandpaper around the blade. This gives you a rigid support for the sandpaper, plus a sanding tool that is easy to handle." (For even more tricky sanding blocks, look in Chapter "S" under *Sanding Blocks*.)

Sandpaper will last several times longer if you tape wide strips of masking tape across the back as reinforcement.

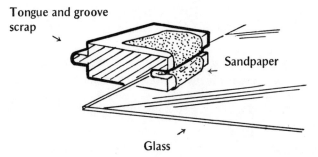

Tongue and groove scrap

Sandpaper

Glass

"After you have cut a sheet of glass, it's often necessary to use an abrasive to smooth off the sharp edges. A small block of hardwood flooring (the kind with grooves in the side) makes an excellent sanding block. Sandpaper fits down into the groove. By running this along the edge of the glass, both edges are sanded at once."

"It's not an easy chore to get a smooth finish when you try to sand rough, porous woods. To attain the kind of finish you want, apply a thin coat of shellac to the wood before sanding. When the shellac is dry, use a fine grade of sandpaper, and the results will be much better."

ACCIDENT PREVENTION   (Some folks would have put this section in the "S" chapter, under *Safety*. I wanted to be sure you learned about the safe way as soon as possible.)

Home and shop accidents can usually be prevented. As you go about your home handyman chores, be ever alert. Don't relax your guard. Think! Here are some accident stoppers from readers.

"We had some steps going out to the garage that were awfully slippery when they were wet. To do away with this hazard, I bought some of those plastic stick-ons designed to go on the bottoms of bath tubs. They are waterproof, so they should wear well outside. The steps are no longer slick, and they really do look pretty."

"If any of your readers have ever walked through the back yard at night and run into the clothesline, they'll want to try this. Dip a sponge in luminous paint and run it over the full length of the line. With the cord visible in the night, there's no longer a hazard."

"Nobody believed me when I showed up with two black eyes and the old story of running into a door. It really did happen when I got up to give the baby his 2:00 A.M. feeding and walked into the edge of a partly open door, using my forehead as a bumper. My wife came up with a solution that will help this not to happen again. She painted the edge of the door with luminous paint. Now if I have my eyes open when I get up, I can see the door."

"I added a safety feature to my ladder that I would like to pass on: I wrapped a piece of burlap on the bottom step, and stapled it on the underside of the step to hold it on. This acts as a shoe scraper, so that there is nothing left on the soles of my shoes that might cause me to slip as I climb on up. It is particularly helpful if there is any dampness to the ground."

"When using a straight ladder against scaffolding, always run a metal pipe strap from a top rung straight in front to the scaffolding and clamp it in place with a C-clamp. With this in place, the strap will not allow the ladder to push away from the scaffold. As a matter of fact, it is a good idea to look for something in front of the ladder to clamp to whenever it is set up. When you are going to be making several trips up and down with paint or tools, this is a good safety margin."

"Power tools need good visibility for safe operation. Dark or unpainted walls won't help, so treat your shop walls to a coat of white or light paint. Besides the safety factor, it will probably look better."

"As you know, a chuck key left on a chuck when a power tool is turned on can be as dangerous as a wild tee shot. I put a built-in memory system on my chuck key so that it cannot be left on the tool. I soldered a small spring onto the key so that it extends over the tip that is inserted into the hole in the chuck. This spring is attached below the gear teeth. The spring should be loose enough to allow you to push the key in place to adjust the chuck. But when you let go, the spring will push against the chuck and pop the key out."

"Statistics show that hand-held tools are responsible for a major number of accidents. There is a very simple way to prevent them. Simply tape the chuck key to the electric cord of the tool, a few inches from the plug end. The tool must then be unplugged before using the key."

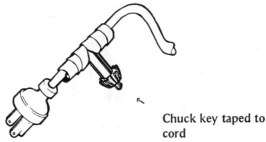

Chuck key taped to cord

"Here is a super safety tip that will take only a few moments. Paint white stripes on all the exposed, moving parts of your power tools. This should include stripes 3″ to 4″ apart on all belts and chains. Also, apply them to saw blades. In this way, when the tool is turned on, the movement will be obvious, and there will be less likelihood of an accident because someone didn't see the machine was in motion."

"It is a good practice to use only a wooden rule around your power tools. If a metal one should get in the way of a saw blade or other moving part, it wouldn't do the tool any good, and it could result in injury."

"As a safety precaution to keep tiny hands from plugging in any of my power tools, I bought a bunch of small padlocks. These are the miniature kind that are for jewelry chests, diaries, and the like. One of these goes through the hole in one of the prongs on the electrical plug for each power tool. This, of course, makes it impossible for the plug to be inserted into an outlet.

"Since all the padlocks are exactly alike, one key fits them all, so that's no problem. I keep it hanging from the shop wall and attached to a large metal washer so it won't get lost."

"I put safety locks on the toggle switches on the various power tools in my shop. The primary reason was to insure that my kids couldn't fool around and turn on a switch. Also, these keep me from accidentally brushing against a switch and turning on a tool."

← Cotter pin thru hole locks cap

Cutaway of film can with toggle switch inside →

"I put all my switches inside those little film cans that 35mm still film comes in. A hole is cut in the bottom of the film can, big enough for the wires to go through but small enough so the switch will hold the can in place when remounted. With the cap screwed on, a hole is drilled through the threads on the can and the top. A nail or cotter pin can then be put through the hole to lock the top on. These are good safety locks that cost nothing and look neat."

Another reader solved the same problem in this way: "I cover the switches with plain old metal U-shaped screen door handles. (Some people call them window bar sash lifts.) These are installed so that the handle runs in the same direction as the switch. It keeps the switch protected from accidental tripping, yet easy to reach with a finger."

'I am not a handyman, but I do have a few power tools. Inevitably, when I did some sort of job with them, I ended up with a few pounds of sawdust in my eyes. Recently, I spied one of the kids' skin-diving masks that had been put away for the winter. This makes a great eye protector."

"My hobby is woodworking, and for the first year of this rewarding pastime it was hard to blow sawdust out of the cracks and crevices without getting some in my eyes. Now, however, I keep a large rubber syringe at my workbench and use it to blow the dust away."

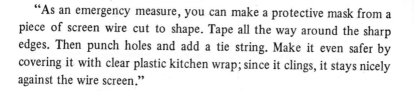

"As an emergency measure, you can make a protective mask from a piece of screen wire cut to shape. Tape all the way around the sharp edges. Then punch holes and add a tie string. Make it even safer by covering it with clear plastic kitchen wrap; since it clings, it stays nicely against the wire screen."

"My shop light is an old adjustable-arm, clamp-on fluorescent drafting table lamp. It is ideal because it can be moved around to almost any area of my workbench. To make it even better, I took a pair of strong spring paper clamps and attached them to the side of the shade away from me, by means of a nut and bolt through the eye. I use these clamps to hold a piece of clear plexiglass, which acts as an invisible shield between me and all of my power tools. It protects me from any chips and bits thrown off by grinding or cutting. It also protects the fluorescent tubes. When I'm not using a power tool, the shield can be removed if it's in the way."

"There are times when you need to use a torch or other heating device on something metal near wooden portions of your house. This raises the danger that you might get the wood hot enough to catch fire. As a safety precaution, take a few moments ahead of time to cover the wood with aluminum foil, which will protect it from overheating. The foil can easily be attached with cellophane tape. Why take chances?"

In case you ever have a fire, here is one reader's precautionary idea: "We added a special hydrant in our utility room and keep an extra-long hose attached to it at all times. The hose is long enough to reach any and every point in our house in case of fire. Even though our fire department is quite efficient, this extra protection would give us a few minutes' head start on a fire, and that can make a whale of a difference.

"Also, we have found several uses for the hose for other chores around the house."

"Here is a safety measure that I hope others will use. All of the bottles in my shop that contain acids and other dangerous substances are made shatterproof with cellophane tape. Wrap the bottles completely with the tape. If they are accidentally dropped, the tape will hold the glass together so that the contents won't run out. The transparent tape allows you to see the level of the contents inside as well as the label on the bottle."

"Almost every workshop ends up with several containers of acid of one sort or another. There is always the danger that a container could be knocked off and cause damage or injury. One way to avoid this is to place the container of acid in a coffee can filled with sand. This not only makes the acid container almost tip-proof but eliminates the possibility of a drip of acid getting on anything it shouldn't. Once you get the container set in the sand, wet the sand down. When it dries, it will form a more or less permanent hole for the container so it can be lifted out and put back in the same place."

"All home handymen know how to keep tools sharp and clean for better performance. After a blade on a sharp knife has been sharpened, however, there is always the risk of taking a layer of skin off while cleaning it. Dip a soft cork into the solvent and use it against the sharp cutting edge. If you are cleaning with a dry cleanser, wet the cork."

"I added a safety feature to my power mower. It consists of a piece of flat metal (6″ x 18″) held onto the back of the mower by two strap hinges. The piece of metal hangs down to approximately ½″ from the ground. The hinges allow the metal shield to swing back when high grass is encountered, and then it drops back into place. This precludes your accidentally getting your foot under the mower, and also deters objects from flying back at you."

ADHESIVES   Much of the fixing-up around the house is done with adhesives. Here's how readers solved some "sticky" problems.

"A few strands of steel wool will give added bite when glueing a joint together. After covering the surface with the adhesive, sprinkle strands of steel wool on and clamp the pieces together. This gives a stronger bond, and there's less likelihood that the joint will slip during the clamping process." (There are clamping tricks galore in the "C" chapter.)

"If you are a messy gluer and get the stuff on your clothes in the process, soak the spots in warm household vinegar. This will take out many glues."

That same warm vinegar was used by one reader to loosen glued joints. "I heated the vinegar to a simmer, and then brushed it on the joints over and over until they loosened."

"When an adhesive in a plastic bottle begins to get low, you can sometimes wait several minutes for the stuff to get down to the spout and come out. I'd rather use this time for something else. So I bored some holes in a shelf in my shop. These are for the glue bottles, and I now store them upside down with the pouring spouts sticking down. (Naturally the spout is closed.) Now the glue is at the spout and ready to come out when I first pick up the bottle."

"For a disposable hand spreader for adhesive or mastic, I take a section of wire window screen and fold it over a couple of times. This makes a spreader that is stiff enough to do the job and still has some flexibility. The holes in the screen also hold lots of glue so that it will spread a long way. Also, the screen is rough enough to leave the glue with a slightly rough finish for a better bond."

"Here is a helpful hint for when you need to spread adhesives over a broad area: Take the flap off a wax-paper dispenser box—one with a metal saw edge for tearing the paper. This will spread the mixture quickly and evenly. The little teeth in the blade allow the adhesive to flow out behind the blade as it is pushed over the surface."

"Tubes of quick-drying adhesives can dry out if you don't keep them capped when not in use. This becomes an aggravation if you have lots of different points to glue. Make yourself a table-top capper by driving an appropriately sized nail through a block of wood. Between glueing operations, put the opening in the tube over the point of the nail, which is always sticking straight up. This seals it up but allows you to use the glue again by just picking up the tube. Then after you have finished all of your glueing jobs, replace the cap."

"When glueing joints together, the clamping pressure will almost always squeeze out some of the glue. This has to be removed unless you want a blob of glue along the edge of each joint. Any way you go about it, the removal process is a pain, and you can end up with a marred finish. However, an ounce of prevention will make it an easy task: Before applying the adhesive, place a strip of cellophane tape along each edge that is to be glued. It will be no problem to lay the tape exactly on the edge. Run your finger back and forth over the tape to

Tiny wire

Dowel

make sure it is stuck down tight against the wood. When the pressure squeezes the glue out, it will be on the tape, and, after it hardens, both tape and glue can be easily peeled away."

"When glueing doweling in place in a hole, a piece of very fine wire can help you get a stronger bond. Wrap the wire around the end of the dowel and on up its full length before applying the glue. Insert dowel and wire in the hole. The wire will allow more glue to stay down in the hole along the tiny space it creates between the dowel and the socket. Clip off the excess wire."

"Roughened glueing surfaces will usually produce a better bond than smooth ones. One of the best tools for roughing up is a 'wiggle nail' (or, if you prefer to use its proper name, a corrugated fastener). Pick out the largest one you have, and it will be big enough to grip and rough enough to scratch. You can even make it into a tool by attaching it to the end of a stick, if you have very much scratching-up to do."

"Here is a 'shot-in-the-arm,' so to speak, for the home handyman who has the problem of getting glue down into a tiny crack. I use one of those disposable hypodermic needles, filled with the glue, to force it in where it should go. The needle is tiny enough to go in most places and sharp enough to be pushed in where it won't fit. If it does leave a tiny hole, this will usually fill up with glue after the needle is removed. This handy glue applicator costs only about 15 cents, so if it gets clogged up after a few uses, it can just be tossed away."

"Did you know that ordinary shellac makes an excellent clear glue? You can use it for glueing wood, metal, glass, leather. In fact, I haven't found anything it doesn't work on. Just wait until it begins to get a little tacky, and put the two pieces together."

Stick with us 'til the "G" chapter for more on glue and glueing.

AEROSOL SPRAY CANS   "Before any of your readers throw away a good partly used can of aerosol spray paint because the nozzle is clogged up, try this: Most of the plastic nozzles slip off the can and, therefore, many are interchangeable. If you don't happen to have another can with a nozzle that fits, buy another of the same brand."

There is also the possibility of soaking the plastic nozzle in a solvent to unclog it—something you sure can't do with it on the can. But a word of caution: There are some that weren't made to come off. If the tip doesn't slip off easily, *don't force it!*

One reader saves all the nozzles of empty spray cans and keeps them in a jar full of solvent. Since so many are interchangeable, he always has an unclogged one on hand.

AIR CONDITIONING UNITS   "A good way to protect the outside part of your air conditioning unit in the wintertime is to tape an old shower curtain down tight over it with masking tape."

ALLEN WRENCHES   "Since Allen screws are often used as set screws, they seem to end up in an out-of-the-way place for those little short Allen wrenches. I adapted a regular screwdriver to give me extra reach for this problem. I drilled a hole in the head of the screwdriver for the small 'L' of the Allen wrench to fit into. Then I slipped a rubber band around the wrench and the screwdriver. Not only do I have the extra reach, but I also have a good amount of turning power from the screwdriver."

Hole drilled in screwdriver tip

ALLIGATOR CLIPS   "If you need an extra alligator clip, a visit to your wife's makeup kit will solve your problem. Borrow her tweezers. Clamp them in place, and before you let go, run a couple of rounds of tape around the tweezers to hold them. They'll work just like an alligator clip."

ANCHORS FOR POSTS   "Here is my idea for an underground anchor for fence posts. I take a face brick (the kind that has holes in it) and attach the guy wire through the center hole. I bury the brick about a foot deep in a hole the proper distance from the post, then I run the guy wire up and attach it to the post. When the dirt sets up around the brick, it becomes a very solid anchor."

Buried brick

ANVILS   For your bench top, here are a couple of anvil ideas to choose from:

"When my wife got a new iron, I pressed the old one into service in my workshop. I removed the bottom plate and drilled a hole at each of the three corners. Mounted flat on my workbench with three countersunk screws, it serves as a built-in anvil—an addition I wouldn't want to do without."

"Since I don't often need an anvil, I have never bought one. However, I have a mini-anvil on my workbench that comes in handy and cost me practically nothing. The anvil is the head of a large railroad spike that I found in a junk yard. It cost me a nickel. I then cut a hole in the top of my workbench the exact size of the shank of the spike when the spike is dropped into the hole. This leaves only the head sticking up, and it comes in handy for all sorts of small bending and forming jobs."

APARTMENT DWELLERS   A reader who is a big-city apartment dweller occasionally has a small project that calls for hammering. He has saved a pair of those thick city phone books to use as a hammering surface. It not only protects his floors from any mars or scratches, but also deadens the sound quite a bit and keeps the neighbors from complaining. If you live in a place where the phone books aren't thick enough to do any good, I bet you have a couple of thick mail order catalogs around.

Here's another trick for the apartment dweller who has to do fix-ups without the benefit of a workshop: "If you need to cut a length of pipe and don't have a pipe vise, get an old magazine. Take a half dozen pages in the center of the magazine and roll these around the pipe as tightly as possible. Then put the magazine down on a chair or flat sawing surface and place your knee on the magazine, up against the hump made by the pipe. You will be amazed at how tightly the magazine will grip the pipe."

"When I need to use a sawhorse, I take a pair of kitchen chairs and put a 2" x 4" in between them, resting on the chair seats. Works fine!"

APPLIANCES   "When we moved into our new home, I created my own 'Homeowner's Manual.' I gathered up all the manufacturers' instruction booklets that came with the appliances, heating system, and other mechanical things in the house, punched holes in them, and put them in a loose-leaf notebook binder. As we've added new appliances and gadgets, the printed material with them has been added. Now when we have a question on anything that goes wrong, we know exactly where to look for the answer." (Also keep the warranty information in your manual.)

"Almost everyone ends up with several of those advertising key chains with plastic ID tags on them. No sense letting them pile up in a catchall drawer. They're ideal to attach to shop equipment, furnaces, and the like as a permanent record of servicing. Each time new things are done, a new card can be slipped in with the vital statistics. The chain makes it a permanent attachment, and the plastic protects the record."

AUTOMOBILES   When it comes to taking care of the family automobile, many people limit their activity to driving the car to the service station or garage. Some will take the next step and occasionally see that it is kept clean. So here are a few ideas that will make that chore easier—also some other helpful hints on taking care of your car.

"Seems as if every vacation area we visited had invested in bumper stickers. Now that our vacation has been over for some time, I decided to remove them. This isn't as easy as it might sound, since heat and time make these things almost a part of the bumper. After trying several methods, I found the best way was to hold a steam iron up next to the sticker. This made both the sticker and the gummy adhesive come off. This way your readers can take off the vacation stickers and make room for the political ones."

Many home handymen who do their own car washing toss away their chamois when it has lost all its softness and no longer performs as it should. Sometimes a chamois can be restored, and since it's not exactly free, this treatment is worth a try. Add one teaspoonful of olive oil to a bucket of warm water and let the chamois skin soak for about 15 minutes. Unless it is too far gone, it will come out soft as new.

"Since I wash my own auto, I've discovered a trick that keeps the metal nozzle on the hose from hurting the car finish, if they should

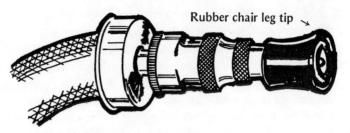

Rubber chair leg tip

accidentally come in contact. I've slipped over the end of the nozzle a rubber chair-leg tip with the end cut out of it. This allows the water to come out, and still allows for the spray to be adjusted.

"A slit length of old garden hose will also protect your car from the nozzle . . . and it can be long enough to cover the entire metal part."

"A baby bottle brush can be used for cleaning parts from engines. Its stiff bristles are excellent for cleaning in threaded parts."

"That garden sprayer that hooks on the end of your water hose is just about the greatest for a quicker car wash, too. Add a couple of ounces of liquid soap to the sprayer jar and fill with water. Then when the hose is turned on, a sudsy spray comes out that cuts the car-bathing time down to practically nothing. After the family buggy is sudsed all over, a quick sponging will remove any stubborn dirt, and then the soap can be hosed off. Be sure to clean the sprayer out really well before you start."

During the rainy season, mud and dirt keep piling up, layer after layer, every time you take the family auto out. You can at least keep it down to one layer at a time with this hint. Before you take the car out of the garage each time, loosen all the dirt by rubbing the car with a soft rag. The rain will then wash it all off, and when you get back in, there will be only the film from that last trip.

"The rubber mats on the floor of our car don't really come clean with a hosing. So when I wash the car, I put the mats into our washing machine. Along with the mats I toss in a few heavy bath towels. As the machine goes to work, the towels do my scrubbing for me. The mats really come out clean."

"By accident, I have discovered a great way to renew the rubber floor mats in a car. The last time I cleaned them, I decided to try to find something that would put a protective coating over the mats. I tried liquid wax shoe polish. It not only puts such a coating on them, it makes the rubber look brand new. They seem to stay new-looking much longer, too."

"Living in an apartment, there was no way to wash my car. So almost every Saturday for eight years, I spent an hour, $2.00, and an extra 15 miles taking my car to the car wash. Then a young couple moved into the apartments, and the husband walked out to the curbside one Saturday with a bucket, and in about ten minutes, he had his car gleaming. Here's his trick that has now saved me a lot of time and money: he uses about a pint of kerosene to a gallon of warm water. He goes over the entire car with this on a sponge. Then he takes a dry cloth and wipes the car dry. It's really amazing."

This mixture even takes off bugs and hard road dirt—another thing, in the rain the water actually beads as if it were on a waxed surface.

"That nylon net that the ladies seem to go out of their way to find uses for can also help the home handyman. I discovered that it is about the best thing going for quick removal of bugs from the grill and windshield of a car. Just wet it and scrub them off."

"Probably the toughest part of an automobile to wash is the grill. My husband solved this problem, and at first I was ready to skin him because of his solution. I walked out to watch him one day as he was washing our car, and found he was using my vegetable brush from the kitchen on the grill. Oh, well, the brush didn't cost much, and it really does whisk the bugs, ants, and road dirt off the grill. So after I got over the shock, I just bought myself another one and let him keep mine."

(I just wonder how many times he had used her brush and sneaked it back into the kitchen before she caught him!)

"The best way I've found to remove bugs from an auto is to use a wet sponge or cloth that's been dipped into baking soda. This seems to cut right through them. It works even better if you wet the car first. The soda won't scratch the finish, either."

"Want your tires to nave that brand-new shine again? Clean them off and then add a coat of clear self-polishing floor wax. The black will shine and glisten with the same glossy look it had when new. The wax will preserve the white sidewalls against the smudges. And the next time you wash your car, the dirt will probably come off with just a blast from the hose. This takes only a few minutes and will save lots of time in the future ... besides providing extra good looks right now!"

"Even after going through the car wash, my white convertible top still had some black marks on it. They didn't bother me, but our son apparently didn't like them. He discovered that they could easily be removed with an art gum eraser. This doesn't leave any eraser marks, either."

(Art gum erasers are available at your school supply store or art store. They also will take many marks off a white vinyl top or dash.)

"When you're on a trip, your auto headlights are usually pretty well covered with road dirt and bugs by the time night falls. This mess is very difficult to clean off while you're out on the road, and the lack of visibility can be a hazard. Each morning before I start out, I cover the headlights with pieces of clear plastic food wrap. This adheres to the glass. When it gets time to turn on the headlights, I pull over to the side of the road and peel off the plastic covers. Then I start my night driving with clean, clear headlights."

As spring comes, it is a good time to give your car a piece of preventive maintenance:

"During the winter, the underside of a car collects salt and other chemicals that have been put down on drives and roads to melt snow. These substances corrode metal. You can wash the underside of your car easily and completely with your lawn soaker. Just lay the soaker out in a rectangular pattern the length and width (inside wheel measurements) of your car. Be sure the holes are aimed up. Hook it to a hose and drive the car over it. Turn it on full blast for five minutes. You will add to your car's life."

And here's some preventive maintenance for chrome:

The chrome on your automobile can make the car look ready for the junk heap if the elements get a foothold and start patches of rust or corrosion. A good way of fighting rust before it begins is to coat the chrome with linseed oil. Clean the surface well and rub the linseed oil on with a soft rag. A light coat is all that is needed. This will even offer protection against air-borne salt if you live on or visit the beach.

About the first place corrosion attacks chrome is along and behind the chrome strips that run the length of the auto. These can collect water, as well as other things that attack the finish. A good way to prevent this is to take liquid wax and pour it along the length of the strip. This will fill in the crevice and keep foreign material out. You may wish to do this every six months or so, if need be.

The radio aerial on your auto can become corroded and not look as well or move up and down as easily as it should. As a measure of preventive maintenance, one home handyman takes a scrap of wax paper and runs it up and down the antenna every few months. This keeps it from corroding, but doesn't build up any residue that might clog. Simple, but a super helper!

If your convertible top has developed a few holes, save yourself a bunch. One smart reader used "those iron-on patches used for mending jeans. My wife held a padded board underneath as I applied the hot iron to press the patches in place. They are made to go through vigorous washings, so the weather doesn't bother them at all. They come in several colors and would probably match most top colors. Mine don't show very much at all . . . and they sure cost a lot less than a new top!"

"The vinyl top on our car began to look like a prune from the wrinkles it was developing. A neighbor suggested that I try this before spending any money on it. He had me hold a heat lamp directly over the wrinkled spots. After a few minutes of heat, the wrinkles could be rubbed away by hand. I started at the center and worked toward the edges, and in a half hour I had a super-smooth top again. This also worked on my vinyl-covered dash."

"We developed a number of unsightly scratches on the finish of our family car. Rather than getting touch-up paint, which always seems to show almost as much as the scratches, I took a wax crayon that matched the car finish. I rubbed the crayon over the scratches and completely covered them. These were then buffed with a cloth. Not only are the scratches gone, but the bare metal is protected from rust by the wax in the crayon."

"There seems to be an endless supply of household items that can be added to the water in your automobile windshield washer unit. Here is one that works well in fighting road film. Add a teaspoonful of cream of tartar to water. If the unit cannot be shaken to mix, premix the powder in water and pour it in along with plain water. It really works."

"Add a teaspoon of liquid detergent to ordinary tap water in the automatic windshield washer container. This mixture cuts any kind of road dirt and costs much less than prepared solutions."

"You can temporarily revive an auto windshield wiper blade that has hardened to the point that it no longer does its job. Rough up the edges of the wiper blade with sandpaper. This will give the rubber enough traction so it no longer will skim over the windshield without removing the water. However, this is strictly a stopgap repair until you can get new blades. If there is no sandpaper handy, try the striker plate from a match book."

"When a windshield wiper blade can no longer do its intended job, it can still come in handy. I keep an old one under the seat of my car to remove the dew that would otherwise prevent my being able to see when I leave for work in the mornings. A few quick sweeps on the rear and side windows, and I'm ready to roll. It's quicker than wiping with a rag."

The fog that forms on the inside of your car windows can easily be wiped off with a rag or almost anything. However, it usually results in a smeared window that has bad visibility. So this is another use for an old wiper blade:

"If you ever have to replace a windshield washer hose on your car, here is a good trick. Make the replacement hose about 6″ longer than the old one. Since these hoses always wear out at the ends, the next time one wears out, all you need to do is trim off the frayed end and put the hose back. The extra 6″ will give you a lot of extra use to the middle part . . . and save time, too."

"While most cars have windshield washers for the front, those side and back windows can become a hazard when they get too much road film on them. If you are vacationing by car, here is a handy way to fight poor visibility out on the road. Save an empty plastic bottle that squirts a stream when squeezed. Fill it with water before you leave on your trip. A few blasts of water on the windows will allow you to clean them out on the road. Wipe off the window with crumpled newspaper. Remember to refill the bottle at the next service station."

"I picked up two scraps of heavy angle iron and keep these in the trunk of my car. When I have to put the car up on a jack, I wedge these

on each side of the tire at the other end of the car. They prevent the car from moving at all, which could cause it to come off the jack. I also use them whenever I park on a steep incline."

"Not long ago, I had a flat tire out on the road and found one of the lugs impossible to remove. Since I had no penetrating oil in the car, it seemed like a bad problem. However, I solved it with my jack. I put the jack in place under the lug wrench and used my foot to jack it up. The steady, sure pressure applied by the jack broke the tough nut loose, and I was able to change the tire."

If you have a cranky lug, and you are in your garage, heat up your soldering iron and put it against the lug. The heat will expand it, and it should break loose. Get the wrench on it quickly, however, before the heat transfers to the bolt and it expands too. If you have a propane torch, a quick blast from it will do the trick.

"Here's a quick way to break a tire from the rim when you have a flat. Place the tire under the bumper of the car. Put the jack on top of the tire and as near the rim as possible. Raise the lift on the jack up against the bumper and keep pumping the jack handle as if you were raising the auto. The base of the jack will push down against the tire, and very shortly the tire will break from the rim."

"Another way to get a flat tire to pop loose from the rim when it is stuck is to pour warm water into the trough made by the rim and the tire. After three to five minutes, try again, and this time the tire will come loose."

"Keep an old nylon stocking in the trunk of your car. Run it around inside the tire, and you will immediately snag the nail or tack that caused the flat. This will keep you from snagging a finger while trying to find the nail. After all, you know how easily your wife's hose gets snagged."

"The next time your readers have hub caps off their cars, tell the n they can pave the way for easier removal of hub caps in the future. A light coat of petroleum jelly on the flanges that fit the hub cap to the wheel will do wonders. It doesn't affect the holding power—it just makes the caps come off easier."

One reader suffered a flat tire, only to find his jack so rusted it wouldn't work properly. "Since I didn't have an oil can, all would have been lost if I hadn't thought of this. I took the dipstick from its place in the engine and let the oil on it drip down onto the jack. After doing this a few times, I got the jack working. It didn't take enough oil from the car to bother it. It occurs to me that this might come in handy in other situations when just a few drops of lubricant are needed out on the road."

Slit hose section on 1″ x 4″ scrap

"After changing a tire, it usually takes as long to get the hub cap back on as it did for all the rest of the chore, unless you have one of those rubber mallets such as garage men use. Anything else you have around to tap it will probably dent the hub cap. However, I made a tool that makes this problem an easy one and won't mar the hub cap. I took a 1″ x 4″ scrap about 8″ long and slipped a slit section of garden hose over one end. When the hub cap is set in place, this block is placed against it, and the other end can be hit with a regular hammer. This sure gets the job done without any dents."

"Rotation of tires is a recommended practice. However, I wonder how many men think to check the air pressure in the tires after rotation. Many cars are supposed to carry different pressure in the front and rear. So if you don't check the pressure, you may be creating a hazard for yourself and the tires."

There are almost as many tire rotation sequences as there are makes of cars. You should follow the method shown in the owner's manual. If you don't have the manual, check your service station operator. He will have a chart for most cars. Be sure you start with the spare, or you'll end up needing two jacks.

"Frankly, I've never figured out why some auto lug wrenches have four different sizes. The only one I ever use is the one that removes the lugs when I change a tire . . . which is why I thought of a handy hint. I painted the one that fits the tire lugs, so that I no longer have to try two or three before I get the right one. The last time I had to change a tire was in zero weather, and I was really glad I didn't have to waste time looking for the right one."

"Maybe one reason our foreign economy car was so economical was that it didn't have a trunk light. I created one by merely drilling holes in the trunk side of the housings for the tail lights. These allow enough light to come in from the tail light bulbs and from both sides."

"Probably the worst possible task that a man has to face is installing tire chains on a cold morning after a sudden snow. When you lay the chains down and try to drive over them, they usually get moved by the car—or the tire holds them down tight, and they won't go on. You can solve this by raising the tire on a jack . . . or with a jig I built to help. The jig is made of a board about a foot long. The width of the board should be just a little less than the width of your chains. Lay the chain down on the board and mark the positions of the cross-chain pieces on the board. Now add $1'' \times 1''$ strips of wood across the board as cleats in between these marks. These can be nailed or screwed in place. To install the chains, place them back on the board with the cross pieces between the cleats. Back your car up on the cleated board, and the chains will be easy to install without a jack or lift."

"Everybody who carries tire chains in the car trunk knows that they rattle around and often scratch up things in the trunk. Sections of an old inner tube about 2' long will solve this. Put the chains in and tie each end with string. Each chain should have an individual inner tube section. The rubber case will stop the rattle and prevent any scratches."

"This is probably going to sound ridiculous, but I use an old worn-out purse my wife was going to throw away as a tool kit for the hand tools I carry in the trunk of my car. It holds them all together and keeps them from rattling. When I need to repair something, I just get my purse out of the trunk, and all the tools are right there." (If any of your friends say anything about this, why not hit 'em with your purse?)

"I like to keep a few tools in my car for minor repairs that might need to be made while out on the road. To keep all my tools together and at the same time eliminate all rattles, I made a tool pouch from an old inner tube. Slit a section of the tube and lay it out flat. Then lay

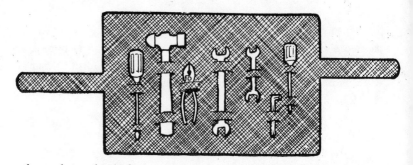

the tools on this before cutting, so you make sure that there's enough
room for all the tools. Then cut out a rectangle of the necessary size,
leaving strips on each side to be used as ties. Then make slits in the
pouch, for the tools to slip into. When they are all in place, the pouch
can be folded up and tied in a neat bundle. No rattle and no loose
tools."

"Auto trunks usually end up with an assortment of dirty tools that
are in the way when you need to put in luggage or something else that
you want to stay clean. I have devised a simple divider for my trunk
that keeps all the tools and messy stuff over on one side (where the
spare is) and leaves the rest of the trunk free of dirt and grime. My
divider is just a piece of hardboard cut to fit and attached to the trunk
floor with angle braces. However, many other things could have been
used."

"I discovered a space behind the grill on my car that is big enough to
accommodate a small tool box, and so I bolted one in place there.
Many cars will have room for this addition, but if you publish this idea,
be sure to warn your readers not to cover up any part of the radiator,
since it must get air through the grill. If you can't find a small tool box,
try a sporting goods store for a small tackle box."

And be sure you wrap these tools so you haven't added a new rattle
to the family car!

"There are many minor repairs and adjustments to your car that you
can take care of out on the road with just a few tools. Therefore, I keep
some tools in my trunk. To keep them from rattling, I shove them
down inside an old work glove. The other glove goes down over the top
of the first, and a rubber band holds the packet together. This way I
also have gloves to keep auto grease off my hands."

"In the glove compartment of my car, I keep a couple of plastic bags
and a couple of rubber bands. When I am out and have to get under the

hood for some sort of repair, I pull the plastic bags up over my arms and hold them in place with the rubber bands. They keep both hands and sleeves clean and allow enough freedom of movement of hands and fingers for performing most tasks."

And speaking of glove compartments, should yours develop the "dropsies," you can expect it to plop open every time you hit a bump. One reader solved the problem without fixing the broken latch. He suggests simply putting a magnet against the metal part inside. When the door to the glove compartment is closed, the magnet holds it in place. However, it is not so strong a magnet that the door won't come open when pulled on. Most cars have metal parts both on the door and inside, so this trick will work.

And from a lady reader: "My husband keeps an old window shade in the trunk of our car. Whenever we have a flat or other car trouble, he merely unrolls it on the ground, and he stays much cleaner while he takes care of the trouble."

"Every driver should have some sort of emergency flares in the car in case of trouble on the road. Mine cost nothing and work quite well. They are just wax milk cartons with a piece of wadded newspaper stuffed inside. The paper makes it easier to light the cartons. When lit, they burn for almost ten minutes and give off an adequate warning light that can be seen from a good distance. I keep several stored in the trunk of my car."

And . . . a few stones in the bottom of each will insure that they don't blow away.

"Many motorists carry a few containers of sand in the trunk of the car in case extra traction is needed in ice or mud. This same container of sand can become an emergency flare by merely siphoning out some gasoline and saturating the sand. When lit, it will burn long and clean. Be sure to put your flare well away from the car and make sure you don't have any gasoline on your hands when lighting it."

"You are always talking about things you should keep in your car in case of an emergency. One thing I recommend is that every motorist keep a roll of reflective tape in the car. This can be a lifesaver in a nighttime emergency. It can quickly be put across the car to warn oncoming traffic. It can be stripped across an obstruction in the road as a warning. It can also be put across your back in case you have to strike out walking for help. It only costs a little to have this extra help on hand in the car."

"I liked the idea someone sent in about putting reflector tape on a gasoline can in case of car trouble at night. Since many people don't carry a gasoline can in the car, they may like my idea. I taped reflective tape on the inside of two of my hub caps. I always have them with me, and they are easy to remove from the wheels. They can then be propped up where they can be spotted by oncoming cars. By having two of them, I can put one in front and one in back of the car."

Another reader painted the insides of hub caps with reflective paint.

Still another reader "put a two-pound coffee can in my trunk after putting strips of reflector tape around it. The can acts as a small tool chest for enough hand tools to take care of most minor repairs. I stuff an old rag into the can to keep the tools from rattling around. This also serves as a cleaning rag for hands and tools after the job is done."

"Here's another way to insure being seen by oncoming motorists, should you have to pull to the side of the road at night. Take reflector tape and apply liberally to surfaces under your hood and trunk lid. There are a number of places on each that face out when these are opened. Usually, car trouble means one or both will be open."

Reflector tape strips

"Put reflector tape strips on the inside face of the door on the driver's side. When the door is opened, the strips are facing the rear of the car, and, therefore, in the path of the headlights of any car that might be coming up from behind. The reflective red tape would alert this driver to the fact that the door was open and allow him to leave plenty of room. Usually when this door is open, someone is getting out of the car, and this could be dangerous at night. It could also save the door, even if no person were there. It is quite easy to do this and well worth the effort."

"If you are like most men, the jumper cables in the trunk of your car usually take a puzzle expert to untangle for each use. Since they are always used parallel to each other, why not tape them together at three or four points? You will be surprised at how much less tangled they will be, next time you use them."

"Do not give up on a car battery that has developed a crack or hole. You may be able to save the battery by mending it with common aquarium cement that can be found at the pet store. It is very inexpensive."

"I have found a method to retard the acid corrosion build-up on the battery posts of my car. I cut out some felt washers from an old hat to fit over the posts. I soaked them with machine oil before attaching the cables again. Every six weeks or so, I again see that these felt washers are well oiled. The result is great ... almost two years without any corrosion."

"I have affixed washers around the battery posts on my auto battery to keep acid build-up from reaching the cables. I cut out the pair of washers from the plastic lids of coffee cans. I made them as large as possible without their getting in the way of the refill caps. This really has helped so far."

A light coat of petroleum jelly both on posts and on cable attachments will also retard corrosion.

"Maybe this is old hat, but I had never heard of it. Recently, there was so much green acid build-up on my auto battery terminal that my car would no longer start. My neighbor cleaned it off with a solution of baking soda and water and a wire brush. He said if I would put a few drops of this on the battery posts every few weeks, I would never be bothered with acid build-up again. So far—and it has been several months—it has worked."

You should make a practice of checking regularly to be sure that the water in your auto battery is at the proper level. If your garage isn't well lighted, you'll find it easier to see where the water line is by looking at it in a hand mirror instead of straight down. This will make it a snap to see at a glance. Try it!

"When someone has car trouble and only needs a push to get started, it really seems a shame not to help. However, there are just too many times when the pushing car can mess up his bumper in doing this good deed. I made me a pair of pusher cushions, and now I can be a 'Good Samaritan' without fear of damage to my car. They are made from sections of an old tire, long enough to completely cover my two front bumper guards. They have ropes on the back so that they hang over the bumper guards. When not in use, they take up very little room in the trunk."

"A tight connection on an automobile hose is certainly desirable. However, if you are a do-it-yourself mechanic trying to get that hose in place, you can often lose your cool before you get the job done. One way to make the hose go on a lot easier is to coat the inside of the lip with a jelly-like soap mixture. Shave a few slivers off a bar of soap and add just enough water to end up with a mixture about the thickness of heavy cream. After the connection is made (without blowing your stack) the soap will dry up and not harm the hose at all."

"The oil from the dip stick in your car can usually find its way onto the many rubber hoses under the hood if you are not careful. This can cause the hose to deteriorate. Since some of the guys at service stations are not as careful as I am, I have wrapped the hoses with aluminum foil for protection. The foil is taped in place with friction tape, and I don't worry about oil or any foreign agent getting on the hoses."

"When a hose on your car wears out, it is usually because it has been rubbing against something. Don't throw the old hose away. Instead, slit it and fit it over the replacement hose at the wear points. This will allow the new one to last many times longer."

"Although I do quite a bit of work on our car, I don't have a creeper to slide under the car. However, the only thing that bothered me was my head resting on the hard concrete floor. So I fixed me a padded cap that took care of that headache. I went to the paint store and got a free paint cap in the largest size they had. Then I took a scrap of foam rubber and glued it into the back and sides of the cap. With this on, my head rests on a pillow of foam. I may look like a fathead, but I'm comfortable."

"The tool boxes used by many auto mechanics are on wheels so they can be rolled under cars for easier access. Since I've learned to do my own mechanical work, I've made my own mobile tool box. It fits nicely on our children's discarded skate board and rolls with me under the car."

"If you're a car tinkerer, here's a way to doctor up your garage floor to give you much greater visibility for the times when you have to slide under the car for work. Take a few moments to paint your garage floor with a white or very light color. You'll be pleasantly surprised at how much light will be reflected up where you need it."

"I bought my own mechanic's creeper, but I added something that makes it a lot more useful. I installed a section of guttering along one side of it. This acts as a tool holder so that when I roll under the car I can carry with me all of the tools I might need. It also prevents my leaving a tool under the car to have to slide back for."

The underside of your auto usually has a rather large collection of dirt particles waiting to drop into your eye the next time you crawl under the car for repairs. Foil these blinders by wearing a pair of shop goggles or a swim mask on your next trip under the car. Protect those eyes so you can keep on referring to this book!

"If you have to do any work under your car while a wheel is off and the car is on a jack, take the spare tire and lay it down flat under the wheel drum. If the car did happen to fall off the jack, the spare under the wheel will keep you from getting crushed. (Best of all, though, figure out how *not* to have to get under your car while it is jacked up.)"

Attention all auto tinkerers! "Here's a trick to protect your carburetor from getting any foreign particles in it when you're working with the air cleaner off. Take a piece of screen wire and lay it over the opening—a simple way to prevent a carburetor cleaning later on."

While we're under the hood, listen to what a professional auto mechanic has to say: "When working under the hood of a car, I always attach a gadget I made to hold small parts so they don't drop down under the car. It's a flat tuna can on which I glued a couple of bar magnets. The magnets attach to almost anything under the hood, so I can position the can close to my work. One of my customers suggested it was a good idea to send to you."

One day I was in a service station and noticed an orange-and-black-striped affair under the hood of a car that was being serviced. On closer examination, it turned out that the radiator cap had been painted this way. I had to ask the owner about this, and it turned out he had done this with a good reason in mind. Not too long ago, the radiator cap had been left off after servicing, and naturally he lost enough water to damage the engine. With the cap painted in bright stripes, he figured that no one would ever overlook it again. He's bound to be right.

"I have a service station and saw a gadget on a car the other day that I think is worthy of passing along.

"On many cars, even I have trouble getting the oil dipstick back into that remote hole. This customer came in with a guide added to his car that would make it easy for even the clumsiest of us to get the dipstick back in place on the first try. He had added a small plastic funnel to the opening. He said it was one he got at the variety store. He got one a shade larger than the opening, and since it had to be forced a bit, it held itself on tight. I wish all my customers would install such a gadget."

If you're working under the dash, you'll want a door open. One reader suggested, however, that "This meant the courtesy light would be 'on for no good reason. A strip of masking tape wrapped from outside the car across the door switch and on inside the car held the button down and the light off. When the job was done, I peeled off the tape, and my battery was not needlessly drained."

"Not long ago, I ran out of gas out in the country. Another car finally came by and offered help. Neither of us had a hose to use for siphoning. Finally, I looked under the hood and removed the hose from my windshield wiper unit and used this. It had clamps on either end, so it came off easily and was put back securely when the siphoning was through."

This will work if you can find a hose under the hood that has clamps. Otherwise, you may not be able to get the hose back on.

"After running out of gas on the freeway because I'd forgotten to fill the tank, I devised a memory jogger for just that purpose. I took an ordinary spring-type clothespin and painted it bright red. Then I printed the word *gas* on it. When I notice the gas gauge getting close to the 'empty' mark, I clip the clothespin on my gearshift. This reminder stays there until I fill up."

And if there's something else you need to remember, the clothespin will hold a note to remind you.

"Okay, so it wasn't too bright for me to strike out on a trip with a leaky radiator. However, I didn't know until the heat got way up, and that happened when I was out in the middle of nowhere. I didn't have a bucket, so I tried to think of some bright way to get water from a nearby stream to the car. I found that in a pinch a hub cap can be a pretty good water carrier."

Another good water carrier is the plastic bag on your windshield washer unit. These bags usually come off, and they hold quite a bit of liquid.

Finally, here's a kooky-sounding idea a youngster wrote me about: "I have to tell you about the weird way our Dad got us back to civilization after we had a water hose break out on the road. He had my sister and me chew up all the gum we had. He took this and smeared it over the place where the hole was, and tied his handkerchief tightly around the whole mess. We then filled up the radiator again, and it wasn't leaking. The cap was not put back on tight, as he said there would be too much pressure on our chewing gum patch. We limped back into a service station for a more conventional repair job. We thought it was a *super* idea."

Ball-Point Pens • Barbells • Batteries (Dry Cell) • Beds
• Beveling • Bikes • Birds • Blind Holes • Boating •
Bricks and Bricklaying • Broken Glass • Brooms •
Brushes—Strikers, Holders, Hangers, and Tricks • Buckets
• Building

B.

BALL-POINT PENS "There always seems to be an abundance of ball-point pens around that won't write. I finally came up with a use for the barrels of the plastic ones. They can be cut into one-inch sections and used as insulated connectors for wiring jobs. Just twist the wires together, insert in the tube, and crimp with pliers."

"I found a good shop use for 'useless' plastic ball-point pens. I magnetized the metal writing tip and use it to hold small screws, ball bearings, and other small metal objects to be put in tight places. It's also handy for retrieving such items. When you're ready for the magnet to let go, just retract the point, and the object falls off."

"Empty ball-point pen refills become small metal tubes when you clip off the point. This tubing came in real handy not long ago when the small hose on my windshield washer unit started leaking. I cut out the defective section of the hose and inserted a section of the tubing. The hose was then clamped to the tubing with two pieces of fine wire."

"Ball-point pens with plastic barrels can be used to make small washers and spacers. Just saw the empty barrel in sections of the desired thickness."

"Remove the empty ink cartridge of an old ball-point pen and use the barrel as a pill carrier. I find it easy to carry in my inside coat pocket along with my pen, and also easy to remember, since I transfer it each day when I change suits."

Instead of looking for things to do with old ball-point pens, you may want to try these methods for getting them to write again. "Tie a 2' piece of string around the non-writing end. With the point out, swing the pen around in a circle. Do this at a fast clip for a minute or two, and the centrifugal force will get all the ink left down into the point. Most pens will have new life." (Even if they don't, it's good exercise.)

"Another ball-point rejuvenating stunt is to hold a lighted match at the point. The heat does the trick." (Be sure you don't melt the plastic barrel.)

BARBELLS   "I decided to do something about my middle age spread. However, when I priced barbells, I decided to improvise. I made my own from a piece of scrap pipe and some concrete mix I had left over from a project. I filled up a two-pound coffee can with the concrete mixture and put the pipe straight down into the can. When the concrete had hardened, I did the same thing on the other end of the pipe. I also made a pair of small dumbbells with smaller cans on smaller pipe sections. As I get stronger, I plan to remake these with larger containers for more weight."

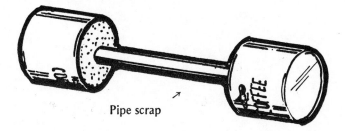

Pipe scrap

BATTERIES (DRY CELL)   "Flashlight batteries being stored can discharge each time they come in contact with metal. This can be prevented by placing a strip of masking tape over the metal center post. Also, don't store them where they will get very hot."

"You know how the terminals on flashlight batteries tend to corrode after a while? This can be stopped with a very light coat of machine oil. Just squirt out a drop on your finger and rub it on the terminals before you put them in the flashlight. It has to be a really light coat, though." (Petroleum jelly helps, too.)

"The batteries in our flashlight went out. We had some spares, but they were the wrong size, as they were intended for a child's toy and were too small around. But I found that if they were wrapped in a layer of cardboard they stayed in place in the flashlight, and it worked fine."

(Batteries from your camera that are too weak to set off a flashbulb will often still be strong enough for a flashlight. They usually need to be wrapped this way to fit.)

"You can often squeeze a few extra hours out of a flashlight battery by just punching about a half dozen holes in the side of the battery with a hammer and nail. The holes need be deep enough only to penetrate the battery shell. Then drop the battery in a pan of hot water and leave for about five minutes. Wipe off the battery, and in most cases the battery will have life again. It will be short-lived, but this will surely help in an emergency."

Here's a tip from a salesman for a battery manufacturing firm. The next time there's a sale on dry cell batteries, don't be afraid to stock up, as they can be kept almost indefinitely by storing them in the freezer. Wrap them in self-adhering plastic wrap or aluminum foil to keep moisture out. If you use foil, tape the terminals. When you're ready to use the batteries, take out and leave them at room temperature for at least a half hour before you unwrap and use. Just make sure your wife doesn't mistake them for a frozen TV snack!

BEDS   "About once a week, a bed slat in our twin boys' bed would fall out. I solved this pesky problem by putting a wide rubber band on the end of each slat, which prevents them from slipping."

"Squeaky bed springs are a real stumper—oiling might stop the noise, but would ruin the mattress with oil stains. The solution is to coat them with spray wax. This stops the noise, but it won't come off on the mattress."

BEVELING   "If you have to cut a beveled edge with a handsaw, here's a tip that'll help make it a lot more accurate. Draw the desired angle on the work, and then with a straightedge extend the line up and position a 2″ x 4″ on the work so the top of the 2″ x 4″ is touching the

straightedge. Clamp the 2″ x 4″ to the work, and it'll act as a fence for your saw and keep the blade cutting at the desired angle."

BIKES   "Let me tell you about the bicycle rack I made from an old metal bedstead that has upright end pieces every 6″ or so. By removing the casters and setting the legs in cement, we had a rack that was as good as the ones in the schoolyard. With the front wheel stuck between the uprights, the children can also lock the bikes to the rack at night."

BIRDS   This may be a super hint or a super hoax. A neighbor has a toy rubber snake coiled around the uppermost branch of a young apple tree. I'd always thought his kids had just put it there, and one day I asked about it. He claims that it keeps birds from eating the apples. I thought he was putting me on, but I watched for several weeks and never saw a bird come near that tree. I asked around, and actually found a nursery man who said he had heard of this, but couldn't tell me why it worked. So with tongue in cheek, I made mention of it in my column. Scores of people wrote in claiming it had worked for them. A rancher says he coils bits of hose up along the rafters in the barns to keep birds out. One reader even claimed he cut out a color picture of a snake and stapled it up in a niche that had attracted a bird family each year, and this kept them out.

If you don't believe it'll work, maybe this one appeals to you. "There is a simple way to keep birds away from fruit trees. Stick a few feathers into a potato and hang this from a branch in the tree. Any breeze will cause the feathers to spin around, and this really does keep the birds away."

Or, if you want 'em back again . .

"An old hollow log can be made into a unique birdhouse. Cut a 10″ to 12″ section from the hollow log. Cut the top at about a 25-degree angle and make a roof from a piece of cedar shingle cut to fit. Another piece of shingle serves as the base. Tiny holes should be drilled in the

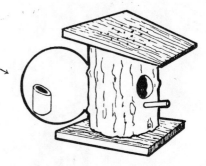

Log cut at angle

roof and floor for ventilation. Bore a hole as the front door, sized to fit the desired bird occupant. Add a perch under the front door, made from a section of doweling, and hang the house in a tree.''

(Not only will you be helping our feathered friends, you'll be protecting your trees and plants from insects, as some birds eat as many as two thousand insects a day.)

BLIND HOLES   "Blind holes that you've drilled or tapped will usually have filings and shavings at the bottom. One way to clean them out is with an old baby-bottle brush. Cut the loop or handle off the brush, leaving only a few inches of the wire shaft above the bristles. Chuck this shaft in your power drill and insert the brush into the hole. This will do the job!''

BOATING   "If you've ever lost the key to your boat while on a fishing trip and had to try to fish it out of 30 feet of water, you'll appreciate my floating key-holder. I took an ordinary wooden slip-over

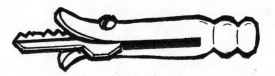

Cork

Screw
eye

clothespin and drilled a hole through both prongs about ½'' from the end. The key goes in between the prongs and a small bolt goes through the holes in the pin and the hole in the key. A nut is put on to keep the bolt in place. The clothespin will keep the key afloat if it's accidentally dropped in the water.''

"I use a cork and an eye screw for my floating key-holder. Insert the eye screw into the cork and put your key chain on the eye screw. If dropped in the water, the cork'll keep your keys afloat. Test it out in your bathtub to be sure that the keys aren't too heavy.''

36   BIRDS

"An empty plastic bleach bottle with the cap on will serve you boatmen as a marker buoy. Just tie a line on the buoy and add a weight that'll reach the bottom of the lake. Or tie the bottle onto an underwater tree to warn boats."

"A corkscrew dog tether makes a great bank anchor when there's nothing along the shore to tie up your boat to. It's a good, sure anchor and easy to remove when you head back out."

"Our small fishing boat always takes on a little water as we scoot across the lake. Most of the water can be bailed out, but there's enough left to make the boat and all our gear messy. I keep a large plastic kitchen sponge in the boat and can get every drop out with this."

"Some people say fish can't hear, but I've never caught a fish when there was much noise around. One of the noisiest sounds on the lake is a squeaking, groaning oarlock. This can easily be silenced by applying a coat of petroleum jelly. After this treatment, you can sneak up on the fish—whether they can hear or not."

"Our small fishing boat is hardly a yacht, but I did give it a touch of luxury by adding beverage holders. They're those inexpensive toothbrush holders that have a place in the middle for a glass. They were easily screwed to the boat at handy places, and this touch of class cost only a few cents. Now, if I'm enjoying a cool one and the fish start biting, I have a place to park my drink."

Tape →

"My boat is kept safe from thieves by a lock and chain. However, I've lost a couple of locks because they got knocked off the chain link while open. I've put a stop to this now by taping the hasp of the lock around the end length of the chain. This keeps the lock firmly attached to the chain, but doesn't interfere with it as a lock."

"Here's a tip for boat owners who keep their rig on a trailer. You can deter thieves from nabbing your trailer by drilling a hole through the part of the trailer hitch that receives the ball. Then put a lock through the holes, and it'll be impossible for a thief to hitch up your rig and flee the scene. When the lock is removed, the holes in no way affect your hitching up."

"We leave our boat tied up at our dock and found that we had been boarded by rats from time to time who were crawling out along the

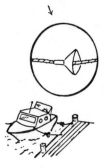
Funnel on rope

ropes. We put a stop to this by putting a large funnel on each rope. The large open end of the funnel faces the dock, and this has stopped them cold." (Make sure the funnels are far enough away from the dock so the rodents can't jump over them.)

"An outboard boat motor should be tested in the water, but most of us don't have a lake in our workshops. I made a great test tank out of a discarded 55-gallon oil drum. I flattened one section of the drum so I could bolt a block of wood to the inside of this section. This gave me a base on which to fasten the motor. The drum should be filled about ¾ full with the motor in the tank. A section of plastic from a cleaner's suit bag is stretched over the opposite side of the top of the drum to act as a splatter shield. A string around the drum will hold the shield in place."

"Lots of times, the repairs we have to make on our mechanical apparatus are due to the abuse we've handed out to it. After having several things go wrong with my outboard motor, I decided it was getting too much punishment from the ride back and forth to the lake. Since I rigged up a cradle for it, I've had no more problems. The cradle is a partially-filled inner tube which is laid in the trunk. The motor rests on this, and now it doesn't get all the bouncing around it used to. The inner tube also acts as a float for the kids, so it's a good thing to have at the lake as well."

BRICKS AND BRICKLAYING   "A mason's line is an absolute necessity for laying a straight course of bricks. However, on a very long wall the line tends to sag in the middle. The sag can be stopped with a

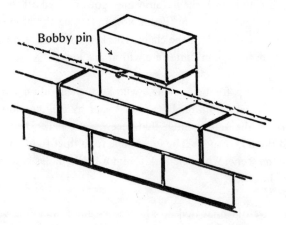
Bobby pin

bobbie pin! Slip this little helper over the line, and then stack a pair of bricks in the middle of the course. Stick the bobbie pin between the two bricks with the eye out, and it will hold the string level. If need be, several bobbie pins can be used in this way. When not in use, the pins can stay on the line."

"When laying bricks or concrete blocks, the best spacers I've found are little glass marbles. They're cheap, and they keep the bricks straight and level without the use of a string or level. They also insure a uniform layer between rows of bricks. After spreading the mortar, push a marble into the mixture near where each corner of the brick will be. Push the brick down against the marbles. Do this about every fourth or fifth brick. When laying concrete blocks, use marbles under each block. These spacers are left in the mortar, and when dry they in no way affect the strength."

"For spacers between rows of bricks, I took lengths of metal tubing and cut them up into bits about 3″ long. These bits were then bent into 'L' shapes. The spacers were covered over with mortar. The brick that was placed on top was pushed down against the spacers, thus forcing the extra mortar out."

When you replace a single brick or two in an existing wall, soak the replacement bricks in a bucket of water for a half hour or so before putting them in place. Also wet down all the surrounding bricks and mortar. This'll help the new mortar to stick better, resulting in a much more permanent repair job.

"Paint spatters on brick can be a real pain to remove. Sometimes if you take another piece of brick and grind it against the paint spots, the brick dust will pick up the paint particles. Even if you're not able to get it all, the dust will probably hide anything that's left."

BROKEN GLASS "If you ever break a glass bottle or jar on your shop floor, here's a very handy trick for getting up all the tiny slivers. After most of the glass has been swept up, a damp facial tissue dabbed on the floor will have all the little slivers clinging to it."

BROOMS "The threaded handle on a wooden-handled push broom often wears down and won't fit tight. For tightening it, I cut a 'V' groove in the end of the threaded part of the handle. Then I make a

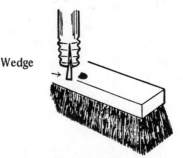

Wedge →

wedge slightly thicker at the bottom than the groove. When the wedge is hammered into the groove, it forces the handle to expand, and the threads will again fit snugly into the broom head."

Another reader solved this problem by wrapping the threads with masking tape. When the handle was again inserted into the socket of the broom, the tape was forced into the threads—this took up the slack and made the handle stay on good and tight.

"When your wife has worn out the straw broom in the house, it'll usually be worn at an angle, and the straws will be bent down toward the end. But by cutting off the straws at the point of the bend, you'll again have a serviceable broom for workshop use. It's easy to cut them off on your table saw if you'll first put a board down on top to act as a compressing clamp to push the straws down. Clamp down about ¼" from where the cut is to be made."

"If you use a regular old broom to sweep out your shop, and your shop floor is concrete, that broom is probably wearing out pretty fast. You can give it a longer life if you'll treat the bristles with thinned shellac. Pour the liquid into a shallow container and dip the broom in. When the shellac dries, the broom will be stronger and last longer. It's also a great way to start out a new broom."

Part of old lid
↓

BRUSHES—STRIKERS, HOLDERS, HANGERS, AND TRICKS   "I made a paintbrush striker plate by cutting the lid of an old paint can in half and bending down the edge slightly to do away with its sharpness. This fits snugly into the rim of the paint can and still leaves plenty of room for dipping the brush."

"For my brush striker, I stretch a large wide rubber band around the can lengthways. The rubber band spans the middle of the opening and not only removes the excess paint, but also serves as a brush rest. To make sure it stays in place, I always put a second rubber band horizontally around the top of the can. I'd suggest you try the rubber band on the can for size before the lid is removed. If it's so tight you have to wrestle it into place, it could cause a spill."

"My striker is made from a strip of tin about 2″ wide and long enough to more than span the width of the paint can. Fold the tin down the middle to form a triangle, and cut notches out toward each end so it rests on the rim. The notches should be spaced so it doesn't rest right in the middle of the can, since its being off center gives you more room to dip the brush. The tin has a sharp edge and does a good job of taking off the excess paint. Since it slants, the paint drips back into the can. It can be used over and over again on the same size paint can."

Pattern for tin brush striker

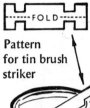

"The easiest way to hold striping brushes in solvent is just to poke the handles through a piece of cardboard. Lay the cardboard over a jar or can which contains solvent. These tiny brushes are so lightweight they'll stay in place suspended in the solvent—and the cardboard will also retard evaporation of the solvent."

If you use such a small brush, take a tiny metal washer and slide it up the handle of the brush. Use a washer with a hole smaller than the diameter of the brush handle, so it'll slide up to a point and wedge. When you need to set the brush down, the washer and the brush end touch the surface, and the bristles are left sticking up in the air.

Washer

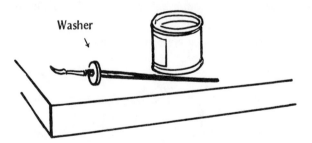

Bobby pin

"Not long ago, I used one of those small artist's brushes in striping a piece of furniture. To soak it in solvent after I was through painting, I clipped a bobbie pin on the handle and laid this across the top of the jar. It held the brush in the liquid at just the depth I wanted."

"About the handiest brush-soaking stunt I've run across is done with a coffee can with a plastic top. First you cut two slits in the plastic top

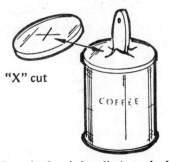

"X" cut

to form an 'X.' When the brush handle is pushed through this 'X,' the lid can be put on the coffee can, and the brush will hang suspended into the solvent. The handle can be adjusted up or down to make sure the bristles are in the solvent without touching the bottom of the can."

"Here's a clever idea to make a tin can into its own brush holder. With tin snips, cut a line straight down from the top of the can, about half way. At the point where this cut stops, make cuts going in each direction parallel to the top of the can. At the up-and-down cut, push the edges back into the can, bending them in a circular fashion. The two circular parts will act as springs, pushing together, and will hold the paint brush handle so the brush will hang down into solvent you put in the bottom of the can. The size of the brush will dictate the size of the can."

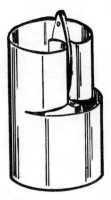

Cut can
bent to hold
brush

"For brush soakers, I use a coffee can to hold the solvent. A pair of spring clips are placed on opposite sides of the rim of the container. I make a rod from a section of wire coat hanger and insert this through the hole in the brush handle and then through the holes in the handles of the clips. This holds the brushes suspended in the solvent."

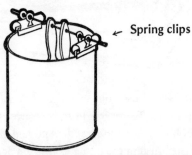

← Spring clips

"Most brush holders require you to use a specially adapted container. My method will allow you to use any container. It's a wooden paint-stirring paddle (the kind that some paint stores give away). A rubber band goes around the handle of the brush to be cleaned and the

Cut-away of can
with rubber band
holding brush to
paint paddle

paddle. Adjust the position of the brush so that the bristles don't quite come to the end of the paddle. Then put paddle and brush into the can of solvent. The paddle rests on the bottom of the tin, and the brush won't be bent out of shape by touching the bottom."

"My brush holder catches drips at the same time. It's a flat pipe-tobacco can with the top removed. It's just the right size to accommodate most medium-sized brushes. This flat tin is taped to the paint can. The lip of the tin can be pushed in or pulled out so the brush will go in as far as the ferrule and rest there to keep the bristles from touching bottom."

Tobacco tin

"When I drained the old permanent-type antifreeze out of the family buggy, I saved a batch of it, and now I use it as a solution in which to store paint brushes overnight. It also serves as a cleaning solvent for the first stages of brush cleaning and saves the use of some of my regular solvent."

After you've soaked your paintbrush in cleaning solvent, you should shake it well to remove most of the liquid, but that can splatter everything in sight. Next time, put the brush inside a paper bag and close the bag up around the handle. Grip the bag as you shake the brush, and you'll sling the solvent no farther than the bag.

"If paint is allowed to stay up under the ferrule, it may start to swell and ruin the brush. I've found a way to get the brush cleaner: I drill small holes in the ferrule to allow the cleaning solvent to get up into the heel."

"For cleaner brushes I fashioned a sort of platform of wire mesh about 1″ off the bottom of the can of cleaning solvent. The wire mesh provides an excellent surface on which to work out leftover paint and work in the cleaning fluid."

"Here's a unique brush holder for any garage with exposed studs. It's made of a length of coat hanger wire that's inserted through holes drilled opposite each other in two of the studs. The wire goes through the holes in the brush handles, and an 'L' bent in one end of the wire keeps the wire from sliding through the studs."

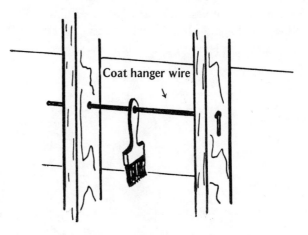

"Hanging brushes after cleaning allows all the solvent to drip out. By leaving them hanging until the next use, the bristles are held down straight by the pull of gravity. My brush hanger is made from a wire coat hanger that has undergone one single cut and a simple twist. The cut is made down at one of the lower angles. The twist is made by putting a 'U' shape in the end of the slanting part of the hanger with the open part of the 'U' aimed up. The horizontal part is perfectly straight, and it's poked through the holes in the brush handles. When all the brushes are on this rod, the end is put into the 'U' to keep the horizontal part from sagging when the hanger is hung up to store the brushes."

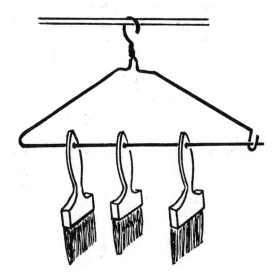

"Sometimes improper care will cause a paintbrush to feather out instead of coming to a point at the end. You can usually remedy this problem by borrowing a can of your wife's hair spray. Spray the brush generously on each side, and then bring the end to a point with your fingers."

"To maintain a pointed edge on my paintbrush, I hang it up in a rather unique way after it's been completely cleaned. My 'hang-up' is an old pants hanger (the clamp kind). I put the point of the brush about ½″ into the hanger. Then I clamp the hanger closed and hang it up on the wall until I'm ready to use the brush again. It comes out with a good point."

"To reshape an old paintbrush, dip the brush into water-soluble glue. While it's still wet, shape it with your hands. When the glue is completely dry, take a piece of fine sandpaper and sand the brush into the taper you want. When it is reshaped, wash out the glue, and your brush'll again be tapered for use."

"This may sound crazy, but I've found that you can reshape a paint brush with an electric razor. First, trim off any uneven bristles at the bottom of the brush. Then go to work on each side of the brush until it's back to the right taper."

"After cleaning a paint brush, put a small amount of turpentine in a plastic sandwich bag. Then put the brush in the bag, and use a rubber band to secure the bag around the handle. Store the brush in the bag; when next needed, it's soft and in perfect shape."

(That plastic sandwich bag is also good when you have to stop in the middle of a paint job, but don't want to clean the brush. Put brush, paint and all, in the bag, and it'll stay soft and moist for two or three hours if necessary.)

"My grandfather was a painter, and always soaked his paintbrushes in vinegar after cleaning them. He claimed that this made them last longer and kept them much more pliable. Although I'm not a painter, I've always done this to my brushes after a home painting chore, and I suddenly realized that I have brushes that are eight to ten years old and just as good as the day they were purchased."

"If you need a small stiff-bristled brush and don't have one, wrap a band of masking tape around the bristles of your regular paintbrush. Put the tape down close to the end of the bristles. This gives you small stiff bristles to work with, and when the task is finished the tape can be peeled off and the brush returned to normal."

"All brushes have some loose bristles, and they can make an otherwise good paint job look bad. I keep an old pocket comb in my shop for the sole purpose of combing new paint brushes before I use them. This gets all of the loose bristles out before they wind up in the fresh paint."

"Usually when it's time to retire a paintbrush, there are still many good bristles left up in under the ferrule. These fibers make excellent small striping brushes. Cut a couple of dozen bristles about 2″ long, hold them together, and tie them to a long fireplace match."

BUCKETS "Here's a tip on re-using empty paint buckets, particularly those that have contained a water-based paint, since they are more easily cleaned. Use a can opener and cut off the rim that all paint cans have. This leaves a nice gallon bucket with a handle; there are many uses for a handy free bucket like this."

BUILDING "We just finished building a new house. You know the access plates in the bathroom and kitchen that let you get to the plumbing? Ours were to have been plywood nailed in place. I got to thinking about how they would look after I'd had to pry them off the first time—and then I came up with a brainstorm. I mounted magnets on the plywood plates and metal tabs on the studs where the plates were to be attached. The plates are held solidly in place by the magnets, and still can be removed without any trouble. My builder said he was going to do this on all the homes he builds in the future."

If you're building or plan to build a new home, here's a simple trick that'll make life easier later on. As soon as the framing is done, get the builder to insert 2" x 4"'s between the studs next to all the windows. Have these placed where you'll be wanting to add the hardware for drapes or blinds. Now the hardware can be installed with screws instead of having to use anchors. If you have very many windows, this will result in a tidy saving of both time and money.

Cabinet Doors • Calculations • Calibrations Renewed • Calipers • Camping • Canvas Goods • Carpet Scraps • Casters • Caulking • Cedar Closets • Cement • Chains • Chairs • Chalk • Charts and Plans • Children and Child Proofing • Christmas • Chuck Keys • Clamps and Clamping • Cleaning Up • Clocks • Coat Hooks • Coffee Cans • Compasses • Concrete • Contour Gauges • Conversion Table • Corks and Corkscrews • Cotter Pins • Countersinking • Curtain Rods • Curving Wood

CABINET DOORS   "If you have cabinets with wooden doors that slide open, the odds are that the doors will strike the wooden frame. After a few years of this, the door edges will be as frayed as your nerves. The simple way to silence this nerve-racker is to use a pair of rubber-headed upholsterers' tacks in the edge of each door. These are easy to install, they do the job, and yet they look fine."

CALCULATIONS   Without getting into a course in math, here are a few easy ways to approach problems in calculation that sometimes face the home handyman.

To find the exact center of a circular object, cut a paper circle the same size as the object. Fold it exactly in half. Now, take the half circle and fold it in half so that the paper is in the shape of a quarter circle. The point of this pie-shaped piece of paper will be the exact center of the original circle.

If you need a very close guess as to the height of a vertical object such as a tall tree and you don't want to have to climb it to measure, here's a way to come up with an answer that's right on the button. Measure the shadow cast by the object. Then place a small stick in the

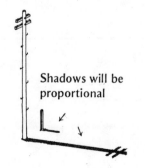

Shadows will be proportional

ground next to the object. Measure the stick, and measure the shadow it casts. Then it becomes a simple matter of mathematics. The shadows will be proportional. Therefore, the height of the object is to its shadow as the height of the stick is to its shadow.

It's no problem calculating the distance to an object that you can't get over to, if you use the principle that two right triangles that each have one leg and one acute angle the same will have all other parts the same. Start at the point from which you wish to measure, and drive a stake. Then run a line at right angles to the direction of measurement. Drive two stakes on this line, with the end one being exactly twice as far from the starting place as the middle one. Now, extend a line at

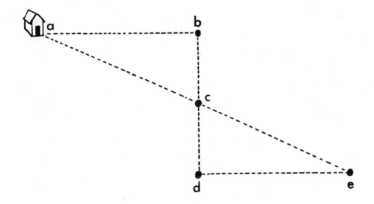

right angles from this end stake and away from the object, until you reach a point at which you can sight across the middle stake to the object. This means that the right triangle formed by the middle point, the end point, and the point you have just sighted from is exactly the same as the right triangle formed by the starting point, the middle point, and the object. Therefore, the distance from the end point to the sighting point is the same as the unknown distance you wanted to find out. Read this over slowly, and you'll get the idea. Try an example:

Let's say the building, A, is on the other side of a creek, and you can't get over to see how far it is from where you are, B. From B, plot a line, B-D, that is at right angles to A-B. Stake the halfway point, C. From point D, go in a line to a place where you can sight across stake C to A. That point, E, forms a line, D-E, that is always the same distance as line A-B.

Sometimes, when laying out a project, you may wish to establish a 90-degree angle for a corner. Even without a square, this can be done

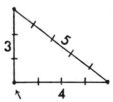

3-4-5 ratio always
makes this angle 90°

easily. All you have to remember is that any triangle that has sides in the proportion of 3 to 4 to 5 is automatically a right triangle. Using a string, mark off 3 feet in one direction and 4 feet in another direction that looks like 90 degrees. Move the end of one of these lines until the distance on the third side is exactly 5 feet, and your corner will be exactly 90 degrees. Even if you do have a square, this trick can make your neighbor think you've mighty sharp eyes if you lay out the angle and then ask him to check your work for accuracy.

Many times the home handyman will want to weaken a concentrated solution. If you know the percent of the solution on hand, there's a formula for weakening. Multiply the amount of solution you have (probably in ounces) by its strength in percent. Now divide this by the strength in percent that you want. Subtract the amount of solution you started with. The result is the amount of water (in ounces) to add to weaken to the desired strength. (For example: You have 10 ounces of 50 percent solution you want to convert to 30 percent. 50 x 10 = 500. 500 ÷ 30 = 16 2/3. 16 2/3 − 10 oz = 6 2/3, and that's the amount of water that should be added to end up with a 30 percent solution.)

Pencil

String

Tacks

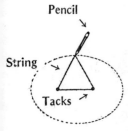

There are times when a shop project will call for cutting out an elliptical-shaped piece. It's easy to draw a perfect ellipse using only a loop of string, a pair of tacks, and a pencil. With the two tacks in the drawing surface, make a triangle of the loop of string by pulling it tight against the tacks with the pencil point. When pulled all the way around the tacks and kept tight against the string, the pencil will draw an ellipse. The length of the ellipse will be governed by the length of string, and the height will be controlled by the distance between the two tacks. Getting these set up the way you wish is a simple matter of adjustment.

Pulleys are great for stepping up or reducing speed from a motor. There's a formula for figuring out the amount of change made by the pulleys. You're dealing with four factors: motor speed, drive pulley diameter, driven pulley diameter, and drive shaft speed. You should know three of these, and, therefore, can easily find the fourth. Just take the pulley of known diameter and speed (this may be either motor speed or desired speed). Multiply speed by diameter and divide the result by the other known factor, diameter or speed (actual or desired). The result is the missing factor. Example: Your motor develops 1800 rpm. You have a tool that needs to run at 3600 rpm. The diameter of the pulley on the motor is 4". 1800 x 4 = 7200. Divide that by 3600, which is the drive shaft speed, and the answer is that you need a 2″ pulley. All problems won't come out that even, but the math will always be the same.

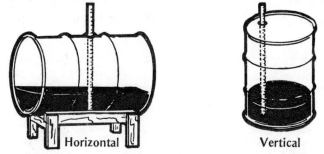

Horizontal   Vertical

Unless you have X-ray vision, about the only way to find out how much is left in that 55-gallon drum is to poke a stick down in it. Even so, all you can tell is how many inches deep it is. But if the drum is sitting upright, there's a formula to tell the volume. Each 2 7/8 inches is 5 gallons. If your drum is horizontal, it's not that easy, but here's a chart to show the volume:

INCHES FROM BOTTOM	GALLONS*
22	55 plus**
21	55
20	54
19	53
18	50
17	47
16	44
15	41
14	38
13	35
12	31
11	28
10	25
9	22
8	18
7	15
6	12
5	9
4	7
3	4
2	2
1	1

* Rounded off to the nearest gallon.

** 55-gallon drums actually hold more than the designated amount, to allow for expansion.

Most of the thermometers around the house are Fahrenheit (F), but most shop projects that call for something to be at a particular temperature use the centigrade (C) scale. To convert from F to C, first subtract 32 from the number of degrees. Then multiply the remainder by 5/9. To convert from C to F, multiply by 9/5 and add 32 to the result.

212°F is boiling—to convert to C:

$$212$$
$$\underline{-32}$$
$$180 \times 5/9 = \frac{900}{9} = 100°C$$

or let's say it's 10°C (brrr)—to convert:

$$10$$
$$\underline{+32}$$
$$42 \times 9/5 = \frac{378}{5} = 75.6°F$$

(not cold after all)

Later in this chapter, you'll find a Super Conversion Table that gives more conversion factors than most people really need to know.

CALIBRATIONS RENEWED   Even if you're not getting old, those tiny calibrations on bits, metal rulers, and other tools can get awfully hard to read. Here's one way to renew their visibility. "Coat the marking with thinned shellac, and then take a piece of white chalk and rub over the marks. Wipe off the excess. When this is dry, the tiny stamped-in numbers will jump out at you and will stay bright for a long time to come. Not only does this save your eyesight, but it will help eliminate mistakes."

Zig-zag sections   "The sizes on drill shafts usually become almost invisible after a while. Renew them easily by rubbing a dab of white paint across the numerals. Then wipe off the shaft, and you'll find that paint has stayed down in the numbers, making them easy to read again. When the paint dries, it will stay put through much use."

CALIPERS   "Almost every home handyman has a broken folding (zig-zag) rule stuck away somewhere. Two of the sections with the hinge in the middle will make excellent calipers. Measure down equidistant from the hinge on both arms of the rule and cut to a point on one arm with a sharp pocketknife. The point should be curved in toward the other section. When it is shaped, make a tracing and flop it over as a pattern for the other. When both blades are finished, the pointed tips should be at the same point when brought together. For inside calipers, move the blades so that the points face out. The hinge will hold dimensions for transfer or measurement."

CAMPING "You can waterproof matches for use on camping trips with boiled linseed oil. Dip a large quantity of match heads into the liquid, and spread them out on a sheet of aluminum foil, leaving them for a couple of days. They'll be completely waterproof."

(Another reader accomplishes this by dipping the match heads in paraffin, while still another uses his wife's fingernail polish.)

"We wrap packages of book matches in pieces of aluminum foil. This keeps them dry so that we never end up without a match to start our campfire."

"To start campfires, even in wet weather, use wax milk cartons as kindling. They flame up enough to get a fire started, and yet burn slowly enough not to go out before your wood has caught fire. They'll burn even though they may be damp. I also use them for starting the fire in our fireplace."

(Just be sure you're using wax-coated cardboard, and not the plastic kind.)

"If your family enjoys corn on the cob, save the cobs for use as fire starters for camp-outs and picnics. After the cobs have dried completely, dip them in a pan of melted parrafin. Not only does the wax keep them dry, it makes them quite easy to light. They'll get your fire started in no time—and you can cook more corn on the cob."

"Here's another sure campfire starter. Before leaving home, take an ordinary brick and put it on a piece of aluminum foil. Pour kerosene or fire starter over the brick so it's well saturated. Then wrap it tightly in the foil and seal out the air. When you're at your campsite, unwrap the brick and place it in the middle of the intended fire. Put your wood around the brick and light it. The brick's retained fuel will burn long enough to start the fire—and will also give you a hotter fire."

"A good way to fashion a wind screen is to take three connected sides of a corrugated box and cover them with aluminum foil. This makes the shield fire-resistant, and the foil will also direct and concentrate the heat in toward the cooking. Pack your foodstuffs in a corrugated box; since all of the contents will be eaten, you don't need the box on the return trip."

"When cooking over an open fire, wrap the bottoms of all pans with aluminum foil. There'll be no sooty black bottoms to slave over afterwards."

"I rub the bottom of my iron camp skillet with a bar of soap. This keeps it from turning black from the campfire."

"Taking a barbecue grill on a camping trip is pretty messy. It's probably too big to carry easily, and the soot can get all over everything. However, food cooked over a charcoal fire tastes even better when you're out in the open. I've solved this by taking only the grate from my barbecue set. This is flat and clean, so it's no problem to take.

Then I also take several empty coffee cans that I've saved. These don't take up extra room, since all sorts of things can be packed in them. Place the cans in a circle, open end down, and push them down into the dirt a little with your foot. Fill up the circle with charcoal briquettes, put the grate on top, and you're ready for cooking."

"We arrived at our campsite with everything we needed for our camp-out—except that we had left behind a box containing all of our cooking pans. Rather than settling for raw food, I went creative. With the aid of coat hangers, I fashioned wire frames and made containers from aluminum foil. I wrapped the foil edges around the wire frame so that when food was placed in the 'pan' the weight held the foil down fast against the edges and prevented it from slipping out. We made a handle from a split branch, fitted it around the wire handle, and tied it with fishing line. This kept our hands from getting burned. We did learn (the hard way) not to stir hard or use a fork to turn food over."

(And such a pan can be thrown away, so there's no washing!)

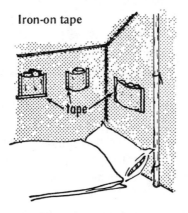

Iron-on tape

tape

"Our tent has been made into a much handier abode by adding pockets on the inside walls to hold all sorts of small items that need to be handy. But anyone who has tried to sew through heavy canvas will know this isn't an easy chore. I put all my pockets on with iron-on mending tape that was meant to be used on denims. The pockets themselves were made from canvas scraps. This is a really easy way to add lots of convenience to the tent."

"If our camp trailer isn't 100 percent level, nothing seems to work right. I can tell when it's level, now that I've added a cup hook in the ceiling and a thumbtack in the floor. Sound crazy? Well, I installed them at home, making sure the trailer was exactly level. A plumb bob hanging from the cup hook told me where to place the tack in the floor. Now when I'm out in the wilds, the plumb bob can be hung up, and when it points to the tack, I know I'm on the level."

"While hunting this winter, I discovered a way to make sleeping on a camp cot much more pleasant. Thin canvas doesn't really do much to keep the sleeper from getting cold from underneath. However, if you convert the underside of the cot into dead air space, your cot will be much, much warmer. This can be done quite simply by draping plastic suit bags off the cot all the way around. Do this early in the day, and when bedtime comes, the dead air space will be warm and so will you."

"I bought a new cheap fountain pen, filled it with antiseptic, and added it to my camping gear. It's airtight, and with the cap on, the point stays clean, and the pen holds the liquid until needed. Any scratches are cleaned with a shot from the fountain pen, and I never have to worry about infection. The pen clips to a pocket, goes with me in the woods, and can be refilled after each trip."

CANVAS GOODS   "When punching holes in canvas for grommets,

Coin taped to finger

place a section of old inner tube under the canvas. The holes punch easier, and the rubber makes the punch bounce back out."

"Some repair work I did on our tent required some sewing, and I soon learned why women use thimbles. But since my wife doesn't sew, we didn't have one. I taped a coin to my finger and pushed the needle through the heavy canvas without hurting myself."

(This is also a good tip for people who have leathercraft as a hobby.)

"Press-on patches are great for repairing tarps, tents, and other canvas goods. They'll usually last until something catches at one of their corners and lifts them away. A good easy way to prevent this is to round off all the corners with a fingernail nipper. A single snip at each corner, and the patches will be less likely to lift off."

CARPET SCRAPS   "Here's a use for leftover carpet scraps. I sewed enough of them together to cover the entire top of my workbench. If you ever try this, you'll never go back to a plain-topped work area. The carpeted surface keeps work with a fine finish safe from mars and scratches when it's placed on the bench. Small objects that used to roll off the bench will now stay put. And this treatment looks so great it has proven a good incentive to keep my entire shop in better order than I ever have before."

Carpet scrap

"If you cut a hole in the middle of a square of carpet and then slit the carpet from the hole out to the edge, it can be placed around the trunk of a small tree to act as mulch. If you don't like the looks of the carpet, scrape out around the tree first, and then cover the scrap with a thin layer of dirt."

"I covered part of the top of my sawhorse with carpet scraps so that any time I want to protect the finish of work, the sawhorse won't mar it. I left some plain surface on the sawhorse in case a project calls for a solid sawhorse surface."

"Carpet scraps are glued to the metal steps on my tractor. If it's the least bit wet, these metal parts can be slippery and a hazard, but the carpet does away with this problem."

"I cut circles from carpet scraps to fit in the bottom of coffee cans. The scraps are saturated with a mixture of equal parts of kerosene and lubricating oil. The cans now act as tool holders, and I can put cold chisels, awls, and other pointed tools point down in the cans. The points rest on the carpet, so they'll not be damaged, and the oil protects the tools from rust."

CASTERS   The "drop out" caster from the leg of a piece of furniture can be fixed so it'll stay put. This can be done by splitting the top of the caster in an "X" with a hacksaw. Then take a screwdriver and spread the splits apart slightly. When you snap the caster back into the socket, it's in there to stay.

CAULKING   "A slip-on pencil eraser is just the right size for capping a caulking-gun nozzle to seal it and keep the contents from drying out. Just wipe the nozzle clean before putting the eraser in place."

"If your caulking compound is a little too thick, thin it with a small quantity of paint. Since you'll probably be painting over the caulking anyway, use this paint. As you thin the caulking compound, you'll also be tinting it close to the final color. Many times the tint will be enough so that you don't have to use two coats of paint to cover the caulk."

CEDAR CLOSETS   "The aroma in a cedar closet or cedar chest gets very faint in time. But a light sanding of the cedar wood will slightly reopen the grain and release the natural cedar oils that provide the aroma. Usually a very light going over each year will keep the odor ever-present."

If you've taken the trouble to cedar-line a closet for the protection of your woolens, take one more small step to make it more effective. Install weatherstripping on the door inside the closet. This'll hold the scented air in the closet and will preserve the cedar scent in the wood for a longer time.

CEMENT   Lots of folks use the term "cement" when they really mean "concrete." Cement is the mixture that's in the bag you buy and the end result is concrete. You'll find all the cement hints later in this chapter under *Concrete*.

CHAINS "I needed to make a single chain from two short pieces of chain I had on hand. Since I didn't have a connector link, I simply took a padlock and used it to join the two pieces together."

"Here's my chain-repair stunt: I use a bolt to go through the two links to be joined, and then tighten a nut down. The diameter of the bolt should be the largest possible that will go through the links of the chain. If it's to be a permanent repair, you'll probably wish to cut the bolt off at the nut and flair the end to lock it in place."

CHAIRS "You've heard the old story about trying to cut off chair legs to even them up and ending with no legs at all. Here's an easy trick on minor leg leveling. Take a small blob of putty and put it on the uneven leg. It can be shaped to look like the leg and painted or stained over when dry."

"If you've ever tried to cut off the legs of a chair, you know the biggest problem is getting them even so the chair will be level at the new height. Here's an easy way to do this. Measure and cut off three of the legs to the desired length. Then set the chair on a table with the uncut leg hanging off. With the three legs flat on the table, mark the fourth even with the table top. When cut, it'll make the chair rest flat on the floor with no wobble."

"Before reglueing a loose chair rung, wrap the end of the rung with a small scrap from a nylon stocking. Cover both nylon and rung with the glue, and you'll come up with a stronger gripping bond."

(Or wrap a few strands of steel wool around the end of the rung. This'll do the same thing.)

CHALK "Most handymen keep a piece of marking chalk in the tool box, but it usually gets broken by the metal tools. Mine doesn't. I always wrap it with masking tape, leaving just the point exposed. Be sure to start wrapping at the top, so that as the chalk is used the tape can be peeled back to expose more chalk. Not only does this keep the chalk from getting broken, it also makes it more dust-free."

CHARTS AND PLANS "To protect shop plans and charts, I put each one between two pieces of plastic kitchen wrap. Even though this type of wrap is supposed to be self-adhering, I run cellophane tape around the edges to be sure they're sealed. This keeps the charts clean and readable no matter how dirty my hands may be."

"I've taped frequently-used shop charts to an old window shade I mounted up over my workbench. When I need to refer to one of them, I pull down the shade. The chart stays right in front of my eyes until I've finished with it, and then it rolls back up out of the way." (This shady idea would also be a good way to keep plans on a project you're working on!)

"Last week, I borrowed a shop manual from a friend and noticed he had a reminder to 'Please return' with his name and address stamped throughout the book. Now, this isn't such an original idea—the public library does it. But I got to thinking of all the plans, workshop manuals, magazines, and other printed things I've lent out to friends who never got around to returning them. Probably a reminder would have gotten most of them back. So I've invested in a rubber stamp."

CHILDREN AND CHILDPROOFING "I want my son to take an interest in woodworking. However, there are times when he gets in the way, and times when it might not be safe for him to be around close to where I'm working. I fixed it so I could have him out in the shop with me, but without his being right under foot, by making him his very own workbench. It's just a simplified, smaller version of mine. He has all of the kid-sized tools that're safe for him to use, and while I'm working on my project, he works on one of his own."

Eventually Dad's workshop should be a place where the kids are welcome, but until they're old enough to be responsible, every precaution should be taken to childproof your shop. Here are a few:

"To keep my kids from opening the drawers on my workbench, I installed some very easy but effective locks. I drilled holes in the top of the workbench at a point just at the end of each drawer. I then inserted a bolt in each hole. The bolts stick down into the drawer and against the inside of the back. The drawer cannot be opened because it's pulled against the bolt. All I have to do when I need to open a drawer is to remove the bolt. I hope by the time the kids are big enough to reach up on the top of the workbench they'll be old enough to handle the things in the drawers."

If you're building a new workshop, here's something to consider When putting in the wiring for your power tools, put them all on a master switch. In this way, they not only will cut off individually, but will be doubly without power when the switch is thrown. This will be added protection against children's messing around with a dangerous tool or misusing your tools when you're not there. Don't let the master switch control the lights, however. Put it up out of the reach of children.

"Here's how I make sure my kids don't mess around with my power tools. There's certainly not room enough for tools in the lockable drawers in my workbench, but I drilled out slots in the top of a drawer big enough for the electric cords to fit into. I put the plugs in the drawer, and when it's locked, they can't come out, and so no one can turn on any of the power tools. This would also make it difficult for anyone to walk off with any of them."

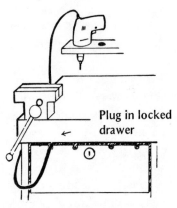

Plug in locked drawer

"As a safety measure, I checked over our children's swing set and was alarmed to find that the chain link at the top was almost worn through. This is, of course, the link that gets all the wear, as it moves against the eye bolt at the top. After removing the bad links, I added a safety chain on each side so that if the top link should ever wear through again, our children wouldn't be thrown out. These safety chains are short lengths attached to the regular chains and then joined

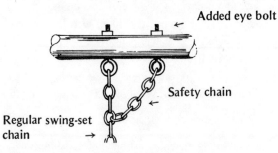

Added eye bolt

Safety chain

Regular swing-set chain

to an additional eye bolt installed about 2″ from the regular eyes. There is just the least bit of slack in the safety chain."

(I urge all parents to give swing sets a safety inspection, and then add these safety chains.)

"Fathers who have to uproot a heavy outdoor swing set to mow the grass around it may profit from my idea. Instead of using the metal stakes that came with our set, I anchored it down with a pair of those big corkscrew stakes used to tether dogs. They can be unscrewed from the ground quite easily, allowing the swing set to be moved. They can be reinstalled just as quickly. Also, they probably hold the set in place better than the straight stakes would."

"After answering our doorbell six times last weekend, only to find the caller wanted one of our kids, I took action. I installed another doorbell a few inches below ours. It's labelled with our children's names, and they've instructed all their friends to use it. It has an entirely different sound than the old one, so that there's no doubt which one is ringing. So far, it's working out great, and doorbells aren't too hard to install."

mr. & mrs. b.e. smith

ricky & david

"Sometimes I feel like I've created a monster, but my idea has given us more good than bad over the long haul. Our youngster isn't tall enough yet to reach the light switch in his bedroom, but after he has been tucked in he can think of lots of good reasons to need the light turned back on. We got tired of having to go in each time, so I devised a handle for his light switch. I drilled a tiny hole in the regular flip-switch handle, and then drilled a similar hole about 1/8″ from the end of a foot-long piece of doweling. I ran a wire through the hole in the switch and then through the hole in the doweling. When twisted tight, the wire holds the dowel up against the switch handle, and can let the handle be flipped up or down. Our child can reach this, of course, and now he works the lights himself. Now if he'll just not come up with quite so many reasons to get up, we'll be in great shape."

Hole drilled in switch

Wire

"Our sliding patio doors are heavy and build up good speed, and I've always been afraid one of our children might get his fingers caught. My husband rigged up a stopper for these doors that put my mind at ease. He put a sponge rubber ball on the end of a small piece of string. The end of the string was attached to a screw set flush in the facing where the door would rest when closed. When the door is slammed shut, it hits the rubber ball which hangs in its path and, therefore, will not close on tiny hands. To close the door completely, it's a simple matter to flip the ball out of the way."

"For a child's sandbox, we got a worn out giant truck tire from the junk pile. By laying it down flat and filling it up with sand, we've a sandbox that cost nothing, with no sharp corners for a child to fall on, and no splinters, as a wooden one might—all big advantages over the kind you buy."

(And when Junior has outgrown the sandbox, it can be rolled back to the junk pile.)

"I put in a sunken sandbox for our kids, and it proved to be a good idea. When kids scattered the sand out of the box, it was easy to sweep the loose sand back in. When the box was not being used, a plywood cover kept rain, trash, and other things out of it. Last week, the kids agreed they had outgrown sandboxes, and so I merely filled in over it with loam and sodded it. You can hardly tell it was ever there."

(If you use this idea next to a patio, when it's time to full it in you might want to cover it with concrete and make it part of the patio.)

"I'm always looking for things I can make for my grandchildren. Last week, I made them an indoor horseshoe pitching set. The horseshoes are made from an old tire. The shape of the tire makes the 1"-thick sections cut from the tire look just like real horseshoes, but they're not as destructive as the metal kind. No real horseshoe-pitchin' expert would get excited over these rubber ones, but the kids sure did."

"My two daughters decided to redecorate their room with those wild posters. Since we have textured dry walls, this presented a problem. Tacks won't stay too well. Wallpaper paste meant that the walls would have to be sanded under the posters. Cellophane tape doesn't look too great. I solved the problem by applying the posters with a generous amount of fairly thin rubber cement, using a wallpaper roller to be sure they were well seated. The real beauty about this is that when the children tire of this fad, the rubber cement will allow us to peel the posters off with absolutely no damage to the walls. Any rubber cement left on the wall can easily be rolled off with a finger."

"I had to go in the house once and tell my four-year-old I'd just run over the tricycle he'd left in the driveway. The fact that it was night, that I couldn't see it, and that it shouldn't have been left there made little difference to him. I was a meanie. I've done something that'll prevent this from happening again. I bought a roll of reflector tape and put strips of it on all the toys he might leave out. Now when I pull in, I can see these things and not become a bad guy again."

CHRISTMAS   A dry Christmas tree is a potential fire hazard. Most people put the base of the tree in a container of water, and this does help. But one additional step will keep the tree green and fresh longer. Before putting the tree up, drill a hole in the bottom of the trunk, using as long a bit as you have. Stuff this hole with cotton, and then put your tree in place with its base in water. The cotton will act like a wick, drinking up the water and carrying it farther up into the trunk.

As a safety precaution for your Christmas tree, invest in one of those battery-initiated fire alarms. They're very inexpensive. Hang the unit on the center trunk of the tree so it won't be seen. If it's a light color, paint it green so it won't stand out. Then if the lights on the tree should begin to overheat, the alarm will let you know in time to prevent a fire.

"If you have to hang Christmas stockings each year, your fireplace mantle can begin to look as if termites have been at it. I mounted cup hooks under our mantle and leave them there year 'round. They're not noticeable, since I painted them the same color as the wood, and if we have more kids, there's plenty of room for more cuphooks."

"If you want to avoid driving nail holes in your mantle to hang Christmas stockings, just use a C-clamp for each stocking. If your clamp is a little beat up, paint it red. It won't hurt the clamp."

"Here's a trick that will help decorate the Christmas tree. Use sections of pipe cleaner to tie tree lights to the branches. They may be dipped in green paint, or sprayed with it, to make them blend in with the tree. They're a lot easier to use than the clips that come on strings of lights."
(In fact, pipe cleaners are great for tieing all sorts of ornaments on the tree.)

"Save divided egg cartons to pack away Christmas ornaments. These boxes will be ideal for storing them safely."
(And a Merry Christmas!)

CHUCK KEYS   "The best holder for my chuck key is a magnet I installed on the wall right in front of my drill press. The key is always handy when needed and quite easy to put back in the right place when I'm through with it."

CLAMPS AND CLAMPING   "I needed a larger C-clamp than I had on hand, and made one by using two smaller ones. I put the stationary face of each of the two clamps against the other. The two *C*'s now form an *S* shape, and the adjustable face of each goes on opposite sides of the work to be clamped. It looks like a Rube Goldberg invention, but it works."

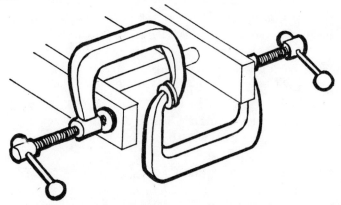

"One of those hard rubber caster cups used under furniture legs makes an ideal pad for a C-clamp needed on wood to be finished. Not only does it protect the wood, but it gives the clamp a better grip because there's more gripping area."

"Since I'm a grandfather with lots of pictures of grandchildren, I've started making my own picture frames with all the decorative moldings available. My glueing holder for the mitered corners is a cigar box with the top taken off, plus two C-clamps. The cigar box fits into the inside of the corner to be glued, and the C-clamps hold the two pieces of the frame to the cigar box until the glue sets up."

Mitered corner held
for glueing by cigar
box and C-clamps

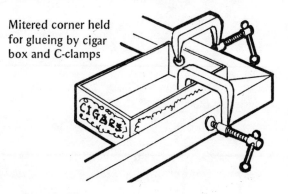

"If you don't have a bar clamp, you can make one of any size with two C-clamps and a length of wire, provided you are clamping a frame or something else with an open area. Make a loop with the wire, which when added to the length of the two C-clamps will be the approximate span to be clamped. With the wire looped around the stationary flanges of the clamps, place the adjustable flanges on the outside of the work to be clamped. As you tighten up the two clamps, the wire is drawn taut between the clamps, pulling them toward each other and making them function as a single one."

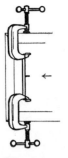

Wire loop pulled taut as C-clamps tightened

"I needed a band clamp but couldn't see that I'd ever use it again, and so I didn't want to buy one. I rigged up one instead, using a pair of ropes instead of a band. They were cut to the proper length, and the ends were inserted into pre-drilled holes in a pair of scrap boards, with

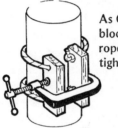

As C-clamp brings blocks together, ropes are pulled tight around work

knots tied to keep the rope from pulling through. With the ropes around the work to be clamped, a C-clamp was then put on the boards in between the holes, so that when the clamp was tightened the two boards were brought toward each other, causing the ropes to be pulled tight against the work. The only thing that I have to be sure of is to have the clamp a little closer to the work than the holes, so that the ropes are pulling against the C-clamp."

"Here's my kooky clamping device. Put a deep drawer or wooden box in front of you, with the open side facing out. Place the work down flat on the bottom of the box. Then place a deflated basketball on top of the work. When blown up, the basketball pushes against the top of the box and down tight against the work. You may never have a use for this one, but you've got to admit it's a wild idea."

When glueing an irregular surface, you may be able to apply enough pressure at all the odd places by putting an ice pack filled with water over the surface being glued. It does have good weight, and it'll conform to whatever shape it's on. If the glue will dry faster at a higher temperature, fill the ice pack with hot water.

Nut & bolt

Spools

"Small clamping jobs can be done with my homemade clamps, made from a pair of wooden spools plus a long skinny bolt with a nut to fit. The bolt must be long enough to go completely through both spools after the work has been put between them. Then the nut is tightened down, causing the flat spool ends to clamp it."

"An old tennis racquet press makes an ideal pressure clamp for glueing together a pair of flat objects."

"If you've a radial arm saw, you might keep in mind that it can sometimes come in handy as a giant-sized clamp. Start by tilting the saw and motor unit a full 90 degrees so the blade is parallel to the table. In most cases, the blade guard will provide a flat surface that can be tightened down on the work by the height-adjustment knob. Great clamping pressure can be applied in this manner."

If you need a really big clamp, "Put your work under the rear bumper of your car. Now take your bumper jack and put it down on the work where you desire pressure. Put the jack in place as if you were about to jack up the car, and raise the jack against the bumper until the required pressure is attained. If pressure is needed over a larger area, put a piece of plywood under the jack."

CLEANING UP   "Since my shop doesn't have a sink in it, I used to leave a trail of grime and dirt in the house on my way to wash up in the bathroom. This, of course, was followed by a trail of abuse from my wife. Then I discovered I could clean up in the shop with a can of aerosol shave cream. I simply spray a small amount on my hands, and it does a fine job of cleaning. Then I remove it with a paper towel, and I'm welcome to go anywhere in the house."

"I filled an empty window spray dispenser with turpentine and keep it in my shop for cleaning my hands after painting. It's a lot easier to spray it on than to spill it from the can."

"I enjoy working on my car, but grease under my fingernails is murder. I've beaten this rap pretty well, though. Before I start to work, I scrape my nails over a dry bar of soap, getting the soap lodged under the nails. When I'm through, the soap washes out easily, and no grease or grime has gotten under my nails."

"My husband is an automobile tinkerer and usually comes into the house with greasy hands. I made a mixture for him that really cuts the grease. First, I make soap gel from leftover slivers of soap. This is kept in a jar right next to a shaker with sugar and sand mixed together (about half-and-half). The shaker is a big saltshaker with the holes enlarged a bit with an ice pick. My husband covers his hands with the soap, and then sprinkles the sugar-sand mixture on and rubs briskly. The mixture rinses off with water, and so does the grease."

"My wife used to hate for me to come up from my basement workshop, because I always tracked in sawdust. To solve this, I got a bunch of old carpet scraps from a builder friend and carpeted the steps leading up from the basement. By the time I've walked up to the top, the carpet has cleaned all the sawdust off, and I no longer track any into the house."

"Here's a clever idea that I've used to keep the sawdust blown away from the hole I'm drilling. I make a small fan out of a circle of cardboard by cutting slits in it and bending them down at an angle and

Cardboard fan →

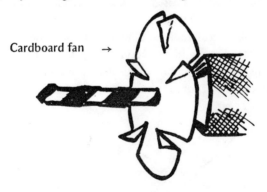

then punching a hole in the center of this circle. The hole is smaller than the diameter of the bit I'm using. Then I force the bit through the hole and push the circle up close to the chuck. When the drill is running, the fan turns and keeps the area clear of sawdust."

Rubber band

Another woodworker solved the problem this way: "Clip fibers about 2″ long from a discarded paintbrush. Place these evenly around the body of the drill bit, and slip a rubber band around to hold them in place. As the bit goes in, the bristles flair out and act as a brush to clear the area of chips."

Brush fibers

"With a handy husband and two teen-age sons, we usually have several projects going at once. This means there can be a dozen or so small screws and other parts scattered around the workbench. My men would never take time to put these scattered parts away, so we've established three 'banks' into which these parts can be deposited—empty jars with slots cut in the tops. One is for washers, one for screws, and a third for miscellaneous small parts. When the jars begin to fill up, we let the two younger children sort out the parts so they can be put away."

CLOCKS "My cheap alarm clock was losing time. I was ready to throw it away, when my mother-in-law claimed she could fix it. She stuck it in the oven and turned the oven to 'warm.' After it had cooked for about three hours, she took it out, and it runs perfectly. Either she's a witch and put a hex on the clock, or some of its working parts had picked up a greasy film that caused them to work slower than they should have—and the heat melted the film and let the clock go at the right speed again."

"My 60-year-old wooden-cased clock keeps perfect time and has not needed repairs for over 20 years. I attribute this to my keeping a small container with about a thimbleful of kerosene inside the clock case. A small piece of rag is partly immersed in the liquid to act as a wick. The fumes from the kerosene inhibit rust in the clock's works and provide just the right amount of lubrication. A thimbleful of kerosene will last nine months to a year."

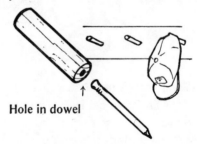

Hole in dowel

COAT HOOKS "Easy finished-looking coat hooks can be made from finishing nails and pieces of dowelling. Pre-drill the dowels through the center to a depth about half the length of the nails. Then drive the nails into place in the wall, leaving about half of each nail sticking out. Put the protruding, almost headless nail into the pre-drilled hole in each dowel, and tap the dowel down so it covers the nail right down to the wall. Only the piece of dowel shows, and this makes for a neat-looking coat hook that can be painted the color of the wall."

COFFEE CANS Many handymen keep various shop items in empty coffee cans. Since so many home workshops are located in garages and basements, these cans are subjected to an undue amount of moisture, and sometimes they leave a rust ring when set on metal work surfaces or cabinets. Save extra plastic lids from those cans and slip them on the bottom of the ones you use as containers. Not only does this eliminate the rust rings, it prevents scratching of work surfaces.

"After I saved enough coffee cans for a project, I forgot to tell the little woman not to save any more. She ended up with a bunch, so I hauled them to our lake cabin. Seven of them banded together, forming

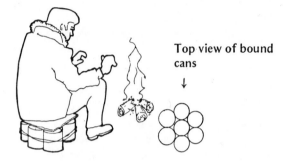

Top view of bound cans
↓

a circle, are just the right height to act as a camp stool for sitting around the campfire. A piece of corrugated board from a box gives a little padding. We banded them together with wire which was tightened by twisting it where it joined."

COMPASSES "I used an old adjustable curtain rod (the kind with a right angle turn at each end) to make a large compass. I taped a nail at one end and a pencil at the other. It makes great big circles and is adjustable."

(Some more ways to use old curtain rods can be found under *Curtain Rods*.)

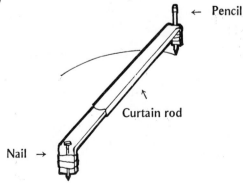

← Pencil

Curtain rod

Nail →

"At those rare times when I need to draw a circle on a shop project, I can never seem to find my compass. However, I always have my pocket comb handy, and it comes to my rescue. By putting a nail in between the teeth at one end of the comb, I have my center point. Then I put a pencil between other teeth at the desired distance from the center. The comb will hold the pencil at this distance while I swing it around the center point, drawing a perfect circle."

CONCRETE   "I was all ready to pour some concrete stepping-stones last weekend, when I remembered I'd failed to get any metal reinforcing. I used three wire coat hangers in each, and have been told by experts that this should work out fine."

"It's easy to pour concrete stepping-stones to make your own backyard walk. We decorated ours in a way that has caused much comment. We call it our 'Family Milestone Walk.' After I had poured the blocks and before the concrete dried, we scratched in the birthdays of each of our three children and had them put their handprints on the appropriate blocks. We put our wedding date and drew a pair of wedding bells on another one. The grandparents were invited over, and a birthday block was made for each of them. It was almost like Grauman's Chinese Theatre. Also, it was fun to write in wet cement, as I had not done this since I was a kid!"

When pouring concrete steps or other such projects where you'll be adding a handrail or posts, the best procedure is to set these attachments in after you've finished the main portion of the job. However, you have to make arrangements ahead of time by leaving holes for these additions. As you pour the mixture for the project, put tin cans where you wish to leave holes. You should fill the cans with sand and coat them on the outside with petroleum jelly. After the concrete hardens, remove the sand and pull the tin cans away from the sides with a pair of pliers. Instead of tin cans, one reader used glass jars which he broke with a hammer, leaving the desired holes.

"Building concrete steps isn't an easy project. First of all, constructing the forms is a pretty good chore. I made steps using pre-cast concrete building blocks, and therefore needed no forms. My steps are two blocks wide. The smooth edges are facing out, and the hollow cores face up. I set the blocks on a four-inch, well-packed bed of sand. The two units were wired together with coat hanger wires besides being mortared together. Then I filled the cores with concrete, and built a one-inch tread up over the top."

"I was halfway through a small concrete job when I realized I didn't have a finishing trowel. I solved my problem nicely with an old metal venetian blind slat. It works as well as anything I've found."

Anchor bolts that are put in concrete as it's being poured will hold even longer if you bend them at about a 40-degree angle before setting them in the concrete. The bend should be made so that it'll be below the surface. The protruding part should be at right angles to the surface. Sometimes when an anchor is left straight up and down, and is subjected to too much force, the concrete fails to hold.

"My next-door neighbor poured a new concrete patio in his back yard. After he got the forms built, he painted the parts to be in contact with the cement with a coat of used motor oil. This prevented any concrete from sticking to forms and made the job of taking up the forms a lot easier."

I stopped to watch a man smoothing off a section of concrete he had poured and noticed that his screed was painted a bright orange. I commented on the colorful tool, and he said it wasn't done just for looks. He had noticed before that as the screed got wet, it also got more difficult to move across the surface. The paint job had solved his problem. His theory was that the paint kept the wooden screed from taking moisture from the wet mixture. Orange just happened to be the only leftover paint he had.

"The fastest way to pour a concrete patio is to make it all one slab. However, this makes for a rather monotonous finish. To make our patio more interesting, I made a design in the finish that was very simple to do. As soon as my husband smoothed off the top, I took different-sized tin cans and pushed them into the wet cement so as to make a circle. By doing this all over, I gave the otherwise plain slab a very interesting pattern."

"Here's my hint for patching cracks in concrete. As you know, the biggest problem is trying to force the mortar into the crack. It's much less of a problem if you fill up a plastic squeeze bottle with the mortar and squirt it in."

"A crack in a concrete porch or patio should be repaired immediately, or moisture will get in the crack, freeze, and widen it. I just discovered such a crack in our patio. It's just too cold to try repairing it at this time of year, but to stop any additional damage I ran a propane torch along the crack to melt the ice and boil out some of the water. Then I filled up the crack with sand to absorb what water was left and taped it up with some wide waterproof freezer tape so that no additional water can get in. When warmer weather arrives, I'll repair it the right way."

CONTOUR GAUGES   A contour gauge is a gadget used to copy the contours of irregularly shaped objects, such as a piece of molding. Most do-it-yourselfers don't own one because the need doesn't come around that often. However, if you're faced with the need to transfer a contour onto a piece of wood that you wish to cut to fit around an irregular surface, here's a good substitute. Take a piece of wire solder and form it over the surface to be copied. It's flexible enough to be easily formed, and yet will hold its shape. Place it down on the work to be cut out and trace the contour off. Then cut.

CONVERSION TABLE

TO CONVERT FROM	TO	MULTIPLY BY
Acres	square feet	43,560
	square yards	4,840
	square miles	0.00156
	square meters	4,046.856
	hectares	0.40468
Barrels	gallons—not petroleum	31.5
	gallons—petroleum	42
Btu	horsepower-hours	0.000393
	kilowatt-hours	0.000293
Btu per hour	horsepower	0.000393
	kilowatts	0.000293
Bushels	dry pints	64
	dry quarts	32
	pecks	4
	cubic feet	1.24445
	liters	35.239
	cubic yards	0.04609
Centimeters	inches	0.3937
	feet	0.0328

TO CONVERT FROM	TO	MULTIPLY BY
Chains (surveyor's)	feet	66
	rods	4
Cubic centimeters	cubic inches	0.06102
Cubic feet	cubic inches	1,728
	cubic meters	0.02831
	cubic yards	0.037037
	gallons	7.48
	liters	28.32
Cubic feet of water	pounds @ 60°F	62.37
	gallons	7.481
Cubic inches	fluid ounces	0.554113
	quarts	0.017316
	gallons	0.004329
	milliliters	16.387064
Cubic meters	cubic feet	35.3145
	cubic yards	1.30795
Cubic yards	cubic feet	27
	cubic meters	0.76456
Cups	teaspoons	48
	tablespoons	16
	ounces	8
Drams	grains	27.34375
	drams (troy or apothecary)	0.45573
	ounces	0.0625
	ounces (troy or apothecary)	0.05697
	grams	1.771845
Drams (troy or apothecary)	grains	60
	drams (avoirdupois)	2.194286
	ounces (avoirdupois)	0.13714
	ounces (troy or apothecary)	0.125 or 1/8
	grams	3.88794
Drams (U.S. fluid)	minims	60
	fluid ounces	0.125 or 1/8
	cubic inches	0.22559
	milliliters	3.6966
Fathoms	feet	6
Feet	centimeters	30.48
	fathoms	0.16667
	hands	3
	miles	0.00019
	kilometers	0.0003

TO CONVERT FROM	TO	MULTIPLY BY
Feet of water	pounds per square foot	62.42
	pounds per square inch	0.4335
	inches of mercury @ 0°C	0.88265
Feet per minute	feet per second	0.01667
Feet per second	miles per hour	0.68182
Gallons	milliliters	3,785
	cubic inches	231
	cubic feet	0.1337
	cubic yards	0.00495
	cubic meters	0.00379
	fluid ounces	128
	quarts	4
	liters	3.7853
	British gallons	0.8327
Gallons of water	pounds of water @ 60°F	8.3453
Gallons (British)	pounds of water @ 62°F	10
	US gallons	1.201
Grains	ounces	0.00229
	ounces (troy or apothecary)	0.00208
	grams	0.0648
Grains per gallon	parts per million (ppm)	17.118
	grams per liter	0.01714
Grams	grains	15.432
	drams	0.56438
	drams (troy or apothecary)	0.25721
	ounces	0.03527
	ounces (troy or apothecary)	0.03215
	pounds	0.0022
	pounds (troy or apothecary)	0.00268
Grams per liter	grains per gallon	58.418
Hectares	square meters	10,000
	acres	2.471
Horsepower	foot-pounds per minute	33,000
	Btu per minute	42.42
	Btu per hour	2,546
	metric horsepower	1.014
	kilowatts	0.7457
Inches	feet	0.08333
	yards	0.02778
	centimeters	2.54
	meters	0.0254

TO CONVERT FROM	TO	MULTIPLY BY
Inches of mercury @ 0°C	pounds per square inch	0.4912
	inches of water	13.6
Inches of water @ 4°C	ounces per square inch	0.582
	inches of mercury	0.0735
Kilograms	grains	15,432.36
	drams	564.3834
	drams (troy or apoth.)	257.21
	ounces	35.27396
	ounces (troy or apoth.)	32.15075
	pounds	2.20462
	pounds (troy or apoth.)	2.67923
	short tons	0.0011
	long tons	0.00098
	metric tons	0.001
Kilometers	feet	3,280.8
	miles	0.62137
Kilowatts	Btu per minute	56.90
	horsepower	1.341
	metric horsepower	1.397
Kilowatt-hours	Btu	3,413
Knots	nautical miles per hour	1
	miles per hour	1.1508
Leagues	miles	3
Links (surveyor's)	feet	0.66
	inches	7.92
	chain	0.01
	rod	0.04
Liters	fluid ounces	33.814
	quarts	1.05669
	gallons	0.2642
	British gallons	0.21998
	cubic inches	61.02374
	cubic feet	0.03531
	cubic meters	0.001
	cubic yards	0.00131
Meters	inches	39.37
	feet	3.2808
	yards	1.094
Miles	nautical miles	0.869
	feet	5,280
	yards	1,760
	meters	1,609.344

TO CONVERT FROM	TO	MULTIPLY BY
Miles (nautical)	statute miles	1.1508
Miles per hour	knots	0.8684
	miles per minute	0.016667
	feet per second	1.467
Miles per minute	knots	52.104
	feet per second	88
Milliliters	minims	16.231
	fluid drams	0.2705
	fluid ounces	0.0338
	cubic inches	0.061
Millimeters	inches	0.03937
Minims	fluid drams	0.01667
	fluid ounces	0.002
	milliliters	0.0616
Ounces	grains	437.5
	drams	16
	drams (troy or apoth.)	7.292
	ounces (troy or apoth.)	0.9146
	pounds	0.0625
	pounds (troy or apoth.)	0.07595
	grams	28.34952
	kilograms	0.02835
Ounces (troy or apoth.)	grains	480
	drams	17.55429
	drams (troy or apoth.)	8
	ounces (avoirdupois)	1.09714
	pounds (troy or apoth.)	0.08333
	pounds	0.06857
	grams	31.1035
	kilograms	0.0311
Ounces (fluid)	minims	480
	pints	0.0625
	quarts	0.03125
	gallons	0.00781
	cubic inches	1.80469
	cubic feet	0.00104
	milliliters	29.57353
	liters	0.02957
	teaspoons	6
	tablespoons	2
Ounces (fluid, British)	fluid ounces, U.S.	0.96
Ounces per sq. in.	pounds per sq. inch	0.0625
	inches of water	1.73
	inches of mercury	0.127

TO CONVERT FROM	TO	MULTIPLY BY
Pecks	bushels	0.25 or 1/4
Pints (dry)	pecks	0.0625
	bushels	0.01562
	cubic inches	33.60031
	cubic feet	0.01944
	liters	0.55061
Pints (fluid)	fluid ounces	16
	fluid quarts	0.5 or 1/2
	gallons	0.125 or 1/8
	cubic inches	28.875
	cubic feet	0.01671
	cups	2
	milliliters	473.17647
	liters	0.47318
Pounds	grains	7,000
	drams	256
	drams (troy or apoth.)	116.6667
	ounces	16
	ounces (troy or apoth.)	14.58333
	pounds (troy or apoth.)	1.21528
	grams	453.59237
	kilograms	0.453592
	short tons	0.0005
	long tons	0.000446
	metric tons	0.0004536
Pounds (troy or apoth.)	grains	5,760
	drams (avoirdupois)	210.6514
	drams (troy or apoth.)	96
	ounces (avoirdupois)	13.16571
	ounces (troy or apoth.)	12
	pounds (avoirdupois)	0.82286
	grams	373.24172
	kilograms	0.45359
Pounds of water	gallons	0.1198
Quarts (dry)	pecks	0.125 or 1/8
	bushels	0.03125
	cubic inches	67.2006
Quarts (fluid)	fluid ounces	32
	cubic inches	57.749
	cubic feet	0.033421
	milliliters	946.358
	liters	0.946333
Rods	chains	0.25 or 1/4
Square centimeters	square inches	0.115
	square feet	0.00108

TO CONVERT FROM	TO	MULTIPLY BY
Square feet	square inches	144
	square yards	0.111111
	square centimeters	929
	square meters	0.0929
Square inches	square centimeters	6.452
Square meters	square feet	10.765
	square yards	1.196
Square miles	acres	640
	square kilometers	2.589998
Square yards	square meters	0.836
Tons (long)	pounds	2,240
	kilograms	1,016.0470
	short tons	1.12
	metric tons	1.016
Tons (short)	pounds	2,000
	kilograms	907.185
	long tons	0.89286
	metric tons	0.907185
Tons (metric)	pounds	2,204.62
	kilograms	1,000
	long tons	0.984206
	short tons	1.10231
Tons of refrigeration	Btu per hour	12,000
Watts	Btu per hour	3.415
	horsepower	0.00134
Watt-hours	Btu	3.413
Yards	centimeters	91.44
	meters	0.9144

This table is quite simple to use. The units are in alphabetical order. All you need do is run down the first column until you find the unit you want. Then move to the second column to find what you want to convert it to. The factor to multiply by will be next to it in the third column.

All weight units are avoirdupois unless shown otherwise. Volume units are U.S. except where indicated.

CORKS AND CORKSCREWS   "I would like to be able to claim that I discovered this handy tip in my workshop, but actually I came upon it when I wanted to open a bottle of wine and our corkscrew had disappeared. I made a corkscrew out of a screw eye with a section of dowel through the eye. If you happened to need a corkscrew in the workshop, it would work there too."

Dowel →

Screw eye

"A cork used to seal a can or bottle can lose its effectiveness if it becomes compressed and no longer fits tight. Such corks can be restored by putting them in a pan of water and bringing it to a boil for several minutes. They'll be as good as new."

"If you've ever accidentally pushed a cork down into a bottle you want to keep, you may want to use my stunt for getting it out. First, you must remove all the liquid. Then pour a half cup of household ammonia into the bottle. Within a week, the ammonia will cause the cork to crumble into small bits. These bits—along with the ammonia—can be poured out, and the bottle can be used again. Of course, you'll need a new cork."

"To remove a cork from a bottle without ruining the cork, get a flat button that's slightly smaller around than the opening in the bottle. Put a strong thin wire through two of the holes in the button and drop the button into the bottle, holding onto the ends of the wire. Turn the bottle upside down until the cork falls into the right position against the neck. Then pull the wire up so the button is flat against the bottom of the cork. Pull gently, and the cork will come on out."

Or, "A bottle brush can be inserted in the bottle, and the bottle then tipped to allow the bristles to get behind the cork. The bristles are strong enough to force the cork into the neck and then on out, but the wire handle isn't big enough to keep the cork from coming through."

COTTER PINS   "Because I didn't have a cotter pin, I was forced to improvise with a big safety pin. Now I wonder if I haven't discovered something that's a lot better than a cotter pin. It's much easier to install and remove, and in the case of a nut that is frequently put on and taken off, it's a real help. Also, the safety pin should last much longer, since cotter pins have a way of getting bent after a few hammerings."

Safety pin

"Almost every home handyman has ruined a cotter pin that had to be hammered into a tight place. The eye will take only so much

Slot

hammering before it bends all out of shape. A tiny precaution will prevent this. Merely stick a nail through the eye, and you can pound away until the pin is in place without bending it. Remove the nail, and you're all set."

"Most of the time, putting in a cotter pin is a matter of searching for the hole. If you can put a road sign on the end of the bolt ahead of time, this can become an easy task. A simple notch filed or sawed in the end and parallel to the line of the cotter pin hole will act as a guide for you to feel which way the hole runs."

COUNTERSINKING "If you don't have the right-size countersink bit, here's a clever trick. Take an extra screw of the right size and cut it off about ¼″ below the head. Place this stub into the pilot hole. With a hammer, tap the stub, and the screw head will be pressed into the wood, forming a countersink of exactly the right size. It's really easy on soft woods, but be sure to take your time on hardwoods."

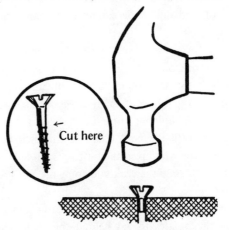

Cut here

"If you don't have a countersink bit, a beer opener will do the job. Just take one of those puncture-type beer openers, and sharpen the point a little with a file. Put the point down into the pilot hole and rotate it in the hole. A few times around, and the opener will cut a countersink. It's actually quicker than changing the bit in a drill."

CURTAIN RODS "Before you throw away an old adjustable curtain rod, remember that it can come in handy as a substitute extension rule for making large-sized inside measurements. It will slide into place and hold the measurement until the rod can be set beside a rule to record the length."

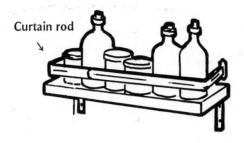

Curtain rod

"Here's another use for the kind of old curtain rod that's curved on each end so it sticks out from the wall. Install it about 2″ above a shop shelf where you keep glass bottles and jars. The rod will act as a guard rail to prevent them from falling off and breaking."

"The long flat parts of old curtain rods are ideal to use in covering up electrical wires that run along a span of baseboard. There's a trough on the underside for the wires to fit into. I glued the rods to the wall with rubber cement, and that way didn't run the risk of driving a screw through the wiring. We've since had the room repainted, and the rods were painted the same color as the walls. They really look quite nice and do hide the wires."

"It really isn't any trouble to figure out where curtain rod holders go, because almost every home handyman will have a wife around to tell him. However getting them in exactly the same position on both sides of the window is another matter. I get them exact with a template

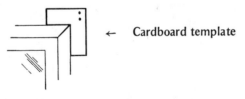

← Cardboard template

that's an L-shaped piece of cardboard. Place the 'L' upside down against the corner of the opening for the window, and mark it to show wnere the bracket should go. Then punch holes in the template where the screws should go. Now flop the 'L' over and you can make marks on the wall at each side of the window which will be exactly the same on both sides."

(Now that the draw drapes are up, they sometimes become a little sluggish. If they're the kind that have a traverse unit that runs in a metal track in the rod, run a candle down the inside of the rod, and the drapes will work great from then on.)

CURVING WOOD   "In putting redwood edging around flower beds, I needed to curve the wood considerably to make it look best. This was done easily and effectively by making a series of saw cuts on the back side of the wood. I made the cuts every ½" or so, about ¾ of the way through the wood (I set the blade on my power table saw so it stuck up just that far)."

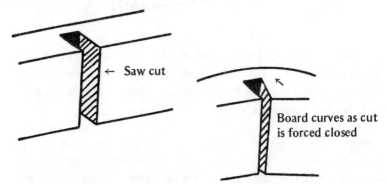

← Saw cut

Board curves as cut is forced closed

(In fact, by spacing the cuts close enough together, you can bend a piece of wood into a complete circle. This is an especially good technique for many ornamental woodworking jobs. Get a piece of wood and play around with this technique—I bet you'll get a kick out of it. This same idea can also be used to make metal bending easier. However, don't use it on metal where the structural strength is critical.)

Decals • Depth Gauges • Doors • Doormats • Dowels • Drawer Pulls • Drilling and Drill Bits • Driveways • Driving Stakes • Dry Ingredients • Dry Wells • Duplicate Cuts

D

DECALS   If you've tried the popular "cuss and scrape" method of removing decals from the car window ... you've probably thought there must be a better way:

"Make a compress out of a couple of thicknesses of rag a bit larger than the decal. Tape the compress over the decal with masking tape. Wet the compress generously with household ammonia, keeping it pressed firmly against the decal and keeping it moist with ammonia. In a short while the ammonia dissolves most of the decal, and the rest wipes off. If it's a stubborn one, just leave the cloth on for 20 or 30 minutes."

(If you don't have any household ammonia around, you can use warmed vinegar on the compress. It does just about as well.)

DEPTH GAUGES   Drilling blind holes that have to be of a uniform depth, a gadget called a depth gauge is needed. Here's a trio of ideas:

"Tell your wife not to throw away any more empty wooden spools from her sewing basket. You can make depth dauges for drill bits by putting a screw eye in at right angles to the hole. This acts as a screw to hold the spool against the bit. For larger bits, drill the hole larger."

"A section of a dried corncob makes a great depth gauge for a drill bit. The cob is easily cut into an inch-thick disc that will slip right on the bit. When it's up on the shank at the right depth, it will stay in place. Another advantage is that the cob is soft enough not to mar the work."

(Folks, this corny idea really works.)

Or—"Wrap tape around the bit at the desired depth. Use enough tape to act as a stop when the drill carries it down to meet the work."

Tape

There are also depth gauges to measure the depth of a blind hole. "Here's my idea for a homemade depth gauge. It's just one of those slip-on pencil clips (that slide up and down) fitted over a piece of dowelling. Put the dowel in the hole to be measured and slip the clip down to the surface, and it shows the depth."

Here's still another kind: "Want to put a toggle or Molly bolt in a masonry or textured wall? The thickness of the wall determines the size of anchor to use. Since you can't see through the wall, here's an easy

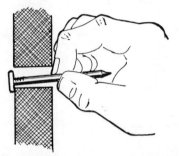

way to determine the thickness. After you've drilled the hole, insert a nail, head first, and hock the head against the back side of the wall. Put your finger on the nail at the point where it comes out of the wall, lift out the nail still holding the finger in position and—son of a gun!—you just measured the thickness of the wall."

"When using a regular saw for cuts that must be of a specific depth, I use a depth gauge made from a pair of yardsticks and a pair of C-clamps. A yardstick is clamped on either side of the saw blade at the desired depth, and then the cutting automatically stops when the work and the yardsticks meet."

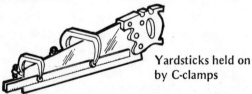

Yardsticks held on
by C-clamps

DOORS   If you're bugged by doors that slam with a bang, why not put tiny cushions in to lessen the noise? Cut small tabs of foam rubber and glue these at about four places along the side stop against which the door closes. These foam pads of 1/8″ thickness will compress enough to allow the door to close and latch, but will keep the door from making contact with the jamb.

A swinger is fun to have around—unless it happens to be a door that swings closed when you want it to stay open. About the quickest way to stop this is to take out the top hinge pin and wrap a strip of cellophane tape around the pin. (Once around will do.) Reinsert the pin, and you probably will have tamed that door.

"We were having trouble with a sticking door, and rather than take the door off to plane it, I merely put a piece of sandpaper on the floor and moved the door back and forth over it. I kept adding shirt boards underneath to raise the sandpaper and keep the pressure on. It worked like a charm."

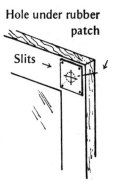

Hole under rubber patch

Slits →

"With an airtight house, the air pressure makes it hard to close storm doors. I've solved this problem with the installation of a small escape valve in each storm door. I drilled a ½" hole through the door—up at the top, so it's not an eyesore. I tacked a square of rubber from an old inner tube over this on the outside of the door. In the center of the rubber patch, I slit an 'X' with a sharp knife. Now, when the door is pulled shut, the air pressure is released through the escape valve. Once the door is shut, the 'X' closes back up and doesn't allow cold air to come in. By allowing the door to close quicker, it lets less cold air in when you go in and out."

"The new door's hung, and the job looks great, but there's one small problem: the latch bolt and the opening in the strike plate don't line up. Before you decide whether to rehang the door or change the plate location, see if the striker plate can't be filed to fit. Usually it's only a matter of a fraction of an inch. Filing it off is much easier than anything else. A little chalk on the edge of the latch bolt will mark on the striker plate exactly where the opening should come to."

"I just have to tell you about how cleverly my husband solved a door problem. We had a door that had warped out of shape in the middle. Instead of removing the door, he simply added a third hinge in between the two regular ones, at the place where the door bowed. When this was tightened down, it forced the door back into shape, and it works perfectly."

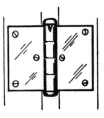

"Doors are easy to take down, once you get a screwdriver in between the pin and the hinge to knock the pin out. However, getting started can be a real chore. A notch cut in the hinge at the point where the head of the hinge-pin fits will give you an ever-present starting place for the screwdriver to fit against the head of the pin. This slit has to be cut while the door is off, naturally, and can easily be done with your hacksaw. It won't be noticeable after the door is put back up."

"Properly lubricated hinge-pins sometimes creep up a bit as the doors are opened and closed. To get them back, a few hammer taps are needed, and this can chip off paint. Remove all the pins and score them in about four places with a triangular file. This doesn't affect the movement of the door, but will absolutely stop the pins from creeping."

(Slightly bending the pin will also stop creeping. Just ever so slightly, or the pin won't go back in.)

"All of the door knobs in our house fit loosely. This didn't make any difference in the way they worked, but there was always a slight rattle and they just didn't feel right. I took them apart and dropped paraffin down in the knob. Now, they have a good solid feel to them as the paraffin holds the knob firmly against the rest of the assembly."

"We had a door that didn't fit tight enough because of a loose-fitting bolt. When there was any air movement in the house, it caused the closed door to rattle against the door stop. Since it only happened spasmodically, it took us forever to find out it wasn't some departed previous resident come to haunt us. But, I eliminated the rattle by cutting a couple of rubber eraser tips off pencils with a sharp razor blade and glueing them to the door stop. When shut, the door rests firmly against the tips . . . and our 'ghost' doesn't rattle any more. Now we're trying to find out what causes the moaning sound from the basement."

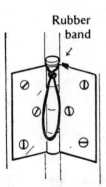

Rubber band

"Here's a simple way to stop many rattling doors. Merely loop a rubber band around the hinge-pin. A knot will hold it around the pin. Let the rest of the rubber band hang down between the two hinge leaves so when the door is closed the rubber band will be in between them with enough padding to keep the door from rattling any more."

"If there is a door that won't stay open, remove the rubber tip on the door stop and replace it with a rubber suction cup. Now when the door is opened, it's pushed against the stop, and the suction cup holds it there until you want to close it."

"You can make an excellent door stop with a wooden spool, a long wood screw, and a rubber crutch tip. Select a spool big enough so that the crutch tip can be forced over the end and will stay there. Insert the screw in the hole through the center of the spool to attach the spool in place on the wall. With the rubber tip placed over the end, your stop is ready for the door. The spool can be painted to match the wall and will look quite nice."

DOORMATS   "By cutting out 2' x 3' sections of an old wood and wire picket fence, you can come up with the best outside door mats you ever saw. We have three kids and live on a farm, and these are the best we've found for scraping off mud. When the mats get too muddy, they can be hosed off and come out clean as a whistle. They look good, too."

DOWELS   "Dowels stay glued better if they're scored to allow the glue to stay up on the dowel and not be forced to the bottom of the hole. The simplest way to do this is to crimp the dowel lightly with a pair of pliers. The pliers will leave some nice glue-holding teeth marks."

Another excellent way to make dowelling stay glued is to wrap a small piece of nylon from a woman's stocking around the end of the dowel. Apply the glue and force both dowel and nylon down into the hole. The nylon will hold the glue up on the dowel, and the bond will be super-strong.

Also, you will get a better joint if the dowels are 100 percent dry. To insure this, place them in a pan in the oven for about 15 minutes. This will take out the moisture, causing them to shrink. After they are in place, they will gradually take on moisture from the air and swell. The shrinking and swelling process is microscopic in size but can make a big difference in the tightness of the joint.

Dowels should fit tight to do their job. Occasionally, the hole will be just a tiny bit larger than the dowel. One way to make it fit tight is to crimp the ends of the dowelling with a pair of pliers, hard enough so the wood is pushed out of round, making it wider. The extra width will make it fit. Use more than the normal amount of glue in a case like this.

"Sometimes a project will call for a dowel to be pointed. This can be done easily with an ordinary pencil sharpener."

Or, "touch a dowel to a moving grinding wheel to bring it to a point."

DRAWER PULLS   "For those who have trouble with pesky screw-on drawer pulls that keep working loose, here's a problem-solver. Cut some round washers out of sandpaper and put these between the drawer and the pull. Cut them small enough so that when the pull is tightened down, they can't be seen. The friction of the sandpaper acts as a sort of lock washer and keeps the pull down tight."

"Here's a neat little trick to stop a wooden drawer knob from coming loose. When it's tightened down well, drive a tiny nail from inside the drawer through the drawer and into the knob. Set the nail off to the side of the knob screw, but be careful that it goes into the knob and doesn't come out so it can be seen. It only has to be long enough to go about ¼″ into the knob to be effective."

DRILLING AND DRILL BITS   Next time you're going to drill holes in thin or soft metal, sandwich it between two scraps of wood. Then drill through the "sandwich," and the wood will eliminate rough edges or bent metal.

Also, in drilling plywood, avoid the splintering you often get on the backside by making an "open-faced sandwich." Just clamp a scrap of wood under the plywood where it is to be drilled. Then, if there's any splintering, it'll be on the backside of the scrap.

When you need to drill in metal, here's a way to start the hole without the bit skidding around on the surface before it takes hold. Just stick a piece of masking tape over the spot to be drilled. Your bit will go right through the tape and into the metal without any problem.

Masonry drill bits have a tendency to crawl away from the marked spot before you can get a good start with your drilling. Prevent this with a block of wood that has a hole drilled in it, the same size as the masonry bit. Stick the block on the brick or concrete with a generous amount of rubber cement. The block not only will keep the drill from crawling, but will eliminate any wobble that would deviate from the perpendicular. After the hole is drilled, a slight prying action will make the rubber cement let go.

"Here's an addition to my power drill that I wouldn't be without. I attached a pen light (one of those skinny flashlights) to the top of the drill with masking tape. This insures always having enough light on the spot where I'm drilling."

Flashlight →

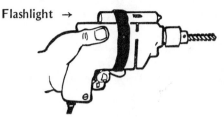

Drill bits that get bent can do a bad job, and the smaller bits are especially prone to having this happen. But they often can be salvaged by a little effort. Take two pieces of hardwood that are smooth and place the bent bit between them. Roll the bit back and forth between the two boards with as much pressure as you can apply against the top board. You'll probably be able to get the bit back as it should be.

"Here's how I find the right-sized bit when getting ready to drill. I measure the item to go into the hole with my adjustable wrench. Then I pick out the bit that fits into the opening. It's a more accurate way than sighting, and the wrench is handier than calipers."

"If the lead-in screw on an auger bit is damaged, it usually ruins the entire bit for accuracy, but such bits can easily be protected by cutting off a few sections from an old broom handle and screwing the points of the lead-in screws into the wood. Once the hole has been made, the bits can be screwed in and out of these protectors by hand." (Small corks would also be good for this protection.)

Door knob holds bit

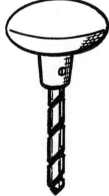

A round peg in a square hole? No problem if you want to use a square-shanked bit in a drill chuck made for round bits. Just wrap it in masking tape. It will then hold without harm to either the bit or the chuck.

"There are places where space doesn't permit the use of a drill, but you need a hole drilled nevertheless. I keep a doorknob in my tool box for these occasions. The bit fits into the doorknob and can be locked in with the doorknob set screw. The doorknob provides a good grip for boring holes, and also works on a screwdriver shank."

"If you have to drill holes in a sheet-rock or plaster wall, here's a tip that will save on clean-up time. Tape a paper sack under the place where you'll be drilling. This won't hamper your drilling, but will probably catch all the chips and dust. Masking tape, of course, will peel right off when you're finished and leave no marks."

"When drilling holes overhead, to prevent shavings from falling in your eyes punch your drill bit through a paper cup, open side toward the point. This catches the shavings and sawdust."

"Many items, such as typewritter ribbon, come in clear plastic containers. I drilled a hole in one and used it as a dust catcher when drilling holes in a plaster ceiling. I made the hole the same size as the drill bit I was using, then inserted the bit in this hole and held the plastic container up flat against the ceiling. It allows you to see what you're doing, so that the drill goes into the right spot, but keeps the dust out of your eyes."

"For pre-drilling starter holes for small screws, I use an ice pick. It's a lot easier than getting out my drill, and it's also easier to stop at the desired depth. However, it doesn't work on wood that's quite hard."

"The old snap-open type eyeglass case makes an ideal case for a set of small drilling bits. These delicate tools can be ruined easily if banged around with other tools. The case will protect them and is handy for carrying in your pocket when you don't want to lug the whole tool chest around."

DRIVEWAYS "After my mother-in-law ruined our lawn for the hundredth time by getting off our circular driveway, I decided I had to take steps. Most of the ones I thought of were illegal, but this one has helped. I painted a white line all around the edge of the drive. This shows up at night and acts as a reminder during the day. She really has stayed on the drive a lot better."

DRIVING STAKES "Driving stakes or posts into the ground can get your goat if the stake splits about halfway down. By putting a tin can over the top of the post, your chances of not splitting it are much better. Get a can whose diameter is as close as possible to that of the post."

"Driving long, thin stakes into the ground is not an easy task. There's not much of a surface to drive on, and if they're hit wrong, the stakes can split or break. Here's a trick that will help. Attach a 2″ x 4″ block to the thin stake with a C-clamp. This gives you a much better driving surface. When the stake is in far enough, clamp the block on to the next stake."

2″ x 4″ clamped to thin stake

"Since I couldn't get my wife to hold the stakes, I used a broom as a holder. Just poke the stake through the straw in about the middle of the straw part of the broom. Lay the broom flat on the ground, and it will hold the stake so you can blast away without the possibility of hurting whoever is holding."

DRY INGREDIENTS   "I like to remove all the dry shop ingredients from the original boxes and keep them in glass jars. They're better protected from moisture, and I know at a glance how much is left. The only disadvantage is in the pouring. I have solved this problem by putting an inner seal of wax paper under the metal screw-on top. First I coated the jar rim with rubber cement to make the wax paper stick on, and then cut off the excess with a sharp knife. This inside top is now much like the inner seal on a jar of instant coffee. Then I cut a pouring spout out of the paper, and this keeps the ingredients from coming out all at once. When the jar needs refilling, the inside top can easily be peeled off."

Wax paper innerseal

Spout

"Here's how I keep dry ingredients such as grout in my shop. I have my wife save the tops off of salt cartons. I cut these to fit inside the rims of jar lids that are the two-piece kind used for home canning. When the jar lid is tightened down, it holds the lid from the salt carton in place, and when I want to pour the ingredients, the spout does a great pouring job."

DRY WELLS   If the runoff of rain from downspouts is washing away soil, dig a hole under the downspout and fill it with rocks and gravel. This sort of installation is called a dry well. The depth of your dry well can vary from a foot to several feet, depending on the amount of runoff. The excess water will seep down among the rocks and soak into the ground below instead of carrying away your topsoil.

"I decided to put in a dry well to take care of a drainage problem. However, there weren't enough rocks around to fill up the hole. Guess what I came up with as a substitute? Bottle caps! They were in abundance behind a local tavern, and so I scooped up a few buckets full and filled up the hole. Then I put what few rocks I had over these for looks. It sure seems to work."

(This will work until they rust, but maybe by then you'll have found enough rocks.)

"A dry well can be made very quickly if you happen to have a discarded automobile wheel rim. Dig a hole big enough for the wheel and deep enough so the wheel can be set in the ground and be flush with the ground. Then fill in around and on top of the rim with gravel. Since the wheel slopes down toward its center, the water will go down into the ground, and, like any good dry well, this will prevent washing the soil away when it rains."

DUPLICATE CUTS   "When you need to make duplicate cuts with your jigsaw, stack the two pieces of wood to be cut, one on top of the other, and bind them together with strips of masking tape. Now the two pieces can be cut at the same time, and the cuts on each piece will be identical. Depending on the size of the stock being used and the size of your saw, you may be able to run more than two pieces through at once if needed."

E
•

EASEL   "My stepladder converts into an easel when I need to work
on screens, plywood sheets, or other large hard-to-manage things. I
drilled a pair of holes opposite each other in the front of the ladder
frame to accomodate a pair of bolts. These bolts support the screen or
other work, which leans back against the frame of the ladder. When the
work is finished, the bolts can be removed."

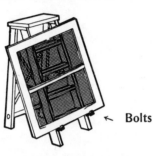

← Bolts

EFFLORESCENCE   Sometimes a white powdery formation shows
up on brick or concrete. This is a chemical reaction called efflorescence.
A mixture of one part muriatic acid to four parts water, applied to the
bricks with a brush, will take care of this problem. After brushing, hose
off the bricks completely. Muriatic acid isn't dangerous *if* you take
proper care, so read the caution notice on the bottle before using.

ELECTRICAL PROBLEMS   "Recently, I had to do some wiring in
our bathroom and wanted to cut off the power at the box in the garage
without having to throw the master switch. However, since I couldn't
see the light in the bathroom from the garage, and with my wife away,
how was I supposed to know when I flipped the right switch? I could
hear, so I plugged in a radio in the bathroom, turned it up good and
loud, and then, when I flipped the right switch, I could no longer hear
the music."

(A noisy vacuum cleaner can also let you know the power is off.)

"In replacing wiring within armored cabling, I taped the new wiring
to the end of the old wires while they were still in place in the armor.
Then it was a simple matter to pull the new cable in while pulling the
old wires out at the other end."

ELECTRICAL PROBLEMS   93

"When you cut BX cable, the hard part is trying to hold the cable. A simple holder can be made with only four fairly good-sized nails and a board. Place two of the nails about an inch apart at one end of the board. Put a section of BX between the two nails and bring it down the middle of the board so that the cable is tight against the nail closest to the center. At a point about 6″ from the nail, hold the BX in place with

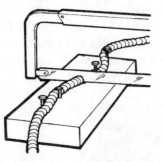

a finger and bend it back up toward the top of the board. This pushes the cable into an 'S' shape. Mark against the cable where you're holding it down and where you can feel good tension about an inch up on the other side. Put the other pair of nails at these marks. Now, the BX will hold itself in place and allow you to saw away."

"Another method for cutting BX is to bend it double until it breaks open. Then twist it so that it opens further. The metal jacket can be cut easily with a BX tool, tin snips, or diagonals. If you wish to cut the conductors too, this can easily be done after the jacket is cut."

"Here's how to remedy a pesky electrical plug that won't make proper contact because the prongs have worn a little thin. Roughen up the prongs with a pair of wire cutters or cutting pliers. Just enough pressure to score the prongs is all you need. Do this in several places on each one."

"After wiring an electrical plug and testing it to be sure it works, I fill the plug with liquid epoxy. This is super insulation, and also insures that the wires will never pull loose. A blob of putty around the wires keeps the epoxy from coming out the bottom of the plug before it's dry."

"My family is alerted to save all of the plastic caps that come on tubes of toothpaste or ointments and to put them in a box in my shop. As they come in various sizes, they make excellent solderless connectors for wiring. I've built up a supply large enough that I can always find the right size."

"My home electrical handiness is limited to very simple things, like replacing a plug. Even at that, I never seem to get the wires tightened down without their being frayed and sticking out from under the screws. After twisting the ends, they still come unraveled. I tried something that worked, and maybe it will help others. I dipped the very end of the twisted wire in a bottle of fingernail polish. Just the tip receives this treatment. After this dries, I have no trouble with the fraying. It may not be a method an electrician uses, but it helped me."

"A bare spot in an electrical wire should be covered immediately. If tape is not handy, dab the spot with fingernail polish, which is an excellent insulator. Make sure the current is off while dabbing. This trick will also come in handy for insulating wires in places that you can't get to readily."

"In stripping rubber insulation away from wires, your task will be a little easier if you use a moistened knife. Just dip the blade into a can of water from time to time and see how much quicker the job goes."

"If you don't have a wire stripping tool, place a claw hammer in a vise with the claw sticking up. The wire to be stripped is then pulled through the 'V' of the claw after the insulation has been cut at the proper place. When the wire is pulled through, the insulation is stripped off."

"We have sort of a master control panel in our basement that's a gang-switch plate with a number of switches. Two of these switches

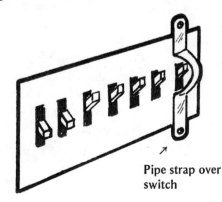

Pipe strap over
switch

would make for bad trouble if they were accidentally turned off—one is the food freezer, and the other is the heating and air conditioning. So I installed a safety cover for these two switches. It's a plumbing pipe strap attached to the wall, and the 'U' fits over the switches. The switches can still be flipped from the side, but there's no chance of hitting the wrong one."

← Tape

No stress here

"The electrical outlet used for power tools in my shop is in a remote spot under my workbench. This means it's a lot easier just to yank on the cord to disconnect a tool. This would eventually pull the wire loose at the plug, except there's no longer any stress at the point where the wire enters the plug. I looped about 4" of the cord back against the plug and taped it in place. Then I pulled the cord back against the loop and taped it again. Now the tugging is at the taped points and not at the connection."

"If you should find you need an electrical grommet and there's not one available, make one from a slip-on pencil eraser. Just cut off the 'roof top' of the eraser. Drill the hole in the metal a shade smaller and insert."

EPOXY   Epoxy glues come in two tubes that require mixing at the time of use. Make sure to put the right cap back on the right tube when the mixing is done. There may be enough of the hardening compound in the cap to start the hardening process in the top of the tube and give it a tough inner seal you don't want!

EXPANSION BOLTS   "If you've ever moved a mirror or other heavy wall hanging, you've probably faced the problem of what to do about the expansion bolt wall anchors that were left. Since they're flared out behind the wall, pulling them back through the wall would leave a hole big enough for a small wall safe. So unless you want this, unscrew the bolt until it lacks only a turn or two before coming out completely. Take a hammer and tap the bolt lightly. This will push the flared part inside the wall away from the wall. If the anchor is a small one, the flared portion will snap off and fall down between the walls. The remaining part can then be taken out of the wall without enlarging the hole. If the flared part didn't snap off, grab the head of the bolt with a pair of pliers and pull out gently. The flat outside flange can now be pulled away from the wall. Cut this off and push the remainder on through the wall so it falls down inside. There will still be a hole in the wall, but only a small one."

EXTENSION AND ELECTRIC CORDS   "When you're using one of your power tools with an extension cord, there's nothing more aggravating than to make a move and pull the cords apart in the middle of your work. There's a simple way to prevent accidental disconnecting. Loop the cords together as if you were going to tie a knot. Instead of completing the knot, however, plug them together. Now you can't unplug them by a sudden pull."

(This is also a good trick for wives who use an extension cord on a vacuum cleaner.)

Those plastic spiral phone cord wrappers that keep the phone cord from kinking will do the same thing for the cords on your power tools.

The electric cords on most shop tools are insulated with heavy-duty rubber that lasts for a long time, but even the toughest rubber can deteriorate after a while. You can give rubber cords an extra measure of protection by coating them with liquid wax shoe polish. Probably once a year will do for most tools. The wax protects the rubber and does neither it nor the tool any harm.

"Electric appliances always seem to have cords that just won't quite make it to the outlet. Of course, there are always extension cords to save the day, but they seem to be 12' long, and that means a huge roll of extra cord to try and get out of the way. I bought several extra plugs and sockets and several feet of wire and made some mini-extension cords that vary from one to three feet in length. They have really come in handy and have allowed my wife to put lamps where she wants them instead of where their cords will reach the outlets."

"I save cardboard tubes from rolls of waxed paper and foil. They're great for keeping the cords on power tools from getting all tangled. Just loop the cords loosely and shove them in the tubes. Extension cords can be stored in these tubes too."

"I've always felt it's safer to unplug all power tools when I'm not using them. However, a couple of times over the years I've ended up with a crushed plug that was stepped on or rolled over. Now I've installed cord holders that are spring-type clothespins nailed to the wall close to the electrical outlet so the plugs are handy when I want to plug them in."

"When rewiring a lamp, the trick is to get the cord up through that tiny pipe. It's simple if you'll tie a string to the end of the old cord before it's removed. As the old cord is pulled out of the lamp, the string will be pulled down through the pipe. Then attach the new cord to the string, and it can be pulled back through the pipe."

EXTRA MUSCLE   "To move a heavy refrigerator across the floor without marring the floor or straining too many muscles, put a bar of soap under the leading edge of the appliance. Push up at the back of the refrigerator as you push, and this makes it slide right across the floor. The soap track is easily removed with a wet mop."

"Under heavy objects you need to move in the workshop or garage or on other hard surfaces, use a few bottle caps. These make great glides, and there's no problem in prying up the edges to slip them under."

"When our new furniture arrived, my husband was recovering from an operation and couldn't help put it in place. However, his brain was working well, and he came up with an idea that enabled me to move the heavy pieces by myself. He suggested I put roller skates under each end, and this made the heavy pieces mobile. I just rolled them into place, and then removed the skates. I've since accused him of coming up with this good idea so he wouldn't have this chore hanging over his head when he got well. At any rate, it allowed me to enjoy my new furniture much sooner."

"After refinishing the hardwood floors in our dining room, I was faced with getting our huge dining room table back in position without scratching up my work. My 96-pound wife was obviously not going to be of much help. We solved the problem by putting wax milk carton 'shoes' on each table leg. The top was cut out of the carton, and each corner of the table was lifted to put the 'shoes' in place. Then the table slid with no mess."

"Keep a few lengths of scrap iron pipe around the workshop to serve as rollers for heavy objects that have to be moved. Just pry up the edges of the object and insert the pipes under the front and back edges. Use at least three sections and on up to four or five. As the object moves along over the pipes, they will roll along too, but will usually keep coming out behind. As one comes out, insert it again at the front. Changing directions can be done by putting the pipe sections in at different angles. With this method, a small handyman can move mighty big things around."

"Every so often most husbands are asked to display their prowess by removing some stubborn bottle cap that won't unscrew. I've found that an old squeeze-type nutcracker will usually do the trick on any metal cap that's small enough for it to grip."

"If your wife has an electric range, touch a stubborn bottle cap to one of the hot cooking coils for a few seconds so that the metal expands, but not the glass underneath. Grip it with a towel, and even the toughest ones will come loose."

"My belt wrench helps remove stubborn jar tops. All it takes is a leather belt and a wooden ruler. Loop the belt around the jar top at about the middle of the belt. Where the belt has made the full circle and again meets itself, place one end of the ruler. Bring the rest of the belt around the other end of the ruler and back toward the jar, pulling it as tight as you can. Grip the ruler with the belt and bring it around in the direction in which the jar lid will unscrew. The added leverage will make the belt grip the lid firmly and will usually open it."

Belt pulled tight around ruler

"If you happen to run across some really tough nails to be pulled, here's a way to get extra muscle. Slip a foot-long length of pipe over the

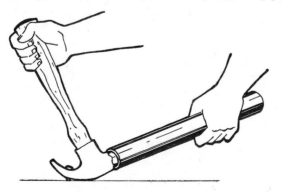

head of your claw hammer. You've now created a V-shaped tool that'll allow you to use both hands and really make the pulling a pushover."

"Those big rolls of building paper are hard for one man to handle, since they roll away each time you tug on them. I borrowed one of the kids' roller skates and turned it upside down. The wheels were adjusted so a roll fits in between, and now the rolls stay put."

EYE HOOKS   "I had a project calling for a number of eye hooks Rather than pre-drill for them, I devised a way to hammer them to get them started without bending the eye. I found a dowel to fit inside the eye and drove each one with the dowel in place."

F

FARM   "On my farm, the pastures are fenced with barbed wire. At
the points where I go through the fence regularly, I use two chunks of
old garden hose as hand- and footholds to save me from ever getting
stuck with a barb. One goes on the top strand of barbed wire, and one
on the bottom one. I raise the top wire up by the piece of hose and
push the bottom down with my foot as I go between them."

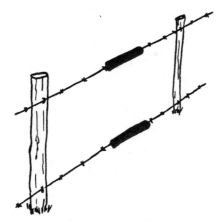

"I needed a temporary fence to separate some livestock and made a
corral for this purpose in about half an hour. First I cut steel rods from
my scrap pile, all about 4' long, and drove them into the ground about
6' apart, outlining the area to be fenced off. Then I put an empty
plastic squeeze bottle down over the top of each rod. (The pint size
that liquid detergent comes in is best, and the spout can be pried out.)
The bottles acted as insulators for the wire that was strung from one
bottle to another. A loop was made around each bottle to keep the wire
in place. When the wires were hooked up to the fence charger, I had a
very effective electrified fence that was easy to put up and easy to take
down and cost very little."

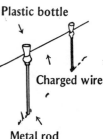

Plastic bottle

Charged wire

Metal rod

FENCES AND FENCE POSTS   "When I put in our fence, I found
myself pulling out the posthole digger several times to insert a yardstick
into the hole to see if it was deep enough. Then I got smart and painted
a line on the handle at the 2' mark (which is how deep I wanted the

holes). Not only did it save me from an extra step, it seemed to make a hard job a little easier because I had a visible goal in front of me at all times. Since then I've painted permanent lines on the handle to mark various depths."

Pitchfork

Tape

"Setting a fence post is usually a two-man job, because you really need a helper to hold the post straight until the concrete is filled in around it. I stick a long-handled pitchfork into the ground at an angle so it slants back over the posthole. Then I put the post in place, and wrap masking tape around both post and fork to hold the post against the fork handle. With the fork stuck into the ground, the post is held straight until you're ready to unclamp it."

(A fork isn't as good a helper as a wife who can tell you what you're doing wrong.)

Driving rods and fence posts into the ground is also a two-man job. If you don't have a human helper, find an old empty nail keg and put it to work. Cut a hole in the bottom of the keg, making it as close to the size of the post as possible. Place the keg over the spot where the post goes and put the post into the hole in the keg. The keg will hold the post while you hammer it in. When the post is driven into place, lift the keg up over the post. If you happen to slip with the hammer, this helper doesn't complain or file suit against you.

To prevent a metal post or pipe set in concrete from working loose, drill a number of holes in the portion of the pipe that will be encased in the concrete. Then when the wet mixture is poured around the post, it will ooze into the holes and hold much tighter.

"When I finished building my fence, the gate latch I ordered still hadn't arrived, so I did what any super handyman would have done— improvise. My 'latch' was made from a common flat L-shaped mending plate which hangs by the hole in one end. By hanging it on the post

Post   Gate

next to the gate, I was able to position it so the right angle extended out over the gate. It was, of course, placed on the side toward which the gate opened. This angle held the gate in a closed position. To open, the 'L' needs only be pulled back toward the post until the gate can clear it. When the gate is closed, gravity keeps the latch in place. A pair of washers, one on each side of the 'L,' makes it work better."

"Here's a unique gate latch that enables us to open the gate from either side. It requires only an ordinary screen-door hook and a little ingenuity. I cut a half circle out of the edge of the gate, and installed

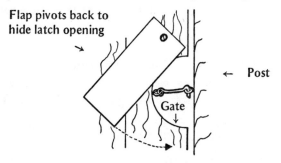

the hook right in the middle of the half circle. I put the eye for the hook on the fence post at a point opposite the hook, and placed a pair of leather flaps on either side of the gate to hide the half circle. It's a good latch and cost very little."

"Painting the bottoms of fences can be tough on a paintbrush; yet it's very important to have this part of the fence painted for protection. I use a dauber out of a bottle of shoe polish for this purpose. It works fine and saves my brush from any damage."

(This is also good for the bottoms of doors.)

"The next time your picket fence needs painting, your wife's dust-pan will come in handy. Slip the dustpan under the fence as you go along, and you'll not have to worry about the paint that drips off. The dustpan is wide enough so that it'll be under several pickets at once and, therefore, will catch the drips. Ever so often, pour the drips back into the paint can, and you'll save lots of otherwise wasted paint. Also, you'll end up with a neater-looking job when it's all done."

"I found a gimmick for picket fence painting that's almost better than Tom Sawyer's method of getting someone else to do it. A wide paint roller covers several of the pickets with each stroke, and actually did as smooth a job as I would have done with the brush. To do the edges, I used a smaller roller and finished the entire job in a third the time it would have taken with a brush."

"Each year, I whitewash our picket fence. I used to mix the whitewash in a bucket, and since this mixture goes on rather fast, it seemed I ran out just as I got started. This year I came up with a brilliant idea that cut down on the mixing time. I mixed the whitewash in my metal wheelbarrow. It holds a number of buckets of mixture, so I mixed enough for the entire job at once. The wheelbarrow could be rolled along the fence as the painting was done. After the job was finished, I hosed the last of the mixture out of the barrow before it dried."

FILES AND FILING Files always work better if kept clean. In using a file card or wire brush to clean your file, always brush along the grain. Otherwise you run the risk of dulling or damaging the teeth.

There are other ways to clean files and rasps. One of these should suit your needs:

"A small ball of putty is the best thing I've found to clean the small particles from between the teeth of a file. Just roll it over the file's surface, and it does the job. The putty can be used over and over, and I store a ball for that purpose in a baby food jar to keep it from drying out. If it starts to dry, a few drops of linseed oil will bring it back to life."

"Stick a piece of masking tape lengthwise over the file. Rub your finger over the tape to press it between the teeth. Then peel it off, and all the sawdust or shavings will stick to the tape."

"Next time you have to file anything made of aluminum, you'll find that by occasionally dipping the file in kerosene you'll eliminate its getting loaded with filings. Any filings that might be washed off into the kerosene go to the bottom, so the liquid may be used for other purposes later."

"Take a piece of plain old blackboard chalk and run it over the file. The chalk dust that sticks in the teeth of the file won't affect its filing qualities, but will keep metal particles from packing on the file."

"To keep your file from clogging up on soft metals, rub a wax candle over the teeth before using. The wax will fill in between the teeth but still leave the points free to file. When the filing is done, melt the wax, and all the filings will be carried off with it, leaving you with a perfectly clean file. Even hot water will melt the wax, so that's no problem."

"Most filing tasks could really be done better by using both hands, but most files have just one handle. I added a handle for such cases by putting a C-clamp on the point. (Remember the point is the end that *isn't* pointed.) To protect the teeth, I wrap the point in a couple of layers of masking tape for the clamp to attach to."

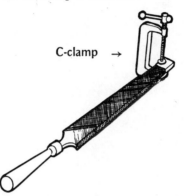

C-clamp →

"Unprotected files have a way of picking up all sorts of grit that can foul up the teeth. If you keep your files in a drawer, wrap them with that clear plastic food wrap that clings to itself. This keeps the teeth protected from grime and grit, and at the same time allows you to see which file is which."

FILTERS "I clean the furnace filter with a vacuum cleaner. However, the suction tends to pull the soft filter material apart. To prevent this, I cut a piece of screen wire the same size as the filter and framed it with wooden strips. When I place this over the filter and vacuum through it, the filter isn't disturbed at all and is cleaned thoroughly."

FINISHING A pair of newlyweds on a very small budget bought unfinished pine furniture and discovered this low-cost stain quite by accident:

"My wife spilled some tea on one of our pieces of furniture before we'd gotten around to finishing it. We really felt badly until we realized that it made a very good-looking finish. We experimented and found that strong tea produces a finish that was just what we had in mind. Sealed with clear shellac, this really looks great."

"If you have a blowtorch, you can achieve a very unusual furniture finish that gives a rustic, antique appearance to brand new pieces. Set the flame very low and run it slowly back and forth along the grain of the wood. Don't leave it on any one spot long enough to catch fire. Additional effects may be had by roughing up the wood with a chain or sharp object before charring the surface. I advise experimenting with a scrap first to get the right touch with the torch. After you've finished with the torch, clean the surface off with a brush and solvent. Then seal it with a coat of clear shellac."

"Instead of sandpaper I use a very fine steel wool to put an extra smooth surface on furniture. Then to be sure I get all the minute slivers of steel wool off the furniture before a finish is applied, I use a magnet. This picks up tiny particles that might otherwise end up stuck in the paint or varnish."

Plastic coffee can lids come in handy for painting furniture legs. When placed under a leg, the lid protects the floor, catches all the excess paint, and still allows you to paint right down to the bottom of the leg. The drippings can then be poured back into the paint can.

The beautiful things that can be turned on a lathe are often fouled up in the finishing process, mainly because they're usually round and knobbly and therefore hard to hold. If possible, while you're finishing the work leave it in the lathe, where it can easily be rotated without handling. This won't help if the piece will be subjected to additional treatment after having been turned.

"Next time you go into the shoe repair shop, ask the man for a few old rubber heels. These are good to have around the shop to protect the finish when you need to use some sort of clamp or vise that might mar. Before using them, be sure the cobbler's nails are removed."

FIRE STARTERS   "Here's a fire starter idea for both fireplace owners and campers. Roll up sections of newspaper, tie them in the middle, and then dip each end into a pot of melted paraffin. When the paraffin is dry, these starters can be stored until needed. For the paraffin, just use the stubs of candles that are too short to look right any longer."

"I keep an open wax milk carton on my workbench as a receptacle for all the small wood scraps left over from my various projects. When the carton gets full, it's folded over and is used later in the fireplace as a fire starter. The combination of the wax carton and the kindling makes an instant fire."

FIREPLACE   "Removing the ashes from the fireplace always stirred up a great cloud of dust which caused me to cough and sputter. It also made the chore of dusting the furniture come due earlier. One day as I started to clean out the fireplace, my husband came in with a plastic detergent bottle filled with water. He sprayed the top layer of ashes lightly with water, and when he reached in with the shovel, no dust came up. By keeping the ashes wet down, the entire job was done without raising any dust."

"I scoop the ashes from the fireplace into a box, but first, I put wet newspaper over the top of the box. As I get a scoopful of ashes, I lift up a corner of the newspaper and dump the ashes in. The wet newspaper not only keeps the dust from coming out, but also catches the dust and seems to settle it down."

"In cleaning out a fireplace, dust can be stirred up that will drift all over the house. Help stop this mess by putting a crumpled paper bag in one back corner of the fireplace. Put a match to it, and as it burns it will create rising heat currents that will draw most of the dust up the chimney."

"To clean the soot out of my chimney, I tie a rope to the end of one of my tire chains and hang this down inside the chimney. When whipped around in a circular motion, the chains loosen nearly all the soot. Of course, you should cover the fireplace with cardboard or a plastic sheet to prevent the soot from getting out into the house. After it has settled down, the loose soot should be scooped up and removed."

"My grandmother used to throw potato peelings into the fireplace and claimed that this removed soot from inside the chimney. When we moved into our new house 11 years ago, I decided to see if this worked. My wife always saved the peels and tossed them into a roaring fire.

Each year when I check the chimney, I'm amazed that very little soot has collected."

(Even if this doesn't work, at least it gets rid of potato peels.)

"I needed to lower the fireplace opening to get the proper draw and came up with a unique way to close off the necessary part of the opening at the top. I bought a section of copper rain guttering, cut exactly to size, along with matching end caps to close it off. It was installed upside down and gives the appearance of a copper hood that had been custom made. I polished the copper and put a protective coating over it to preserve the shine."

"Add a pair of rope handles to a small section of picket fence, and you've an ideal log carrier. The pickets should be about 3' or 4' long, and the width should be about the same. The logs go parallel to the pickets. You can carry several logs at one time without messing up your clothes."

"The biggest problem about splitting logs for the fireplace is that when you stand them up on end, they fall over either before your first axe blow or immediately afterward. I made a great log holder from an old tire. A section of tire about a foot long is nailed to the end of a 2" x 6" that is a couple of feet long, and this forms a right angle. With the board on the ground the piece of tire will hold the log up straight."

"If you have a fireplace and air conditioning, don't forget to close the chimney damper in the summer. No sense in trying to cool down the entire neighborhood."

FISHING   This idea for storing fishhooks in a tackle box does away with the danger of snagging a finger and also keeps the hooks sharp:

"I take a strip of masking tape and lay the hooks down on one half the length of the tape on the sticky side and fold the other half back

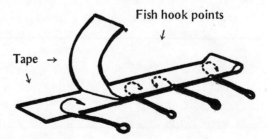

Fish hook points
↓

Tape →
↓

over the top of the hooks. This means there's sticky tape face to face, and seals in the points of the hooks. As you need to use them, they can be removed one by one by peeling the tape back."

(This same storage idea will be good for a set of screws or other sharp, small objects.)

A smart 12-year-old angler discovered that the filter tips from cigarettes could be used on the points of his fishhooks to keep them from hooking the wrong things when not in use.

"I cover my fishing rod tips with a short piece of old garden hose to protect both the rod and whoever might be in the car or boat. This is also a good place in which to stick fishhooks not being used."

"Many men leave fishing rods leaning in a corner. This can result in damage to either the rod or the loops that guide the line. Mine hang on

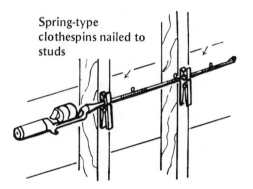

Spring-type
clothespins nailed to
studs

the garage wall, held by a pair of spring-type clothespins that are nailed to the studs high enough so nothing comes in contact with them. The clothespins already have a curved cut-out that accomodates the rod."

"Fishing worms always get down to the very bottom of the can, which means you have to dig for them. Take a coffee can and cut off the bottom, and then put a plastic cap on both ends. Each time you need to bait your hook, just turn the can upside down, and the worms are on top."

"Once I really did have some nice fish, but I had to resort to fish tales because my stringer accidentally came loose from the boat, and I lost my entire catch. Now, as a precaution, I've attached an empty plastic bleach bottle to the stringer. The stringer still attaches to the boat or dock, but if it accidentally comes loose, my bleach bottle float shows me where the fish are going, and it's a cinch to retrieve float, stringer, and fish."

"I made a fish scaler by tacking bottle caps to a stick, rough side out. It really works."

"An easy way to rid your hands of that fish odor that seems to linger forever is to rub your wet hands with bicarbonate of soda. After a good workout with this, the smell will be gone."
(It may even help sell your wife on cleaning the fish.)

"If you need a quick anchor for your small fishing boat, fill a plastic bleach bottle with cement. When this hardens, you'll have a handy weight to use for an anchor, and the handle of the jug is ideal for tying on the anchor rope. If you don't have cement, fill 'er up with sand."

FLAGPOLES "If you have a flagpole, the rope will last a lot longer if it's protected with a thin coat of linseed oil. 'That's a good tip,' you say, 'but since my pole has been up for years, you're a little late with that. After all, I'm no flagpole climber.' That's where my next tip comes in. Rig up a pan with linseed oil in it and put it up high enough so the rope hangs into it. Then as the rope is pulled, it will all pass through the pan of oil and coat itself."

"We always display the flag on proper holidays, but when we moved I forgot to remove the bracket that held the flag. When I tried to find one at the stores, I discovered they don't carry such things, so I decided

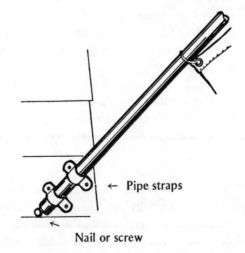

← Pipe straps

Nail or screw

to become creative. I found that a pair of pipe straps held the flagstaff just as well as the bracket. I put them in a line about 3″ apart; the pole slips in and is held in place by a large nail driven part way in under the bottom pipe strap."

FLASHLIGHTS "An adjustable flashlight holder can be made by using a funnel and a rubber band. The funnel mouth rests flat on the ground. The rubber band holds the flashlight against the slanting side of the funnel. The slant allows you to adjust the flashlight beam to any desired angle, and the flashlight will stay in place."

"Another holder can be made by sticking an open pair of pliers into the ground. The flashlight rests in the cradle formed by the pliers, with the back end of the flashlight resting on the ground. Adjust it to beam the light where needed."

"Since there are many times when a flashlight is needed in the course of a repair job, I carry one in my toolbox. To protect the lens from the other tools, I created a simple cover from a hollow rubber ball by making a pair of slits in the shape of an 'X' big enough for the flashlight to fit into. When the flashlight is pushed into the ball, the pieces formed by the slits keep it from slipping off."

Slits in rubber ball

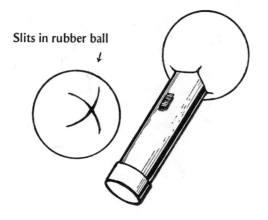

"I keep the flashlight in my toolbox in an old heavy sock with a loose knot tied in the end. This not only protects the glass, but keeps the case from getting scratched. I also use a few other socks to hold various groups of tools, which makes for a quieter toolbox and protects the contents."

"Carry a spare flashlight bulb in the case, under the spring in the bottom. The spring protects it from getting broken."

"Maybe you have a flashlight you would like to make waterproof. If so, brush all the seams with rubber cement. This will keep out the water, and yet can be broken loose when you need to get inside. So as not to cover the lens, just put a thin line around the edge."

This won't work on a flashlight that has a loose-fitting switch. But here's another suggestion:

"Put your flashlight in a plastic bag with a tight rubber band to close the opening. The light can be switched on right through the plastic."

"My flashlight can shine around corners, with the help of an old bicycle rear view mirror. The clamp that was designed to go around the bike handlebar was installed around the barrel of the flashlight. The mirror can be adjusted at almost any angle in front of the flashlight, and the beam can be reflected around corners. I rigged this up when I couldn't get light to the work spot in a pump engine. Since then, I've found dozens of other uses for my light bender."

FLOOR FURNACES   "Floor furnaces are a real liability during the summertime because they're just big pits waiting for dust and dirt. Mine aren't dust catchers any more, as I wrapped the grills with pieces of that clear plastic that comes from the cleaners. Transparent plastic tape holds the covers in place. They look fine, and the plastic keeps out all the dirt."

"I've made a cover for each grill on my floor furnaces from a piece of plywood cut to fit and covered with a scrap of the same carpet as used in each room. When the cover is in place, it can hardly be seen."

(If you have vinyl floors, cover the plywood with that.)

FLOORS   Before you go into the more complicated ways to stop squeaking boards on a hardwood floor, give this quick method a try. It's quite simple, and will cure the squeaks nine times out of ten. Locate the two boards that are causing the noise. Then take a squeeze bottle of white all-purpose glue, squirt this down into the crack, and wipe up the excess. This will probably solve your problem, but if it doesn't you haven't spent much time or money trying to do it the easy way.

Or:

"Sweep talcum powder between the squeaky boards."

"When one of the vinyl squares in our bathroom came loose, I put strips of double-coated tape—the kind that's sticky on both sides—on the bottom of the square and put it back in place. That's been four or five months ago, and it's still in place."

If one of the square asphalt tiles on a floor comes loose, there's a good possibility that others might be coming loose too. While you have the stuff out to replace one, wouldn't it be great if you knew which of the others were loose? By placing the suction cup of your plumber's friend down on each tile square, you can quickly find out. Pull straight up to see if the tile comes up. If not, push the friend over to the side to release the suction cup.

"Try this for almost perfectly matched repairs of gouges in vinyl or linoleum floors. Pick a spot on a scrap piece of the material that matches the color that has been marred. Shave off a thin layer, and then chop it up very fine with a sharp knife. When it's about the texture of coarse salt, mix it with shellac to form a paste. Fill in the holes with this paste. When this is dry, wax and polish it, and you'll have to use a magnifying glass to find the repair."

"I don't know what the pros use when laying vinyl floor tiles, but I found the best way to press them down was with my wife's rolling pin. This allowed me to put force across the entire square with a good amount of pressure. It sure gave us a fine-looking floor that I know is stuck down tight."

"When varnishing floors, place a flashlight down on the floor so it shines across the path where you've been working. The light will help you to see any places that you've missed with the varnish brush, and allows you to avoid skips. Be sure you don't end up with your flashlight over in a corner you can't get to until the varnish dries."

"If floor tiles all have to go a certain way for the pattern to come out right, lots of time can be wasted trying to get them right. I solve this before ever removing the tiles from the box. They're all facing the right way in the box, and all I do is run a chalk of contrasting color across the ends. Now all I have to do is lay the tiles with the chalk marks aimed in the same direction."

Installing a floor can mean many hours of knee torture. Here's how one man saved his knees:

"I rigged up some knee pads from two big plastic sponges. I attached each to my pants legs with a pair of large safety pins. It was like kneeling on a pillow, and after I was through, the sponges were still good for cleaning."

Sponges held on by safety pins

"The new linoleum rug for the kitchen came rolled up, so quite naturally it didn't lie down flat when I went to lay it out. I put an electric blanket down on top of it and turned it up high. In a very short time, the heat from the electric blanket softened up the linoleum so it lay flat on the floor."

FOAM RUBBER "Trying to cut foam rubber accurately can cause many a handyman to come forth with some 'shop talk' that would make a sailor blush. Avoid the problem by compressing the foam rubber tightly with a pair of boards clamped to the cutting surface. Clamp the boards along the line to be cut, with only enough space for a razor-sharp knife blade. The more compressed the foam rubber, the easier the cutting job will be."

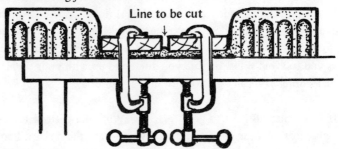

Line to be cut

Flower pot

FUNNELS "A good emergency funnel that you can usually find around the house is a small clay flowerpot. Fit the hole in the bottom of the flowerpot over the receptacle and pour."

"With the caulking compound gone, an empty caulking gun cartridge will serve as a small funnel. Because of the long tube, this funnel can be used many times when a 'store bought' funnel wouldn't do as well."

"When you need a one-shot funnel, make one from one of those plastic lids from a coffee can. Simply cut or punch a hole in the middle and then slit the lid from the edge into the hole. By overlapping at the slit, the lid forms a funnel. It's held in the funnel shape by the finger and thumb of one hand as you pour with the other."

"Cut the bottom out of an empty machine oil can, and it's transformed into a tiny funnel for which you'll find many uses. An old lighter fluid can will work too."

"When pouring a liquid through a funnel into a narrow-necked container, the pouring process is often slowed down because the funnel fills up the opening completely, and there's no escape hatch for the air inside. Slip one of your wife's bobby pins over the rim of the funnel spout. Now when the spout is inserted into the neck of the container, the bobby pin won't allow the funnel to go all the way down to the top of the container and seal in the air."

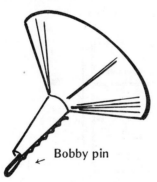

Bobby pin

"An old spring from inside an upholstered piece of furniture is a great funnel holder, as it will fit over most bottle necks and steady the funnel in place."

FURNITURE   "We have a fine sectional group that makes an L-shaped sofa in our den. However, we had trouble with the sections' sliding away from one another and getting out of place. I fixed this by joining them together with sets of screen door hooks and eyes put underneath the furniture where they can't be seen. They unhook for floor cleaning."

"We put newspapers over the top of our end table to protect it from the Christmas tree and ended up with a layer of newspaper we couldn't get off the table. My mother-in-law poured olive oil over the surface, and after letting it stand for an hour, she wiped it off and all the paper came off, leaving a sparkling top again."

"We have a tall china cabinet that never seemed quite steady because the baseboard at the floor wouldn't allow the cabinet to push up flush against the wall. A pair of screen door hooks now hold the cabinet completely steady. We screwed the hooks into the wall, and put the eyes into the cabinet. When we need to move the cabinet, we just unhook it."

"We had a couch that slid back against the wall every time anyone sat down on it. Needless to say, this marred the paneled wall I worked so hard to put up. I eliminated this by installing a pair of screw-in rubber-tipped door stops on the legs of the couch. Now when the couch slides back, the bumpers hit the wall instead."

"While sliding furniture around in his room, our son managed to break off one of the legs on his chest of drawers. My husband removed the other three legs and replaced them with new ones he made from

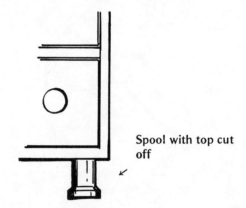

Spool with top cut off

ordinary wooden spools. He cut one end off the spools, and then countersunk the other end. The new legs could then be put on the chest with long wood screws with flat heads, and only the wooden spool would touch the floor. When painted to match the chest, they look great. And they cost us nothing."

FUSE BOXES "Have you ever had a fuse blow and then have to try to find out in the dark which one it was? I keep a pen light tied by a string to the knob on the fuse box so I can easily find the culprit. It hangs out of the way when not needed."

Garages • Garbage • Garden Hose • Gardening • Gas
Cans • Gaskets • Gauges • Glass, Glass Cutting, and
Glazing • Glue and Glueing • Golf • Good Shop Practices
• Grease • Grinding Wheels • Grout • Gutters and
Downspouts • Guy Wires

GARAGES   That oil spot under the old family car sure makes for an
unsightly garage floor. One very simple and usually effective way to
"pick up" the oil is to sprinkle dry portland cement on the spot. Build
up at least ¼" layer of the cement. Let it stay this way for a couple of
days, sweep it up, and the stain should be gone. If there are any
stubborn spots, scrub them with a cleaning solvent to remove the last
traces. If you can't repair the leak in the car right away, put something
under the car to catch the drippings and save the floor.

G.

However, if you just want to hide your mess, read on:
"Our garage faces the front of our house, and when it was open,
everyone could see the oil drips that came from our car. My wife
managed to call this to my attention every day, but no more! I painted
a neat black stripe the width of the space between the wheels of the
car. The oil drippings fall on the black stripe and can't be seen. Also,
the stripe acts as a sight line when my wife tries to park the car in the
garage."

"To protect the door edge of our new car from getting nicked
against the garage wall, I installed a bumper on the wall. It's made from
a section of garden hose long enough to catch either the front or back
door. The hose is slit the full length and nailed to the wall with the slit
down. I was careful to center the strip at the point where the doors
stick out the farthest."

"Our cinderblock garage wall was taking its toll on our car door until
I cemented a foot-wide scrap of foam rubber carpet padding to the
wall."

"We had just about used all the storage space we could, and still our
new, smaller home was not going to hold all those things my wife
wouldn't let me throw away. Then one of my new neighbors helped me
build a cabinet in a completely unused space I might never have
thought of The space is in the garage up over the hood of the car. The

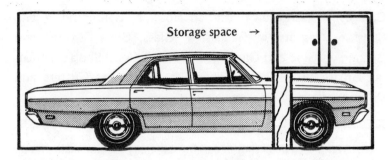

Storage space →

car still goes in the same spot, but the hood drives right under my new cabinets. We rigged them so they go all the way to the ceiling, and the supports come down to the floor on either side of the car. The only drawback is that the first few times you drive in, you think the car is going to hit the cabinet."

"Remember the TV commercial where Dad comes home and blows his stack because Billy's tricycle is where the car should go? We used to have similar problems until I took a page from the book of parking-lot planners and painted white lines on our garage floor. Now my wife parks her car in a set area and always leaves me enough room. The kids never leave anything in the parking area because it's clearly marked. Even I am helped by the lines, since now I don't leave tools in the wrong area."

Spool

GARBAGE "We have a city ordinance against dogs running loose, but some still do. They like to knock over my garbage cans, scattering garbage all over the neighborhood. I solved this by getting old tires from our service station dealer. The cans fit down into these, and the broad base makes them impossible to knock over—making the neighborhood cleaner and helping contain both the garbage and my temper."

"My mother-in-law bolted a wooden spool through the center of her garbage can lid on the underside. When placed over the rim of the can, this provides a hook. Sure beats having to bend over to pick up the lid when you need both hands to get the junk in the can."

Would you believe a metal garbage can that's left outside all the time and has lasted nine years without even the tiniest hole in the bottom? When the owner bought the cans, he painted the bottoms inside and out with a generous coat of plastic asphalt roofing sealer. This is the black stuff that's used to seal around flashing and at other possible trouble spots. The compound is of trowel consistency, goes on easily, and leaves a smooth finish. A quart can of this costs less than a dollar and is more than enough to do three garbage cans.

Another homeowner doesn't think on such a long-term basis:

"About all you can hope for is to keep your metal garbage cans from rusting or corroding before the garbage pick-up crew bends them beyond recognition. When I get new cans, I take about five minutes to paint them inside and out with boiled linseed oil. This not only protects the metal, but also keeps garbage from sticking to the sides."

"Tell your readers not to throw away an old garbage can just because the bottom starts to rot out. A new bottom can be installed by cutting a circle out of hardboard to fit down into the can. Coat the edges of the circle with epoxy before putting it in place, and it will stay for as long as the sides of the can last. The circle doesn't have to be perfect, since the can bottom usually starts to rot in the middle."

"Instead of retiring our old garbage can to the garbage dump when the bottom rusted out, I put it back in service as an outside incinerator. All I needed to do was to punch plenty of holes in the side for ventilation. A scrap piece of expanded steel or wire mesh serves as a top, and the earth serves as the bottom. We're all set to burn those leaves that will be falling off the trees this autumn."

(Just make sure your town ordinances allow this.)

This prompted another reader to suggest, "An old bicycle wheel will work as a sturdier top than the wire mesh."

"Our kitchen sink garbage disposal quit on us, and we called a plumber. He must be the most honest one in the business, because he suggested we stick the end of a broom handle down into the unit (he cautioned us to be sure the unit was off) and call him back if it still wouldn't work. The broom handle apparently pushes against the cutter blades in the bottom. Although it only moves the cutter blades the tiniest bit, when the broom was removed and our unit was turned on, it worked again.

"The repairman explained that these units can sometimes be stopped by a bit of grit left from the last grinding job, and the little movement will be enough to release it."

(This will work on many disposal units. Also, check the reset button to see if it needs pushing, as this kind of overload can cause it to kick out.)

GARDEN HOSE "Here's a real space saver. Take seven empty two-pound coffee cans and nail them to the garage or storeroom wall. Hang your garden hose around the circle, and use the cans as storage bins for all sorts of small items."

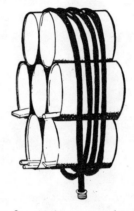

"I use a coat hanger for storing my garden hose. After coiling the hose, I put a wooden coat hanger through the coil, and then hook the hangel into an eye hook on my garage wall."

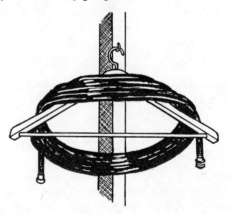

"I store my garden hose in an old tire. The hose rolls up nicely inside the tire, and this can be hung on a nail or just leaned against a wall in the garage. When I need to use the hose, I can roll the tire and hose to where it's needed."

"The very best hose holder I've ever had is one I made from an old automobile wheel. It was easily mounted on my garage wall and is an

ideal size to wrap a hose around. My neighbor liked the idea, but
mounted his on a post outside. He painted it, and it looks fine."

"I mounted an old washtub on my garage wall and wrap garden
hoses around it. Inside the tub, I built shelves, and I use these to store
all sorts of hand garden tools."

(If you've been leaving the hoses out, and they're already ruined,
some great ways you can still use them are described in Chapter "H."
Look for *Hose Uses*.)

"When I put our garden hose away for the winter, I noticed the
rubber washer fell out. I figured there was an awfully good chance that
it would end up missing before next spring rolled around, so I coated
one side of the washer with rubber cement and glued it in place inside
the coupling."

"When there's a leak at a garden hose connection and you don't have
a replacement washer, try this trick. Remove the old washer, reverse it,
and put it back in place. This will usually stop the leak. However, since
the surface of one side of the washer is damaged, this will only be a
temporary repair. Pick up a new washer soon."

"For the other folks who are always loosing the nozzle for the
garden hose, this will be a lifesaver. I installed a broom clip on the wall
right next to the outside water hydrant. Whenever it's necessary to take

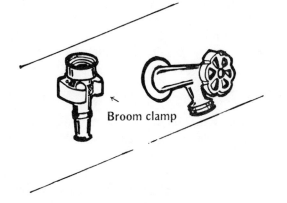

Broom clamp

the nozzle off the hose, it's put into the clip and is held there until time
to put it back on the hose. It's never been lost since I put this idea to
work."

GARDENING "Many of the seeds that are to be planted in rows in a vegetable garden need only be dropped into trenches no more than ¼" deep. Instead of digging a trench, I place a broom handle along the line I want for the row of seeds. Then I push this handle down into the dirt with my foot. This works down to about an inch in depth. This way, you have a perfectly straight row of plants, and the seeds are all planted at the same depth. The furrow is then covered over with a few strokes of a rake." (Premark the broom handle at the proper planting intervals so you drop the seeds at the right distance apart.)

"When seeds need to be planted in a straight row, try this. First, mix up a batch of flour-and-water paste. Dip a piece of string the length of the intended row into the paste. Now put the paste-covered string down onto a paper on which the seeds have been spread. The paste will pick up seeds all along the string. Now plant string and all in a predug trench, and you'll have a completely straight row. When wet down, the flour paste dissolves, and the seeds can grow."

"Other husbands may have the same problem I do every spring. My wife keeps bringing home dozens of plants in little pots, for transplanting into our yard. After several years of this, I've found the best digger to use in these small pots is not a trowel at all but a shoe spoon. It's just the right size to reach down into the pot and scoop out the plant and dirt all at once. Also, the spoon is curved to hold the dirt for transplant."

"After pulling up seedlings by the roots while trying to get them out of their pots for transplanting, I decided there must be a better way. This year, instead of pots, I used coffee cans with both ends cut out. I put the plastic top back on as a bottom, with holes cut for drainage. At transplant time, I removed the bottoms, and the contents—dirt and all—easily pushed up and out."

"For those handy gardeners who will soon be starting seedlings and cuttings, here's a clever trick. Cut the bottoms out of several pop-top beverage cans. Plant your seedlings in these pots. With the pop-top hole at the bottom, you'll have a ready made drain hole for the excess water to go through. When it's time to transplant, the entire planting, dirt and all, can be pushed up and out of the can by putting a dowel or other round object in through the hole at the bottom. Then your free pots can be discarded."

"If you have plants that must be brought in for the winter and put in pots, here's a maneuver that will save time next spring. First line the pot with a large piece of plastic from a cleaner's suit bag. Leave the edges out over the edge of the pot. After the plant is in and the pot is filled with dirt, trim off the excess plastic, leaving about an inch above the dirt. Bury this tab. Next spring when you carry the plant outside again, all you have to do to transplant it is to lift out the plant, dirt and all, by the plastic."

"Last winter when I ran out of things to do, I sat in front of the fire and filed notches on the garden trowel. The notches are 1″ apart for 5″ up the blade. Now when my wife is planting seeds and bulbs, she can tell exactly how deep she's dug with her built-in ruler."

"When I filled my new heavy-duty four-gallon garden spray, I soon learned that it wasn't as portable as it had seemed in the store. I improvised with the aid of my golf caddy cart and put the sprayer on wheels. Not only did it make my job easier, but it reminded my wife that I hadn't been out on the course for a while—and she actually suggested I should go play when I finished my spraying."

"My addition to the garden sprayer is a U-shaped stiff wire extension taped to the handle. It sticks out over the nozzle and acts as a lifter. It's longer than the nozzle and slants up from the handle so that at the end

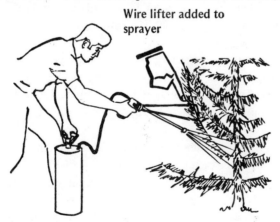

Wire lifter added to sprayer

it's about 6″ above the spray head. With it, I can lift branches up so I can spray down at the roots of bushes or underneath where the spray might be more effective. Most sprayers are two-handed jobs anyway, but even if you have one that requires only one hand, this gadget eliminates the need to get your free hand on the foliage, where it could come in contact with poisonous spray."

"Instead of stabbing my hands when I prune those thorny bushes, I get the biggest pair of pliers from my shop and use these to grab hold of the thorny limbs."

"Here's a use for discarded antenna rods. I find these tubular aluminum crosspieces the best garden stakes around. Cut them to the desired lengths and flatten one end so they can be driven into the ground more easily. They can be moved easily, too, and they never rust."

GAS CANS   "To make the spout on your gasoline can dripless, wrap a pipe cleaner tight around the spout, as close to the end as possible. Then when you're through pouring, the last dribbles will be absorbed by the pipe cleaner instead of falling on the housing of your mower or whatever you're fueling."

GASKETS   "Usually when there's a break in a gasket, a new one has to be installed. However, a small break may often be mended with the aid of some cork, plus gasket compound. First, liberate your wife's vegetable grater from the kitchen. Grate the cork as finely as you can. Blend this cork dust into the compound until it has reached a putty-like consistency. Then work it into the break with a putty knife. The final step is to sneak your wife's grater back into the kitchen."

"When you have to replace a gasket in a motor, use the worn old one as a pattern for the new one. Just lay the old one out on the cork gasket sheet. Then give it a short blast of quick-drying spray paint. You'll have a perfect pattern to cut by."

GAUGES   "I made a marking gauge using only the metal cutting edge off a waxpaper carton and a square block of wood. I attached the cutting edge to the block of wood with two small screws. Then I placed the block against the edge of the board to be marked so the blade lay flat on the surface to be marked, with the teeth facing the intended direction of marking. The 'V' of the teeth holds your scribe or pencil in a straight path as you move the gadget along. Since there are many teeth, you can place the pencil anywhere along the blade at the desired distance from the edge."

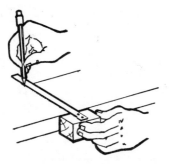

Or: "Take a wooden spool and find a dowel that will fit through the hole in the spool. Drive a nail through one end of the dowel, and then put a screw eye through a predrilled hole in the center of the shank of the spool. This locks the dowel inside the spool at the desired place. The spool then runs along the material to be marked, and the nail scribes the desired line."

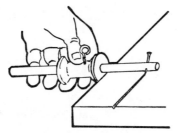

GLASS, GLASS CUTTING, AND GLAZING   "Plastic toothbrush cases are just the right size for storing a glass cutter. I stick a wad of cotton soaked in oil in the bottom of the case. The blade of the glass cutter pushes down into the cotton and is lubricated as well as protected while being stored."

"The rubber bulb on an old medicine dropper makes an ideal protective shield for storing a glass cutter."

"I made a wall holder for my glass cutter that's also a small oil reservoir. I used a short length of copper tubing big enough around for the tool to fit into, and crimped it at one end and sealed it with solder to hold the oil. I left a tab of the tubing at the top to attach the holder to the shop wall. I leave the glass cutter in the holder until I'm ready to use it, and then I merely wipe off the excess oil."

"If you have an older glass cutter, it won't have a shaped rest for your index finger and can be pretty uncomfortable. I taped a metal

thimble to my glass cutter, and this enables me to apply the proper pressure without putting blisters on my fingers."

One of the best ways to be sure you're cutting glass to the exact size and shape is to make a pattern on paper ahead of time. Place this under the glass, and it will be easy to follow and out of the way. If the glass is to be moved around, use cellophane tape to keep the pattern in place on the underside.

One of the tricks of good glass cutting is to be sure your straightedge doesn't slip—and this is difficult, as the best straightedge to use is a metal one. You can prevent this slipping by putting strips of friction tape along the underside of your rule. Double-sided pressure-sensitive tape also works well on this chore.

"Your straightedge won't slip on the glass you're cutting if you'll run a dry bar of soap over the area where the rule is to be placed. The soap will hold it there while you run the glass cutter along the line. A wet rag will remove the soap when the glass is cut."

(Also, rub the bottom side of the straightedge with a bar of soap before using it.)

If you're using a wooden yardstick as a straightedge when cutting glass, you can make it much less likely to move at the wrong time merely by wetting it with water before putting it down on the glass surface.

"For best results, keep the glass cutter perfectly straight and at right angles to the glass. I do this with a holder I made—merely a block of wood with a notch in it. The notch is the exact size of the cutter handle. The block slides along the glass, and the block forces you to keep the glass cutter straight. It also gives you a better grip than the cutter by itself."

Notched block

Just before you run your glass cutter over the glass to be cut, dip a small artist's brush in some oil or turpentine. Brush this along the glass where the cut is to be made, and this will help prevent chipping and flaking.

"The principal advantage to glazier's pliers is the larger-surfaced bite. Since I would only use them once in a blue moon, I made a pair from an ordinary door hinge and my regular pliers. When the two plates on the hinge are parallel, there's a gap just about the same thickness as window glass. Place the hinge around the glass and grip the hinge with the pliers. A strip of tape on each plate gives an even better grip. You'll actually have a wider bite than you get with most glazier's pliers."

(If a hinge is not handy, your regular pliers plus a folded piece of newspaper to give a little more even grip will do, but not as well as a hinge.)

Hinge in pliers

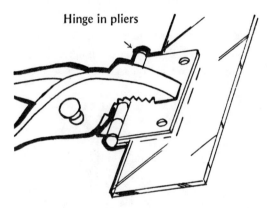

"The removal of old putty is usually the toughest part of replacing a broken windowpane. I've discovered that lacquer thinner will soften putty enough in a few minutes so it can be scraped out with ease. One word of caution—don't get the lacquer thinner on a painted surface unless you plan to repaint."

"Another way of removing old putty from around windowpanes is just to brush a little muriatic acid on and let it sit for a few minutes. You'll find the putty has softened up and will be easy to remove."

Heat helps to loosen up putty that has to be removed in the process of replacing a windowpane. One home handyman trick is to wrap the end of your soldering gun tip with aluminum foil and run this across the putty. The foil keeps the putty from fouling up the tip, and heat will get the putty soft and easy to scrape off.

The removal of a broken pane of glass can be troublesome and possibly dangerous. Here's a stunt to make it easier and safer. Cut two pieces of paper the same size as the pane and stick a sheet of paper on each side of the pane with rubber cement. Now the entire pane can be taken out without loose glass being scattered around and without danger of cutting your hands. In fact, you may find the pane will come out still more easily if you give it a few taps with a hammer to break it away from the frame.

If you can't immediately replace a pane with a hole in it, you might find this stunt helps keep loose pieces from falling out. Borrow two large buttons from your wife's sewing basket and a wire hairpin from her makeup kit. Place a button on each side of the hole and run the hairpin through the holes in the buttons and twist it down tight. The glass slivers will be held in place until you are ready to do the job the right way. During the button-down be careful not to cut yourself.

"To make it easier to drive in those small glazier's points, use a small butt hinge as a helper. By folding the hinge back until the two leaves form an 'L,' you'll have a tool to use as a sort of driver. It will fit

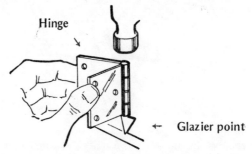

Hinge

← Glazier point

against the point and provide a much broader target for your hammer. This makes tapping the point home a much easier job, with less likelihood of breaking the pane."

"Put a coat of heavy mineral oil on the side of a glazier's point next to the pane, and it holds the point to the glass. Any heavy oil would do as well, and you can cover up any oil spots with putty."

"Driving in glazier's points can be a little rough on the fingers if you aren't careful. To make this job a lot simpler, hold the point in place with the eraser end of a pencil. It will stay in place, allow your fingers to keep a safe distance from the hammer, and also enable you to see better what you're doing."

"Since I never throw anything away, I've had a bunch of old phonograph needles in my junk drawer for about ten years. I had to replace a window pane and found I had no glazier's points. Rather than go into town, I came up with the idea of using the old phonograph needles for this job. They work very well, and I think they're easier to handle than the regular ones."

(They would also be good as fasteners to hold pictures and backing in picture frames.)

GLUE AND GLUEING   "The bottom end of a tube of glue makes a great spreader. It's wide enough to do a fast spread job, and the little crimps where the tube is fastened to the end allow the glue to flow out as it's pulled along. Afterwards, wipe off the end of the tube with a rag so it won't stick to the shelf."

"Recently, I found a use for an old wiper blade off my car. I was getting ready to glue a new top on an old table. The wiper blade allowed me to spread the glue over the entire table in just a few moments."

"When glueing joints together, there's always the possibility that the pressure will force out some of the glue onto a surface where you don't want it. I always run a strip of cellophane tape along the edges in such a case, so any glue forced out will come out on the tape. When the glueing is done, the tape can be peeled off, leaving the finish free from excess glue."

"To loosen glued joints, use plain old household vinegar. Heat the vinegar to a simmer on the stove, and then brush it on the joints over and over until they loosen."

(Vinegar won't work on all kinds of glue, but it's worth a try, since it does soften up so many kinds. It'll also take some glues out of work clothes.)

A few strands of fine steel wool will give added bite when glueing a joint together. After covering the surface with the adhesive, sprinkle the strands of steel wool on, and then clamp the pieces together. Not only will the end result be a stronger bond, but there's less likelihood that the parts will slip in the clamping process.

"Before inserting a dowel into a hole for glueing, turn a tap into the hole to thread it. This gives a much better bond between the dowel and the wood, because the glue stays in the threads instead of being pushed on down to the bottom of the hole."

Glueing usually requires clamping, and the last thing you want to do is glue your clamping device to your work. Preclude this possibility by always separating the clamp from the work with a piece of waxpaper from the kitchen. Then if any of the adhesive gets where it shouldn't be, the waxpaper won't stick to it.

One way to get pressure over a wide area of work—such as when glueing on a veneer—is with bricks. They can be piled all around to give uniform pressure, or, if need be, can be stacked to give extra weight in a particular spot. With enough bricks, you can provide all the weight needed, even if it be in the hundreds of pounds. Since they're lifted on and off individually, you don't have to be a Samson to use this type of press.

Spring-type paper clamp holds cans

"A double boiler is the best setup for heating glue, but my wife has never wanted her kitchen pans to be used for this purpose. As a substitute, I use a pair of different-sized tin cans. I put water in the larger can, and the smaller can is held up by a spring-type paper clamp over the rim of both cans so it rests in the water without touching the bottom of the larger can. When I'm through glueing, my makeshift double boiler can be thrown away."

Epoxy glues, as well as others, require mixing, and usually you only need a small amount. Whatever you use as a mixing container is better off being thrown away when you're through. If you don't have a throw-away container, make one from a scrap of aluminum foil. Just bend up the edges all the way around to make sort of a mixing box. It can be made any size you need. In addition to being disposable, it has a surface which makes it easy to mix as well as remove the mixture.

GOLF   "A handy tip for golfers: If you're lucky enough to get a new set of woods, take time to put a coat of paste-type shoe polish over the wooden parts. When it dries, buff it. Your woods will retain that new-look luster almost forever."

"Rain doesn't stop me from going out on the golf course—but my wife threatened to, because of the muddy mess my golf caddy cart made in the trunk of the car. I solved this sticky problem by swiping a pair of plastic bowl covers from the kitchen, large enough to go over the wheels of the cart. I slip them on just before I put the cart in the trunk."

"I carry a 2″ strip of corrugated board in my golf bag as a tee holder. The tees stick in the holes in the corrugation and are always easy to find."

GOOD SHOP PRACTICES   "When I put up pegboard and hooks to hang most of my hand tools, I had a fairly neat shop area. However, as I used and forgot to rehang tools, I found that I couldn't remember where they all went. When I finally got everything rehung, I got smart. I took a can of paint and an artist's small brush and drew an outline around all the tools. Now I know exactly where everything goes."

(Another idea is to cut out the shapes of tools from pressure-sensitive contact paper and stick them on the wall. Or, give each tool a blast of spray paint while it's hanging in place.)

"I confiscated an old hanging shoe bag for my workshop. It hangs on the inside of a closet door, and I use it to hold bottles of shop liquid, jars, small cans, and other related small items. The shoe bag actually holds as much as one full shelf, and this way the things can never be knocked off and broken."

"If your wife ever decides to throw away an old Lazy Susan, latch onto it. It makes an ideal rotating work area that's particularly good for working on small appliances or anything that requires attacking the problem from all sides."

(Even if your wife isn't tossing Susan out, borrow it and cover it with foil to protect it.)

"An old hot plate that my wife had discarded was still in working order, so I took it to the workshop. I use it for such shop functions as warming glues and preheating, and, of course, it means that I always have plenty of coffee to see me through the shop chores."

A shower curtain ring can be used on the shop wall as a hanger for planes. The small end of the ring goes over a hook screwed into the wall. The plane is then hung from the wall by putting the knob through the larger round part. The flat bottom of the plane rests against the shop wall."

"I've come up with a couple of good uses for old record album covers. They're great for storing circular saw blades and keep them well protected. Album covers are also good to keep sheets of sandpaper flat. One of our radio stations gave me a good supply of record jackets, and the regular inexpensive metal record racks hold the jackets nicely in my shop."

"Rather than throw away an old hacksaw blade, make a shop memo pad holder. A pair of stove bolts are put up through the workbench and through the holes in the blade. Before tightening the bolts down, place a supply of paper between the blade and the bench. The saw-toothed blade makes it easy to tear off sheets from the pad."

"One of the most-used shop tools is a pencil. When I considered how many times I had to retrieve my pencil after it had rolled off the bench where I parked it, I decided to put brakes on it. I wrapped a plastic

← Plastic bandage

bandage around the pencil so that the two sticky ends came together face to face. This meant there was a sort of flap sticking out, and this positively prevented the pencil from rolling. Saves me time, but I miss the bending exercise."

"I'm never at a loss for a shop pencil, because of my handy holder. I glued a magnet under my workbench and stuck a tack in the tend of the pencil eraser, which allows the magnet to hold the pencil ready for use."

Magnet

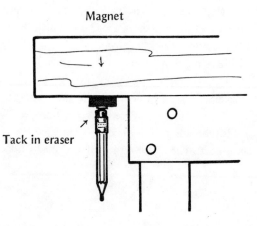

Tack in eraser

"How do you like my hanger for circular saw blades? I take an ordinary wire coat hanger and bend the middle of the crossbar up toward the hook, forming an upside down 'V.' Then I bend the two outside corners (where the shoulders of a coat rest) toward each other, forming a pair of V's. I put a rubber band from this upside down V up around the hook, and the blades can rest down in the other two V's and be held there by the rubber band. To avoid the blades' being against metal, the V points are wrapped with masking tape. The hanger is hung from an eye hook on the shop wall."

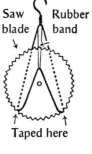

Saw blade Rubber band

Taped here

"Even when my yardstick is hung up for storage, it's ready to be used. I hang it along the edge of my workbench, and things can be measured by just placing them down on the edge of the bench next to the yardstick. To hang it, I made keyhole slots about an inch from each end, and held it tight against the bench by a pair of screws. (The keyhole slots are the kind with a hole big enough for the head of the screw to go through at the bottom, but only the size of the shank of the screw at the top.) It needs only to be lifted up to remove it for other uses."

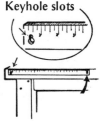

Keyhole slots

"Probably my most cumbersome tool was the hose for my shop vacuum. However, I made a simple hanger for the hose out of a wire coat hanger. The two ends of the hanger (where the shoulders would go) are bent around until they are parallel with their original line and the two ends are about 4" apart. The curve made when bending should be big enough to hold the hose. With the hose looped around the regular coat hanger hook and through the bent-up ends of the hanger, it can be hung on a nail, out of the way."

"To hang my power tool electric cord so it's up out of the way, I loop rubber bands made from an old inner tube around the cord and hang it on a nail. By attaching the bands to the cord with a simple hitch, they're quickly put on at any point along the cord. Also, the rubber hooks are much safer than hooking cord over a nail that could damage it or short out the cord."

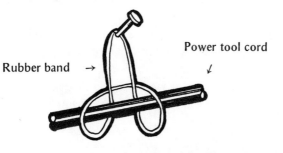

Rubber band →   Power tool cord

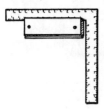

"I rigged a place to hang my large metal square on the shop wall, and you might be able to use the idea. I nailed a foot-long scrap of tongue-and-groove flooring on the wall. With the groove side up, one blade of the square fits into the groove, and the other hangs down against the wall."

"After pulling the drawer in my workbench out all the way and dumping the contents on my feet, I added a 'stop' to the drawer so it can't be pulled all the way out. The stop is simply a block of wood

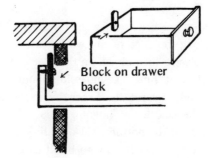

Block on drawer back

attached to the back of the drawer by a screw. The block sticks up higher than the back of the drawer, so when the drawer is pulled out, the block hits against the inside facing of the front of the bench. The screw is easy to take out if the drawer should ever have to be removed completely."

"To prevent my pulling the drawers in my workbench all the way out, I added 'reminders'—bright lines I painted on the sides of the drawers. I know I can pull out the drawer safely until I see the bright red lines, and then I know it's time to stop or dump a few hundred pounds of junk on my foot. It's certainly an easier solution than rigging up drawer stops."

Clothespin mounted on pegboard

"One problem facing the mechanized handyman is a maze of wires that supply electricity to his power tools. They have a habit of getting in the way, and this can be both bothersome and dangerous. I've all but eliminated the problem by bolting a series of spring-type clothespins to the pegboard wall in my shop. They're high up on the wall and form a line leading to my electrical outlets—and are excellent for holding wires up off my work table and out of the way. One group holds the wires of stationary tools, and there are extra ones I use for a portable power tool. Usually only a pair of clothespins are required to do the job. Before I added the pegboard, I tacked the clothespins to my shop wall."

"As a safety habit, I always unplug my shop machinery when not in use. So that I don't have to crawl around and look for the plug, I installed eye hooks in the wall near the outlet to hold the wire and plug. Of course, I had to force the eye open to get the plug through it."

Screw eye

"Many home workshops are equipped with small glass babyfood jars to hold screws, washers, tacks, and small nails. If the shop has lots of these small items in jars, it may be difficult to tell one size from another. The best way to know you're getting the right-sized screw ahead of time is to label the jars, and the best way to label them is to tear the label off the box the items come in and stick it in the jar. Hold it up against the inside of the jar (like the slip on a doctor's prescription bottle) so when the items are poured in, the label will still be visible."

"I use babyfood jars to keep screws, nuts, and other things in. That's not a new idea, but my adaptation is. I place the tops of two jars flat against each other and solder them together. This means I now have two jars that always stay together, and these are used for related items—bolts in one jar and nuts to fit in the other, for instance. This is a small detail, but makes for a better-organized workshop."

"The best containers I've run across to hold small items in workbench drawers are empty sardine cans. Since they're squareish, they fit nicely into the drawers, and they're an ideal size to hold nails, bolts, screws, and other small things that I always save." (Men, be sure to get all these cans you need before the little woman discovers how good they are for buttons and other small items *she* keeps!)

"When you're putting work through a power saw, and your fingers get too close to the blade, good safety practices call for the use of a push stick of some sort. Mine is a section of doweling with a rubber slip-on eraser on the end. The rubber won't slip as wood against wood might. Since it has a couple of nicks out of it, I'm glad I use it instead of my fingers."

"I've rigged up a foldaway bench stop on my workbench to use when planing the edge of a board. It's simply a hinge with one leaf attached to the side of the workbench top. The other leaf can be raised up, and the board to be planed is attached to it by a C-clamp. With this set-up, the board can be held in a vertical position."

Hinge on bench
folds up & clamps to
work

"This is a small problem, but most shops don't have a place to keep rubber bands handy and neatly together. I drove a pair of nails into studs in my shop wall and stretch the rubber bands over them. The bands are easy to get off to use and easy to put on to store." (A pair of nails driven into the sides of a drawer also accomplishes this nicely. In fact, it may be a help to your wife in keeping her supply of rubber bands neat.)

"My wife's kitchen has a pull-out dough board that adds to the counter top when pulled out. I made similar pull-out boards for my workbench. They give quite a bit of additional work area and were simple to make. They're out of the way when not needed."

"I mounted sections of leftover aluminum guttering on the ends of my workbench. These serve as handy trays to hold all sorts of small objects I'm working with, leaving the surface of my bench clear for more working room. I also used sections of guttering (with end plates added) nailed to the wall as storage bins for nails, screws, and so on."

"They say that behind every successful man there's a woman, and sure enough, I keep my husband's shop organized. Here's one idea he liked. We saved all the metal and plastic cylindrical tops off aerosol spray cans. The ones I'm talking about are 1½" to 2" high and about 2" across. After I'd collected enough all the same size, I glued them to a flat board, and this unit fits into a shop drawer. These containers hold lots and lots of small screws, nails, and parts. When you need to clean the drawers, the unit lifts out."

(Most men keep their shop organized by keeping wives *out*. Maybe that's been a mistake.)

"When tearing down small motors, I keep a clean workbench by installing a throw-away pad made from a section of our daily paper. I take an entire section, lay it flat on the bench and staple it at all four corners. The parts are laid out on this. As the surface gets too dirty or greasy, I tear off the top sheet, and there's a new, clean one underneath. The white paper makes it easier to spot small parts and screws."

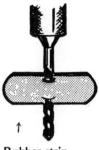

"One problem in using a power drill is that the shavings get in your way and block your view—but not if you use my fan blade. The fan is made of a strip of rubber from an old inner tube, about ½" wide and 3" to 4" long. The strip is slit so the drill bit fits down into it and holds it in place. When the drill is turned on, the fan naturally turns around too. As it does, it blows away the shavings created by the drill."

Rubber strip

"I put reference marks and guidelines on my power saw table by laying down strips of masking tape at right angles and at 45-degree angles. If need be, measurement marks can be made right on the tape and can be erased when no longer needed. Special strips can be added at unusual angles as necessary. When the strips get too marked up or start to peel off, it's a simple matter to replace them."

Anybody who's running a power tool that's potentially dangerous needs all the visibility he can get. Yet many shops I've visited have dark or unpainted walls. If yours is one of these, why not do your eyes a favor and give the shop a coat of whitewash—or at least a light-colored paint job? The added visibility makes for a safer shop, and the place will certainly look better. You'll probably end up saving on electricity, as you won't need to bring in extra lights on occasion.

"Rig up a movable shop light over your workbench with the aid of a spool and a wire. String the wire through the hole in the spool and stretch the wire up above the bench. Tape or tie the socket of an extension cord to the spool, and as the spool will slide along the wire, your light can be moved along the wire to the point that best suits your work."

"In the shop of a friend, all the containers have a bright red rubber band around them. The bands show the level of the contents, and as a portion is used, he moves the band down to the new level."

"Many times when I'm working in my shop, I'll realize things I need, but I never used to be able to remember these wanted items until the next time I needed them. However, I've solved that problem by installing a small blackboard at my workbench. I keep a piece of chalk on a string tied nearby, and when I realize I need something, I jot it down on the blackboard. Then when I'm going to the hardware store, I copy down from my 'want' list all the things I need."

If you haven't put an extension phone in your workshop, here's a trick that may help you hear the one in the house. Put the phone on top of a large cake pan or bucket which has been turned upside down. When the phone rings, you'll be surprised how much the hollow container will amplify the bell. This still won't help if you've got a power tool going full blast, but otherwise you may get a call you might have missed.

Here's a way to test the straightness of a piece of work. Place the edge in question up against a metal rule or other known straightedge. In this position, hold them up with a strong light behind. If the work isn't absolutely straight, you'll be able to see a sliver of light between the work and the straightedge. This'll tell you where the problem should be attacked.

"Before you junk an old frayed leather belt, cut off a 4" or 5" strip and glue it to a larger board. It will make an excellent strap for sharpening chisels, shop knives, and the like."

"Don't throw away an old paint brush. The flared, feathery ends can be clipped off, leaving a dust brush for the workbench. It'll get into those corners and keep the working surface clean. Since the brushes have a hole in the handle, they can be hung on the side of the bench—ready for action."

GREASE   "The pump-type tops that come on jars of chocolate syrup are ideal for dispensers of heavy grease. This is much neater than having to reach into the grease container with your fingers."

GRINDING WHEELS   "A wet sponge kept under the grinding wheel in your shop will collect most of the particles of grit thrown down by the grinding wheel. It sure makes for a lot neater working surface, and when you're through the sponge can be rinsed off."

"An old hacksaw blade is ideal for dressing your grinding wheel. With the wheel turned on, gradually bring the blade against the wheel, making sure it's straight with the original surface of the wheel. It will true up any uneven places on the grindstone, making it almost as good as new."

GROUT   "I use one of those round typewriter erasers to clean the grout in between the tiles in the bathroom. They contain some kind of pumice and will cut right through any sort of guck on the grout and make it white again. Another nice thing is that the eraser is just about the same width as the grout and will fit down in the depressions."

"After replacing the pieces of grout that had fallen from between our bathroom tiles, I found that the new grout was quite a bit whiter than all the rest. I had my wife go to work on the walls with bleach, but there was still a difference. She solved the problem by getting out the white liquid shoe polish and running the dauber over the grout lines. She took no pains, because the polish that got on the tiles came off with a wet rag. When the job was done, the grout looked as it did when we moved into the house."

GUTTERS AND DOWNSPOUTS   "Our gutters were starting to sag in several places and wouldn't allow the water to drain out. The reason for the sagging was that the nails had worked loose, and I figured they would work loose again, so I devised a method of permanent repair. I put screw eyes in the roof about 3' up from the edge at the sag points. I made sure the eyes went into the slats under the shingles and then dabbed roofing cement around each eye to prevent leaking. Then I put a turnbuckle between wires from the eye to a hole drilled in the gutter. This enabled me to pull the gutters up to their proper level, where they'll stay."

"In repairing our rain gutters, I used spray-on auto undercoating. It's good for sealing the gaps where sections are joined together and also for patching. In patching holes, put a piece of screen wire over the hole, and then spray."

"I added an extension on the elbow at the bottom of the down-spouts to prevent big gushes of water that wash out all the dirt. The extension is a 3' section of regular straight downspout. Before adding it, I crimped the end shut, and drilled holes all along the sides and top of the section. Now the rain water squirts out of all these holes and is dispersed all around instead of gushing out in one big stream."

(Just be sure to drill enough holes to take care of all the water, or you'll have a back-up problem.)

"Rather than doing my famous but dangerous balancing act on the ladder this year to clean leaves out of my rain gutters, I rigged a contraption that allows me to stay on the ground. I attached a tin can by a 3'-long wire to a pole long enough to reach the roof. The can should be small enough to fit in the gutter; as it's dragged along, most of the leaves and debris will fly out. The rest will be collected at the end, and there's only one climb up the ladder."

"Leafproof your gutters and downspouts by putting strips of screen wire over the top of the gutters."

GUY WIRES   "Guy wires are necessary to keep tall structures such as TV antennas from falling or being blown over. However, they seem to blend into the scenery and can be very dangerous if someone should trip over one. Here's a way to make them less invisible. Take a section of old garden hose and slit it so it will fit over the guy wire. Then wrap the hose with a strip of reflective tape, and it will make the wire show up better, both night and day."

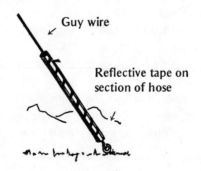

Guy wire

Reflective tape on section of hose

Hacksaw Blades • Hammers • Hand Savers • Handles—
Loose • Hang Ups • Hasp • Hauling • Heated Blade
Cutting • Heating • Hedges • Hobbies and Model Making
• Hoisting • Hold-Downs • Holsters • Hose Uses •
House Numbers • Humidity Fighters • Hydrants

H

HACKSAW BLADES   Sometimes you want to cut a wider slot with
your hacksaw than it normally will cut. If so, you can put two or more
blades together and widen the kerf to suit your purpose. In some cases,
parallel cuts can be made at one time by using two blades with spacers
in between.

"Don't throw away that broken hacksaw blade. It can be very useful
as a small saw to reach those sawing jobs that won't allow room for the
regular hacksaw frame. All you have to do is add a handle, and this can
be done by simply wrapping part of the blade with a few rounds of
friction tape. If you'll put one of these in your tool box, I bet you'll be
surprised at the number of times it will be of more help than your
complete saw."

(If you don't have a broken blade, and the frame is in the way, try
this trick with a spare blade. After you're through the tape handle can
easily be removed.)

Tape →

Broken hacksaw
blade

"If you're about to saw a pipe, and there isn't enough room above
the work, remember that the blade can be turned upside down."

An excellent place to store an extra hacksaw blade is right on the
saw itself. Just tape it along the side of the top of the frame. The frame
on most hacksaws is a shade wider than a blade, so that the teeth are
held flat against the frame. This trick also works well for coping saw
blades.

HAMMERS   "Installing a new hammer handle is an easy chore and
here's a way to make sure the handle never develops any wiggle. Just
before you're ready to insert the new handle into the eye of the
hammer, coat it with epoxy glue, and it will really be set."

"There always seems to be a collection of old keys around that no
longer are of any use. Not long ago, I devised a use for two of them.
While installing a new handle on my hammer, I discovered I'd misplaced

the metal wedges that had come out of the old handle. The keys were made into wedges with just a little grinding."

Here's a good temporary tightening job for a loose hammerhead. Pull a section of screen wire tight over the end of the handle, and then reinsert this in the hammerhead. The screen wire will give the handle new holding power until a new handle can be installed. This trick also works for other tools, such as a pick. However, any time there's the least chance that the head of a tool may come off in use, extra care should be taken for your own safety and that of people around you.

A hammerhead face that has worn to the extent that it's rounded off can lose its effectiveness. The nails just slip off to the side when struck. This can and should be remedied. Put the hammer in your vise and dress the face with a file until the center of the face is flat again.

→ Rubber
band
& nails

"I keep a tight rubber band around the upper part of my hammer handle to hold nails. I just insert as many as I can under the band before I start nailing, and they're easily extracted from the band as needed. This is certainly much safer than the age-old practice of putting nails in your mouth."

(Be sure you have a tight rubber band or the impact from hammering makes the nails fly out.)

"To protect the finish of work when I'm hammering, I use a square of inner tube with a slit in it. The slit fits over the nail until it's driven all the way down to the inner tube. Then the tube is slipped off, and one more hammer tap puts the nail in all the way."

(This same patch of inner tube, when placed around a screw being tightened down, protects the finish from a possible slip of the screwdriver.)

"Don't throw away those hard rubber wedge-shaped door stops. They come in handy in several ways. A wedge can act as a good fulcrum to put under your hammer, and it also provides protection for the work underneath the hammer. There have been several times when I've needed a temporary wedge for a project. I've also used one as a pad to put down on work when I needed a mallet but had to make do with a hammer."

"How about this hammer cover to protect work from mars and scratches when pulling nails? It's a strip of rubber from an old inner

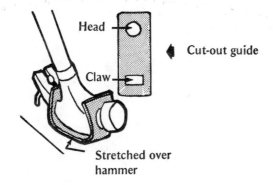

Head

Cut-out guide

Claw

Stretched over
hammer

tube, with a round hole in one end for the hammerhead to slip into and a square hole at the other end for the claw to slip into. When this is stretched over the hammer, only the rubber protector comes in contact with the work."

"I altered my claw hammer for easier and faster nail clinching. I merely drilled a hole in one of the claws; this slips over the nail to be clinched. A slight yank, and the nail is bent and can then be hammered on over."

If you've tried to hammer a nail into a surface right next to a wall or other finished area, you know the risks of the hammer's marring the finish. A cardboard shirt board from the laundry, held up against the wall, will let you hammer away.

HAND SAVERS "A pair of worn-out kitchen sponges comes in handy as pads for your hands when using a file. Just wrap the sponges around the metal, and you won't have to worry about nicking your hands."

They're also handy for other gripping chores. For example, when you run into a tough job with your screwdriver, try putting a sponge around the handle. It will absorb any moisture from perspiring hands. Also the ridges on most screwdriver handles can be a little rough on the fingers, and the sponge will eliminate this without your losing your grip.

The shock from hammering on a cold chisel or star drill can really begin to bug you after a few minutes. Most of this will be absorbed if you take a kid's ordinary sponge rubber ball and put a hole through it so it fits over the handle. You'll still have a tight grip, but you'll feel much less shock.

"The handle on a bucket can be a real hand-killer if you have much heavy carrying to do. Here's a quick way to provide a grip for the handle that will take out the 'ouch.' Just wrap the bail with soldering wire from your shop. The solder is flexible enough to easily wrap around and form a grip that's easy on your hand. After the bucket brigade is over, the solder can still be used for its original purpose.

Wrench

Or: "Take an open-end wrench—any size will do, as long as it's large enough for your complete hand to grip the handle. Let the handle of the bucket run through each end of the open-end wrench, and then pick up the bucket by the wrench. The wire handle will no longer cut through your hand."

Horseshoe with bike handle grip

"Lugging concrete building blocks around is tough on any man's hands. Wearing gloves is OK for the carrying, but the gloves can get in the way when it comes to putting the blocks in place. I've found an old horseshoe makes an ideal handle for this chore. One prong of the horseshoe fits into the hollow core opening at one end of the block, leaving the other prong sticking out as a handle. If you slip a bike handle grip over the carrying prong, there's no need to wear gloves. A pair of horseshoes can be used so two blocks can be carried at the same time."

Spools

"Get your wife to save all those empty wooden spools from her sewing basket. They come in handy for many things. For example, my file has never had a handle. I glued two spools together with epoxy, and then used this as a handle. The tang of the file is pushed up into the hole in the end of the spools. The spools are then tapped, forcing them down against the heel. If you want this to be a permanent handle, pour epoxy down into the hole, and when it sets up, the handle can't be blasted off."

HANDLES—LOOSE Loose handles can be dangerous and often make a tool less effective than it was meant to be. Many times you can remedy a loose handle on a small hand tool such as a file or awl by installing a plastic wall anchor in the handle. Since these come in a variety of sizes, you'll probably find one to fit inside the handle. When the tool is reinserted in the handle with the anchor inside, it will be tight as a drum. Of course, this won't work on a tool that's turned in use, such as a screwdriver.

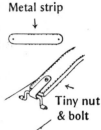

Metal strip

Tiny nut & bolt

"Certain kinds of suitcase handles can easily be repaired. If the handle is the flat kind that loops around a metal piece, cut two strips of metal not quite as wide as the handle. These should be about 3″ to 4″ long. Loop the strips around the metal strap holder as an outside layer to the handle. Drill a hole through both ends of the metal strip and the handle at the same time. Insert a small bolt and fasten it on with a nut. This is even good as a reinforcing measure for intact handles."

HANG-UPS "The ring pulls from those easy-open beverage cans make really good picture hangers that cost nothing. If your frame has room to attach a tack, you can use the aluminum ring by itself. If you wish the hanger to be attached to the cardboard backing behind the picture, however, you'll need to use the ring plus the tab. The tab can be looped through a pair of slits in the cardboard and held in place by a staple. It's best to put in an extra backing to protect the picture from being damaged by the staple or tab."

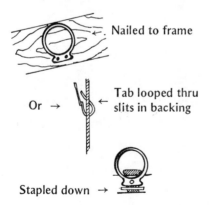

Nailed to frame

Or → Tab looped thru ← slits in backing

Stapled down →

"To hang something on a brick wall with concave mortar joints, you may not have to go through the tedious job of drilling and setting wall anchors. If the joints are deep enough, you can drive beveled blocks of wood in between the bricks and fasten on to these. It's a lot easier, and when your wife decides to take the object down, you don't end up with holes in the wall."

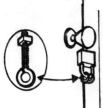

HASP "Two eyebolts will make a quick hasp for a door or gate. Install one in the door and the other on the facing right next to it. When they're set, the lock goes through the eyes, and the door is locked."

HAULING "The standard 4′ x 8′ size for plywood, pegboard, and other materials makes it difficult to haul these things home with an ordinary passenger car. To solve this problem, I take along four C-clamps when I go to the lumberyard. I attach these to all four corners of the plywood. This gives me tie holds for ropes that can then be lashed to any of several parts of the car. To protect the finish on the top of the car, I put several rolled up newspapers between the car and the material."

Another approach is to "have a pair of old inner tubes for that purpose. These can be inflated and placed on the roof of the car with the plywood atop them. A pair of ropes are then run over the top of the plywood and through the car windows and tied where they meet.

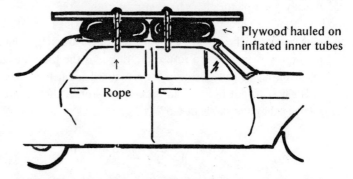

← Plywood hauled on inflated inner tubes

Rope

The ropes can be pulled very tight against the inflated tubes without bringing the wood down where it would touch the car."

(An equally clever fellow substituted swim floats for the inner tubes.)

"When you have to haul things in the trunk of your car that are too big for the trunk lid to close, use an ordinary screen door spring and attach an S-hook to each end to hold the trunk lid down. No matter what make or model of car you have, there's a place for this to attach. It's quick to hook on and stretches to the desired length."

"Punch extra holes all along an old belt and stow it in the trunk of your car. The next time you haul something in the trunk that prevents closing it, the belt will provide an excellent tie-down. The extra holes make it adjustable to take care of various-sized loads. Sure is easier than either wire or rope."

"I was faced with the task of hauling dirt in my pickup truck. Rather than shovel all the dirt out, I made a simple drag board that made it possible to dump each load easily. The drag board was made

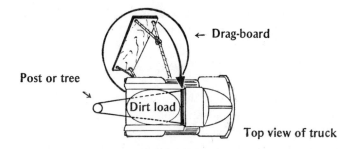

← Drag-board

Post or tree

Dirt load

Top view of truck

from a piece of 1″ x 12″ the width of the truck bed, with ropes attached through holes at each corner. The four ropes were joined together to another that was several feet longer than the truck bed. I placed the board in the truck bed, flat upright against the cab, and the rope trailed out the back end. The dirt was loaded on top of the rope. When the truck was backed into place where the dirt was to go, I tied the rope around a tree and pulled the truck slowly forward. This pulled the drag board out through the length of the truck bed, and it pulled the dirt with it, dumping it on the ground behind the truck."

(If there's not a tree in the right place, it may be worth your while to set a post to attach the drag board to.)

HEATED BLADE CUTTING   Several materials can be cut much better with a heated blade. If this is called for, you can improvise one with a razor blade and a soldering gun. Simply attach the blade to the end of the element with a small nut and bolt. Turn the gun on, and you have a heated blade.

HEATING   Almost every home central heating installation has a filter that can be changed by the home handyman. Most will also require other minor attention such as lubrication. Doing these chores at the regular intervals prescribed by the manufacturer will usually provide greater efficiency at lower cost. You'll always know when these duties were last attended to if you keep a record by writing the dates of each chore on a small piece of masking tape and sticking it right on the unit.

Do this for any other motors you have around the house that should have regular attention.

If your heating system isn't giving off as much heat as it should, your problem may be that soot has collected at the point where the ducts turn to go into the chimney. There's a simple way to check for an accumulation of soot even while the unit is running. The soot will settle at the bottom of a horizontal run of pipe or ductwork and will act as insulation Therefore, the bottom of the duct will feel cooler than the top. Make it a quick touch so you don't burn your hands. If it does feel cooler, your best bet is to shut down the unit and clean out the soot. You'll be warmer and at smaller cost.

"Last winter I found that the thermostat was registering the desired temperature but the room was actually too hot. I finally figured out that the problem wasn't in the thermostat, but rather that the hole for the wires going into the wall was allowing cold air from inside the walls to come in and affect the thermostat. By sticking a dab of modelling clay into the hole, I stopped the flow of air and made the thermostat govern the heater properly."

(This is one of the first places to check when you feel the thermostat is out of whack, as any air coming in the back will register. The modelling clay is a good idea—so is anything that will plug up the hole.)

"My husband greatly increased the heat from our radiators by taping aluminum foil on the walls behind them. This reflected the heat out into the room and made a big difference."

HEDGES   "To make sure that my wife had the latest in labor-saving devices, I bought her an electric hedge trimmer. Like any kid with a new toy, I had to try it out, and when I stepped back to admire my handiwork, I found the hedges slanted down at one end. I started cutting again, and instead of evening everything up, I discovered I had taken a little too much off the other end. Before this developed into a fiasco that might mean whacking the hedges right off to the ground, I got out a line level and string. By setting this up as a guide, I ended with the most level hedges on the block."

(Even stretching a string along at the desired height will help solve this problem.)

HOBBIES AND MODEL MAKING   "I use an old safety razor as a miniature vise. It's held in a regular vise with the razor handle sticking out so it can be tightened."

All model builders do a better job at their hobby with a constantly sharp knife. The most economical knife sharpener to keep at your work table is the striker plate from a book of matches. These free sharpeners are always around and do a surprisingly good job.

A sixth-grader came up with this idea: "I've borrowed several of my mother's earrings and find they make ideal miniature clamps for my model building. They are, of course, the kind that screw on the ears."

Another youngster thought up this one: "Here's an idea to share with model builders. I put the parts, in the order in which I'll use them, on a strip of masking tape. The tape holds the small parts so they don't fall off and get lost."

"I've never run across a tiny grease gun, and so I made one from an old mechanical pencil and a short piece of dowel. The works are removed from the pencil, leaving only the barrel with the point. This is filled with grease, and the dowel is inserted into the barrel. As it's pushed down into the barrel, the grease is forced out of the hole at the point."

HOISTING   "When my neighbor stained his roof, he lifted the bucket of stain by a hook on a rope. I would have wasted a lot of time fishing with the hook for the handle on the bucket, and then have had to call my wife to come hook it for me. Not him. Before he got on the

← Rubber band on bail

roof, he stretched a wide rubber band around the handle of the bucket while it was in an upright position. With the rubber band pushed down against the top of the can, the handle stayed upright. It was an easy matter to lower the rope from the roof and hook the bucket."

"I saw some men working on a roof and thought their method of hoisting up the rolls of roofing paper was clever. When you stop to think about it, such a roll wouldn't be easy to tie for lifting. They had a foot-long section of iron pipe tied on the end of a rope. When put

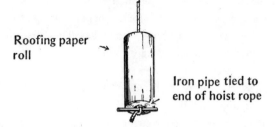

Roofing paper roll

Iron pipe tied to end of hoist rope

through the roll, the pipe would be pulled up flat against one end of the roll and couldn't be pulled back through. The rope then ran **through** the roll and up to the man on the roof who hoisted it up. This lifter was easy to put on and take off and certainly secured the roll for lifting."

Rubber band

Suction cup

HOLD-DOWNS "With so many gadgets made to be glued to walls, I think my clever hold-down will probably help many handymen while the glue is drying. I use a pair of rubber suction cups with a strong rubber band attached between them. With the suction cups stuck to the wall on either side, the rubber band stretches over the object, clamping it firmly against the wall."

Shower curtain ring

HOLSTERS "A shower curtain ring also serves as a holster for a hammer. The narrow part that fastens like a safety pin is clamped onto a belt loop. Then, when I poke the hammer handle down into the bigger round part, the hammer hangs at my side until needed. I've been practicing on a fast draw and am known around the house as the 'fastest hammer in the west.' "

"If you need a holster for nails, screws, or tiny parts, a paper drinking cup can be put to work. Make two vertical slits in the cup, about an inch apart. Start just below the rim and come down as far as your belt is wide. With the slits slipped over the belt, you have a holder for these parts at your side. In fact, if you have to use several sizes of nails, put several of these holsters on your belt."

← Slits

If you carry your hand tools around in a holster on a belt, be sure to wear it pushed around toward the back instead of at the front. Then if you should fall, you needn't worry about a sharp screwdriver coming through the leather and gouging your leg.

HOSE USES Don't throw away an old worn-out garden hose. Here are ways to use 103′ of the stuff.

"I made a wall holder for rope and wire in my garage from scrap  **Slit hose**
sections of hose about 6″ long. The hose is slit and then nailed
horizontally to the garage wall. The wire or rope is rolled up, and one
section of the coil is slipped into the slit hose. This will hold the coil of
rope or wire flat against the wall, as shown."

"I shock-proofed the handle on my electrical switch box. In my
case, I didn't even have to split the length of hose. I just flattened it
out, and it slipped over the handle. If need be, however, it could be slit
to make it fit over the handle."

"A 3″ or 4″ piece of old garden hose makes an excellent handle for a
file. It slips right over the file and saves your hands."

"I slit sections of old garden hose about 8″ long and nail them
vertically to the shop wall. They are great holders for chisels and
screwdrivers and keep the points protected. They can also be used in
the tool shed to hold rakes and hoes. The handle fits inside the hose,
and the blade of the hoe rests on the top."

"Slit two strips of hose to fit over the steps of a shovel or fork. This
is much easier on the feet."

**Hose section on saw
blade**

"Protect your axe blade and the people around you by slipping two
slit pieces of hose over the cutting edges. Hold them in place with
rubber bands."

"If you have a pruning saw or bow saw with large sharp teeth, you'll
find that a split section of hose placed over the teeth the length of the
blade offers a good sheath to protect you and the saw when it's not in
use."

"I put a length of hose over the blades of handsaws I have hanging."

"We have patio furniture made with metal frames that form runners instead of legs. These runners are noisy when moved, scratch up the patio, and can leave rust spots. I slit lengths of old hose and slipped these around the runners, providing much less wear and tear on both the patio and the chairs. And no more noise."

"I slit sections of hose and cut them to fit over the edges of the wooden seats on our children's outdoor swing set. When the swing is in motion, it could severely injure a child if he should carelessly run in front of it and be hit. With the rubber hose as a cushion, the injury would be much less. The hose will stay in place if it's just clamped over the seat."

"You boat owners can slit a couple of sections of hose and slip them on the line you use to tie the boat to the dock. Slide them in place at the two wear points where the rope hits the dock and the boat, to keep

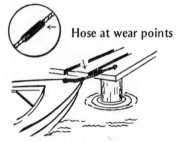

Hose at wear points

the line from wearing out because of rubbing at these places. If you don't dock at the same place all the time, the protectors will slip to any point on the rope."

"I put old garden hose all around the top board on the sides of my pick-up truck. I'm constantly in and out of the back of the truck, and the hose keeps me from picking up the splinters I used to get."

"I made weatherstripping for our garage door out of hose. The door is on a track and raises to open. I cut a piece of hose the entire length of the door and slit the hose from one end to the other. The slit edge was tacked to the inside of the bottom of the door, and the rest of the hose was wrapped around underneath. At the top, a piece of hose is fastened on the front of the door and wraps around the top. My door didn't need any weatherstripping along the sides. The hose not only keeps the garage warmer in the winter, it keeps lots of debris from blowing under the door."

"A couple of slit pieces of hose make great grippers when you need to carry a piece of plate glass."

"Door stops can be cut out of a leftover piece of old garden hose. Cut some triangular wedges, leaving about an inch of the hose still completely round on the end. They can be tailored to fit."

↑
Hose sections

"Rather than chop that worn-out garden hose into little pieces, I took an ice pick and punched holes all along the hose. Then, by turning the nozzle to 'off,' I had a doggone good lawn sprinkler for parkways, flower beds, and other narrow areas."

"If trees need wire bracing, use a length of hose at the point of contact to prevent the wire from cutting into the tree."

"I slip a slit section of plastic hose over the clothesline when I hang out blankets or bedspreads on the line so there's no crease from the wire. Use plastic, since a rubber hose might leave a black mark."

Before you chop up that old plastic garden hose to use for all these super ideas, try this. Holes in plastic hose can often be mended with a solder gun. Hold the gun up to the hole in the hose until the plastic begins to melt. Spread the molten plastic back and forth so it goes into the hole and seals it. This won't help on large splits, but for little holes it's great.

HOUSE NUMBERS   "I made a very unusual house number sign for our home. I bought the cheapest metal numbers and put these on a board I cut to the desired size. Then I ran my propane torch back and forth across the board, burning away a good portion of the top surface of the wood. However, the wood under the metal numerals wasn't burned, and when they were removed, our house number stood out with an unusual rustic charred background."

"One of the teenagers in our neighborhood came by and asked me to save my old·auto license plates for him. He was cutting out the numerals, mounting them on pieces of wood, and selling them as house numbers throughout the area. Maybe you won't want to go into that business, but if you need an extra set of house numbers, scour the neighborhood at license-changing time and get the numbers you need. There are all sorts of ways to mount them."

"Our front porch light went out when we had company coming, so I devised a lighted house number that has been on duty ever since. I cut the numbers out of dark paper and taped them to the shade of a lamp that sits on a table in the front window. With the lamp on, the house number was quite easy to see from the street."

HUMIDITY FIGHTERS   Some of the tools in your toolbox aren't used too often, and many times the moisture in the air will start them on the road to rust and ruin. A large piece of chalk kept in the bottom of your toolbox will absorb the moisture instead of letting it go to work on your equipment. The large cones of carpenters' chalk are ideal for this. When the chalk begins to feel a little damp, you can dry it out by putting it in the oven for about 15 minutes.

"The piano tuner told us that one possible reason our piano kept getting out of tune was our excessive humidity. My remedy was to install an electric outlet in the bottom of the case and keep a small bulb burning inside at all times. The bulb is only 25 watts and therefore doesn't create enough heat to affect the piano, but it does keep the moisture down."

Hard-to-open wooden drawers often result from swelling due to moisture and can usually be fixed by drying the wood. A simple but effective way to do this is to put a lighted bulb in the drawer. The heat will dry out the moisture and allow the drawer to move easily again. Then prevent the moisture problem from bothering the drawer again by applying a coat of linseed oil to the sides. Rub or brush it on and let it sit for an hour or so; then rub off the excess with a dry cloth. This seals the wood against future moisture absorption.

HYDRANTS   Somehow we lost a handle off our backyard hydrant. I discovered that an ordinary doorknob fits in its place. The set screws for the doorknob hold it on tightly."

(One lady adapted this idea in her guest bath when she removed the two handles on the wash basin and replaced them with a pair of antique doorknobs!)

IDENTIFICATION PLATES "With all the hubbub about companies mailing out unwanted credit cards, I've my own solution to the problem. Most of these plastic plates have my name and address on them. I cut these sections out and make excellent use of them as identification plates. One is glued to my tool box. I drill holes in some and sew them in place to such things as tents, tarps, and jackets. The name by itself fits into the slot on our mail box. After I get just a few more, they can go ahead and do something about the problem."

INDOOR PLANTS "For those who have made patio planters out of wooden barrel halves, here's a way to insure against the fungus that can get started in the wood. Before you put the dirt in, pour fire-starter or lighter fluid on the bottom and sides of the barrel. Stand well back, and toss in a lighted match. This will char the inside of the barrel and preclude the fungus from getting a start."

(Just be sure you don't burn up the whole planter in the process.)

"Our apartment was greatly enhanced by our many potted plants—until we got a kitten that decided the pots were more convenient than the sandbox we'd provided. Chemicals are supposed to keep cats away from things, but they didn't even phase Tiger. Finally I put my creative genius to work and came up with an idea that let us keep both the cat and the plants. I cut pieces from wire mesh hardware cloth to fit over the dirt of each plant, and I cut holes out of the center of each for the plants to fit through. Then I cut a slit from the edge to the center so the mesh could be slipped in place. I bent the edges so the mesh stood about ½" off the dirt. This may have only frustrated the cat in the beginning, but now she uses only the sandbox."

INSULATION If you're doing a small insulation job using batts and don't have special shears for cutting them, drag out the hedge trimmers. They'll do a fast, neat job on the batts, and it won't hurt the blades of the clippers.

J.

JIGS   There are many workshop contrivances that help you use a tool by acting as a shield, guide, template, or holder. Generally known as jigs, they may enable you to turn out a number of exactly duplicated pieces or do a job more accurately. Here are some jigs you can rig up yourself.

"When cutting dowels to a certain length on my bandsaw, I clamp a guide fence the proper distance from the blade. A straight scrap of wood and a C-clamp will serve this purpose. Then I use a square block to push the dowel through the blade. With the block against the fence, the blade goes squarely through the dowel."

"A jig for setting the height of a table saw blade can easily be made from scraps of 1/8″ hardboard. Start with a piece about 6″ long and cut each succeeding piece a half inch longer. Glue them together in stair step fashion (as shown). When the shortest side is placed on the saw table, the blade may be turned up until it touches the desired height. I glued a scrap ruler section on mine, so I don't have to count layers to arrive at the correct height."

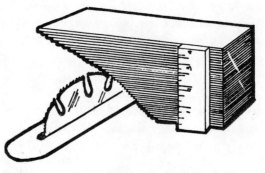

"I have a drill jig I made to allow me to start the drill at right angles to the surface being drilled. It's a 'V' notched 2″ x 4″. When the point of the 'V' is placed on the spot to be drilled, the drill bit can be held against the block and is guided straight into the work and at the right spot."

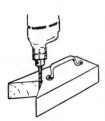

(And, you could add a screen door handle to the block to make it easier to hold.)

JOINTS AND JOINING   Sometimes a home handyman project will call for holes to be lined up exactly on two boards that are to be fitted together. Here's a trick that will help line them up. Take a lead BB shot and place it on the center mark on one of the boards. Tap it into the wood, and it will stick there. Now take the other piece of wood and place it in position as it will be when finished. Tap it lightly until it becomes flush with the first piece. When the two boards are separated and the BB is removed, there will be a pair of indentations exactly opposite each other on the boards. These dots will allow you to follow through with the next step, knowing that the joining will be exact.

"I make dowel joints stronger by drilling several tiny holes in the dowel before inserting for glueing. Glue gets in the holes and creates a stronger bond."

"When joining pieces that are not to be at right angles, I still use a regular metal corner brace. I put the brace in my vise and bend it to the proper angle. Even if one or both pieces are curved, the brace can be shaped to fit."

K.

KEYS "Never again will I lock myself out of the house. I've buried an extra key in our yard, inside one of those 35mm film cans."

(Another good way is to wrap the key in aluminum foil before burying it.)

"I glued a small magnet to an outside water hydrant that's out of sight because of a hedge. The magnet holds my extra key where I can always find it, but in a place where no one else would think to look."

"Lots of folks hide a spare car key by holding it somewhere in the car with a magnet. I've always been afraid it might be jarred off, and so I came up with what I think is a much better method. I drop a car key and also a spare house key into the water bag that goes with the windshield-washer system. The keys fall to the bottom, and in no way hamper the washer. Since the keys are made from a rust-proof metal, there's no problem on that score. If the emergency should arise, the plastic bag will be quite simple to empty to get the keys."

"I have an extra car key and apartment key hidden right on my car. They're behind the license plate, held there by the same two screws that hold the plate in place. The keys are between the plate and the holder on the car and look as if they were washers, although they can just barely be seen at all."

"I got tired of fumbling around for the right key to open my house at night and solved the problem by altering the door key. I drilled a hole over at the side of the key, and placed the key ring through this new hole. When the keys hang down, all the others hang down straight, but the off-center hole in my door key makes it hang at an angle so it sticks out and is easily found in the dark."

New hole off center

"We have quite a number of padlocks on gates, outbuildings, and storage cabinets, and I used to have to fiddle around before I came up with the right key. Now I don't have any problem, because I've color-coded all the locks and keys. I used enamel and painted a different-colored stripe around each lock and the corresponding key."

"We have an outside door that uses a skeleton key for locking. As long as the key is in place, another skeleton key can't be inserted by a stranger. However, there's no problem in pushing this type of key out

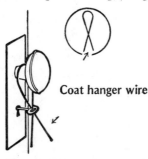

Coat hanger wire

from the other side and then using your own key to gain entry. At least not until I rigged up my gadget to hold the key in place. With the key sideways in the lock, I looped a section of coat-hanger wire around the door handle and ran the ends through the hole in the key. The key can't be pushed out, and when we wish to open the door, the wire gadget is simple to remove."

"Here's one way I utilize handles from old toothbrushes. We have a drawer full of loose keys for such things as gates, trunks, the garage, and storage cabinets. Here's where the toothbrush handles come in

Toothbrush handle (cut off here) →

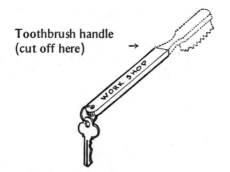

handy. A wire through the hole in the key and the hole in the handle connects the two. A hot icepick burns identification of the key's use into the plastic handle. It's also almost impossible to lose a key or forget to return it to the drawer."

L
●

LADDERS   Whenever you use a ladder, think of safety. Here are some steps you'll want to keep in mind.

Did you ever wonder why you don't see many painted ladders? There's a very good reason for this. Paint could hide any cracks or splits that might be developing. Feel free to apply a good coat of linseed oil to your wooden ladder, however, to act as a preservative. Metal ladders should not require any maintenance, but all ladders should be checked carefully before each use.

Here's a quick way to give your straight ladder a safety check before using it. Lay the ladder flat on the ground and walk the entire length, stepping on each rung as you go. This is a sure test of the soundness of the entire ladder and a particularly good idea for the home handyman who doesn't use his ladder very often. The few moments this test takes could save you from a few months in a cast.

A broken rung need not be the swan song for your ladder. If the rest of the ladder is still in good shape, you can replace the rung in question with a section of ¾″ iron pipe. Use enough pipe to go completely through both sides of the ladder and stick out a little on each side. Thread each end and tighten these down against the sides with pipe caps. If done right, this method makes a good strong repair.

"There's a lot to be said for those lightweight aluminum ladders. However, they cannot take as much abuse as wooden ladders, and mine ended up with a bent side rail that was folded over between the bottom

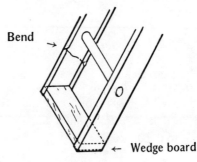

Bend →

Wedge board →

step and the end of the rail. The rail was easy to straighten out, but obviously it might bend again while someone was standing on the ladder. So, with the rail straight, I cut a board to fit exactly in between the two rails (like a new step right on the ground) and wedged it down in place. Then I drilled holes in each rail, and put in screws to prevent the piece from coming out. With this board in between, the rail can't collapse, and the ladder is safe."

(This is also good preventive maintenance to keep the ladder rail from getting bent. The method of repair mentioned above works for rails that are bent *in*—which is the way most are. If you had a ladder rail that bent *out*, you might put on some sort of turnbuckle to pull the two rails toward each other.)

"Placing a straight ladder up against a tree or pole can be dangerous, as the straight rungs don't fit too well around curves and the ladder has no stability. To eliminate that hazard, I put in a new top rung made from a length of chain covered with a piece of discarded rubber hose. The chain is attached to the ladder by a pair of eyebolts. The flexibility afforded by this new rung allows the ladder to fit against rounded objects for a firmer stance. The rubber hose keeps the ladder from sliding down. It's a lot safer!"

Hose over chain

(This will also work if your ladder has to be placed against the corner of your house. As always when you drill holes in your ladder, be sure you don't leave it structurally unsound.)

A ladder can sink down in soft ground. Don't take a chance, when there's an easy way to make your ladder much safer under such conditions. Get yourself a piece of scrap lumber that will span the distance between the two feet. If the scrap of wood sticks out on each side, so much the better. Now, take a pair of C-clamps large enough to attach the board across from one leg to the other at the bottom. This will prevent the ladder from sinking into the soft ground, and maybe prevent you from having a sinking spell, too.

"With a pair of angle braces, I made some safety feet for my straight ladder that prevent it from slipping when it's resting on the ground. One part of each brace has been bent back at a right angle and filed to a point. This makes the brace into a 'Z' shape. The unaltered half of the brace can be attached to the face of the ladder leg. The other half conforms to the bottom of the leg. This leaves the point sticking down where it can be pushed into the ground. The braces are attached with nuts and bolts so they can be removed."

Bent down

Filed to point

Another idea for feet is: "Use a pair of tunafish cans for the feet of the ladder to rest in. Drive a large spike through the bottom of each can into the ground. With the cans anchored by the long spikes, the ladder cannot slip."

"When I need to use a ladder on a slick surface, I put a pair of 'shoes' on the feet of the ladder. The shoes are canvas bags filled with sand. After the feet of the ladder are well down into the bags, I wire them on. The sandbags will keep the ladder in place and make it skid-free."

"On each leg of my ladder, I put a common door barrel bolt and slightly sharpened the points. When the ladder is set in place, the bolts are stuck in the ground and locked in place. When not in use, the bolts are locked back out of the way."

Barrel bolt

And there are some steps to make ladders less harmful to things around them:

"So as not to mar the finish when I use my straight ladder up against the house, I glued strips of carpet scraps over the ends. The carpet scraps are soft enough not to scratch, yet still allow the ladder to rest firmly against the house."

"I've added an accessory to my straight ladder that makes it safer and prevents marring. I got two large suction cups that were designed for holding racks to car tops. Attached to the ends of the ladder, they stick to the wall and keep the ladder attached without scratching. After I'm through, the suction cups pop loose from the wall easily with a twist of the ladder."

"When working around windows, you need something to span the window, as your straight ladder can't lean against the pane. I drilled holes at the top of the ladder, large enough for a 1″ pipe to go through both uprights. This way, the pipe rests on the window frame and holds the ladder away from the window itself. If it's a double window, I use a pipe long enough to span both."

"When you're using a saw on a stepladder, there's really no place to put it down for an instant. I cut a groove with a saber saw in the top of my ladder about ½" from the back edge, as a saw-holding slot."

"To hold my yardstick to the side of my ladder, I took a pair of three-inch-square patches of rubber from an old inner tube and stapled them to the side of the ladder. They're positioned so that when the yardstick is laid down flat against the side of the ladder, each end will fit under one of the rubber tabs. It's out of the way but comes loose very easily when needed."

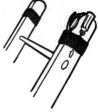

"A wide rubber band cut from a bike inner tube and put around the top of each of the side pieces on a straight ladder acts as a holder for small hand tools. Just slip the tools under the rubber bands. As a matter of fact, slip them in the holder before putting the ladder up, and they are there when you get to the top."

Here is a similar holder for hand tools on a stepladder: "Slip a pair of large rubber bands on the ends of the top step of the ladder. Instead of just putting the tools down on the step when not in use, slip them under one of the bands."

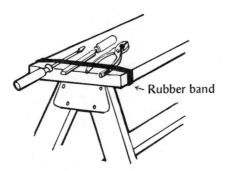

← Rubber band

← Broom clamp

"Those mop and broom holders also have a good handyman use when installed on the top step of a ladder. They serve as holders for many small hand tools. Put 'em on the ends so they'll be out of the way."

"I've almost doubled the area of the top step of my stepladder with a very easy swing-out shelf. First I cut out the shelf the same size as the top step of the ladder. Then I drilled a hole over in one corner through

← Swing-out shelf

Bolt

both the shelf and the stepladder. I attached the shelf to the step by means of a nut, a bolt, and washers, left loose enough so the step could swing out. This extra space really comes in handy to take care of all the tools, cans, or brushes I need for a particular job."

"I've bored various-sized holes in the top step of my stepladder. Now the tools I need fit into the holes instead of falling off on the floor every time I put them down."

"Put quarter-round molding around the edge of your ladder top, and you've got a tray that will prevent things from getting away from you."

"I installed an old towel rack on the back of the top step of my stepladder for holding rags when I'm cleaning windows or painting. It also will hold several kinds of tools, and it doesn't get in the way when I'm just using the ladder for climbing."

"If you're looking for a clever way to hang a paint bucket on a ladder rung, put a shower curtain ring over the rung at the most convenient height, and then put the bucket handle on the ring. Snap the ring closed, and the can can't be accidentally dropped."

"I've devised a whiz of a paint can holder for the top of my ladder. First I bored a hole in the top step of my ladder, over to the far side. Then I got a foot-long piece of dowelling the same size as the hole and

forced it down into the hole. A rubber band from an old inner tube holds the paint steady against the dowel. When the dowel is not in use, I drive it down flush with the step."

"Here's how I solve the problem of using a tippy paint bucket on the top step of a ladder. I found an old cake pan that's just the right size for a gallon paint can to fit into and soldered a large nail by its head to the bottom. A hole in the top step of the ladder receives the nail, and my bucket holder is in place until I am through. Not only does it prevent my tipping over the can, it catches drips and keeps the paint from getting all over the ladder. It also serves as a small tool tray. Since it comes off when not needed, it doesn't change the ladder for normal usage."

(How about this same idea using a tuna can for small cans of paint?)

Sections are bolted together

Middle stay added

Bottom piece optional

"I converted my 20' extension ladder into a sort of stepladder—but with advantages over the conventional ones. The two 10' sections are joined at one end by ¼" stove bolts and wing nuts. A middle stay made of 1" x 2" board is installed between the sections, about 3' up from the ground. Mine is about 3' long. This gives it a stepladder effect, with the sections spread apart at the bottom and coming to a point at the top. I also added a 1" x 4" bottom piece with chocks to one side for greater stability on uneven ground. It can be quickly put up or taken down with the use of the wing nuts. The middle stay can be left attached to one section after disassembling, and the bottom piece left in place all the time. It is quite handy for pruning trees, picking fruit, and other jobs when there is no place to lean a ladder. You can climb up either side and face in or out as you work. Your neighbors will prove they admire it by borrowing it often, as mine have."

"Hanging ladders on nails along the wall is a good way to store them. If hit, however, they can be knocked off on someone's head. I've guarded against this—and at the same time used an item that would otherwise have had to be discarded—by attaching an old leather belt to the wall between the two nails. This is buckled completely around the ladder, and the ladder can no longer fall down. Yet it's a simple matter to take off the belt when I need my ladder."

"Although quite simple, my stepladder holder idea has been admired and used by many friends. A regular wire coat hanger and an eye screw are all that's needed. Twist the hook of the coat hanger around the eye

Wire hanger in screw-eye →

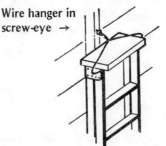

screw, installed on the garage wall at the right height. Position it so that when the ladder is standing against the wall, the horizontal wire of the hanger will slip over the top step. The hanger will hold the ladder in an almost straight-up position against the wall and keep it from falling over. If the step is bigger than the horizontal wire, this can easily be bent to fit."

"When being carried or stored, a stepladder should stay closed. To make sure mine does, I installed a common window latch to keep it locked shut. It's installed on the side out of the way, and the two parts of the latch are on opposite parts of the ladder for a secure lock."

"Although ladders aren't usually very heavy, they are cumbersome to handle. I made my ladder a lot easier to carry by putting a screen door handle on the side, right in the center. It works great."

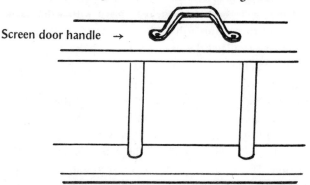

Screen door handle →

LAG SCREWS   An easy way to install a lag screw is to chuck it in a hand brace and turn it into a predrilled hole. This is a real work-saver if you've several lag screws to put in place. Use the brace to turn the screw down to the wood, and then finish tightening it with a wrench.

LAMPS   "After our garage sale, we still had Aunt Minnie's old dining room table—the one with the carvy legs. I cut off the legs and made a great pair of lamps out of two of them. I drilled a hole down through them for the wires and mounted them on blocks which were also drilled. A finish, the proper hardware, and shades completed the lamps. After all, those carvy furniture legs are usually fine wood." (And you still have legs enough for another pair of lamps—with different bases and finish.)

LAWNS   "I'd heard about this, and it worked. To prevent the birds from eating my grass seed when I sowed my new lawn, I soaked the seeds in a solution of bluing and water until they were blue. Then I cast them and the birds didn't bother them. Why? I guess blue bothers birds. The bluing didn't affect the fertility of the seeds."

"No sense feeding your lawn grass seeds to the birds. Here's a fast but effective 'scarecrow' that really keeps them away. Stretch a strong string across the newly seeded area. Then take 1"-wide strips of aluminum foil about a foot long. Staple these to the cord a foot or so apart. These strips will twist and flash with practically no breeze at all and will keep the birds away. Soon as the grass starts to come up, the 'scarecrow' can come down in moments."

"One of life's big disappointments is to plant seeds and have them wash or blow away. My system spares me that. I cover the seeded area with old burlap bags, holding them in place with a thin layer of dirt scattered over them. This will allow water to reach the seeds without washing them away, and the bags are also good mulch. Plants will grow right up through the loose burlap."

"Many people who turn on a sprinkler to water the yard don't leave it in place long enough to do the job. I've made sure each area gets the proper amount by using a tunafish can as a rain gauge. I know exactly how deep the water should be in the can to have done the proper watering job. This would vary, of course, according to the type of grass and soil, but once you determine the proper level, this simple gauge takes the guesswork out of watering."

"Here's a tip that will save many moments of frustration for all those who have soaker hoses. As you know, the biggest problem is to get the soaker to lie flat. The problem can be easily solved by taping thin strips of wood—I used some old yardsticks I had picked up over the years—to the side without the holes. These strips also allow you to fold the soaker for storage."

"One stretch in our lawn is too short for the lawn soaker we have. I tried tying a knot in the soaker, but this didn't work out too well. So I went to my 'discarded gadgets' box and found an old pants hanger that works like a clamp. It actually works better than most types of clamps since it has a felt padding that was designed to protect pants, and doesn't cut the soaker."

"By installing an underground sprinkler system, I eliminated one yard task but created a new one—trimming the grass around the sprinkler heads. As you can imagine, this is a hand clipping job—or was until I found a tin can that was a shade bigger around than the sprinkler heads and sharpened the open edge on my grinding wheel. I ran a cord through holes punched in the top of the can. Now, I just put the can over the sprinkler heads and press down with my foot. It cuts the grass around the head in a neat circle. The string forms a long handle and enables me to pick up the edger without even bending over."

"The plants under my roof overhang were sheltered from the rain. It was difficult to set up a sprinkler to water them properly without watering the walls too. I took care of this with an old garden hose as long as my flower beds: I capped over one end and punched holes about every 2". I mounted this under the eave of the house, with the holes pointing down. The remainder of the hose comes on down to the hydrant. When I wish to water this bed, I connect the hose, and a gentle rain-like watering job is under way."

"Here's a safety tip for electric lawn mowers. Get a roll of brightly colored plastic tape and wrap the mower's electric cord in a sort of barber pole fashion. This will make the cord visible enough so that you won't run the risk of running over it. This is also a good safety move for the electric hedge trimmer cord."

"My front and rear yards are on different levels, which means I have to lift my power mower up and down some steps. As you know, mowers aren't the handiest things in the world to carry, but mine is much easier now. I mounted a screen door handle on the front of the mower. With this, plus a grip on the regular handle, it's a cinch to lift."

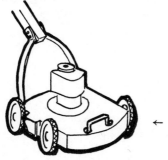 ← Screen door handle

"Now that I have a power lawn mower and a power eager, my lawn trimming is a breeze. However, I discovered that it took me longer to sweep up than it had to mow and edge. Now I just run my mower back over the walks and drives after I have finished, and it cleans up for me. Most of the trimmings are pulled up by the movement of the blade and thrown into the grass catcher. It's almost as good as sweeping and takes a tenth of the time."

"My power lawn mower always used to run out of gas in the most remote part of my yard, so I devised a gas gauge which I think is pretty ingenious and really quite simple. I stuck a wire into a cork so that it stood straight up. Then I drilled a hole through the cap on the tank and put the cork inside so that it floats on the gasoline. The wire sticks straight up through the hole in the cap, and as the gasoline goes out of the tank, the part of wire sticking out gets shorter. I marked the wire at several spots so I can always tell exactly how much gasoline is left in the mower."

"I'm retired, but still do my own yard work. However, the power lawn mower is the kind that requires pulling a rope to turn over the engine. It was about to become too much for me to start. My son welded a ring on the front of the mower and put a metal stake in cement at the edge of the garage apron. Hooking the ring over the stake holds the mower in place, and now I can use both hands to pull. Also, I can get into a better position, since I no longer have to put a foot on the housing to keep the mower in place. To get the ring on and off the stake, the front end of the mower lifts up easily by pushing the handle down and using the back wheels as a pivot. Without this, I probably wouldn't be able to do the mowing unless someone else started the mower for me."

"Edging up next to our fence was quite aggravating until I laid down a strip of plastic beside the fence. The strip was about 4″ wide and was made from folded-up plastic garment bags we got from the cleaners. As I put down the plastic, I covered it with a layer of dirt about ¼″ thick. This isn't enough for grass to root in and keeps all but a few stray runners away from the fence—and these are easily hand clipped from time to time."

LEAKS   "Here's a way of fixing a small gas leak until the utility company answers your call. Dab the pipe with some of your wife's fingernail polish. It's thick enough and dries fast enough to seal up most small leaks. If it doesn't get it the first time, give it another coat. If you're not sure you have the leak stopped, cut off the flow at the meter."

The standard way to locate a gas leak is to apply thick soapsuds to joints or suspected areas. If there's a leak, the escaping gas will cause the soap to bubble up. But here's a great new wrinkle. Instead of regular soap, use shaving cream from an aerosol spray can. It's the greatest.

"Here's an emergency measure that I suggest to all who have gas piped to their homes. I bought a cheap wrench to fit the cut-off valve at the gas meter and tied this onto the meter with plastic cord. Now, if we should have any sort of emergency that would require cutting off the flow of gas to the house, I could do so in minutes. I know from a previous emergency how long it can take to go to the shop and locate a wrench for this purpose—too long!"

(An excellent idea for any sort of emergency cutoff that requires a tool.)

LEVELS   "Since the bubble vial on a shop level is glass, it should be protected when the level isn't being used. I wrap mine in a kitchen sponge, and then put rubber bands around the sponge to hold it in place."

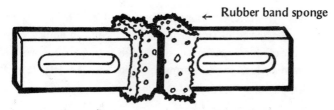

← Rubber band sponge

"A level that's out of whack can be disastrous. If you've any doubts about yours, give it this simple test. Pick out a smooth inclined surface, lay the level down, and mark the position of the bubble. Now, reverse the level end-for-end. If the level is accurate, the bubble should be in exactly the same position on the other side."

"Those long metal levels are great to work with, except that when you try to hold them against a smooth wall, they have a tendency to slip. If you glue small squares of sandpaper along the sides of the level, the grit will help keep the level from slipping. This will also help steady a metal rule. Use rubber cement, and the sandpaper patches can be peeled off when not needed."

"There are times when you don't want your work level, but you do want it inclined at the same pitch at all times. You can still use your level to keep the same pitch if you make one minor adjustment. When you get the bubble set at the desired position away from the center

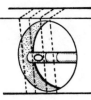

lines, make new lines with two strips of tape. Put one strip on each side of the bubble. Now, all you have to do to keep the same pitch is line up the bubble between the tapes. When the job is done, take off the tape."

"I needed to level the ground for a walk and devised a very simple grade-leveling tool from my garden rake. I attached a long board to the teeth of the rake by driving nails into the board and clinching them over the teeth. This tool did a fine job of leveling. When the job was done, it was a simple matter to restore the rake to normal."

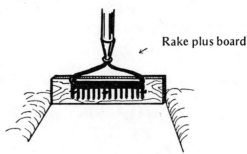

Rake plus board

"An easy way to level furniture is to put small lag screws in each leg. When these are screwed in almost all the way, you can adjust them to get the piece of furniture level. Since this can be done with the furniture on the floor in its normal position, it's an easy task. Put casters under the lag screws to protect the floor."

"If you don't have a level handy, here's a tricky way to find out if the surface in question is level. Take a yardstick and lay it flat on the surface. Place a marble next to the ruler. The marble will naturally roll along the straightedge toward the lower part. When the surface has been levelled, the marble will stay in place."

Painted line
↓

→ ↓
Plumb bob

"I made a level that works great. It's made from a straight board, a nail, and a plumb bob. I used a 4' long 1" x 2". (Be sure to get a straight one.) In the center, I laid a right angle and drew a line perpendicular to the length of the 1" x 2". At the top of this line, I drove the nail in. From this, I hung up the plumb bob. When the string on the plumb bob lines up with the line drawn on the 1" x 2", the board is level. The beauty about this is that you can use a longer board if you need a level to span several feet."

"If you need a level and there isn't one handy, improvise with the aid of a measuring cup from the kitchen—the kind that is calibrated on both sides. Fill the cup up to a point where it's even with one of the markings. Then put it on the object you want to test for levelness. If it's level, the waterline will be on the same mark on either side of the measuring cup. If you don't have a measuring cup, any glass container could be marked at points opposite each other. Measure up from the bottom and mark with a felt-tipped marker."

"If you don't happen to have a pocket level, you can make one quite easily. Buy one of those replacement bubble vials for a level and tape this to a pencil that has a flat top and bottom. You can use a six-sided pencil or a flat carpenter's pencil. Test your level on a known level surface. If the level is off, shim up the vial with tape. Once you have zeroed in, the level can be carried in the pocket, and will prove to be a very handy little gadget."

Level bubble vial

LICENSE PLATES "When the new auto license plates come out, there are many rusted, corroded nuts and bolts that'll have to be wrestled loose. I used to have this problem until I learned this trick. Soon as I get the nut loosely down on the bolt, I coat them both well with rubber cement. While the cement is still wet, I tighten the nut down. This seals the nut to the bolt and keeps out all the elements that might cause rust or corrosion. Also, there's never a chance of its coming loose and starting to rattle. When it's time to put on the new plates, the rubber cement lets go with very little pressure."

LIGHT BULBS AND LIGHTING "With my bulb-changing tool you can replace a burned-out light bulb without having to climb up on anything. I removed the bulb clamp from inside an old lamp shade and clipped off the braces leading to the shade. I then attached the clamp to the end of an old broom handle. With this, you can reach up and clamp onto the bulb. These clamps have a springing action and, therefore, will spread apart to go around the bulb. I wrapped the parts that touch the bulb with masking tape to give better gripping power."

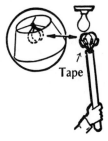

Tape

"Here's how I change light bulbs that are out of reach. I've saved an arrow from a child's archery set, the kind that has a rubber suction cup on the end. This can be stuck to the burned-out light bulb and is like adding a handle to the bulb. A gentle turn of the shaft will unscrew the bulb. After the new bulb is screwed in place in the socket, a quick downward twist pulls the suction cup off. It sure beats climbing up on a chair!"

"If you should break a light bulb, there's a safe way to remove it without cutting your fingers or shocking yourself. Use a rubber-handled screwdriver and jam the end of the handle firmly against the base of the bulb. Turn it so it backs the base out of the socket."

"A broken light-bulb base is difficult to remove from the socket because there's no safe place to grab it. Don't worry. Just jam a bar of soap into the base and twist. It will come out."

"Here's another way to save some cut fingers. Stick a large cork up into the base of the broken bulb and twist it out. The cork will hold onto the sharp protrusions and save your pinkies."

Which brought this response: "In this day when more and more items are being made of plastics, a large cork is more of a museum piece than a household item. A raw potato pushed onto the broken edges of the bulb makes a good handle for safe removal."

"If you have a pesky light bulb that flickers for no reason, it may be that the contact point on the base is worn and is making a bad connection. If so, a drop of solder on the base will improve the contact and do away with the flickers."

"Usually, when a three-way light bulb burns out, only one element goes. This means it still gives light, but on only one setting. You don't want to throw it away, but it's an aggravation and defeats the purpose to leave it in the three-way socket. By connecting the center terminal to the outer terminal with a thin coat of solder, you can make the bulb work in a regular one-way socket like any ordinary bulb."

"My basement workshop is lit by a single fixture. Imagine my dilemma when the bulb burned out recently. I barked my shins on everything in the basement before I could find the stairs. To prevent this from happening again, I replaced the single bulb with a double socket that houses two bulbs. The likelihood of both bulbs going at once is very small; so if one goes, the other will still light my way. Just in case this great idea of mine doesn't work, I also bought a new flashlight for my shop."

(A good idea for the garage or any outbuilding that has a single bulb where you would be left in the dark if that one bulb should burn out.)

"Our front porch light burned out and had to be replaced during the coldest month in our history. To hedge against this happening again, I replace all of our outside light bulbs with brand new ones in the fall before the weather gets bad. There's practically no chance that I'll have any burn out during the winter. The bulbs I took out are still good, and I'm using them inside the house."

"Our attic has a single light fixture in the middle of the room, controlled by a pull chain. Needless to say, when one of us takes a load of stuff in, it's like running an obstacle course to get over to the pull chain. Or at least it was until I rigged up my elbow switch. I ran a string from the pull chain over to a screw eye that I'd installed in the door facing. The eye is about shoulder height, so that when someone walks in, he can turn on the light by merely putting an elbow over the string and pushing it down. Even with an armload, an elbow is free to light the way."

"For less than a dollar I've installed a safety light that's always on duty in my basement to guide me down the stairs. It's a luminescent light that puts out a greenish glow from a small screen put in the wall outlet at the bottom of the steps. Such a light costs practically nothing to leave in continuous operation, and lasts a long time."

(Those lights will supposedly last over 15,000 hours, and give enough light to help out in any dark room that doesn't have a light switch at the entrance.)

LIQUIDS "Many times when you pour out of a bottle or can, some of the contents run down the side of the container and miss the mark. I've learned a trick that pretty well solves this problem. Just place a pencil or nail over the opening, and the liquid follows this down to your target.

"Those flat gallon cans and other cans with the screw-on cap can make you look pretty clumsy when it comes to pouring. You'll eliminate most of the sloshing and dribbling off the side of the can if you'll keep the hole at the top. This allows air to enter the can as the liquid comes out, and lets you pour with a smooth, regular stream. If it's a small flat can with the hole in the middle, hold it so the long part is horizontal to the ground."

"If you're like me, you use a bucket to mix all sorts of chemicals for the yard and house. These include insecticides, plant foods, cleaning compounds, and many others. I finally got smart and painted some graduation marks on the inside of the bucket. I marked off a line for a pint, a quart, and two quarts, and for gallons up to the top of the bucket. Now I don't have to guess or use a measuring cup. Be sure to use a paint that won't dissolve in water."

Drawer knob screwed onto cork

"Before I uncap a can of liquid, I put a large rubber band around the can. After the lid is removed, it's slipped under the rubber band and held tight against the can so I don't have to wonder where the lid is when I'm through. My wife also adopted this one for use on the various household liquids."

"If you have a frequently used bottle that's capped with a cork, here's a time- and effort-saver. Install a small drawer knob on the cork as a permanent corkscrew. The knob has a screw in it, so it can easily be screwed into the cork. This one-time installation eliminates grappling with the cork each time."

"When you have a partially-filled can of solvent, pour water into the solvent to bring it up to the desired level to reach your brushes. After a little while, the solvent will all rise to the top. All the residue removed by the solvent will fall to the bottom, and the solvent can be poured off the top and reused."

"Here's a trick for getting the most out of the last drops of solvent. Take a small tin can and cut the top almost all the way off. Bend an 'L'

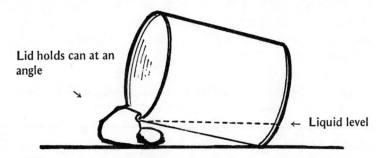

Lid holds can at an angle

← Liquid level

in the top, and it will hold the can at about a 20- to 30-degree angle. Pour the little dab of liquid into the can. At this angle, your brush will come in contact with a lot more liquid than if the container were upright."

"If you need to strain a shop liquid and don't have any screen wire around, get one of those throw-away aluminum pans that frozen TV dinners come in. You can quickly punch lots of holes in the pan with an ice pick or nail. This will act as a strainer—and it can be made without any strain on your part."

You're probably familiar with the famous quotation "Don't cry over spilled chemicals." Almost any glass bottle or jar is liable to slip out of your hand and break all over the floor. A few rubber bands around the bottle will provide a sure grip. This is a particularly good idea when the liquid is oily.

"I store left-over shop liquids in glass jars with screw-on tops. To seal them against air, I run a quick coat of rubber cement on the threads of the jar before putting the cap on. Although this seal guards the contents against air, it can easily be broken by twisting when you need to use the left-over again. This is particularly good for left-over paint, as it will still be good after even a year of storage."

LITTER BAG FOR SHOP   "I've helped stop my shop litter problem by making a litter bag basket that fits on one end of my workbench. It was made by cutting a bushel basket in half. This leaves a flat side open, which is covered by stapling a piece of canvas all around to form this side. A wide whisk broom across the bench tops sweeps all the dust, shavings, and particles into the litter bag. I put a pair of tent grommets in the canvas to hang on a pair of nails driven into the bench, so the half basket is easily removed when full, but any number of ways could be used to hang it."

Half of bushel basket

Canvas back stapled on

LOCKS   "Our overhead garage door lock went on the blink, and we were not able to lock the door. Since my shop tools are in the garage—which is attached to the house—I had to come up with something. I merely put a C-clamp on the tracks on each side right at the top of the door when it was down. This makes it impossible to raise the door until the clamps are removed from the inside. Even if your lock works, this is added protection against intruders."

"I devised a positive lock on our overhead garage door by drilling a hole through the bar that moves through the door track and normally locks the door. After the door is closed and locked, the bar has been moved through the track. I then insert a large nail with a flat head through the hole. This makes the bar impossible to move out of the track from the outside. To keep the nail handy, I tied a string around it and attached this to another nail driven into the wall above where the first nail is to be used."

Locks need lubrication every six months or so. If you don't have powdered graphite around, take an ordinary lead pencil and rub it against the key on both sides until the key is well covered with the pencil dust. Run the key in and out of the lock a few times, and you'll have given it a good lube job.

LUBRICATING   "It seems that motor manufacturers delight in putting the oiling points in hard-to-reach spots. Since many are covered with those tiny spring caps, lube time can be very frustrating. I soldered

Washer on oiler spout

a small washer to the end of my oil can spout, and now any cap I can reach with the spout can easily be flipped up with the washer. Once up, the caps will stay until flipped back."

(Another good way to foil those fiendish oiling point hiders is to file a small notch on the oiler spout. The notch will catch on the cap and flip it open.)

To get oil in a tight spot, try coating a pipe-cleaner with the lubricant and putting the end down into the right place. The cleaner will hold the lubricant long enough to do this, but will allow it to run on off slowly. If possible, rub the pipe cleaner over the spot to be lubricated, and the process will be done much quicker.

Sometimes too much oil is just as bad as too little. If you are about to do a very delicate oiling job, here's a way to adapt the spout of a spare metal oil can so the flow is slowed. Insert a straight pin into the spout and crimp the spout down against the pin. With the spout crimped, push the pin down flush with the top of the spout. Now, only the tiniest droplet will come out.

"Often oil needs to be rubbed on a tool instead of being poured or squirted on. For that purpose, I keep an old shoe polish bottle—the kind with the dauber in the stopper—full of machine oil."

"Most kitchen appliances need lubrication eventually. Ordinary machine oil is usually OK, but if you're not careful, foods will end up with a subtle oil taste, and this won't win any cooking awards. I discovered recently that cooking oil will do the lubrication, but is tasteless and odorless and just has to be better on the digestive tract than machine oil. I've used it on the cutting mechanism of our electric can opener, with good results. It should also work for mixers, beaters, and other such appliances."

"We don't throw away leftover cooking fat after frying. I take it out to my workshop and use it in a number of lubricating tasks. I keep a can of it in which I store my drill bits. I just push them into the can of fat, and they stay lubricated. When it comes time to use one of the bits, I pull it out and wipe off the excess. I also use this free lubricant to rub on saw blades, to dip nails into, and to do other small lube chores. Just be sure that the grease doesn't come in contact with wood surfaces to be finished, as it can sometimes leave a stain."

"Those little plastic containers that house Polaroid print coaters are waterproof. I keep one filled with oil and store it in with my drill bits. It's much more compact than an oil can and is always handy when I need to lube a bit while drilling. I also carry one of these containers with me when fishing, to make sure I always have dry matches."

"You've suggested soap as a lube for nails and screws. Shaving cream from an aerosol can works better, since it can cover much quicker and more completely. Also, I use this as a lube for my saw blade. It spreads on quickly and easily and doesn't stain the work."

When it's time to drag out that electric fan, you'll want to oil it. To be sure you don't sling little drops of oil out all over the place, put a large grocery bag over the entire fan and place the fan over a piece of newspaper. Switch the fan off and on several times, and all the oil will be slung out nside the bag instead of in your house.

"A little-used hinge can easily be forgotten and not lubricated often enough. Remove the pin on such a hinge and file one edge off flat.

Reinsert the pin, and before it's pushed down all the way, fill up the filed-off space with lube. Now there's a reservoir of liquid in the hinge. Each time it is used, the turning of the hinge around the pin makes it self-lubricating."

"Here's a trick I learned from my teen-age son, who's a hot rod nut. He lubricated the speedometer cable on his car with the aid of a paper cup. He put a quantity of graphite grease in the cup, then punched a hole in the bottom of the cup and fed the speedometer cable down into its housing through the hole. This meant it also went through the grease and lubricated itself as it went. It was a neat job and wasted none of the graphite."

LUGGAGE RACK   "We were all ready to leave on a camping trip when we discovered there wasn't enough room in the car for all our gear. In about 15 minutes, my husband had solved our problem by making a car-top luggage rack. He nailed together a simple wooden frame from scraps of lumber. Then he installed four rubber-tipped door stops at the four corners of the frame to protect the finish on the car top. The rack and extra grear were then tied on, and we were on our way. He has since bought regular luggage rack straps and painted the frame so that it even looks good."

(This idea can also protect your car top when you're handling those big sheets of plywood.)

LUMBER   "Several readers have come up with uses for old tires. I use them in my shop as a base for stacking lumber and sheets of plywood. They keep this valuable stuff off the damp floor, and prevent it from getting ruined by moisture."

"If you're working with lumber that has knots in it and one of them falls out, don't toss the piece of wood aside for another. Chances are, you will be able to put the knot back to stay by dipping it in shellac and replacing it. Until the shellac dries, the knot should be held in with some sort of clamp. Usually masking tape will do."

M

●

MAGNETS   "If you've ever used a magnet to clean up small metal shavings, you know that the next problem is getting these sma'l particles off the magnet. Next time, slip your magnet into a plastic sandwich bag. The magnet still pulls through the plastic; when the job is done, just peel the bag and metal bits off with no trouble."

"If you have a metal bench or work surface, you may want to remember that a strong magnet will attract all the way through the metal top. It may be to your advantage to use magnets on the bottom side of the surface to hold a part or piece in place on top. I recently found use for this trick when soldering some pieces together. The magnet held the parts in place without cluttering up the top itself."

"A friend of mine glues a tiny magnet to the housing of the electric plug of each of his power tools. When the tool is not being used, he disconnects the plug as a safety measure to make sure his children do not accidentally turn on the machine. The magnet allows him to put the plug against some metal part of the machine, and thus be up off the floor. This way, there is no risk of the plug's getting smashed or stepped on, and it's also a lot handier when he wishes to plug it in."

"Did you ever spill a box of tacks or small nails out on the workbench? It sure does take a while to get them all back in the box. My little stunt helps in this regard. Into each container of small items like this in my shop I drop one of those small magnets. If the container is tipped over, the magnet usually holds the contents together. Even if some of the small items get away from the magnet's grasp, the magnet can help get them back in tow."

"One of the best and quickest ways to make stops or guides on a metal power tool table is with bar magnets. Just be careful not to use such a guide too near a blade or other moving part."

"Whenever I get a can of some liquid out to use, I also grab one of the small magnets I keep on my workbench and place it on the lid of the can. When the lid is taken off for pouring, the magnet holds it right on the side of the can so I never have to worry about the lid's being mislaid."

"Here's a very helpful addition I've made to both my sawhorse and my stepladder. I installed magnetic knife holders designed for the kitchen. These kitchen gadgets have very strong magnets and will hold almost any hand tool, even with the vibration exerted on the sawhorse from the use of a power saw. I don't know how I ever got along without them."

MALLETS   "Probably the easiest way to put a temporary rubber face on a regular hammer is with an extra-wide rubber band cut from an old inner tube. Knot one end of the loop and hook this in the 'V' of the

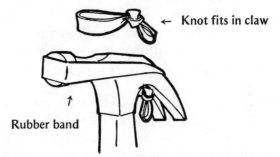

← Knot fits in claw

↑
Rubber band

claw. Stretch the other part over the hammerhead, and you will have a padded head. If that is not quite enough padding, stick an extra square of rubber under the band, and the band will hold it in place."

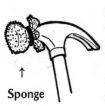

↑
Sponge

"I needed a mallet recently, but since I don't own one, I decided to improvise. I borrowed a kitchen sponge and put it around the head of my regular hammer with a rubber band. It did the job."

MASKING   "One of the best movable masking devices for painting is one of those rectangular metal cement finishing trowels. [This tool is

actually called a 'steel float.'] The float has a handle and can be moved easily right along with your painting. When you are through painting, paint can be removed from the metal easily with turpentine."

Short piece tape on
V-notch

"When you need to mask large areas in painting, the use of masking tape can run into some money. To cut down on the use of tape, I take strips of newspaper and cut little V-shaped notches every 5" or 6". The newspaper can then be stuck in place by putting small pieces of masking tape over the V's. Saves lots of tape and works great."

... You'll find more masking tips in the *Paint* section.

MASONRY "Drilling in masonry will turn out a little easier and a lot better if you make a pilot hole with a masonry nail at the exact spot where you want the hole. Be sure you don't drive the nail in far enough to make it difficult to remove."

"If you have ever done any chipping or chiseling of rocks or concrete, you know the dangers of flying particles. Placing a section of screen wire over the place where you are working will protect you from all the flying bits without hampering your view of the work or the use of your tools."

MEASURES AND MEASURING "With a yardstick or zigzag rule, you can measure higher than you can reach, merely by extending the rigid measure. However, if you don't have one of these, a tape measure or retractable steel flexible tape can be made to do the same thing by taping the end to a piece of molding. This prevents your having to climb up on a ladder."

"I keep a few lengths of masking tape stuck to the yardstick to write down measurements so I don't forget them. When the strips are all used up, I remove and replace them."

"If you need to split lumber half in two, find the center in seconds. Lay a 1' ruler diagonally across the board so that each end is at the edge of the board. No matter what size board, the 6" mark is the center of the board."

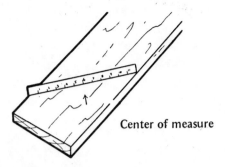

Center of measure

(In fact, any size or part of ruler or yardstick will do. Just find the halfway mark on the measure, and that is the middle. This diagonal principle also works if you want to divide a piece into thirds, or other portions.)

With wear, most of the gauges or measures stamped on metal tools get hard to read. Renew the readability by rubbing a crayon of contrasting color over the stamped calibrations. Rub lightly with a rag dampened with turpentine; the surface crayon rubs off, but that which is down in the stamped area remains. A coat of clear shellac will keep it readable longer."

"I put one of those metal screen door handles in the middle of my yardstick and now I can slip it down flat for measuring and pick it up with ease."

"Many times it helps to know approximately how long, high, or wide something is, but there is no ruler handy. From having measured a long time ago I know that when I spread my fingers as wide apart as they will go, the distance between my little finger and my index finger is approximately 6″. By walking my hand across the surface to be measured, I can tell quickly about what it measures. I would guess I have used this method for quick measuring hundreds of times."

If you're using a metal rule and need to mark certain measurements for transfer, use a tiny magnet to mark the place on the rule. Keep one of these markers on the rule at all times . . . it won't be in the way when you don't need it.

"If your wife won't let you steal her kitchen measuring cup, make your own. Put a strip of masking tape vertically on the side of a fruit jar. Use her measuring cup only long enough to pour different amounts into your jar. Mark these as you go, and you will end up with what you need."

"From a piece of lightweight tin about ½" wide I made a sliding metal band that goes all around my shop yardstick. Such a band can be formed by bending the strip around the ruler. Be sure there is a little slack so it can slide along the yardstick. This enables you to transfer measurements from one spot to another with much more ease. Just slide the band up to the measurement and hold it in place with your thumb while the rule is moved."

(The strip from a can opened with a key is ideal as the band. Just flatten it out and cut it off to fit around your yardstick.)

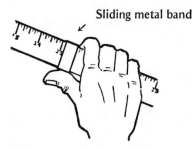

Sliding metal band

Lots of times you would like to know approximate measurements but don't have a measuring device with you—or so you think. Unless your wife has relieved you of all your money, chances are you do have one in your pocket. A dollar bill is 1/8" over a half foot in length, so that it's a handy 6" rule. In width, it is exactly 2½". A quarter is good for smaller jobs, since it lacks only 1/16" of being an even inch. This won't pass engineering standards, but it sure helps when you want a close "guesstimate."

METAL—CUTTING, BENDING, FOLDING   "It is very difficult to cut soft metal pipes and tubing such as copper and aluminum, since the pressure from the saw can bend the pipe and cause it to pinch the saw blade. Also, a bent pipe or tube may not be as usable as if it were straight. This problem can be solved by inserting a dowel into the tube and cutting through both pipe and dowel. Use a dowel the same size as the opening. A small scrap can be used, as long as it is pushed down to where the cut is to be made. Use a wire or rod for pushing the scrap in and back out."

"To bend metal tubing to shape without the risk of kinking it, just fill the tubing with damp sand while shaping it. When the tubing is in the proper shape, the sand can be tapped out. If the tubing is then to be used to carry liquid or gas, it should be thoroughly flushed out to make sure there is no sand left to foul up an engine or something."

"You can make your own metal-polishing attachment for a power drill. Chuck a wooden dowel in the drill and dip the dowel into rubber cement. Now take a good-sized swatch of steel wool and wrap this around the dowel. Be sure the wrapping is done in the same direction that the drill turns. When the cement dries, this will be a good metal-polishing tool. As the steel wool wears away, more can be added. Do your polishing in short bursts for best results."

"Don't throw away an old glass cutter just because the blade is worn out. It makes an ideal tool to score a piece of sheet metal. It runs easily along a straightedge and makes a good clean line."

"Here is a trick for making a sharp bend in a large piece of sheet metal. As you know, a vise will not be wide enough to hold a very wide piece, and yet you need to have the metal anchored down. I take a pair of boards as wide as or wider than the sheet metal and put them in the vise with the metal between. The vise is then clamped down on the boards, and they provide the edge over which the metal can be bent."

"Here's a safety reminder for the next time you're drilling in metal. Be sure the work is well clamped, as there is always the possibility that the bit may bind and force the work to spin. I always clamp in two places instead of just one–and with the clamps on either side of the drilling spot."

"Hacksawing metal is easier if you file a notch in the metal before you start. If you do much hacksawing, you will find it well worth your while to weld a section of a small triangular file on top of your hacksaw frame. It makes for a much handier operation."

"We got a new electric knife sharpener, and so my wife no longer had any use for the old hand sharpener. It's the type that sharpens when the blade is drawn through two rows of metal discs. I find it's great to de-burr the edges of any kind of sheet metal that has been cut."

"Did you know that a great way to clean copper is with a lemon wedge rubbed in salt?"

Many home handymen cut a piece of angle iron by sawing down one leg and then across the other. The better way is to start the hacksaw at the corner. This means fewer strokes and a smoother cut. It will take added care to put the angle iron in the vise this way, but is well worth the effort.

"To polish metal objects with intricate, hard-to-reach designs, I have found the ideal tool is one of those cotton swabs that come on a stick. When the swab is broken off one end, the stick can be chucked in your power drill, and a swab dipped into the polishing compound gets into all the close quarters. After this has been done, put in another clean swab to polish."

"When working with sheet metal with a polished surface, there is the ever-present hazard of scratching up that surface. One good way to protect the finish is to cover it with heavy kraft paper stuck in place by rubber cement. The rubber cement releases the paper easily when you are through working, and any rubber cement left can be rolled off with your finger."

MINI-TOOLS   "Those keys that are used to open sardine and other types of cans are great to use as small screwdrivers. Their handles allow

you to turn in very tight places. The blade is small enough for most of the tiny screws that manufacturers put in out-of-the-way places. If the blade isn't small enough, it can be dressed down to size with a file."

"I fell heir to one of those swivel penholder desk sets without a pen in it. Before I had a chance to find a new pen, I discovered a better use for it in the workshop. With the aid of a spring-type clothespin and a rubber band, I made a swivel holder for all sorts of small shop jobs. It's great for holding small items for soldering or wiring and can be moved around to the best angle for the particular job at hand. I didn't really need a desk set anyway."

Screwdriver tips

"It's always handy to have a small screwdriver in your pocket, and I made one that's great. I took an old skeleton key and ground off the end into a screwdriver tip and did the same thing to the flange that sticks out to turn the lock. This gives me two sizes of screwdrivers, and it's carried on my key chain."

"I made one of those screwdrivers out of a can key. In case any of your readers haven't realized it, these handy keys can be kept on your regular key ring so you'll always have a screwdriver handy even when you are away from the workbench."

MIRRORS   "Bathroom mirrors subjected to moisture are likely to have some of their silvering flake off. There are a couple of easy things you can do, either of which will prevent moisture from getting in under the silvering and attacking it. Apply a coat of clear shellac or, easier still, spray the back with that clear plastic spray now on the market. Cover the mirrored back completely, and all moisture will be sealed out."

"From reading your column my wife is convinced that there's nothing in the way of a do-it-yourself project that a semi-intelligent husband can't do. In trying to keep her sold on my semi-intelligence, I have tackled them all. Recently, she decided I should resilver a scratched mirror. I outfoxed her, however, with this trick: I took little scraps of aluminum foil, placed them on the back of the mirror over the scratches, and stuck them in place with cellophane tape. While this wouldn't work on a bathroom mirror that is looked into closely, it made the scratches disappear from this mirror, and my wife was impressed."

MITERING   "Many times your handyman chore calls for the use of a miter box when you are away from your workbench, with only a sawhorse to use as a work surface. You can steady your miter box and do a better job by clamping it to the end of the sawhorse with a C-clamp."

"Right-angle mitered corners such as are found on picture frames need to be clamped for glueing. If you don't happen to have a picture frame clamp, all you need is an angle iron mending plate (L-brace) and a pair of C-clamps. With the mitered pieces held in place, put the L-brace up against the right angle made by the two pieces. Hold it in place by attaching a C-clamp around each of the mitered pieces and the L-brace. This will hold the joint tight while the glue sets up."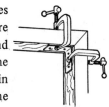

"Instead of sawing down into your wooden miter box, keep a scrap piece of wood in as sort of a false bottom. Then when the saw goes through the piece being mitered, it will cut into the scrap instead of your miter box. When the scrap gets all chewed up, replace it with another . . . and as you replace it, think of how bad off your miter box would be if you hadn't done this."

"As a general rule, a backsaw is best for mitering. Its reinforced back allows you to apply downward pressure with your left hand. If you don't have such a saw, you can use your regular crosscut saw. Add a section of old garden hose to the back of the saw blade so that you can apply the necessary pressure without ruining your hand."

Hose section

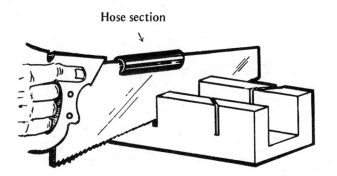

(Another difference is that most crosscut saws are not going to give you as fine a cut as a backsaw. Most mitering should be precision work, so if you don't have a backsaw I would recommend using a hacksaw over an ordinary saw. However, in the absence of both hack and back, this idea is on the right track.)

MIXING   "A small can of liquid that requires mixing before each use can usually be mixed pretty well by a good shaking. But it will be mixed better if you drop a steel ball into the can before the big shake-up. Leave the ball bearing in the container until all the liquid is gone, and it will be ready to mix up each time you want to use it. When the can is empty, drop the ball bearing into solvent and clean it for reuse."

When using some sort of compound from a tube it's a good practice to make sure it is properly mixed. Many times the components will separate in the tube, and therefore the compound may not do what it is intended to. Mixing can usually be done by squeezing the tube from top to bottom several times. It will only take a moment and could save your having to redo the job later on.

"Since my wife would not let me have one of the blades from her kitchen blender to mix paint with, I improvised. I took a piece of dowelling and drove about six large-headed nails into it at different angles to form blades. I put the other into the hand drill. However, when I put it in the paint and turned it on, zowie! Paint flew out all over the place. My wife solved this by making a hood from a plastic bag, attaching it by a rubber band around the drill on one end and the paint bucket on the other. I think both of us had good ideas."

"I find the best way to mix paint is to bend a piece of wire into a flat 'S' shape a little less wide than the bucket, leaving a straight shank a little taller than the bucket. Then punch a hole in the lid of the paint can. Bring the wire through this opening and insert the wire in your electric drill. Then reseal the can and turn on your drill. It does a good job of stirring and cannot splatter. If you have some paint left over and need to store it, just put a patch of masking tape over the hole in the lid."

"The best homemade mixing container for paints as well as other liquids is a plastic milk carton. Cut the top off, of course. In pouring the paint back and forth, you will be pleasantly surprised to find that the paint does not adhere to the plastic, so that you can pour all of the paint back to be used."

MOLDING   "I repapered almost every room in the house, and that meant removing all the molding. At first, I started prying it with a screwdriver ... much damage. Then I tried a wide putty knife and didn't damage any more molding. Maybe this hint will save some of your readers from the trial-and-error portion of such a job."

Removing and replacing molding can be very frustrating, particularly if it is old molding. Instead of hammering out the old nails, snip them off even with wire cutters. This eliminates the inevitable splintering on the molding face, and there are no holes to putty.

MOVING DAY   Our next-door neighbor moved away, and I was a little surprised when he came over to borrow some charcoal briquets on moving day. He explained that the charcoal was for the refrigerator. Charcoal will absorb any moisture left in the box and keep mildew from starting. The mover claimed that fresh coffee also takes up moisture. Even if your move will only take a few days, it is much nicer to have a clean-smelling refrigerator when you move into your new home.

"We rented a trailer to move with, and I found my conventional rear-view mirror was inadequate. I improvised by taping a pair of dimestore mirrors to the side vents. Then I opened these to the right angle and adjusted them so that I could see what was going on behind. This saved me from having to drill holes in my car and making a permanent installation of rear-view mirrors I didn't otherwise need."

"It wasn't possible for us to be on hand when the movers arrived at our new home across the country. When we got there a few days later, however, all the furniture was in place where my wife had wanted it. We had given the movers a floor plan of the new house with squares marked where pieces of furniture were to go. Each square had a number in it, and each room was tinted a different color. Then each piece of furniture was tagged with tinted and numbered tags. It was a cinch for the moving men. Maybe this will help others who are transferred."

... And then, two weeks later, your wife decides the piano ought to be moved over here, and the couch. .... And if she does, here are a couple of furniture-moving helps:

"Like all wives, mine decides to rearrange all the furniture in our house about once a year. Since we've been married 25 years, that is a bunch of moving. I save our hardwood floors from scratching by putting old socks on the furniture legs. Also makes sliding across the floor a lot easier."

Another idea is to put a coat of wax on the bottom of each leg. This is great for chairs that are moved all the time, as in the case of breakfast room chairs.

N.

NAILS—DRIVING, PULLING, CLINCHING The fastener used most by the average home handyman is the nail. There are almost as many types of nails as there are people to use them. A few basics about different kinds of nails are given in the following chart.

1. The old stand-by for general rough construction work.

2. Looks a lot like the common nail but with a smaller shank.

3. For finished construction work. The brad-type head is driven flush with work.

4. Also for finished construction work but the head lends itself to countersinking and thus a more finished look.

5. Used for temporary construction. The head allows easy clawing to remove.

6. A flat nail that looks a lot like a horseshoe nail.

7. For roof installation.

8. For fastening in masonry.

9. Many types come threaded or grooved for extra holding power in certain materials.

10. The one not to hammer on.

SUPER HANDYMAN NAIL CHART

PENNY	LENGTH INCHES	APPROXIMATE NUMBER PER POUND			
		COMMON	BOX	CASING	FINISHING
2d	1	876	1010	1010	1351
3d	1¼	568	635	635	807
4d	1½	316	437	437	584
5d	1¾	271	406	406	500
6d	2	181	236	236	309
7d	2¼	161	210	210	238
8d	2½	106	145	145	189
9d	2¾	96	132	132	172
10d	3	69	94	94	121
12d	3¼	64	87	87	113
16d	3½	49	71	71	90
20d	4	31	52	52	62
30d	4½	24	46	46	
40d	5	18	35	35	
50d	5½	16			
60d	6	11			

penny = d

There are lots of different ways to use nails, too. Here are a few.

"How about this for a nail carrier when you have to be moving around while nailing? Take a paper cup from the kitchen and fasten it to your belt with a spring-type clothespin. It's a lot easier to get nails out of a paper cup than a pocket, and also easier on your pockets."

"If you have to drive any nails into a plaster wall, try heating them beforehand. They go in much smoother, without chipping the plaster. Don't ask me why, but it does work. If you have quite a few to drive in, put them in a pan and heat them on the stove. However, if it's a single-nail job, hold it over a flame."

(Don't get the nails too hot to handle; just good and warm will do.)

"On a hot day, sweaty hands make holding onto nails a problem. If you have much nailing to do, a handful of sawdust in the apron pocket along with the nails will stop perspiration problems."

"If you've never been faced with driving a nail under water, you may not realize how near impossible this is. However, if you will magnetize the tip of a section of ¼" steel rod that's long enough to reach the work and still stick out above the water, you'll be able to drive the nail much easier. With the magnet holding the nail head in place, put the point down where the nail is to go and hammer the rod down. This is also a handy way to drive nails in other hard-to-reach places."

"In addition to countersinking nails, here's another method used by many craftsmen to hide them when finishing. Around the point where the nail is to be driven, raise a chip of wood with a chisel or wood-

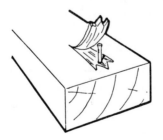

carving tool. Do not cut the shaving all the way off, however. Lift up the edge of this chip and drive in the finishing nail, making sure the nail is down flush with the wood. Now glue the shaving back into place over the nail, and if it's done with care, it will be impossible to tell where the operation took place."

"When using finishing nails, I drive the nails through the holes in a scrap piece of peg board, so if I miss (and I do occasionally), I don't mar the wood. When each nail is driven in, the peg board lifts off and the nailing can be finished with a nail set."

"Sometimes you need to drive a nail so close to the edge of your work that you run the risk of splitting the wood. If a finishing nail is called for, why not chuck it into a hand drill and turn it into the wood as far as you can? It can then be tapped down flush with a hammer and nail set without splitting the wood. In chucking the nail, be sure it's in the drill straight, or it will ream out too big a hole. A smaller pilot hole will make the nail go in easier."

"Since I never use my nail set without my hammer, I have an ideal storage arrangement. I drilled a hole in the hammer handle deep enough to hold the nail set. This is closed up with a cork. Now the nail set is always where it ought to be—with my hammer."

Hole drilled in hammer

"There are almost as many ways of clinching nails as there are hammer owners. I like mine, and maybe some of your other fans will like it too. I drilled a hole all the way through the top of the poll of the hammer. All I have to do to clinch a nail is to slip the hole in the hammer over the nail and push the hammer in the direction in which I wish to clinch. This bends the nail, and it can then be hammered down."

Slit in eraser

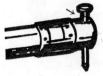

"No sense in banging your fingers while trying to drive a small nail or brad. Just slit the edge of a pencil eraser and use that as a holder. The nail will slip in, and your fingers can hold it from the other end of the pencil. When the nail is started, the eraser will let go with a slight tug."

"You've always heard that a woman can do anything with a hairpin. I've discovered a way to save wear and tear on my fingers when I have to drive small nails—by using a bobby pin as a holder."

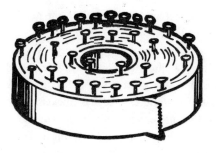

"Here's a tricky holder for tacks or small nails that will really help the home handyman who needs his supply right in front of him, instead of having to dig into a pocket. Just take the tacks and insert them in the edge of a roll of tape (masking or friction tape will do). The points will go between the layers of tape and stay there until you extract them. Put all of them in one side. The roll will lie flat in front of you, and you don't have to worry about digging for, dropping, or swallowing tacks. This is particularly good if you're working up on a stepladder."

"I magnetized a thimble and use it as a holder for very small nails. It lets me use my fingers to pick them up. Once the nail's in place, I need only my thimbled finger to hold it there until it's started. Sure saves bruises, 'cause if I should miss, the thimble protects my fingers."

"Instead of banging your fingers when starting to nail sprigs and tiny nails, use a common pocket comb as a holder. Just slip the nail in between two teeth at one end of the comb and hold it in place by the other end."

Another small-nail starter is: "Stick a blob of modeling clay around the nail and put it down where the nail is to go. Modeling clay will stick to any finish and will hold the nail in the desired position until the nail is started. Then the clay can be removed, and the nail can be driven home."

Half of sponge
rubber ball

If the head comes off a nail while it's being pulled, here's a tip that may save the day. Get a good hold on the shank of the nail with a pair of locking-grip pliers. You won't need but a fraction of an inch of shank. Tighten down the pliers, and then use your claw to pry against the pliers. If you have a good hold, the nail will come out.

"When you have a lot of nails to pull, you waste much time moving and placing a block to keep from marring surfaces with your hammer.

By glueing half of a small hard-rubber ball to the head of your hammer, you cut out that time-waster."

"One of the items I liberated from my wife's kitchen is a rubber plate-scraper. This makes a great cushion for the claw hammer when pulling nails on finished work. One edge is thicker than the other, and it acts as a fulcrum. I've also made a slit in the end, so it can hold small nails in place for starting. It does save my fingers from getting banged up."

If you've ever tried to pull nails from a corrugated metal roof, you know that the hammer will bend the roof up pretty badly. However, if you'll take a length of pipe and place it down in the valleys, it'll serve as a fulcrum and make the task much easier, and gentler on the metal. Just be sure that the pipe is large enough to stick up above the peaks in the corrugation.

"Here's a tool that can't be bought. It's a right-angle triangular scrap of 2" x 4". The base should be from 3" to 5", and the corner angle 15 to 25 degrees. Make a saw cut from this point as if you were going to

Saw kerf

slice the block in half and make a pair of 1" triangles. Stop the cut about an inch before the blade reaches the vertical. Now you've created a wedge that will act as a fulcrum for nail pulling. Start the nail, and push the wedge into place so the nail is in the slot (kerf). As the nail is pulled out, push the wedge in so the claw hammer always has its best leverage. This is, of course, designed for use on longer nails."

NUTS "A Sunday repair job, and a bolt without the right-sized nut! Sounds like a disaster, but here's what I did. I found a nut a size too big for the bolt and coated the bolt with petroleum jelly. Next, I put the oversized nut over the bolt and filled in the gap all the way around with epoxy. The epoxy conforms to the threads on the bolt. The greased bolt allows the nut to be removed when hardened, as if it were a regular one."

"Here's a simple way to lock a nut in place. Let a few drops of solder flow around the threads up next to the nut. To remove the nut, the solder, of course, can easily be melted away with a solder gun."

"There may be times when a home handyman would like to secure a nut on a bolt so that he can be 100 percent sure it'll never come loose. There's a simple way to do this. After the nut has been tightened down, take a hacksaw and slit the bolt down to the top of the nut. Slit it again to form an 'X,' and then with a ball peen hammer, strike the 'X.' This'll spread the bolt out over the nut, locking it so it can never work loose."

X-slit cut in bolt . . . then hit with ball-peen hammer to spread

(If the bolt sticks out more than ¼" above the nut, it would be better to cut it off some before slitting it.)

"Another way to lock a bolt in place is to slit the end after the bolt and the nut are in place. Slit it right down to the nut, and then take a metal wedge-shaped object and spread it. An old screwdriver can do the spreading."

(Don't do this if you know you'll have to remove the bolt later on.)

"Often the bolt fasteners used on license plates become rusted or corroded and are very difficult to remove. Before putting on new plates each year, slit the end of the bolts with a hacksaw. The nut goes on as it would have normally. If at the end of the year the nut won't come off because of rust or corrosion, crimp the slit bolt with a pair of pliers, and the nut is a snap to get off. Then replace the bolt.

(This works on any bolt that may have rusted by the time you want to take it off.)

Pre-slit bolt crimped to remove nut

O

ODORS   After you've used turpentine or kerosene, you've probably noticed that the memory lingers on in the form of a not-so-slight odor on your hands—even after you've scrubbed with soap and water. But a final rinsing in vinegar will remove the last of the smell.

"When you finish painting a room, you can get rid of that awful paint odor overnight. All you have to do is cut a large raw onion in half and put it in a pan of water. Place this in the newly painted room, and the onion will absorb all of the paint odor. Don't worry—it doesn't leave any bad onion odor instead."

"Even the best of fireplaces sometimes brings smoke into a room if the conditions are wrong. Just put a saucer of vinegar in the room, and the smoke odor will go away in a hurry."

OIL CANS   "The plastic top off a one-pound coffee can fits exactly over a quart oil can. Since I always have two or three different grades of oil open around my shop, this means I can keep the oil in the can clean and never have to fish out the rolled-up clump of newspaper I used to stuff in the opened can."

"Buying machine oil in bulk is cheaper than buying it in the small dispenser cans. However, those little cans with the spouts are sure handy when it comes to getting the oil in the right place. I've discovered how they can be refilled. All you need is a large glass bottle with a

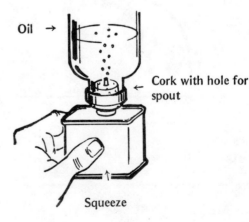

Oil →

Cork with hole for spout ←

Squeeze

cork. Drill a hole through the cork, large enough for the spout of the small can. Fill the bottle with oil, then push the spout tight into the cork and turn the bottle upside down. By squeezing the sides of the can, air will be forced out, and the oil in the bottle will be drawn into the can."

"My wife barred my oil can from the house because I put it down on a rug and it left an oily ring. Now, however, it's fixed so it has its own drip catcher, and she no longer has to worry. The catcher is a plastic lid from a one-pound coffee can, glued to the bottom of the oil can. Before glueing it in place, I cut a hole in the center so I could still get my thumb against the can for squirting pressure. Then I used enough glue to make sure there was a tight seal between the plastic lid and the oil can."

"My husband has several squirt-type oil cans around, and after using one, I noticed oil had dripped off on the floor because there was no cap on the can. I discovered that none of the cans had caps, so I solved the problem by saving the caps off lighter fluid cans. They fit—and stop the drip."

Here's another drip solver. "I keep the oil in an old nosedrop bottle that has a dropper in the top. The dropper works fine for applying the oil, and there's no drip problem at all."

(Just be sure to label the bottle so someone doesn't oil his sinuses.)

OILSTONES   "An oilstone will give a much sharper edge to knives and tools if you keep it soaking in kerosene at all times. When you need to sharpen something, take the stone out of the fluid and just shake off the excess."

"A sardine can is the right size and shape to be a soaking tray for an oilstone."

"A dirty whetstone loses its effectiveness. I've found that most of the dirt can be removed by boiling the stone in plain water for about eight or ten minutes. A particularly gummy stone may need to be boiled again in clean water. You'll be pleasantly surprised at how much better your whetstone will work after this treatment."

"As a substitute whetstone for sharpening knives and other tools, use a clay flower pot. Keep the section of pot wet as you draw the blade across. If it's a piece of a pot or one you won't be using again, use an oil to lube with. Otherwise, keep it moist with water. This won't be as good as a whetstone, but it sure beats nothing at all."

OUTDOOR COOKING "A true handyman has to be a great patio chef too. Here's a trick I learned for starting charcoal fires. I keep a two-pound coffee can with lighter fuel in it. Instead of dousing the charcoal briquets with fuel, I drop them in the can for a few minutes, where they really soak up the fuel. Removed with tongs, they light in a hurry. Be sure to keep the coffee can tightly closed when not in use."

Notch filed in beer can opener

"A clean barbecue grill is a must for best-tasting results. I created a tool to scrape the spokes of the grill so tough spots and food particles loosen or chip off. Then it's an easy task to scrub the grill clean. The tool is made from a beer opener. File a notch on the end opposite the pointed end. Use a round file, and the notch can be made almost the same size as the spoke. I tied mine to the grill so it's always handy. Also, the opener can still be used to open a cold beer."

"Keep an empty plastic squeeze bottle (the kind liquid detergents come in) out with the barbecue grill to use as a bellows in getting the coals going. After they've caught fire a little, give them blasts of air by pressing on the squeeze bottle, and in less than half the normal time the charcoal is ready for cooking."

"I made notches in my spatula the same distance apart as the wire bars on my grill. This enables the spatula to fit down between the bars and get in under the meat for much easier turning."

Notches in spatula

"Use tongs to turn meat instead of stabbing it with a fork. The fork punches holes that allow juices and flavor to drip out."

"I've found an additional use for the old disposable filters that come out of furnaces. I used the fiberglass stuffings out of one to line the inside bottom of my outdoor charcoal cooker. Cut it to fit, and it gives a much hotter fire with fewer coals. It's porous enough to allow the proper draft to come through the vents in the bottom, but still protects the bottom from hot drippings."

"Have you ever tried using the sawdust from your shop in cooking on your outdoor grill? I have, and find it gives meat a great new flavor. I soak a handful of sawdust in water and put it on the charcoals just before the meat is put on the grill. No matter what kind of wood you've been cutting, it flavors the meat."

OUTDOOR FURNITURE "Metal patio chairs will collect rain water in the curves in the seat, and if the water is left there, rust isn't far behind. I put a small bit in my power drill and drilled holes in the lowest places in each patio chair. Now the water drains out, and I never have to worry about rust."

"Right about now there are hundreds of husbands whose wives have noticed that the metal legs on the patio furniture have cut all the way through the rubber tips. This makes scratches on the patio, and the wives want them fixed. Men, you'll never have to fix them again if you follow my advice. When you get the new tips to put on, also get a supply of metal washers that will fit in the bottom of the rubber tips. With these in place, the tubular metal legs cannot cut through the rubber."

(One lady didn't have any metal washers, so she went to her coin purse and found that a nickel worked just fine. She looks upon it as a great way to save money.)

"Some of those plastic stoppers that come on many bottles are just the right size to fit over the legs of metal patio furniture. Seems the rubber feet that come on the legs are always getting lost, and so I save these tops for such occasions."

"Aluminum yard furniture can look pretty ancient when it comes out of hibernation. Just crumple up a piece of aluminum foil from the kitchen and rub this over the aluminum parts. It restores that new bright look like magic."

"The small coiled springs that hold the cross braces under the cushions of patio furniture often pinch the fabric on the cushions. Before exposing new cushions to this spring torture, apply a few rounds of electrician's tape to the springs. This still allows them to give when someone sits down, but keeps the cushions from getting pinched."

(Or try a section of garden hose slipped over the springs to separate the fabric from the pinch.)

"Our patio lounger has rubber tires on the back so it can be moved around easily. But our sundeck is of painted wood, and the two don't go well together, since the rubber tires leave marks on the painted surface. I covered each tire with a strip of masking tape. Now there are no marks, and yet the lounger still rolls around as easily as it always did."

(Folks, this will work on any furniture or appliance that rolls. Even though the masking tape will wear out after a while, it's no trouble to replace.)

OUTDOOR LIGHTS "For those who have outdoor yard lights, here's a tip. A very light coat of machine oil on the metal part of the bulb will prevent rust. Just take a rag with machine oil on it and rub it around the threads. Make sure the coat of oil is thin enough not to run."

(As a matter of fact, a thin coat of petroleum jelly will do the same thing.)

"Recently I put up some outside lighting, and to make sure the switch was protected from rain, I added a case around the switch. The case is a one-quart plastic ice cream carton with a plastic lid. I drilled a hole in the bottom of the carton for the wires to enter, and mounted the fixture against the carton, holding it in place. With the plastic top on, all moisture is kept from the switch. It's quite simple to remove the top to operate the switch."

Packages and Packing • Painting • Patching • Patterns •
Pencils in the Shop • Penetrating Oil • Perforated Hard-
board • Pests • Pets • Pictures and Picture Hanging •
Ping-Pong Balls • Planes and Planing • Plastering • Plastic
Bleach Bottles • Plastics • Pliers • Plumb Bob • Plumb-
er's Friend • Plumbing • Plywood • Poisons • Pulleys
• Puttying

PACKAGES AND PACKAGING "Here's a trick that will allow you to tie packages much tighter. Just before you start tying, wet the string. Then go ahead and tie up the package as you would ordinarily. When the string dries, it will shrink just enough to leave the package tied up good and tight."

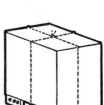

"Here's a simple trick that may help some of your readers with the task of putting cord around a bulky package. If you place the package on top of four bricks or wooden blocks, you can do the complete job without having to wrestle the cord around the bottom side of the box. With a brick at each corner, there's room to run the cord under the box with your hand."

Space under box

Here's a trick that helps a lot in unpacking:
"As we tape up each box, we place a piece of kite string under the tape, with an inch or so left sticking out. When it comes time to unpack, a quick pull on the strings slits right through the tape, and the boxes are opened instantly."

"When we moved recently, we saved quite a tidy sum of money by doing all the packing ourselves, in corrugated boxes sealed up with paper tape. To avoid licking several hundred yards of bad-tasting glue, I cut an uncooked Irish potato in half, and the moisture it contained wet the tape enough to get it to stick down. As the potato begins to dry, you can either dip it into a pan of water or cut a slice off and get to another moist section. Also, a potato is usually big enough to cover the wide tape completely."

(This works, friends ... but it sure does ruin the flavor of the potato.)

PAINTING   "When you don t have a color card, and you wonder just how paint is going to look when it's dry, use my trick. Brush a streak on a blotter. The oils in the paint will soak into the blotter, and the color will be the same as it would be if dry."

"This may seem like a dumb idea, but it does save elbow grease. Whenever I buy paint, I put it in the trunk of my car and lay the cans on their sides. This means they're free to roll around while I drive home. By the time I get home, a big part of the mixing has already been done."

Mending plate

(And if you start traveling by pogo stick, you'll have *all* the mixing done by the time you get home.)

"Starting on a paint job, the very first tool that you use is an opener to pry the lid off the paint can. Next comes a paint stirrer. I found it a very handy arrangement to combine these two tools. I took a small metal mending plate and bolted it on the end of the handle of my paint paddle."

"When that rim around the paint can eventually fills up, the paint starts running down the side of the can. As soon as I open a can of paint, I take a nail and punch several holes in the groove. The paint

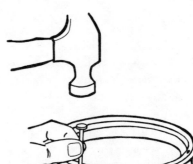

then runs back into the can . . . and since the lid seals against the side of the groove, this doesn't create a new problem."

"Here's a simple trick that makes paint mixing go a lot faster. Just bore five or six holes in the business end of the paddle, and the stirring is quicker and easier."

"The best paint paddle I've run across is the old kitchen fork I salvaged. The tines of the fork allow you to really mix the paint. Try it, and you'll never against waste time boring holes in a wooden paint paddle."

(... A good idea, but a fork isn't long enough to reach into the bottom of a gallon can. Good for a quart or less, though.)

If you have one of those electric-drill attachments that stirs paint, you probably also have a pair of pants with splatters all over them. Next time you want to stir things up, take a paper plate and poke a hole in the center of it. Put the stirrer attachment through the hole before putting it in the drill chuck, and then adjust it so it fits over the top of the paint can. It will catch all the splatters, and you'll stay neat and clean.

"Trying to stir a full can of paint usually sloshes some of the liquid out. This doesn't happen with a can that isn't full—so I just raise up the sides of the paint can. I take a piece of heavy paper and wrap it around the top of the can so it sticks 5″ or 6″ above the top, and hold it in place by slipping a rubber band around the paper and the can. Now I can stir like crazy and never slosh paint out. I even leave this paper on until I've used an inch or so out of the can so the brush doesn't splash any out."

"Here's a tip for pouring paint. Before you start, put a strip of masking tape over about half of the rim of the can. Do your pouring over the part of the can that has the tape on it. After you're through pouring, peel the tape off, and there will be a clean rim underneath. Then you can reseal without the lid's forcing paint out of the rim and down the side of the can."

"When straining paint (or any other shop liquid) through a cloth, the straining net is always trying to fall down into the container. However, you can beat this problem with a plastic-topped coffee can. Just cut all but the rim of the plastic top out. When the net is stretched over the top of the can, place this plastic rim over the top of the can, and it will hold the net firmly in place. You can paint right from the coffee can."

"Rather than strain a can of paint that's all lumpy, try this. After stirring the paint, take a circle you've cut from an old piece of wire screen. Lay it on top of the paint. As it sinks to the bottom, it carries all the lumps with it. The top of the paint can makes a pattern for cutting the circle, which needs to be a shade smaller so it doesn't hang on the sides of the can."

"How do you like my simple drip-catching paint tray? When I get ready to paint, I take a large empty cereal or detergent box and cut a round hole in the side big enough for my paint container to fit in. Not

only do all the drippings go into the box, but also it's impossible to tip the paint can over. Additionally, there is room on the box to lay down the brush when you take a coffee break."

"Before I open a new can of paint, I get a big paper plate and put a few drops of rubber cement on it. Then I put the paint can down on the plate and let it stick. Now my paint can has a permanent drip catcher, and if there's leftover paint, the can and drip catcher can be shelved until needed again."

One reader liked that idea and told his wife about it, since she was planning to do some painting:

"Apparently, I didn't get through to her completely. When I got home, she had cut a hole in the plate and had mounted it around the top of the can. But this meant there was a flared top from the plate

← Paper plate

that allowed the drips to run back into the can. Her misunderstanding actually worked out to be a pretty good trick."

(Wish all mistakes turned out that good! This way, the sides of the can will stay clean.)

Screen door spring

"The best brush striker for a paint can is one I made from an old screen door spring. The spring stretches across the opening of the can, and a rubber band hooked on either end and run under the bottom of the can holds the spring in place. It's rigid enough to allow me to strike excess paint off the brush, and yet has some give to conform to the shape of the brush. Also, when I'm finished, this handy gadget can be removed and used on another paint can."

"I use a striker wire that saves much of the ordinary paint mess. It's a piece of coat hanger wire long enough to reach across the top of the paint can, with an inch-long tab at right angles on each end. I punch a pair of holes in the rim of the paint can, and the tabs fit down into these holes. This means the drippings from the brush go back into the can instead of into the rim. The striker also serves as a rest for the brush when I need to stop for a moment."

"When I have to use two or more brushes, I tape and attach a tin can to my paint bucket with masking tape. I make sure that the bottom of the can is even with the bottom of the bucket. This not only gives me a place to keep the extra brush, but also gives the bucket extra stability when it needs to be set down on the top of the ladder."

"My wife calls this idea my 'nontipping, nondripping tip.' When using a small can of paint, I cut a hole in an old kitchen sponge the same size as the paint can. Placed around the bottom of the can, it keeps it from tipping over and catches all the paint drips. The sponge can be saved and reused."

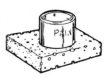

"Always clamp a hand screw on the bottom of a paint can while painting. This gives you a nontip container, because of the broader base the clamp affords. When working with small containers, use a C-clamp instead."

"A Sunday roll-on paint job was almost called off when I discovered someone had lifted my paint tray. However, I fabricated one from an empty detergent box. I cut out one side and lined the box with aluminum foil. The foil made it waterproof, and I was able to do the painting."

(... And you can throw it away when you're done!)

"Here's one more way to hang a paint bucket from your straight ladder without altering the ladder—use a C-clamp. Select one that is large enough for the rung of the ladder to be inside when it's closed. When it's completely closed around the rung and the bail of the paint bucket, your paint will be hanging in a convenient place. It can also be moved up or down the ladder with little effort."

(Make sure the bail is not against the part where the clamp closes together. It just might slip through, and then you'll have to figure a clever way to clean up spilled paint.)

"Before starting a paint job, I always tape a scrap block of square molding to one side of the ferrule of the brush. This allows me to put my brush down during the painting; it will rest on this block and the tip

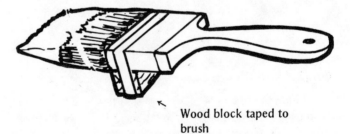

Wood block taped to brush

of the handle, with the bristles sticking up. In that way, the brush can be put down anywhere without getting paint on a surface where it shouldn't be. When the painting is done, the prop is peeled off and discarded."

"This may look a little silly, but when I'm painting with one of those tiny paint cans with no handle, I drop it into an old coffee mug.

This gives me a handle and also catches all the drips. If the mug is cleaned before the paint is dry, it can even be used for drinking again. Mine is one I set aside for just that purpose, so I don't even have to clean it."

(Just be sure you don't get absentminded and take a swig from the cup while you're painting.)

"Here's a painter's trick that will help you avoid skips when painting walls and ceilings. Start next to windows and doors and work back toward the darker parts of the room. The reflections off the new wet surface will flag any skips. If you don't have a door or window to work from, set up an electric light source."

"Recently, I painted the ceilings of our house. Rather than take down the light fixtures, I taped plastic suit bags from the cleaners around them. Not one drop of paint on the light fixtures."

"Besides spreading out newspapers when I'm going to paint in the house, I put a coat of wax on the floors. However, I don't buff them until after the paint job is finished. Then if there are any spatters, they're on the wax and they buff right out."

"If you're like me, you feel naked without your watch on. This can be bad if you happen to be a painter as I am. It doesn't take many splatters to make it impossible to tell what time it is. I've solved the problem in true Super Handyman fashion. Each morning before I start to work, I wrap my watch in clear plastic freezer wrap. This allows me to see the face, but keeps the paint off the watch and band."

Here's a good one from a gal:
"When painting, I slip a pair of my husband's old socks right over my shoes to protect them from paint spots. Also, I can wipe little spots off the floor with my foot without having to bend over. My husband thought this was such a good idea that he now does it when he paints."

(What most men would like to know is how her husband got her to do the painting!)

"Next time you want to carry several paint cans, just take a wooden coat hanger and turn it upside down. One can hangs from the hook in the center, and another from each end of the hanger. You carry it by a

crosspiece. This leaves the other hand free for other things or for another hanger full of paint cans."

"Whenever I'm painting from my stepladder, I bolt a pie pan to the top step. This acts as a holder for the paint can, to keep it from slipping off and also to catch the drippings. When the job is finished, I remove the pie pan and store the nut and bolt back in the hole in the step until the next paint job."

(This would also make a good holder for nails and small tools.)

"When painting from a stepladder, I use a pair of short coil springs with hooks on each end. A screen door spring cut in half is ideal. One end of each is hooked to the can. The other end of each spring attaches to a pair of eye hooks on each end of the top step of my ladder. These anchor the paint can down and prevent it from tipping."

"When painting must be done from a ladder, a partially filled paint can is a lot better than a full one. First of all, there is much less likelihood of spilling. Next, you don't have to look down if the brush can be dipped in until it touches the bottom of the can without paint getting up too far on the brush. Also, with a partially filled can, if a quick stop is needed, you don't have to worry about where to put the brush down. It can be stood up in the can for a few minutes without hurting the bristles."

"To paint our garage door at the top, I devised a scaffold that gave me just the right amount of extra reach. I took three gallon-size paint cans and put my scaffolding board across these. They will hold lots of weight and are ideal when you need only a short scaffold."

(This will probably be all the extra height most men will need for getting a better shot at painting a ceiling.)

"To speed up my outside painting chores, I get a large empty squeeze bottle (the kind liquid detergent comes in) and fill it with paint. Holding this in my left hand, and my brush in my right, I'm ready to paint. I squeeze the paint out of the bottle, and then spread it with the brush."

(You may have to enlarge the opening.)

"The dropcloths that painters use over shrubbery are fairly expensive for the home handyman who repaints the outside of his house only every couple of years. I got mine free by saving the plastic suit bags that come from the dry cleaners. These can be put together with cellophane tape to form a drop cloth as large as you need. If the weather is very windy, rocks can be put in the bags closest to the ground for the needed weight. When the paint job is done, the dropcloths go into the garbage, and there is no unsightly paint to damage grass or plants."

"Not long ago, I was painting the exterior of our house and needed some weights to hold down the tarps I was using. My wife supplied me with plastic bleach bottles that she had filled with water. This was really a good idea (even if it did come from my wife), because we had saved lots of these empty bottles and so we could quickly have as many of these weights as we needed. Also, when we're through using them, the water can be dumped out, and there's no strain in hauling them around."

(. . . A good idea no matter what your "weighty" problem.)

"Paint roller pans aren't too handy to use atop a stepladder, and so I welded a pair of L-shaped angle iron braces to the pan so that one of the angles ran parallel to the top of the pan. I left a gap of the width of

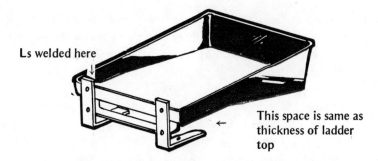

Ls welded here

This space is same as thickness of ladder top

the top of the stepladder between the stand on the shallow end of the pan and the angle brace. Then the pan can rest on the top of the ladder with the metal piece underneath to keep it in place."

(That also gives you something to hang the tray by when not in use.)

"The very best way I have found to clean paint rollers is by using a quart milk carton. It is exactly the right height for the roller that I have. I just put the roller inside, fill up the carton with the cleaning solvent, and then close the carton back up. After I'm sure that it's tightly closed, I shake it up well and then let it set for a few hours. When the roller is removed, it is free of all paint."

"I found an ideal container for cleaning a paint roller—a tennis ball can. The roller fits right down in there."

"Our paint roller doesn't have a handle long enough to reach our ceilings. I made an extension handle by rolling up a section of the newspaper and attaching it to the regular handle with rubber bands. Just be sure to use a thick enough section to hold the roller up. As I was painting, I noticed your column on the 'handle,' and it reminded me to share this idea with you and your readers."

(That's a strange way to catch up on news.)

"If you want to improve the smoothness of your paint roller a great deal, cut a section of wire screen the same size as the paint tray and place this in the bottom of the tray. As you dip your roller in the paint and roll it across the wire screen, the roller loads with paint much more evenly. And because the roller is loaded more evenly, the paint flows on the wall more evenly."

"Before pouring paint into the roller tray, spread a plastic suit bag from the cleaners over the tray to act as a liner. When the painting is done, pour the leftover paint back into the bucket, lift the liner out, and throw it away. The tray is still spotless, and you've eliminated a messy clean-up job."

(Many folks line roller trays with aluminum foil to stop the mess.)

"My wife saves those aluminum containers that frozen foods come in. When painting a ceiling, take one of these aluminum pans and punch a hole through it. Stick the paint brush handle through the hole, with the open side of the pan up. This catches paint drips and splatters. Helps me do a neater job and also helps get rid of a pan every so often."

"If any of your readers had caught me painting our ceilings, they might have thought they had run across a man from Mars. I used a roller and soon found that my eyes needed protection from the paint fallout. The only thing I could think of was my old swim mask, and so I put it on. It did look weird, but sure saved the eyes."

"Most coats of primer paint are white. When the finish coat is to be a fairly dark color, it can be quite difficult to cover over that first white coat. The smart handyman will add a tube of tint to the primer so that it is closer to the desired finish color. Even though it isn't a match to the finish, it will be much easier to cover."

If you paint over a screw, the paint may seal it in so you'll have to blast it to get it out later. Simply back the screw off a few turns while you are painting. Then after the paint is dry, tighten it down again, and it will be an easy matter to remove when the need arises.

(Or, use   screwdriver as a chisel to remove dry paint from a painted-over screw groove. A few taps with a hammer on the end of the handle will usually do the trick.)

If you have just finished painting one side of a removable shelf and are reading this book as you wait for that part to dry, you should have read this to begin with. You could have painted both sides, as well as the ends, at one sitting, merely by driving a pair of nails into each end of the shelf. The shelf can then be held up by resting the nails on a pair of sawhorses. After the top side is painted, the shelf can be turned over by handling the nails only. The other side can then be painted immediately.

Heavy coat hanger

"If you've ever had to paint the gutters along your roof, you'll certainly appreciate my idea for a paint can hanger made from an old wire coat hanger. First make a hook out of one end of the coat hanger, big enough to fit down into your gutters. Then bend the hanger around, forming a loop big enough for your hand to go through. With the remaining part, form another hook at the bottom for holding the paint can. Now you are ready to go to work. The holder will slide along the gutters as you work and carry the paint with it."

(This is a good idea, but be sure that you use a heavy-duty coat hanger and bend it around so the hooks are composed of several thicknesses of wire. A partially full bucket might also be a good idea. All the time you saved will be lost if the bucket falls.)

"When I started painting our apartment, I discovered there was no way to get the roller—or a brush for that matter—behind our radiators. We would have ended up with a sloppy-looking job, but I made a 'brush by stapling a section of kitchen sponge on the end of a yardstick. This gave me the length I needed and was skinny enough to go in behind the radiator. It also gave us a pretty smooth finish."

(This should also be a help for getting in behind that big old refrigerator and in back of the stove.)

Board
↓

"Painting screens is much easier and neater if you can raise the screens up off the ground. I make an easel by putting a wide plank from the second step of the ladder down to the ground. The part that touches the ground should be braced against something so it won't slip. The work sits on top of the plank and rests back against the ladder. If you need to raise the work, the board can be moved up to the desired step."

(Folks, this is a good easel for any big flat work!)

"For painting window screens, the best thing I've found is a common kitchen sponge. It holds a good quantity of paint, and does the job quickly. If you get too much paint and fill in some of the tiny squares, just squeeze out the sponge and rub it back over the screen to remove the excess."

(Or a carpet scrap tacked to a wood block is also good. So is a piece of foam rubber.)

Did you ever have to paint a picture frame? The big problem is that there is no way to move the frame around to reach all sides without getting paint on your fingers ... *unless* you "Tack a strip of scrap wood on the back of the frame so that 6″ or so of it sticks out to form a handle. Now, you can turn the frame around in any direction and even spray paint without getting any paint on your fingers."

(Drill a hole in the end of the handle, and when you're through painting, you'll have a place to hang the frame by for drying.)

"Each spring, I repaint all of our flower pots so the little woman can move all our plants out to our screened-in porch. This year I ran a piece of rope through the hole in the bottom of each pot, and tied a knot so the rope could not come back through the hole. Then I suspended each pot from the rafters in our basement so that it hung upside down from the rope. This made it a snap to spray-paint each pot by walking around it. The pots hung this way until dry."

"To paint a small object—say the size of a chair or smaller—I make a turntable from a piece of corrugated cardboard nailed in the center to my work table. The nail acts as an axis. The work sits on the cardboard and can be turned around as the painting is done. This way, you never have to touch the work or move yourself and the paint around the work."

(A "Lazy Susan" for lazy but smart painters!)

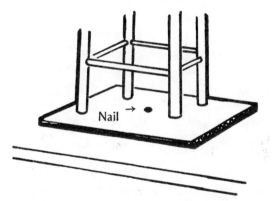

Nail

"We have one of those barbecue grills with the grill that can be rotated. I found that it also makes a good spray paint table: The object being painted can be turned around for a shot at all sides. Any paint that gets on the grill is then burned off at your next cookout."

"When you paint a chair, the natural thing to do is to put a newspaper underneath to catch the drips. But after the paint dries, the newspaper naturally sticks to the chair legs. I put the chair on stilts so this doesn't happen. Before painting, I drive a small nail into the bottom of each each leg, just far enough to hold. This keeps the legs up off the newspaper, and the nails can easily be pulled out when the paint is dry."

To keep newspapers from sticking to the wet paint, you can also use small squares of aluminum foil under each leg. The foil will still catch all the paint that runs down the leg, but will not stick to the painted surface. Go ahead and spread the newspapers under the entire piece of furniture to catch any splatters, but let the foil be under the legs.

Or: "Here's a use for those versatile plastic lids from coffee cans. Put one under each leg of a piece of furniture when painting. This is much better at catching drips than newspaper because it doesn't stick to the wet painted surface as newspaper does."

Sometimes molding has to be painted before it's installed. Because of the small size of the molding, this is not the world's easiest painting chore. You can cut the task in half, however, by painting two pieces at the same time. Put the backs of the pieces together and hold them that way—either with nails partly driven in or with a few dabs of rubber cement. Because you have a larger target, the task becomes easier; you can do both pieces with one stroke of the brush.

"We have a friend who painted the stairs leading down to his basement. When he finished and looked up to admire his workmanship, he realized he had trapped himself downstairs. If you have to paint stairs, paint every other one. This will allow you to use the stairway while the paint is drying. Then come back when the painted steps are dry and paint the rest."

(Another way is to paint half of each step at a time, and use the unpainted half to walk on.)

"Much as I hate to admit it, my wife is a 'Super Handyman' too. She watched while I tried to paint our chain-link fence, first with a brush, then with a sprayer. She suggested a roller; and it was so easy, I was amazed."

When you spray-paint a picket fence or any kind of fence with spaces for the paint to go through, make a simple fence shield to be hung from the side opposite the one from which you are painting. The shield can be made from a large corrugated box. It should be the same height as the fence, but can be any width you desire. Fashion hooks from pieces of wire, and the shield can be moved along the fence as you paint.

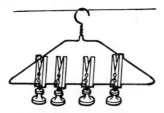

"Wooden drawer knobs are a pain to paint and an even bigger problem to dry. I think my trick solves both problems rather well. I hang the knobs from a wire coat hanger by means of a spring-type clothespin. I leave the screws in the knobs, and the clothespins hold the knobs by the screw heads. When the coat hanger is hung from a clothesline, the knobs can then be easily spray-painted. Then I just leave them hanging until they're dry."

←   Pipe cleaner

"If I have a small paint or touch-up job, I make a throw-away brush out of a pipe cleaner. I bend the cleaner around at one end to form a triangle, which acts as the brush part. This can be formed to the best size for the job. The rest of the pipe cleaner acts as a handle. The fuzz on the cleaner holds quite a bit of paint, and gives a surprisingly smooth coat after a little practice."

Flatten side of
coffee can   →

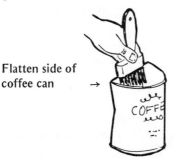

"For a small paint job, I often mix the paint in an old coffee can for easier handling. To make the can more of a help, I take a pair of pliers and flatten out a section at the top. The flattened part needs to be slightly wider than the brush I will be using. I use this flattened section to wipe off the excess paint as I take the brush out for painting. It only takes a few moments to do this, and it's a real help."

"When you stop painting for a moment, there's always the problem of what to do with the brush. If you lay it across the top of the paint bucket, a certain amount of paint is going to drip down the side. If you put the brush in the bucket, it often sinks too far down in the paint. I have solved this problem by driving a nail in the brush handle at right angles to the handle, just above or in the metal fiber holder. When I stop painting, the head of the nail fits into the rim around the edge of the pail. The brush doesn't go too far down, and the drips go back in the bucket."

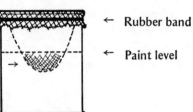

← Rubber band

Net hangs below paint level

← Paint level

"If you need a few brushfuls of paint from a partly used can, it's a nuisance to have to strain the entire can of paint. However, by putting a piece of a lady's old stocking over the top of the paint can with enough give to reach down into the paint, you won't have to do any straining. Leave enough stocking outside so that a rubber band can be put around to hold it in place. Your brush will push the net down into the paint, and the paint that the brush dips into will have come through the stocking—and, therefore, will be strained."

If you've mixed a little dab of paint in a small tin can and find that the brush you need to use is too wide to fit into the can, don't despair. By simply squeezing it, you can compress the mouth of the can into an oval shape which should then be big enough to accomodate the wider brush. This may sound like an awfully simple idea, but I've known some folks to spend 15 minutes looking for another container, or resorting to a too-small brush.

Many a home handyman has dripped so much paint on the outside of a can that he couldn't read the label. One reader removes the label before he opens the can, cuts off the important part, and tapes this to the top of the lid. This part never gets dripped on, and therefore he can always tell the kind and color of the paint in the can.

If your springtime paint-up includes painting your screen doors, here's a tip that will make it a lot easier to paint that spring that pulls the screen shut. Hook it on a pair of nails far enough apart to spread the coils, and by painting it while it is stretched out, you'll be able to paint much more of the coils. In other words, paint on a sprung spring spreads better.

Paint will adhere to galvanized metal much better if you rub the surface with vinegar before painting. Just rub on a light coat with a rag, and since the vinegar dries rapidly, you can come right along behind with your painting.

"My kids really love ice cream on a stick, so we always have a rather large collection of used sticks. I found a very good use for some of them recently when we repainted our house. I made a visual history of the paint job that should really prove valuable in the future. For each room we painted, I dipped a stick into the paint about an inch. When this color sample was dry, I then recorded on each stick, with a ball point, the amount of paint used, the color, the brand, and the date, and then designated the room or area for each. I then stapled the sticks to the inside door of my paint cabinet. When we're ready for a repaint, I'll know exactly how much of what paint to get. The date will also let me know whether I got a good paint job or should change brands."

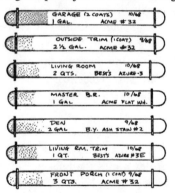

"We all know how effective masking tape is in keeping paint off a surface not to be painted. However, when you have a curved or rounded surface, the masking tape is hard to apply. Forget it! Give the area not to be painted a coat of rubber cement. A brush will allow you to follow any contour, and any paint that gets on the rubber cement will be taken up when the rubber cement is rubbed off. (It can easily be removed by rubbing a finger over it.)"

"Next time you do-it-yourself painters are painting around windows outside, forget the masking tape. Get a nice big bar of the cheapest soap you can find and run this around the edge of the windows. (It is so easy to do I even got volunteer help from the kids.) The film of soap keeps the paint off the glass. After the paint has dried, turn the hose on the windows, and the soap dissolves. Using a brush makes the removal even faster—and you probably needed to clean the windows anyway!"

"When you paint up against a surface that is not to be painted and you need a shield that can be moved along, drag out your wife's dustpan. It has a handle that makes it easy to hold. It's flat, so you can paint right up to the edge. After you're through painting, the paint won't hurt the dustpan at all. As a matter of fact, my wife thinks her multicolored dust pan is prettier than it was before."

"When painting a door, almost everyone wants to mask the door-knob somehow to keep paint off. But the doorknobs of the doors that are *not* being painted are usually the ones that get paint on them—the paint that gets on your hands and then on the doorknob when you have to open the door. Before you start the paint job, put a plastic sandwich bag over every knob, and slip a rubber band over the bag to hold it on."

Bet you'd like to be able to see through those partly used paint cans to know how much of what color is in the can. No need for X-ray eyes. Next time, before closing the can, paint an inch-wide stripe on the outside of the can from the top down to the paint level. You'll know how much and what color at a glance. When you use some more paint, just extend the stripe down to the new level.

"I use a dip stick to tell me how much paint of what color I have left in a can. Just before I cap up a can, I take a straight twig about a foot long and dip it straight down into the bucket. This gives me the exact depth of the paint. When it dries, I attach it to the outside of the can with a rubber band. It is always easy to see, and if I want to compare the color, I need only take the twig to see if it matches."

Stick dipped in can

"As a home builder, I have my painters do something that I think would also be helpful to the home handyman. If we have paint left over, I have the painter put a swipe of paint on the lid of the can. Then he takes a matchstick and scratches into the swipe the room and the use for the paint in the can. This way, the home-owner can tell at a glance which can to get for the inevitable touch-up jobs that come later."

"When I cap a can of paint, I don't worry about it's drying up or developing a skin on top. I pour hot paraffin over the paint to seal it in. I figured if it worked for my wife in her jelly canning, it would work on my paint, and it does."

"Here's an added step to seal off that partly used can of paint from the outside air. Lay a piece of clear plastic food wrap over the top of the open can. Make sure the plastic extends an inch or so over the edge. Now put the can lid in place and tap it down into the grooves in the rim. It will push the plastic down into the rim as it goes in, providing an extra seal against the air."

"You know how important it is to seal up paint cans good and tight. I clean the rim out, and then put a coat of rubber cement around the rim of the lid. This gives me an airtight seal, and yet is quite easy to break when I want to reopen the can."

"Epoxy paint is too costly to throw away if you happened to have mixed more than you need. I have discovered that the drying process is greatly retarded if I store leftover paint in the freezer. In fact, it will still be usable after several weeks of cold storage in a tightly capped jar. In case there is need for a touch-up, you will be all set . . . but the paint won't."

"Have your wife save those empty fingernail polish bottles. Then each time you finish a paint job, fill one up with leftover paint. If you ever have a tiny touch-up job, the paint and brush are ready and waiting."

Another reader came up with this bottled idea. "It has always bothered me that the soft drink people now use those no-return bottles. But I store small amounts of paint in them. They make it possible for me to see at a glance the color I want. Regular bottle caps can be pushed back on to seal them. I also store these bottles in the cartons, which keeps them from being easy to knock off the shelf. I wonder if you or your readers have any other uses for them?"

(This, like any other idea, must be weighed for safety. Just make sure soft drink bottles that have been refilled are kept well away from kids. It's also a must to label all containers put to another use.)

"Whenever I finish any kind of paint job, I pour a dab of the leftover paint into an empty shoe polish bottle—the kind with the dauber in the stopper. Then if I ever have a touch-up to do, I can quickly mix the paint by shaking, and there is already a brush in the bottle."

"If you've been painting and get ready to clean your hands, only to find you don't have any turp to clean with, grab a handful of sawdust and rub your hands together with the sawdust in between. Then take a handful and rub this in with your regular soap and water. When it's time to rinse, you'll be pleasantly surprised to find you have clean hands."

"When the painter finished our house, I noticed that after he put the lids back on the leftover cans of paint, he turned each can upside down for a few moments. I just had to ask what this was for. He explained that the paint would act as a seal for the lid so that no air could get in and dry out the paint. Sounds like a good idea to me."

"Last weekend, I finished painting and found that the level of solvent in my brush soaker can wasn't high enough to reach the brushes. I solved the problem by dropping enough pebbles into the can: This raised the solvent level up to where I wanted it."

"I reuse cleaning solvent for paintbrushes over and over again. The secret is to remove all the sediment after each use. The quickest and easiest way I have found is to pour the solvent into a plastic bleach bottle first. Then I take a patch of steel wool and place this over the opening. (Use a patch big enough to lap over the opening so that a rubber band will hold it in place.) Then I pour the solvent out, and the steel wool does the straining."

"No matter how careful you are, a paint job results in messy hands. Usually about the time you are well under way, the telephone rings, and by the time you've cleaned your hands it's too late to catch the phone. Next time, before you start to paint, wrap a section of an old rag around the phone handle. A pair of rubber bands will hold it in place. Then when the call comes, you can answer it without leaving paint samples."

"When I'm painting, I keep a spare plastic sandwich bag handy. Then if the phone rings or someone comes to the door, I slip my hand in the bag as if it were a glove, and I don't have to worry about paint's getting on anything I might have to touch."

"When we got our last kid out of the bottle stage, we gave away all the bottles and equipment but still ended up with a bottle brush. Rather than throw it away, I stuck it in a catch-all box in my shop with the idea that I would find a use for it later. Not long ago, I read that painting the bottoms of doors is really hard on brushes. I decided to try my bottle brush on this task and found it worked out fine. Saved a paint brush and is easier, too!"

PATCHING   "The so-called plumber's friend can also be the plasterer's friend. With the suction cup facing up, you have a handy holder for the mixture. The container is good for mixing as well as carrying to the job, and the rubber's easy to clean after use."

"If your wife changes her mind about where pictures should hang as often as mine does, you'll end up with lots of unsightly holes in the wall. I patch up the holes in our plaster walls with an ordinary piece of blackboard chalk I've sharpened to a point. I push the point into the hole, and when it's in good and tight, break it off. Next I sand it off flush with the wall, and touch the spot with shellac. When dry, it's painted to match the wall."

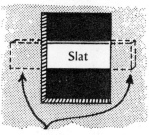

Glued inside wall as base for patch

"Patching a hole in a sheet rock wall is no problem if you have exposed studs to attach the new patch piece to. But I had a hole between the studs, with nothing to attach the patch to. I took a strip of thin wood long enough to span the hole and overlap and inch or so on each side. I put fast-drying glue on each end and held it in place inside the wall until it was dry enough to stick by itself. When it was completely dry, I put glue across the back of the sheet rock patch and held it against the thin wood with masking tape. When it was dry, I filled the crack with compound and textured over it."

"I've discovered the ideal pallet on which to carry the patching mixture for those small patching jobs on a plaster wall—the top of one of your wife's old saucepans. The mixture rests nicely in the inside of the lid, and the knob acts as a fine handle which can be held easily and which allows you to turn the pallet around for the best angle."

"After refinishing several pieces of furniture, I've learned to collect some of the sawdust in a glass jar. This can then be mixed with glue and used to fill cracks and nail holes later on. Nothing blends as well with the natural wood as a few 'chips off the old block.'"

Here's a real cavity fighter: "My wife decided to move some of the wall hangings around. The result was several holes in the wall where she no longer wanted pictures. Now I wouldn't even know where to go to buy patching compound or what to ask for if I got there. [It's called spackling, by the way.] However, I patched up the holes with tooth-paste. After it dried, you couldn't find the holes. In one room where the walls are not white, I touched up the toothpaste patches with a dot of water color, and now they're hidden too."

A trip to the kitchen will get you some quick patching compound for any small holes in your plaster wall. A half spoonful each of starch and salt with enough water to form a putty-like mixture is all you need. If you're painting with water-based paint, you don't even need to wait for the patch to dry before painting over it. Otherwise, you should.

"Tiny holes in wood to be finished are usually more difficult to fill than the larger ones. Maybe you don't need to fill them. Take a damp cloth and lay it over the wood where the holes are. Then take a hot iron and press the cloth until almost dry. The steam will expand the fibers in the wood and close the hole. Then if you apply the finishing coat fairly soon, you will never know the holes were there. This method also takes out small dents and other surface mars."

"Nail holes in wood can sometimes be patched up with this trick. Dip the end of a round toothpick into some glue and insert this into the hole. After the glue is dry, break or cut the projecting toothpick off and sand it down flush with the surface of the wood. When refinished, these patches will hardly be noticed. For any of you men who have a drawing board in your shop, this is an ideal way to take care of all the thumbtack holes and make the board smooth again."

"If you have to fill a very large cavity with wood putty or some other such compound, insert staples in the bottom of the cavity. Leave them sticking up but not above the surface. This way, the compound has something to stick to and it will give you a much better bond."

PATTERNS   "Recently I needed a pattern for a shop project and got a big assist from a gadget I found in my wife's sewing basket, called a tracing wheel—a handle with a wheel that has little spikes around it. When rolled, it punches holes in paper. I drew the pattern on a big sheet of paper, then used this gadget, taped the paper to the wood to be cut, and went over the pattern with a can of spray paint. When the paper was removed, the design was all laid out with dots of paint that had come through the holes the gadget left. Quick-drying paint made it possible to start cutting right away."

PENCILS IN THE SHOP   "If you've put pencil lines on a piece of wood that's to be finished, don't try to remove the marks by sanding. Often the graphite particles will just go down deeper into the wood and can never be removed. The best thing to do is to use an eraser on the lines, and usually all of the markings will disappear. If all are not removed after erasing, it will then be all right to use sandpaper, as most of the graphite will be gone."

"A good sharp pencil will always be handy if you glue one of those dime-store plastic pencil sharpeners to your metal rule. Since the straightedge and pencil are go-together items, this means the pencil sharpener is usually handy. Even if I am not using the rule, I at least always know where the sharpener is."

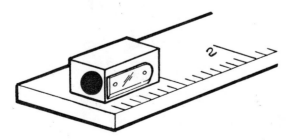

Drill holes here

"Keeping up with a pencil would be a problem for me if I hadn't come up with a handy holder for both my workbench and my sawhorse. Simple to make but not so simple to describe, my pencil holder is a 1" x 4" square block of scrap wood with a 'V' cut on the top the full width of the scrap. In the center of the 'V' a hole is drilled almost to the bottom of the block, big enough to accommodate a pencil. Another hole is drilled through the block at the very bottom of the pencil-holding hole to keep it from getting clogged up with sawdust."

PENETRATING OIL   "Have just discovered another good substitute in case you have a stubborn screw or bolt and have run out of penetrating oil. A few drops of hydrogen peroxide from the medicine chest will usually cut through the problem in a few minutes."

"Did you know that iodine from the medicine chest is a good substitute for penetrating oil? Next time you've got a cranky bolt or screw, try it."

PERFORATED HARDBOARD   "Since so many workshops have pegboard walls, you may want to tell your handy friends about my brainstorm. I welded pegboard hooks onto several foot-long sections of guttering. These hang from the wall and provide handy trays for all sorts of shop items. I'm surprised the people who make the pegboard hooks haven't put out a line of trays. Mine are great."

"I made tool holders on my pegboard wall by weaving plastic clothesline in and out of the holes. This formed loops, and the tools hang in the loops against the wall. To keep the line in place, a knot is tied on the back at each end."

(This won't work in all cases, because you have to be able to get to the back of the board to weave the line.)

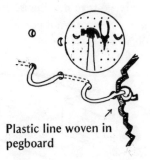

Plastic line woven in pegboard

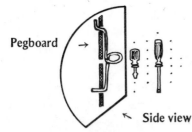

Pegboard → Side view

"I saved a fair amount of money by making some of the hanger fixtures for my pegboard workshop walls from coat hanger wires. The most effective ones are those with loops to hold screwdrivers, chisels, and other such tools. The loop is formed around a pipe, and the tip that goes into the holes in the pegboard is bent out with a pair of pliers. They are made to span two holes. I wrapped the tips with tape to make them fit a bit tighter."

"In spite of all the clever hooks for pegboard that cost very little, they seem to be all gone when you need one. Maybe this will save the day. Go to your golf bag and dig out a few tees, either wooden or plastic. These little gems fit nicely into the holes and wedge in so they will stay. Just be sure that you leave enough to tee off with next weekend."

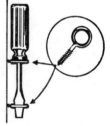

"You're always talking about pegboard walls and how handy they are. Well, my shop wall is solid, so I had to figure something else out. For all of my screwdrivers, chisels, and the like, I installed a pair of screw eyes, one below the other. The tools fit down into the eyes. The bottom screw eye isn't really necessary except to keep the tools hanging straight. While pegboard is a convenience, there are advantages to having a solid wall."

PESTS "How many paint jobs have you seen marred by insects that came in contact with the wet surface? I now mix two tablespoons of insect repellent into a gallon of paint, and this is one problem that doesn't bug me any more. The repellent doesn't seem to affect the paint."

"Sometimes those old home remedies you have heard of really work. A family of moles started a subway system under our yard. I had always heard that you could run them off by throwing a few mothballs down in their holes. I tried it, and sure enough, they're gone."

(This old remedy usually does drive moles and gophers away. They probably just moved over to one of your neighbors' yards to set up housekeeping, so don't go around bragging about your eviction.)

"We discovered a mole colony had set up underground quarters in our yard. I sentenced them to the gas chamber, and I think it was an ingenious way. I covered up all the holes I found, except for one. Then I connected a hose to the exhaust on my power mower and inserted it in this hole, packing rags around the hose to make it tight. When I started the power mower, the exhaust fumes went all through Moles-ville, and either gassed all the moles or ran them off. We haven't been bothered since."

(I could not try this since my lawn has no moles. If you want to avoid having these pests, don't provide underground restaurant facilities. Moles feed on white grubs and other insects, and there are many good insecticides for the control of this mole food. Even if the moles do not come to dinner, these insects are probably not doing your yard any good.)

PETS "This fall, I buried mothballs around a tree to kill borers. I soon noticed our dog avoided that tree, though it had once been a favorite of his. Now I've mixed mothballs in the dirt in our flower beds, and there is no more problem with the dog's digging in them."

(This also keeps garden snakes out of flower beds.)

Screen door spring

"If you're bothered by man's best friend knocking over your garbage can, here's another way to keep your garbage from being scattered all over the neighborhood. Get an appropriate-sized screen door spring and permanently fasten it to one handle of the can. Bend out the loop on the other end of the spring so it becomes a hook. When the spring is brought through the handle on the lid and hooked to the can handle on the other side, there is no way a dog can get the lid off. However, it is a simple matter for the pickup man to get the spring undone to dump the contents into his truck."

"My dog is smart as a whip out in the field, but in the backyard he always knocked over his water dish. I solved the problem by swiping an old angel food cake pan from the kitchen. This water dish fits over a stake driven into the ground and cannot be knocked over."

"If you own a dog, you may have had to wash him in the bathtub at some time. This can result in splashing water all over. Here's how I solved this problem. I took an old shower curtain that my wife had decided to retire and cut a pair of armholes in it, about tub high. Then I cut a head hole so I could look in to see what was going on. With this shower curtain hanging in place, I can reach in and scrub my dog and never splash a drop out on the floor or me. After the tub is drained, I can also reach in and towel him dry before taking him out."

"No need to throw away a worn rubber auto floor mat. It makes an ideal mat on which to keep your pet-food dishes. Even the best-mannered dog or cat will slop out food and water, but the rubber mat will keep it from messing up the floor. The mat can be easily picked up and washed off under the sink faucet when necessary, and it looks a lot better than papers."

"If you need a temporary fence to keep your puppy in until you can put up a permanent one, wedge 2″ x 4″ posts into the openings in concrete blocks. This can easily be done with scraps of lumber wedged in to hold the posts firmly. Place these around the area to be fenced, about 5′ or 6′ apart. Then take a roll of chicken wire and staple this to the posts. Make sure it comes down to the ground. We fashioned a gate by putting the last two posts next to the house only two feet apart. When we were through with this temporary fence, we still had the chicken wire, the 2 x 4's, and the concrete blocks intact for other uses later on—only we haven't thought of any other uses as yet."

Here's what a 14-year-old lad wrote me: "One night my dog got run over by a car. I guess the driver just couldn't see him in time. Our new dog will have a better chance at night, because I've wrapped his collar with strips of reflector tape that really do show up at night."

PICTURES AND PICTURE HANGING   "After framing a few pictures and losing time and temper from those tiny brads that go in the back of the frame, I decided there must be a better way. Masking tape around all four sides of the backing cardboard so that it overlaps the frame will not only hold the picture in but also seal out all dust. It sure is a lot easier."

"To keep a picture straight and true after it's been hung, put a loop in the hanger wire right in the center. Then when the wire goes over the hook, the weight of the picture will pull the loop tight around the hook, and the picture won't slide around."

PING-PONG BALLS   "Our family has taken up Ping-Pong in a big way. Since those little plastic balls cost about 12 cents apiece, I was happy to learn that Ping-Pong balls that have dents but are not cracked can be cured. Just drop the balls into a pan of boiling water to which a pinch of salt has been added. Keep turning the balls over for a few minutes, and the dents will pop out."

(Our neighbor, Stanley, who has a Ping-Pong set, tried this . . . and said they were delicious.)

PLANES AND PLANING   "Getting ready to plane a large hardwood surface? Dampen it first with a wet sponge. This will make the grain rise a wee bit, and the plane will bite better, thereby making the job much easier."

"My improvised bench stop is made from one of those rubber-bumper door stops that are installed into the wall. If one of these is bent to form a right angle about an inch from the base and is screwed into the workbench, it becomes a great bench stop. The work rests against the rubber bumper. For wider work, two or even three door stops can be lined up on your workbench."

Door stop

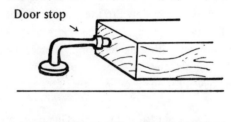

"If you've ever tried to plane the edges of a piece of plywood, you know it's a real tough row to hoe. When trying to fit two sections of plywood together, forget about trying to plane them to get a perfect fit. Merely push them tightly together, and then tack them down on a scrap board and run a power saw through the seam. When untacked, the two sections will fit together exactly. This even works on joints that are not straight. After they're cut as nearly as possible to fit, use this method and cut along the seam with your saber saw. Whatever your path, the two will fit."

Nail
↓

"I find I do more planing away from the workbench, and so here is how I put a bench stop on my sawhorse. A few inches from the end of the horse, I cut a slit only about ¼″ deep that slants back away from the end. This holds a wiggle nail (corrugated fastener), and the work to be planed stops up against this. The corrugations also hold the fastener in place in the slit. When the stop is not needed, the wiggle nail comes out."

PLASTERING   "If you're having trouble with plaster that's getting hard before you can get through working with it, try adding a little vinegar. This will retard the hardening process. A half teaspoon in a quart of mixture is about the right amount."

PLASTIC BLEACH BOTTLES   Many readers have sent in clever ideas for those plastic bleach bottles. It's amazing what a wide variety of things can be done with them. Only a few are included here. Before you start, it might be helpful to know the best ways to go about preparing them. First of all, you will want to clean them out inside. If the project calls for the bottle to be dry, let it sit upside down so it drips dry. For drawing designs on the bottle, a soft lead pencil is best. Cutting can be done well either with a single-edge razor blade or with a pair of scissors. If you use scissors, you will have to punch a hole first and a heated ice pick is best. If you need the plastic to be more flexible and pliable while working on it, soak it in very hot water. Most paints will adhere to this type of plastic.

"I made my trouble light from one of those plastic jugs. First I cut off the bottom half and threw it away. Then I ran an extension cord with a socket through the spout, so that the socket was inside the jug. I pulled the socket down tight into the neck, and tied the cord to the handle to keep it that way. This lamp has a handle to carry it by or to hang it up by. The white plastic reflects the light nicely, and the price is certainly right "

(If you don't get a bright enough light, wrap the inside with foil for extra reflection.)

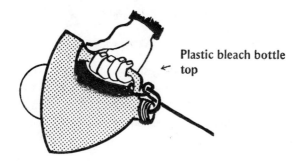

Plastic bleach bottle
← top

"One of the best throw-away paint buckets can be made from a plastic bleach bottle. Starting about 6" from the bottom, cut a line up toward the handle. Leave the handle on, but cut the spout portion off. This leaves you a paint container that can be easily carried, has plenty of room for you to dip in your brush, and can be either thrown away or cleaned and used again. The handle makes the container a lot easier to use than a bucket—which leaves your hand in the way of the brush—and makes pouring a lot easier."

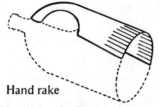

Hand rake

"From a plastic bleach bottle, I've made a small hand rake for my wife to use in the flower beds. The handle of the bottle remains as the handle of my rake. By cutting straight down from where the handle meets the neck of the bottle to the bottom of the jug, I formed the rake shape. Next I cut out the bottom, and made slits about ½" apart and about 3" deep. These form the teeth of the rake. My wife swears by it."

"Cut out the bottom section from a gallon jug, leaving a container about 5" or 6" high. Turn it upside down, and cut holes in the bottom. When this is put on the top of the workbench, it makes a handy holder for all sorts of little hand tools. If you decide ahead of time which tools it is to hold, you can cut all the holes to fit."

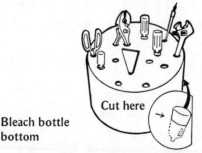

Cut here

Bleach bottle bottom

One time I jokingly suggested using the leftover top of a plastic bleach bottle as a megaphone for the handyman to use in yelling at his wife. It brought forth this response: "Part of my teaching duties includes the running of our school pep squad. I had each of my 60 girls make a bleach bottle megaphone. Since our school colors are blue and white, we tied blue ribbons on the handles, and they really look great. After they made their debut at the first football game, more and more other students and parents began showing up with them. The kids even call them Super Handyphones. Thanks for a great idea! We haven't lost a game since we started using them."

PLASTICS   "Did you know that liquid brass polish will also take out tiny scratches on most clear plastics? Rub the polish on gently with a soft cloth for a minute or so. Then remove the polish with a dry rag, and the scratches will have disappeared."

PLIERS   "I've created a rather unique and handy grip for pliers with a length of rubber hose about 14″ long. Slipping it over the ends of the handles makes the pliers a lot more comfortable on the hands. Also, when you loosen your hold, the hose causes the pliers to spring open, ready to grip something else."

(In addition, this gimmick insulates your pliers for any electrical work.)

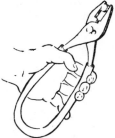

"The jaws of pliers are made for gripping, and consequently may leave unwanted marks on work with a fine finish. Cut a couple of fingers off an old pair of gloves and slip them over your pliers the next time you need to protect the finish. They will still grip, but with a gentler touch."

"If you're using pliers on a material that will be easily marred, cushion the jaws with a couple of strips of masking tape. If you'll be working for some time, you may need a double thickness."

PLUMB BOB   "Any home handyman with a plumb bob will want to use my adaptation. I've attached a rubber suction cup on the end of the string—the kind of cup that has a threaded hole and bolt in it, but any kind would do—and substituted an eye bolt for the regular bolt. Now I'm never at a loss for something from which to hang the plumb bob,

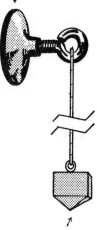

Rubber suction cup

Plumb bob

since the suction cup will stick to just about everything. I've even had occasion to stick it on the ceiling, which is a big advantage over a regular plumb bob."

"How do you like my idea for a plumb bob carrying case? It is a 4″ section of old radiator hose from a car. The ends are V-notched so the string can be wrapped from end to end. The bob rests inside the length of hose."

String through hole in pencil eraser ↓

Nail set →

"We didn't have a plumb bob, so I made one. I took a slip-on rubber pencil eraser and punched a hole in the end. I pushed a string through, and a knot tied on the inside kept the string from going through the hole. Then I inserted my nail set, which fit tight into the eraser. You couldn't buy a better plumb bob!"

Or if you don't have an eraser . . . "Maybe my makeshift plumb bob will help some home handyman. You need only a yardstick and a small nail. Drive the nail through the yardstick as near to the end as possible. Measure the width and be sure the nail is centered. To use the stick as a plumb bob, tap the nail into the surface you need to check. (The smallest nail is desirable so it will leave a tiny hole.) Just put it in far enough to hold the weight of the yardstick, leaving the stick free to swing back and forth. It will hang straight up and down, of course. If there is a ledge, the nail can just hang over this and need not be driven in."

Nail

We got a great kick out of a reader's very funny letter about his trials and tribulations in his recent fence-building project. One problem he ran into was that his plumb bob kept blowing back and forth in strong gusts of wind. This could have been remedied with a bucket of water. Just put the bucket so the weight on the plumb bob hangs into the water, and it will just about cut out the swinging.

PLUMBER'S FRIEND   "The plumber's friend can become an even more useful helper. Before using it next time, smear a little petroleum jelly all around the rim of the plunger. This makes it have much greater suction, because it gives it a better seal. When you've finished the chore, wipe off the remaining petroleum jelly with a paper towel."

"If your plumber's friend has developed a loose handle, nail a soft-drink bottle cap to the end of the handle where the plunger goes. Put the zigzag side of the cap up toward the handle. Now reinsert the handle, and the zigzags on the bottle top will grip the rubber plunger and keep it from coming loose."

Or try this one: "I repaired our plumber's friend by putting an adjustable hose clamp around the plunger and the handle and turning it down tight. Now the plunger won't come off any more."

"We have a glass top on our dresser. When I want to wax underneath, it's very difficult to lift up the glass because it's cut exactly to fit. However, the suction from the 'friend' enables me to lift it up and get a hand under to remove it. It also proved to be a pal when the pull broke off a drawer. The suction from the plumber's friend allowed me to open the drawer without prying."

PLUMBING   "Even though I'm a professional plumber, I really don't mind the hints you pass along that let your readers do-it-themselves. I would much rather take care of the big jobs and let the home-owner do the little ones. In fact, here is a temporary pipe patch job one customer used that kept his call from being an emergency. His patching equipment includes a split section of rubber hose about 4″ long and a C-clamp. The hose was slipped around the hole in the pipe, and the clamp was placed against the hose at exactly the location of the hole. When he applied the clamping pressure, the hose stopped the water. While this wouldn't last forever, it sure did the job until I arrived."

Or, until you can permanently repair a leak or replace a section of water pipe, "cut off the water at the source, if possible. Take a strip of inner tube about a foot long and an inch or so wide. Start wrapping the pipe with this about 6″ from the leak. Stretch the rubber as you go and make sure each turn overlaps about half the previous turn. When you have reached the end of the rubber strip, tie a cord around that end and wrap the length of the rubber strip with cord. The laps with the cord should be fairly close together, with at least two laps for each lap of inner tube. The secret is to stretch and wrap the rubber as tight as possible and pull the string tight too. This will take care of the leak until a more permanent repair can be made."

"I discovered a long stretch of pipe that had developed a sag because of a joint in the middle. It was not situated so it could easily be raised by a pipe strap, so I got a long piece of angle iron and used this as a sort of splint under the sagging section. The splint was held in place by tape."

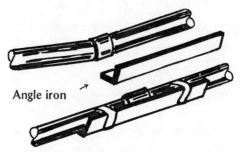

Angle iron

'Let me reveal an old plumber's trick to help in measuring pipe. A 2' section of auto radiator hose will clamp the end of your steel tape around a pipe and allow you to measure on down the line. Similar sections will also help on a curve or bend that needs to be measured, holding the flexible steel tape in place against the curve."

"I made a pipe de-burring tool out of one of those V-type beer-can openers. All I had to do was file the edges of the 'V' so they were sharp. It takes the burrs out of the pipe and cost me not one cent."

"Usually when a sink is clogged or slow draining it's because of grease in the trap. When it happened to me, I got our heat (infrared) lamp and directed it on the trap under the sink. Soon it had melted the grease, and by running hot water through it I cleaned it out good."

"Next time you have to remove the drains under your sink, coat the threads on the pipe and inside the union with petroleum jelly before replacing them. This will accomplish two things: (1) The connection will be better sealed, and thus dripless, and (2) the union will be much easier to remove the next time."

"If any of your other readers need to locate a buried plastic drainpipe, as I did recently, my trick may come in handy. I ran a plumber's snake into the drainpipe and then went out to the yard with my magnetic treasure-finder. The metal snake showed up on the finder gauge, telling me where the pipe was. Oddly enough, the pipe was nowhere near where I had thought it would be; so if I had been guessing, I would probably have dug my pond in the wrong place and plowed right into the pipe."

"After I cut through a water pipe while digging holes for fence posts, I decided to protect the new pipes from myself and anyone else who might dig around in the yard. After the pipe was in place and before the trench was filled in, I placed slats of scrap redwood, creosoted for extra protection against decay, over the entire length of the pipe. Then the dirt was filled in over the top of the slats. Now anything sharp being used for digging will strike the wood before the pipe can be reached. Already it may have paid off. We had a new tree set out, and the nurseryman would have hit the pipe if it were not for my protectors."

"A discarded length of BX electrical cable will perform just about as well as a plumber's snake. It's flexible enough to be fed into the pipes and around the curves. A slight rotation as the cable is fed in will help it along. After you reach the trouble spot, rotate the cable until it bores through. You may wish to flare out the end a bit so it will gouge into the blockage. Don't flare it too much, or the cable will have trouble negotiating the curves."

"Often when water continues to flow after flushing the toilet, residue has formed on the rubber float inside the tank and weighted it down. If about three tablespoons of ordinary soap flakes is put in the water closet and allowed to stand overnight, the soap will remove the corrosion. Other parts of the water closet will also be improved. By applying the soap this way in my bathrooms every few months for the past several years, I have not had to replace a single rubber float."

"Here is an emergency repair trick for the hollow float-ball in a water closet. With the water supply turned off, drain the tank. Remove the float-ball and drain all the water from it. Replace it and get a plastic bag large enough to cover the ball and extend about halfway up the float-ball rod. Tie the end of the plastic bag securely around the rod. If it is tied right, it will keep water away from the float-ball and last until you have a chance to get a new float-ball."

"The metal float-ball inside our toilet developed a leak. I took it into the plant, and our supervisor let me fix it for nothing. So the family still had a working flush toilet while I was at work, I taped a plastic detergent bottle with the cap on to the float arm, and this acted as well as the float-ball. If you try it, just be sure to get a bottle big enough to raise the float arm and yet not big enough to get in the way of anything else. Tape several inches of the bottle to the arm, and, of course, use a waterproof tape."

"A loose tank top on a commode is subject to being cracked from the movement against the tank. One quick way to stop movement is to put a coat of rubber cement around the rim of the tank. This will not seal the top on permanently—just stop it from banging around."

PLYWOOD   "Sometimes when you're cutting a sheet of plywood, you get a splintery edge. You can eliminate this completely by putting a strip of masking tape along the intended cutting line. You'll saw right through the paper tape, and when you strip it off, you'll have a clean-cut edge."

Waterfalling makes the surface grain on finished wood appear to flow over the edge of the wood. A reader tells how to waterfall plywood, and at the same time hide the plywood edge: "Cut the plywood oversized on all sides to be finished. Cut off a strip at least as wide as the plywood is thick. Then cut off the first layer of veneer. Glue this on the edge, and you will have an almost perfect waterfall."

In the use of plywood paneling outside, many home handymen will skip over one very important step: sealing the back and edges of the plywood. Even though these parts are not actually exposed to weather, moisture has a way of getting to these areas too, and this can cause trouble in years to come. A primer is all that is needed for the back, but the edges should be given a coat of exterior paint that will seal them up.

POISONS   "Ant poison can attract not only ants, but children or pets. My holder made from a pair of bottle caps keeps this poison away from all but the insects. First, take a block of scrap wood. Place one bottle cap upside down on the wood and put the other on top of it rightside up. Then drive a nail through both bottle caps. Before driving the nail all the way down, place the ant poison into the bottom bottle cap. Then drive the nail on down, leaving only a fraction of an inch

Bottle caps →

between the two caps. To make sure the ants can get in, place a toothpick between the two caps to form a gap. If you can put the poison out on a surface that can stand a nail hole, nail down the block so it cannot be turned over. Then nothing but an ant can get to the poison."

"To safeguard mouse poison, I merely cut a hole in the side of a coffee can. The hole should be about the size of a silver dollar. With the poison on the inside and the plastic top back on the can, our pets cannot get into the small hole, but the mice can. To make sure the can is not tipped over, it could be nailed down to the floor in a cabinet or on a spot where the nail hole won't show."

(... Or, the can could be stuck to the floor by running rubber cement around the rim. However, that silver-dollar-sized hole would keep out some of the Texas-sized mice.)

Opening

"One of the dangers of putting out poison to get rid of rats and mice is the possibility that a cat or dog will take the bait instead. I put the poison in an empty one-gallon turpentine can and lay it down on its side with the opening down nearest the ground. A mouse can get in the can without any problem, but your pet cannot."

(This is a good safe place for the bait. Be sure to clean the can, though, as the turpentine odor may keep mice away.)

"If you have an accumulation of jars and bottles that contain poison, here is an added precaution. On the highest shelf in your shop or garage, mount some empty coffee cans by means of a screw through the bottom of the can and into the shelf. Store the bottles inside these, with the plastic lids on the cans. This will eliminate the possibility of accidentally knocking off a glass bottle, and also will keep children from getting into poisons. If looks count, paint the cans."

PULLEYS Pulleys are usually hung up high and hard to get to. Since they're usually metal, they occasionally need oiling. Here's a tricky way to get the oil to the pulley. Tie a sponge tightly around the

rope and soak it with oil. Then pull the rope so the sponge goes through the pulley. As the sponge is pulled through, the oil will be squeezed out and will lubricate the pulley. Pull it back and forth through the pulley several times. This is an idea you can run up the flagpole!

"If you ever need a small pulley and don't have one, confiscate an empty wooden spool from your wife's sewing basket. This can be held on a frame made from coat hanger wire. The wire frame goes through the hole in the spool so the spool can rotate around it. The top of the frame need only be a loop from which the pulley is suspended. Hang it up, and you have a homemade pulley."

(Of course, this makeshift pulley can't be used for hoisting car engines, but it sure is a clever idea for a lightweight job like awnings that need to be raised and lowered.)

PUTTYING   "Next time you knead putty, don't worry about getting the stuff all over your hands. Put it in a plastic bag along with a few drops of linseed oil. If you just have to get the feel of putty on your hands, put flour on them first, and it won't stick. If you have much puttying to do, take along extra flour and keep your hands dusted as you work."

"When puttying, one thing that must be done is to keep the putty knife clean. This can be done by using a putty can that has had a slit cut in the side the same width as the thickness of the putty knife blade. To clean off the blade, all you need do is insert it in the slit at the handle, and then pull it straight out. The putty on the blade will be scraped off into the can for reuse, and the blade will be clean as a whistle."

Slit

Another way to keep your knife clean is by palming a small piece of steel wool in your left hand. Presoak it in linseed oil. Now as you work, keep rubbing the blade of the putty knife into the steel wool as putty starts to stick, and your chore will go much faster and more smoothly.

Putting in new window panes works better if all the old putty is removed. After most of it has been scraped away, apply the brush attachment on your power drill around the window frame. A quick swipe with this will remove the last traces and make for a much better glazing job. But do it fast, so as not to allow the brush to dig into the wood.

"Old, dried-out putty is often difficult to remove. Try heating it with your soldering iron, and it will come loose much easier. Actually touch the surface with the iron, but keep it moving. Then come right along behind it with your scraper. The putty still retains some of its oil, and the heat brings it back to life and softens the putty."

"If you're puttying in a wood-framed window, here is a trick that will improve the bond of the putty. Borrow your wife's tracing wheel from her sewing basket. Run this along the strip on the window frame where you plan to putty. As the putty is worked into place, it will be forced into the little holes made by the spiked wheel and have added 'roots' when dry."

"Anyone knows that putty is much more pliable when warm. When it is still cool outdoors, maybe this will help any of your readers who have to do some puttying. Put a brick in the oven until it is hot. Carry this in a bucket and keep your putty container on top of the brick while you're working. The brick holds the heat for a long time, and the putty stays quite pliable."

"Here's a hint that will save time when you're painting and run across nail holes that need to be filled. If you use putty, the recommended procedure is to wait until the putty dries. However, by making your own putty from cornstarch and the paint you're using, you can fill in the holes and paint over them immediately. Just add enough cornstarch to a tablespoon of paint so that you develop a mixture the consistency of putty, and push it in place with your thumb."

"If you sometime need only a tiny amount of putty, you can make up a small batch at home from linseed oil and talcum powder. Add a few drops of linseed oil to the powder, and mix. Keep adding oil until the mixture reaches the texture and consistency of putty. This can be worked into holes just like putty and painted over when dry "

Q

QUICKIES   Many times something can be done a quick way that will "get by" even though it may not be the best way. Hence this group of quickies.

"Need a fast scaffold? Maybe your picnic table will serve the purpose. It has plenty of working space and is a good sturdy place to stand."

"For quick measurement of long lumber, convert your shop floor into a giant rule by marking off 6″ intervals for 8′ or 10′. Start at a wall that can be used to butt the board against. For odd inches, keep a small rule handy."

Dull shop shears or tin snips will often do more harm than good. If you don't have the time or tools to do a proper job, quickie sharpening can be done by cutting through a sheet of fine sandpaper several times. This works best if you put two sheets back to back.

"If you don't have a shop apron, make a one-shot job out of one of those plastic suit bags from the cleaners. Cut holes for arms and head, and when the apron has been slipped on, fold up the excess at the bottom to form a pocket for small parts and tools. Tape the pockets in place."

"Some of us aren't fast enough, and while we're working with a compound, it dries out before we use it up. I'm a slowpoke, but have found a quick way to revive some compounds. Spackling compound can be restored by adding white glue until it's back to the right consistency. Plastic wood can be made plastic again with lacquer thinner, polish remover, or lighter fluid."

"We keep a big looseleaf book called *Where It's At*. Each time we store something away, we note in this book where we put it. Now we have a quick reference instead of having to look through half a dozen boxes."

"I have quick light in case of a power failure, because I've stashed inexpensive flashlights at strategic places throughout the house. To be sure I can find the flashlights, I put luminous paint on them so they can still be seen if the lights go out."

"Not long ago, I ran across an odd-sized nut that none of my wrenches would fit. I went over to borrow one from my neighbor, and although he didn't have the right size either, we quickly made a wrench that was a perfect fit. We took a piece of scrap iron the size of a large mending plate and made a pair of cuts with a hacksaw. The distance between the cuts was the same as the width of the nut, and the cuts were made about ½″ deep. The strip between the two cuts was then bent back. The space this left was just right to fit the odd nut, and it was then turned with ease."

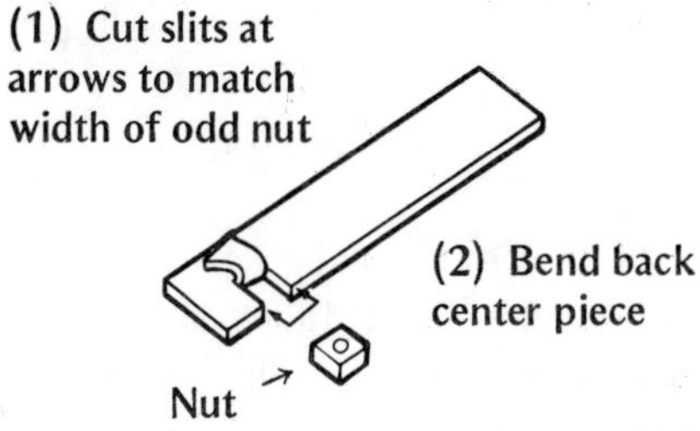

(1) Cut slits at arrows to match width of odd nut

(2) Bend back center piece

Nut

Rags • Rasps • Razor Blades • Razor Care • Razor Uses
• Reassembly • Remodeling • Retaining Wall • Rivets
• Roof • Rope • Router Bits • Rubber Bands •
Rubber Cement • Rubber Suction Cup • Rugs • Rust

R.

RAGS   Home handymen are always in need of rags to use in cleaning, wiping, applying, and scores of other tasks. Here's a tip to save you
some headaches: When you get ready to retire those old pajamas and
decide to make shop rags, cut them out with a pair of pinking shears
instead of tearing them to size. You'll find that they're much less likely
to unravel and, therefore, won't leave threads on your new paint job or
in some other disastrous place. (As a matter of fact, gals, why not do
this for your handy husbands? It will leave them more time to fix that
squeaking door.)

RASPS   "I got a bargain on some hacksaw blades, so I bought a
bunch of them. To store them, I bolted them all together. By accident,
I discovered that these blades bolted together make a really good rasp.
If any of your readers ever need a rasp and don't have one, this is a
good substitute. Just be sure all the teeth are aimed the same way
before the blades are bolted together."

RAZOR BLADES   "Rather than having to buy single-edged razor
blades for shop use, if you shave with a double-edged razor, use my
trick and eliminate the danger to fingers from using double-edged
blades. I save the striker part from book matches, and this makes a
good handle and hand-protector for a double-edged blade."

Matchbook cover

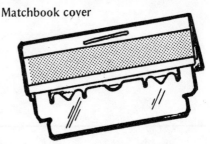

Here's another way: "I use a small butt hinge as a holder for the
blade. Mine is about the same size as the blade. The blade is placed
between the two leaves of the hinge, held tightly together by a pair of
tiny bolts through the corresponding holes in the two hinge leaves and
the slot in the blade. This gives me a good grip, too."

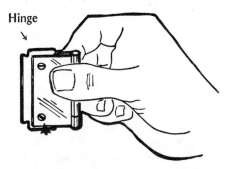

Hinge

"Almost every home handyman uses razor blades quite regularly in the workshop. I installed a holder for them over on the corner of my workbench so they're always where I can find them. I took a scrap of wood and made slots with my saw to hold the razor blades. The block is a little wider than the blades, and the slots are about ½" deep. The saw kerf is plenty wide enough to accommodate the razor blades. They stay sharp longer because they don't come in contact with other tools and get nicked."

(Add a piece of masking tape around the outside of the block, and you'll form a frame that will keep the razor blades from being accidentally knocked out sideways.)

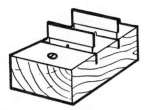

"I just glued a big old cork on the shop wall and use it to stick my razor blade in. The blade stays put when in place in the cork, but comes out easily. When the cork wears out, it can be replaced, but mine has lasted for a long time."

Here's a way to keep a razor blade from running around loose in your tool box or drawer: Take an empty match folder, stick the blade down in behind the match striker, and close the cover. The blade will be easier to find and less likely to get damaged, and you won't run the risk of slicing your finger while digging around for something else.

RAZOR CARE "Any man who uses a blade to shave with will find this to be a help in getting more and better shaves from any kind of blade. Between shaves, I store my razor—with the blade in it—in a small glass jar that has about an inch of rubbing alcohol inside. The jar is capped to keep the alcohol from evaporating. This keeps both the blade and the razor from developing any rust or corrosion, and thus makes for a keener edge. The alcohol also kills any bacteria, and prevents any facial infection. If you'll try this, you'll find it a great improvement."

RAZOR USES "I just bought a new razor and was delighted with the shop use I came up with for the old one. I made a twine cutter that's installed in a stud in my shop wall. I drilled a hole the same size as the handle of the razor. The hole is at a slight angle and is shallow enough so that about an inch of the handle still sticks out. I also drilled a hole through the handle in the part that sticks out; this is for the string to go through. Then I coated the handle with adhesive, inserted it into the hole, and twisted it so the blade would be at the best angle. It looks neat and works well."

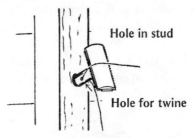

Hole in stud

Hole for twine

(This will only work if your razor allows for blade changes from the top. However, you can probably figure out how to adapt this good idea to any type of old razor . . . except an electric.)

"Here's another use for an old safety razor. I made a bench stop from one. At the proper spot, I drilled a hole in my workbench the right size for the handle of the razor. When the razor is dropped in, the head sticks out, and by putting the work up against the end of the razor, you have a fine stop."

REASSEMBLY "According to the old clock on the wall, there was something wrong, and so I decided to take it apart and see what kept it from ticking. Well aware that I had no idea what I was doing, I used this helper to keep all the parts in order. I put a piece of masking tape down with the sticky side up. As each part was removed, I placed it on the tape and it stuck there. I placed the parts in the order in which they were removed, which made the reassembly a snap. All the pieces got back in the proper place. (No, the clock still doesn't work, but I felt the tape idea was worth passing on.)"

"Anytime I have to work over any kind of motor, the biggest problem is to get it put back together again. I've learned to go in ahead of time and code everything I will need to disconnect. I do this with a tiny artist's brush. If the surface is large enough, I number the two connections. If it is too small, I color-code them. The insides of all our household and shop gadgets look a little funny, but I don't end up with a bunch of parts I can't find a place for."

"There are probably thousands of radios that have been torn down for repair that the home handyman never quite got back together. (I have one.) The next time I decided to repair one, I took steps that helped in reassembly. I put masking tape on each wire as I removed it from a tube or connection. On the tape, I wrote where the piece was taken from, so it could go back there. The tubes were also taped with identification tags: a different-colored dot of paint at the base of each and a corresponding dot on the chassis told me exactly where they were to go and in what position to put them. These simple guidelines helped me to get the radio back together and working."

REMODELING   "We remodeled our house and decided to do away with a seldom-used door in our kitchen. However, instead of just walling over the door, we did something that we modestly think is *super*. We walled up the opening of the door and left the door itself, which opens into the kitchen. This means we ended up with a closet that is only the thickness of the wall in depth. We put shelves from top to bottom and have an ideal pantry for canned goods. It will hold over a hundred cans and boxes of food."

(Even if you have a door you want to do away with in another room, this idea would be well worth considering, as there are lots of small items that could go into a skinny closet like this.)

RETAINING WALL   "We needed a retaining wall at the rear of our property. My method for building this was unique. The wall was made of bags of cement, placed in courses like bricks. As each course was laid, it was placed right up against the slope. Each ensuing course was put so the joints were staggered. As I went along, I drove scraps of reinforcing steel down through the bags. Each piece of steel was long enough to go vertically through at least three bags. When the stack was finished, I turned a hose on it to fully saturate the cement. After it set up, we had a strong wall at very little cost and effort. To hide it, we have planted vines."

(Entire houses are now being built using this method, which is called stack-sack construction.)

RIVETS   "Spent .22 shells make excellent rivets. Insert the shells into predrilled holes in the work to be riveted. Cut them off about 1/16″ longer than the thickness of the work. The shells can then be flared by placing a ball bearing in the opening and tapping with a hammer. These will give you a highly professional-looking rivet. Next time you're around a rifle range, stick a handful of empties in your pocket for future use."

ROOF   If you have an emergency roof repair during cold weather, and it calls for plastic patching cement, your biggest problem will probably be keeping the compound spreadable. Cold temperatures act adversely on the character of this material. Warm it up before you go on the roof, but also take along a small container of kerosene. Keep dipping the spreader into the kerosene, and the cement will remain much more spreadable. A hot brick wrapped in cloth will also help to keep the mixture warmer longer.

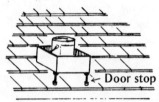

Here's a rooftop paint bucket and tool-holder idea: "As you can see, it's merely a small wooden box I got from a grocery store, with a pair of rubber-tipped door stops. The door stops (the kind you screw into the wall) are screwed into the bottom of the box so that, when placed on the slanting roof, they keep the box level. You need to take the box up on the roof before installing the door stops, so that they can be placed at the right spot on the box to make it level. It sure makes roof staining a lot easier."

"When working on a roof or other sloping area, there's nothing more exasperating than to have your hammer slide off. Besides, it could hit someone below. It's a good idea to make your hammer slideproof by taping the shank of the head with several rounds of friction tape."

Tape

"My temporary roof repair method has worked rather well. I had some split shingles and no flashing to slip under them. I made flashing out of plastic bags with a piece of cardboard slipped inside to make them rigid enough to slide under the damaged shingles. I've tested out the places where these temporary repairs were made, and so far, there has been no failure."

ROPE   If you want to prevent a knot in the end of a rope from untieing, dip it into a container of thinned shellac or thinned glue. If you ever have to undo the knot, dip it in a solvent that will dissolve the glue or shellac—and get ready to cuss quite a bit.

"Most of us have rope stuck back somewhere that is used only once in a while. After a time, a rope will get too stiff to use. Usually a simple bath in hot soapy water is all it will need to regain the softness and therefore the flexibility it should have. Once you get it back into shape, it will stay that way even longer if you will dip it in linseed oil."

A too-short rope can be almost as bad as no rope at all . . . unless you can add on to it. One way to splice rope is with a short length of soft metal tubing. Insert the ends of the two pieces of rope into the tube. Crimp the tubing with pliers to flatten it. This will clamp the two pieces together, and you will have a fairly strong bond. However, this type of splice is not recommended for use in mountain climbing or for cattle rustling.

Pencil sharpener cutter shaft

ROUTER BITS   "I used the two rotary cutters from a discarded desk-type pencil sharpener to make a pair of useful shop tools. Each cutter was welded to a metal shaft, and they're now very inexpensive router bits. They do a very smooth job of routing and curved sanding when used in a power drill."

RUBBER BANDS   "Next time your wife wears out a pair of rubber gloves, don't let her throw them away. They can be cut into rubber bands of any width you want and almost any size. Very small ones can be cut from the fingers, on up to bigger ones from the palm. I'm always finding a shop use for an odd-sized rubber band."

RUBBER CEMENT   "When rubber cement gets too thick and you've run out of thinner, a little cigarette lighter fluid will thin it down just the way it should be. Maybe some of your readers quit smoking as I did and ended up with a can of lighter fluid that they can now put to good use."

RUBBER SUCTION CUP "The next time you need to fasten something to a wall by means of a rubber suction cup, apply a little soft soap to make it behave. Just rub the suction cup over a wet bar of soap before you put it on the wall. You'll find it will stay in place a lot better—and it will leave less of a ring on the wall if it should be removed later."

"Rubber suction cups sometimes lose their grip because the rim dries out and then becomes ragged. We had one that had suffered this fate, and before tossing it out I decided to trim the edges and see if it could be restored. As soon as the frayed edges were gone, it could grab a surface again, and it worked as good as new. A coat of liquid wax or a silicone spray will keep cups from getting into this shape."

RUGS "Like most rugs, ours had the affliction of curling up at the corners. I would like to pass along my husband's method for solving this common household problem. From scraps of pegboard, he cut four right triangles. Using the holes already in the pegboard, he sewed one of these triangles to the underside of each corner of the rug. They prevent curling, but don't show from the top."

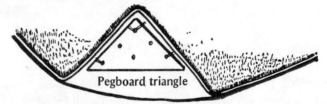

Pegboard triangle

"Cut a triangular piece of asphalt or rubber tile for each corner of the rug. Glue a triangle on the underside of each corner, and the rug will lie flat. Use rubber cement so the tiles can be removed for cleaning."

"I coat the entire bottom of the rug with thin rubber cement. When it dries, it stiffens the corners and makes the rug stay in place on the floor."

RUST "The handiest thing I've found for removing small rust spots is a secretarial typing eraser. If you use the pencil kind, it will enable you to get into all sorts of hard-to-reach places. This is a particularly good tool for electrical tinkering on spots that must be cleaned for contact."

These typewriter erasers also come on the end of a ball-point pen for office use, and can be tightened down in the chuck of your electric drill, thus giving you a power buffer. An ordinary eraser can also be chucked for polishing metal. With either kind of eraser, be sure that there's plenty of eraser left, so the metal holder doesn't scratch the metalwork.

"When you have metal parts that must be stored, they need to be protected against rust. Most people use heavy grease, which works but is quite messy. I've found that I accomplish the same thing by spraying the parts with rust-preventive paint. When it's time to take the parts 'out of mothballs,' the paint can easily be removed with paint-removing solvent if it has to come off. No rust and no mess."

"For really stubborn rust, you'll find this trick very helpful: Dip a steel wool pad into kerosene and go to work on the rust spots with this. Even the toughest ones will come loose with this attack."

Sand • Sanding • Sanding Blocks • Sandpaper • Saw-bucks • Sawdust • Sawhorses • Saws • Scaffolding • Scissors • Scrapers • Scratches • Screens • Screwdrivers • Screw Eyes • Screws—Loose, Botched, Frozen • Scribe • Set Screws • Shelves • Signs • Siphoning • Soldering • Speakers • Sports • Spray Cans and Sprayers • Squares • Staples and Stapling • Steel Wool • Storage • Straightedges • String • Stud Finders • Studs • Swimming

S.

SAND   "When you're sifting sand, it invariably has lumps that won't break up until you hit them with your shovel. Most of these lumps will break up as you sift if you throw a length of heavy chain on the screen along with the sand. If you don't have chain handy, put a half shovelful of medium-sized gravel on the screen."

SANDING   "Here is a groovey trick that may come in handy when you need to sand down in a groove. Back the sandpaper with a lump of modeling clay. It can be molded to any shape and will shape the sandpaper to fit the groove better."

There are times when you need to sand small items. Most sanding blocks will not give you a very delicate touch, and often will do away with the visibility you need. In such cases, you will probably do better to clamp the block into your vise and move the work over the abrasive.

"Many home handymen borrow emery boards from their wives for use as small rasps in sanding or as files in the shop. However, shop use is pretty rough on them, and the edges wear out awfully fast. These frayed edges can be trimmed off with a pair of scissors, and then the emery board can be used again. Each time the edge becomes ragged, it can be trimmed again."

SANDING BLOCKS   Next time you visit a site where a new house is going up, see if there's a scrap of handrail around. This will make an excellent sanding block. It has a top already shaped for your hand to grip and a flat side around which you can place sandpaper (held onto the block with a rubber band). This is actually better-shaped for your hand than many of the sanding blocks on the market, and better priced too—free!

"I converted one good shop tool to another good use. I made my plane into a sanding block, and this works out great. It allows you to sand with both hands and with an excellent grip. All I did was remove the blade from the plane, cut a strip of sandpaper about ½″ longer than the plane bottom, apply a coat of rubber cement to the back of the sandpaper, and stick the paper to the plane bottom. About ¼″ of the paper should be folded up on the leading and trailing edges—this keeps it from being pulled loose as you move it back and forth. When the sanding is done, the paper and rubber cement are easily peeled off the plane."

"Here is my sanding block creation that is easy to make and works well. A pair of 1 x 4's are cut to an easy-to-handle size. A strip of leather is used as a hinge on the end of the two blocks. Now a series of inch-long nails is driven into the top board along each side and about ½″ from the edge. The nails will go through the top board, of course, and into the bottom. Now, when the sandpaper is wrapped around the bottom block, and the top block is clamped down, the nails in the top block will go down into the holes they made and hold the sandpaper in place for sanding."

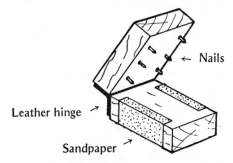

← Nails

Leather hinge ↗

Sandpaper ↗

"Maybe some other handymen can use my idea for sanding inside a curved area. I merely roll up a magazine, and then roll the sandpaper around it. This gives me a sanding surface rigid enough to get the job done, and yet flexible enough to conform to the curves. It is also adjustable in size to fit the job."

"Here's a card trick: For sanding down in a curved place, just put sandpaper around a deck of playing cards. The cards push down to follow the contour of the wood. Then when you grip the deck tightly, it holds the shape, and you have a perfectly contoured sanding block."

Another reader felt that sawdust and playing cards don't mix. Here's his idea: "Take a strip of corrugated board. It rolls up nicely. When the roll is large enough, cut off the rest and wrap the sandpaper around the roll. It is stiff enough to sand with, and yet can be molded a bit to size. It is also easy to get a grip on."

"Don't throw away a worn-out shoeshine brush. It makes a great sanding block for irregular surfaces. The sandpaper should be wrapped around the brush part and can be held in place by your hands while sanding. There's enough give to the brush for sanding uneven places."

(And if you don't have a shoebrush, a kitchen scrub brush may do the job.)

Here's a clever idea for a specially curved sanding block: Borrow an old teaspoon from the kitchen and wrap a small piece of sandpaper around the bottom. Your forefinger placed in the bowl of the spoon will hold the sandpaper tight around the spoon and also apply pressure as you're sanding. Keep this one in mind, and maybe it will be just right for a future curved sanding job.

"Here's another small sanding block that you'll find very helpful and handy. Take a section of a flat telescoping curtain rod. You can use a long skinny section, or a very short one. Your sandpaper can be cut to fit around the outside piece with enough over to fit inside this section. The smaller rod that slides inside can then be put in, and this will hold the abrasive paper in place. A long section of curtain rod can become a sanding stick if a small piece of sandpaper is put on the end. This can give you lots of extra reach for a small sanding task in a hard-to-reach spot."

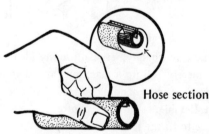

Hose section

And another curved sanding block "is made from a section of old garden hose about 4″ long. Slit the hose along a straight line the full length of the section. Cut a piece of sandpaper to a size a little more than enough to fit around the section of hose. Fold the edge of the sandpaper down and slip the fold down into the slit. Wrap the paper tight around the hose and fold the remainder down into the slit from the other side. The hose will naturally spring back together at the slit and hold the paper in place. The hose is easy to grip, too."

"One of the best creative sanding blocks I've run across is a rubber heel off an old shoe. First, you cut a slit in opposite edges of the heel. This is for the sheet of sandpaper to fit into. The rubber then allows you to open the slit to accommodate the sandpaper. Once the paper is in, the heel will hold it in place. The ideal part about it is that it's a hand-sized sanding block. Also, the rubber allows a little flexibility that is sometimes helpful."

"I made a unique small curved sanding block that may help someone else on some project. I used an old discarded safety razor. The sandpaper fits around the outside edge and can be clamped in place fairly tightly by closing the razor on the paper."

SANDPAPER   "If you need a finer grade of sandpaper than you happen to have on hand, you can actually 'fine up' the grit by carefully running the sandpaper across your grinding wheel. You really must use your very lightest touch or you'll make it so fine that it's just paper. It's better to start with the right grit, of course, but this trick will work in a pinch."

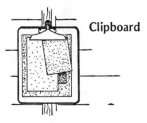

Clipboard

"An old retired clipboard can be put back in service by using it as a holder for sheets of sandpaper. After putting the sheets in the clip, add a piece of heavy cardboard as a top layer to keep the sandpaper from curling out. Then hang the clipboard on the shop wall by a nail, so it's out of the way but in easy reach. When you need sandpaper, the entire holder can be taken off the wall and carried to your project."

SAWBUCKS   If you're ever stumped for a sawbuck, here's an idea. "If you've an old tree stump that's big enough, it can be converted to a great sawbuck. Cut it off flat on the top, and then cut a big 'V' across the center. A saw slot should be cut at right angles to the V. The timber to be cut is laid down in the V."

Or, "My sawbuck is a 55-gallon oil drum with a pair of V's cut in the rim to hold the logs for cutting. The drum is filled with sand for weight."

SAWDUST   "I'm always looking for ways to use things most people throw away. Finally I've learned of a great use for the accumulation of sawdust from my workshop—it makes excellent mulch for flower beds and plants. I checked it out with a nurseryman, and he says it's very good."

SAWHORSES   There are many times when I've wished my sawhorse were wider, so that it would provide a bigger working area. One of my neighbors solved this problem with a removable top for his sawhorse. It's quite simple to make and well worth the time. He cut a 1" x 12" board to the same length as his sawhorse. In a line along the middle of the board, he installed three tire bolts about 2' apart. (You'll recall that tire bolts have heads that can be countersunk.) In his sawhorse, he drilled three holes all the way through to match the bolts. When he needs a wider sawhorse, he puts the top on and tightens it down with nuts under the sawhorse. Since the bolts are countersunk, the top still has a smooth surface. When he's through with the wide top, it lifts out, and the holes in the sawhorse don't interfere with its regular uses.

Hinges →

Folding leg brace →

Rope

"My workshop is in my garage, and with the car in, there isn't enough room for all the things I would like for the various shop projects. One way I've conserved space is with my collapsible sawhorses. They can be stored flat against the wall, hanging from nails. They're made from two pieces of plywood about 2½' high by 4' wide, hinged together at the top. A folding leg brace (the kind of gadget found on folding card tables) is attached to each about halfway down. A rope handle is attached through a pair of holes in the top of one of the pieces of plywood. This is used for carrying as well as hanging. These folding horses are capable of holding a good work load, and yet are lightweight and can be made flat for storage."

"Most home handymen have so many saw cuts in their sawhorses that the top is rougher than a washboard. I've made a top for my sawhorse out of two boards. When I nailed them on, I left a 2" gap between them. When I am sawing so that the blade would normally hit the sawhorse, I just arrange so the blade goes down into the gap."

"In an emergency, you can turn your stepladder over on its side and open it up fully, and you'll have an excellent sawhorse. It's a little bit lower than a regular horse, but will work fine."

SAWS   Keep a bar of soap in your workshop, and lubricate your saw blades with this instead of machine oil. Just rub the dry bar over the blade and leave a thin film. With soap there's never a stain on the wood being cut.

"When sharpening a saw, it's all too easy to skip a tooth or two along the way. If you run a dauber with liquid shoe polish (a dark color) along the teeth, you'll have no problem telling which has and which hasn't been filed on."

Here's another stunt for the handyman who sharpens his own saw. Before you start, take a lighted candle and run it along the saw teeth until a coat of soot covers them. This will enable you to tell which teeth you've sharpened on, since your file will remove the soot as you go along.

"In using a saber saw, there are times when the blade sticks down far enough through the work to hit something underneath. This happened to me recently, and I made a U-shaped block out of ½" plywood that I attached to the base of my saber saw. This, in effect, shortened the blade ½". However, the blade still extended far enough beyond the new base to cut through the work."

A section of garden hose can be used as a pad to allow the home handyman to put downward pressure on a saw. Another Super Handyman accomplished the same thing in another way. "I use a scrap of tongue-and-groove flooring about 5" long. The groove part fits over the top of the saw blade, and you can apply all the hand pressure to the blade that might be needed. It won't work any better than the hose section, but some of us have already used up our old hose on all those other ideas you've published."

"When cutting large sheets of plywood on a table saw, it helps to have a sawhorse taller than normal to rest the work on. I solved this problem by stacking my two sawhorses one on top of the other. Then, since this still was not quite level, I used a pair of C-clamps to hold the legs on one side of the top horse to those on the bottom one. I raised the top one until it was high enough, and then tightened down the clamps."

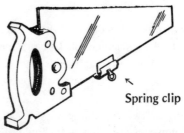

Spring clip

"When working with a saw, many a home handyman will damage it by laying it down so the teeth hit against some surface. When I lay my saw down, it rests on its back with the teeth pointed up, so that there is no danger they will hit anything. Also, there is no danger of setting something down on the blade that would hurt it. The saw is able to stand up because I clip a spring-type clip on the back side of the blade. Place the clip far enough away from the saw handle so that the two clip handles and the saw handle form a tripod on which the saw will rest. The clip will stay in place while you use the saw."

"When you're sawing through plywood or ripping a warped board, the wood is probably going to bind the saw blade. I prevent this by dropping a pocket knife into the kerf. It will not fall through the slit and will keep it apart so it won't bind the blade."

Cutting intricate designs out of plywood will often result in splintering along the edges. A coat of shellac around the design will banish the chipping and splintering. If the work is to be finished later, put the shellac on the back or underneath.

"Another way to keep plywood from chipping and splintering when being cut is to score the line to be cut. If possible, score both sides of the plywood. (This can be done when you're making a straight cut.) I find this really makes for a smoother cut."

"When sawing with a hand saw, here's a way to get a smoother cut and stay right on the intended line: Instead of using a pencil to mark the intended cut, use a small triangular-shaped file. Run this along the straight edge with enough downward pressure to make a groove on the work. This is another one you can 'file' away for future reference."

If your handsaw consistently strays away from the straight and narrow line you're trying to follow, there's a simple remedy. The saw probably needs a very slight dressing along the edge of the teeth on the side *toward* which it strays. Run your finest oilstone ever so lightly along the teeth. Chances are, your saw will wander no more.

SCAFFOLDING   "Here's a simple safety step: Paint a broad, bright band at each end of your paint scaffolding. This will serve as a warning that you're reaching the danger zone. About a 4″ to 6″ stripe will be enough for you to be sure that you never work too close to the edge."

Pipe strap   →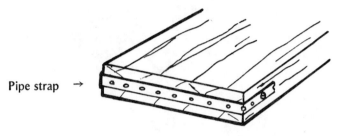

"Any home handyman who has scaffolding boards will want to use this reinforcing idea I picked up from a professional painter. Boards are most vulnerable at the ends. By running a strip of perforated pipe strap around the end edges, these areas will be reinforced. Attach the strip with wood screws. The strap will act as a clamp and prevent the board from splitting on the ends. Also, the metal strap will take the banging around better than the wood."

"The few times a home handyman would have use for scaffolding may make this kind of equipment a bad investment. However, a sturdy scaffold can be made by using a pair of stepladders and a straight ladder. After the straight ladder has been placed across the stepladders, a wide board can be laid down on the rungs to form the platform. Since the ladder is designed to hold your weight anyway, there is no problem V notches with it breaking with you on it, as there might be with a board by ↓ itself."

SCISSORS   "A pair of long-nosed scissors can become a useful tool box addition. File a 'V' notch in the very end of each blade, and you'll have a handy tool for holding small parts such as nuts and screws in position in tight places. Also, the scissors are still able to do some cutting chores around the shop."

SCRAPERS   If you have to scrape off flaking paint, here's a scrapeɪ you can make in just a few minutes that does an excellent job. Take a piece of wire screen and a block of wood that's big enough to grip well. Wrap the screen around the block and fasten it on the back with nails or staples. This will make quick work of paint flakes.

"I took an old paintbrush and cut the bristles off right up next to the metal ferrule. I then wrapped wire mesh (hardware cloth) around the brush stub and stapled it to the wood part above the metal band. This gave me a paint scraper with a handle."

Hardware cloth wrapped around brush stub →

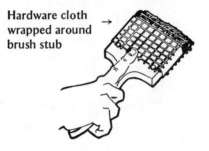

SCRATCHES   "I've discovered a good cover-up for scratches on finished wood. I use a felt marking pen. This type of pen comes in so many different colors that it's a sure bet you'll find one that matches. After you're through covering up scratches, the marking pen is still good for its intended use."

SCREENS   "With the storm windows put away and the screens back up, it might be a good time to check screens for any small holes. Screens with holes of about ¼″ to ½″ need not be repaired with the time-consuming weaving process. Take some clear nail polish and dab it around the hole. As soon as it's dry, dab it again. Keep this up until the hole is covered. Since polish dries very fast, you'll be able to put on several layers in a matter of minutes."

SCREWDRIVERS   "Those of you that keep your screwdrivers in holders with only the handles showing have probably reached for a standard screwdriver and pulled back a phillips head instead . . . or maybe you had to pull up more than one to find the size you wanted. No need for wasting time, if you mark the tops of the handles. Put a '+' for phillips heads, and a '−' for standards. Graduate the size of the mark with the size of the screwdriver tip. One of the best ways for either wood or plastic handles is to burn the mark on with a red-hot ice pick. Sure does away with the guessing contest."

When you run across a stubborn screw, give your screwdriver extra bite by coating the tip with chalk. This will cut down on the possibility of its slipping out of the slot. Regular old blackboard chalk is as good as any for this. Be sure to use the proper size and kind of screwdriver, too, as this also helps to prevent slipping.

"Here's a neat trick to get more leverage in a screwdriver. Drill a hole through the handle, big enough to accommodate a large nail. With the nail through the handle, you can grasp the nail, and you get a lot of extra power, just as you do with a longer handle on a socket wrench."

"Here's another way to get more leverage on a screwdriver. Use a square-shaft screwdriver and put a small- or medium-size crescent wrench on the shaft. This will let you add all the power the screw slot can take without breaking."

"Since I'm a widow, I do all the handyman chores around our house. You've really given me some good ideas, but here's one I learned from my father. A woman usually needs extra strength when using a screw-driver on a tough screw. A claw hammer can provide lots of extra leverage. Put the claw down on the tip of the screwdriver. Move the 'V' of the claw up tight against the tip of the screwdriver. Now you can grip the handle of the hammer with your right hand, and this gives great leverage."

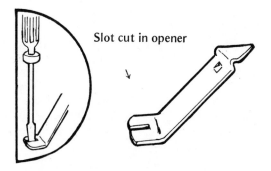

Slot cut in opener

"From an old beer-can opener, I've made a screwdriver wrench. It is so designed that it fits on the flat tip of the screwdriver and gives me a lot of extra leverage. All I did was to cut a slit in the rounded end that was formerly used to remove bottle caps. The slit is big enough to fit snugly over the tip of the screwdriver. The remainder of the beer opener is wrapped with electrician's tape to make it easier on the hands. That little bit of extra leverage really does a lot toward breaking loose a stubborn screw."

"Sometimes it is necessary to count the turns applied by your screwdriver. Unless you want to make a mistake, you will need to slow down your turning speed. You can speed it up some by having a reference line at some point on the handle of the screwdriver. Either a strip of thin bright plastic tape or a painted line makes counting the turns a lot easier."

Washer chucked in
drill

"If you need a magnetic screwdriver and don't have one the right size, try this handy substitute. Rub the tip of your screwdriver over a wet bar of soap. Now you will find that the screw will stay in place on the screwdriver until you get it started. This works great on small-sized screws, and will even work on larger ones with a lot of soap and a little patience."

"If you don't have a screwdriver bit for your drill brace, here's a quick way to make one: Just insert a metal washer into the chuck and tighten the chuck down. The edge of the washer will fit into a screw slot, and the brace can easily turn screws up or down. The ordinary workbench will have a variety of washers to fit all sizes of screw slots.

"This is great! Even the guy who has a screwdriver bit for his brace won't have one to fit all screws . . . but he probably will have a washer to substitute."

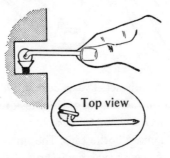

Top view

"Got a problem getting to a screw in a recessed area? By taking a long nail and bending it at a 90-degree angle about ¼" below the head, I created an offset screwdriver. If you can't get a wide enough turning arc, you can alternate this tool with a nail that is not bent."

File off

"I always have a pocket screwdriver on hand since I altered a key to do this job. With my grinding wheel, I filed off one side of the key handle so it's shaped like a screwdriver tip. It can even be used while still on my key ring."

(This beats using a coin, as I find the vending machine people don't like what screws do to coins. They sure let me know about it when I ran that "helpful" idea in the column. So don't use a coin!)

SCREW EYES   "If you've ever had to install a bunch of screw eyes, you know you need some sort of gadget to turn them down. I sawed a slot in the end of one of my plastic screwdriver handles and now have a handy tool anytime I need to install eyes or hooks. The slot slips down over the eye, which can then be quickly turned down. The slot doesn't interfere with the normal use of the screwdriver."

Slot in handle

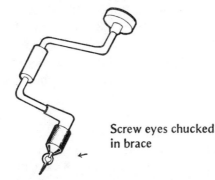

Screw eyes chucked
in brace

"Installing screw eyes is a much easier job since I discovered I can let Chuck do it. The Chuck I am talking about is the one on the end of my brace and bit. As the chuck is tightened down, the jaws come out and will grab hold of a screw eye. When I operate the brace just as I would if I were drilling, the screw eye goes in easily and quickly."

"One of the handiest 'wrenches' for turning down screw eyes is your pocket knife. With the blade closed, the end of a pocket knife has a slot for the blade to slide into when open. On most knives, this slot is just about the right size to fit over several sizes of small-eye screws. The knife is large enough to provide a good turning handle."

SCREWS–LOOSE, BOTCHED, FROZEN   "Here's my method for replacing a loose screw that has to go back into the same, too-big hole. Clip a piece or two of small plastic-covered electrical wire. It should be almost as long as the screw. Insert the wire in the hole, and then reinsert the screw. When turned down, it will be as tight as it should have been originally."

...And from another Handyma'am: "I have even created a few super tricks of my own. Like my way to retighten a wood screw that has worked loose because the hole has become too big. I take a tiny piece of cotton and soak it with fingernail polish. I poke this into the hole, then replace the screw. And between the cotton and the holding power of the polish when it dries, it is in to stay."

"Here's a quick way to reinsert a screw in a hole that has become too large to hold it properly. Take a small scrap of aluminum foil and wrap it around the threads. When you reinsert the screw, you'll find it can again be turned down tight."

"The next time you run across a loose metal screw, try this. Take one of those tissue-paper-thin drops of solder and wrap a piece of it around the threads. If it is thin enough, it will conform to the threads, and the screw can be reinserted. This will take up the gap and probably take care of the looseness. However, if you want it to be doubly tight, touch the top of the screw with a hot soldering iron for a few seconds. This will carry heat through the screw and cause the solder to melt enough to solder the screw in place. When it comes time to remove it, another heat treatment will loosen the solder."

"I put a coat hook on our bathroom door. A week later, the screws worked loose, and the hook fell out. The reason was that it was a hollow-core door. My husband then put it back, only he used slightly larger screws that were made for use in sheet metal. It has been almost a year, and the hook is still in place."

"Here's a trick that may come in handy to some of your readers: A stubborn round-headed screw or bolt that has a stripped screw slot can be doctored so that it can be removed with an open-end wrench. Just file off the sides of the head so there are two parallel straight sides for the wrench to take hold of—simple but effective!"

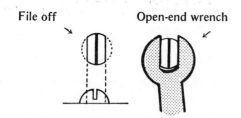

File off   Open-end wrench

"A screw with a round, oval, or fillister head that has a botched up screw slot will still be easy to remove. All you need to do is take a hacksaw and cut a new slot in the head at right angles to the original slot. Then, with the help of your screwdriver, it can be unscrewed easily. A flat-headed screw which is turned down flush can't be re-slotted with a saw, so you'll have to try another trick. One way is to stamp a new slot with a sharp hammer blow on a metal chisel."

"A good way to set that wood screw permanently and at the same time eliminate future rust is to dip it in clear shellac just before putting it in."

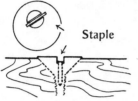

Staple

"Did you know that you can lock a wood screw down in place with nothing more than a stapler? Just tighten the screw down, and then shoot the staple into the wood so that it fits down into the screw slot with the points going into the wood on either side of the screw. This will absolutely keep it from working loose. If you need to remove the screw later, however, the staple can easily be pried out."

"Here is a super-lock for a screw that should stay permanently in place. After the screw is down in place, take your tiniest drill bit and drill a hole in the edge of the screw head. Then insert a tiny nail into the hole and drive it down flush with the screw head. The screw cannot be turned as long as the nail is in place. Should you ever need to remove the screw, just pry up the nail."

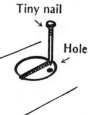

Tiny nail

Hole

Sometimes your soldering iron may be closer to hand than the penetrating oil for a stubborn bolt or screw. If so, hold the hot iron to the head of the bolt or screw for a few moments. Then remove it and let the fastener cool. The expansion-and-contraction process will most often break loose the screw so it can be removed.

SCRIBE   "For a metal scribe, I took an old automatic pencil and inserted a tiny drill bit instead of a piece of lead. When not in use, the bit retracts back into the barrel."

"A ball-point pen that's ready for the scrap heap can be made into a handy scriber. Remove the point from the barrel and sharpen it on a grinding wheel. You'll find it to be an excellent scriber, as well as one that's easy to carry clipped to your pocket. Be sure to retract the point when not in use."

SET SCREWS   Some manufacturers will come up with a set screw that tightens down against a threaded part. That's fine if you never have to remove this part, but if you do, you can find that the set screw has botched up the threads. This can make for new problems. If you run across this situation, snip off a piece of wire solder and drop this in before you put the set screw in place. The solder will take the form of the threads and act as a cushion against the set screw. Another thread-saver would be to insert a square piece cut from a wide rubber band. Even if the set screw does not come down against threads, the rubber patch will keep it tighter longer.

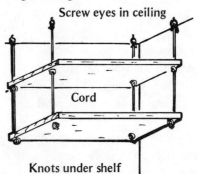

Screw eyes in ceiling

Cord

Knots under shelf

SHELVES   Here's a swinging idea: "We made some quick shelves that certainly should qualify us to become honorary handymen, even though we are three airline stewardesses who share an apartment. These shelves are suspended from the ceiling by means of four screw eyes. Colorful plastic clothesline was tied to the eyes and goes down through holes we drilled in the shelf. The plastic line is knotted under the shelf.' This is a good shop shelf idea, too.

"Although I am neither handy nor a man, I would like to share my bookshelf idea with you and your readers. My roommates and I had more books than bookshelves. Even if we'd been handy enough to have built shelves, we couldn't have installed them, since we live in an apartment and the landlord frowns on anything attached to the walls. So I put in shelves that exactly fit the wall space where we wanted shelves. And I built them without cutting a board, driving a nail, or turning a screw. I used 1″ x 12″ boards as the shelves, and bricks for the supports and spacers. The lumberyard cut the boards to the right length. The bricks are stacked at either end of the boards to the desired height, and then a shelf is laid across them. They are quite stable, most inexpensive, and very attractive."

"If you're building a new garage, basement, or workshop and plan to add shelves at a later date, here's an idea that will help. Instead of the regular 2′ x 4′ studs, have the builder use 2 x 8's. The extra material won't cost much, but will certainly make the shelves you add later a lot more sturdy. You need to use the extra-wide material only on the one wall where you might want to add shelves."

"There were some old curtain rods in our garage, and before throwing them away I decided to see what new use I could find for them. These were the kind that are made of metal and are flat on the front side. The back has a ridge running the length of the rods where one section telescopes into the other. This ridge holds a ¼″ piece of plywood, and therefore the rods made great brackets for shelves. I attached sections of the rods in the corners of the garage and cut triangular shelves of plywood which slipped in the brackets. It took only minutes to install more shelves than we needed . . . and they look great."

Curtain rod section

Plywood fits in slot

"Here's how I made some quick shelves in my garage. I had intended them to be only temporary, but I like them so well that I plan just to leave them. I took a strip of chicken wire and stapled it crossways to the joists in the garage. Since there's very little span between the joists, there's practically no sag, and these wire shelves will hold a pretty fair load. What convinced me to leave them up permanently was the fact that you can see through them and tell at a glance where everything is. I've added them along the other wall, too."

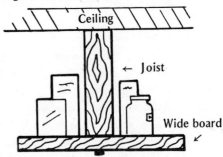

"Here is how I added a number of shelves in my garage with a minimum of effort. With lag screws, I attached wide, rough boards to the joists in the garage ceiling. I used 1″ x 12″ boards, which meant that I ended up with approximately 5″ shelves on each side of the joist. Since the joists are 2″ x 8″, my shelves will accommodate items up to almost 8″ high."

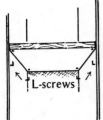

"The installation of additional shelves in our kitchen cabinets was accomplished in practically no time with the method I devised. I used 4 L-screws under each shelf. The L-screws were put into the cabinets on each side where I wanted the shelf to fit. The 'L' part pointed up. I then marked the bottom of the shelf where the L's hit and drilled a blind hole at each of these 4 points. The shelf fits down on the L's and is set in place. However, a shelf can easily be moved if desired."

"While remodeling my garage storage cabinets, I was faced with a problem of no temporary shelves on which to store all the things I had to remove from the old cabinets. I think my solution is worthy of space in your fine column. Each shelf consists of a pair of ordinary wire coat hangers attached to the ceiling beams in the garage, with a board resting on the hanger part of the two hangers. They are quick to install but quite effective."

SIGNS "Recently, we had need to put up a yard sign to give away another litter of Tabby's kittens. Until now, I've always driven the signpost into the ground. But often the post gets splintered up, or the sign gets hit and becomes loose in the hole. Also, this method always leaves a hole in our yard that I forget to fill up until I step in it or the lawn mower wheel gets stuck in it. This time I used a concrete building block and inserted the sign into one of the holes in it. I drove in wooden wedges next to the post to keep it in tight. The weight of the concrete block wouldn't allow the sign to blow over, and when we finally got rid of all the kittens, there was no hole left in the yard."

"When we had our garage sale, I had painted a really beautiful sign to go in front of the house. No sooner had it been put out than it started to rain. Since I had used tempera paints, I knew the rain would cause the paint to run and ruin my art work. I quickly retrieved my sign, and we wrapped it with clear plastic food wrap. When it was put back out, we no longer had to worry about the rain and could concentrate our efforts on getting rid of all that junk in the garage."

"When our church had a bazaar, I was in charge of publicity—which meant I nailed up placards all over town. After I had some trouble with them tearing loose from their nails, I learned a handy trick. I collected a batch of old bottle caps and drove a nail through each cap. Then I used these to nail up the placards. I found that the extra width of the bottle caps kept the signs from being torn loose. This trick will really be a help to those who have to post election signs."

"When we have any sort of a church function, we always post notices all over the church. We used to have trouble prying the staples out when the posters were due to come down. However, one of our members came up with an idea that prevents the stapler from putting

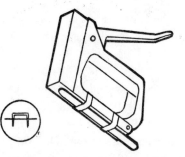

the staples in all the way, so that there's no problem in getting a prying tool under to remove them. All you need to do is to tape a stick from an ice cream bar to the bottom of the stapler. This raises the stapler machine away from the surface so the staples go in far enough to hold but still leave prying room."

"Our scout troop was all set for our garage sale when we realized we had all the merchandise ready but no signs around the neighborhood to tell where it was. With only one lettering-sized paintbrush, we could have wasted a lot of time, but we made several quick brushes so that everyone could get into the act. We used the filter ends of cigarette butts. When these are dipped into the watercolors, they make excellent lettering brushes."

SIPHONING   Siphoning is the best way to get a little bit of gasoline out of the tank of your car for whatever you might need it for around the house. However, gasoline doesn't taste all that good. Instead of starting the siphoning process with suction from your mouth, find a small plastic squeeze bottle and let it choke on the gasoline. Insert the spout tightly into the hose, and with the other end well under the level of the gasoline in the tank, give the bottle a quick squeeze. When the squeeze is released, the extra air in the tank, coupled with the vacuum caused by the bottle snapping back into shape, will draw the gasoline through the tube. If it doesn't come all the way through the first time, give it another squeeze. Of course, you'll remember that the container into which you're siphoning has to be lower than the tank.

SOLDERING   "Next time you run across a scrap of asbestos shingle or siding, save it. It will come in handy if you have to solder and want to use a vise to hold the work. As you know, many times heat is transferred to the metal vise, and thus dissipated, making it difficult to solder. Put a square from the asbestos scrap against each jaw of the vise.

With the work between two pieces of asbestos, no heat is dissipated. If you have several soldering projects and you want the asbestos pieces to stay on when the vise is open, stick them on with rubber cement. They will stay until you want to peel them off."

"Need a really inexpensive, quickly-made holder for a soldering iron? Take a scrap of wood and drive two nails at an angle to form an 'X.' The iron rests in the 'X' and not on the workbench."

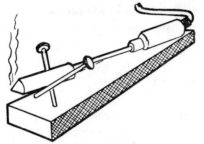

Or: "Take one of those metal cellulose-tape dispensers, after the tape is gone. The hole in the center keeps the point of the iron off your workbench."

"I got one of those large spring-type paper clamps. It fits around the iron just below the heating head, and you never have to look for the holder. It stays with the iron."

"Another good stand to hold your soldering iron up off of the work surface can be made from an empty typewriter ribbon reel. All that needs to be done to the reel is to bend the two sides out from the center of the spool at right angles to their original plane. This forms a flat surface for the holder to stand on, and the iron is then placed in the ribbon slot at the top. If the iron is too fat to fit, this slot can be bent out too."

"I never run the risk of taking out my soldering gun and getting all ready to solder, only to discover that I forgot to get the solder out. I keep an emergency supply always handy by wrapping a 6" strip of wire solder around the electric cord of the solder gun. It wraps on easily and doesn't get in the way "

"Tinning" is an electrician's word, meaning to coat with a very thin layer of solder. If you need to tin some connector wires, one problem is the receptacle to hold the solder and keep it in a molten state. Here is a super hint: If you have a solder gun, take an empty .22 cartridge and wedge this in the loop of the heating element. With the gun turned on, the cartridge will heat enough to melt solder. Now you can dip the wires into the cartridge to tin them.

"I keep a mousetrap in my soldering kit and put it to good use as a clamp for all sorts of small soldering jobs. I removed the little doodad that holds the cheese and the wire trigger. Then I wrapped the wooden base with a piece of foil to prevent the heat from the solder iron from burning it. It really is a handy clamp to have around."

"When you have small parts to solder, an ideal way to hold them in place is with magnets. I keep several small magnets in my soldering iron case just for that purpose."

Another reader uses Silly Putty® to hold wires. It acts as a heat sink, as well (stops heat dissipation). Since this stuff doesn't dry out, keep a blob in your soldering kit.

"Here is a good 'vise' to hold small objects for soldering: Just borrow some of your kids' modeling clay. Put the objects to be soldered in it, and it will hold them nicely. The clay also allows you to move the objects into a better position if necessary."

Coil spring

"Inside the case that holds my soldering gun, I keep a handy item I made to hold wires when they're being soldered. It consists of a section of spring from a screen door. It's about 3" long and is tacked to a small piece of wood. When the wires to be soldered are slipped between coils at either end of the spring, they're held in place until the soldering has been completed. This won't be applicable in all cases, but it's a useful third hand for many soldering projects."

"If you need to solder along a narrow seam, your handiwork will look much better if you can manage to confine the solder to the seam. Here's a trick that will help keep you on the straight and narrow. Tape a pair of ordinary crayons together and run these along the line. The two marks are to straddle the line to be soldered. Any solder that gets on the crayon line will not stick, but will come up with the crayon."

It really pays to "hide your light under a bushel" ... if you're mending tiny holes in a bucket, washtub, or other container. A light under the container will show you where to apply the mending material. For best results, use an extension cord with a fairly good-sized bulb.

Since several readers have sent in this next tip, I assume it is widely used—and I want to suggest that it ought *not* to be. The tip was to paint with rubber cement the area around where you're going to solder, the theory being that any drops of solder that fall will not stick to or ruin a painted place. The rubber cement could then be rubbed up, leaving the area clean. But these well-intentioned handymen forget that rubber cement will burn. While it would not catch from the heat of the solder, it might accidentally do so from the iron. This could cause far more trouble than the drops of solder.

"When you need to solder on a large metal sheet, the heat is often dissipated over the area of the sheet. You can concentrate the heat by borrowing your wife's iron. Turn it on and place it directly under the area to be soldered. When it is hot, you will have no trouble with the dissipation problem. Of course, if you get any solder or flux on your wife's iron, you will have some problems from her."

"We don't believe in wasting anything around our house. When there are only a couple of inches left on a roll of solder, many handymen would throw it away, since using it would probably result in burned fingers. Not me. I keep a cork with a slit in it to act as a holder and can use the solder right up to the last."

(A slice of raw potato will also do this job.)

"Removing solder is done quite simply by heating it with your soldering iron. Sometimes, however, it rehardens before you can get it off. An empty plastic squeeze bottle can be used to form a small 'vacuum cleaner' to pick up the liquid solder while you keep it hot with the iron. Slip the metal barrel from an old ball-point pen over the original spout to keep the heat from melting your 'vacuum cleaner.' Squeeze in on the bottle, and as you release, the solder will be sucked up into the bottle."

"Here's a trick to use when soldering two wires together. First, just heat the solder over a hard surface and let the drops fall. As you know, they flatten out into little flat circles, which can easily be shaped around the two pieces of twisted wires. Then all you have to do to solder them is reheat the circles, and the solder will melt down all around the wires."

"Here's a simple stunt that will make your soldering of a pipe much more effective. Wrap the section to be soldered with a few turns of thin copper wire. Let the wire extend past the area by ¼" on each side. Tie the wire down tight. Now the solder will flow down in between and all around the thin wires. The solder will have a better bond and will not drip off the pipe as you apply it."

"Steel wool is excellent for cleaning off the tip of a soldering iron. Each time I start a soldering job, I staple a patch of steel wool right on my workbench next to my project. The staples hold it in place, so the cleaning operation requires only one hand. When the job is finished, the steel wool can be removed."

"In an emergency, you can solder without a soldering iron, provided you have wire solder and a cigarette lighter. First heat the metal with your lighter, in the area to be soldered. Then hold the wire solder in the flame and as close as possible to the soldering area. Make sure the area doesn't cool off."

SPEAKERS   "I just ran an extension speaker from my hi-fi to our patio. After pricing the speaker wall cases, I decided to make one myself. In the process, I came up with a clever method of stretching the speaker cloth. I used a pair of wooden crochet hoops. Since they snap one inside the other, they held the speaker cloth nice and tight. This unit was then easy to attach between the face of the case and the speaker."

SPORTS   "With people taking transistor radios to ball games, on hunting trips, and to so many other places where they are apt to get rained on, you may want to pass along my 'radio-rain-gear' idea. When I go hunting, I drop my pocket transistor into a plastic sandwich bag and close up the top tight with a small rubber band. This makes the radio completely waterproof. The plastic bag is so thin that the radio can be operated without taking it out of the bag. Not only can it be turned off and on, the volume can be regulated and the stations can be changed through the rain gear. And the sound is not lost at all."

"We have a basketball backboard and hoop outside for the boys to shoot baskets. The weather and wear-and-tear took their toll on the net under the basket, so that it needed to be changed about every year. That was until I soaked the net in linseed oil before installing it the last time. This gives it a built-in protection against the weather, and I think makes the net much tougher. At any rate, this one is in its second year and looks brand new."

SPRAY CANS AND SPRAYERS   "As you know, spray painting results in a smoother finish when the paint gun is kept at about the same distance from the surface throughout the spraying. I always tape to the paint spray a stick that's about an inch short of the desired distance from the wall. It's quite easy to keep the end of the stick about an inch from the wall, and, therefore, easier for me to get a smooth paint job."

"I just discovered that we have a paint spray booth built right in our home. It also doubles as a fireplace. I found that by using the fireplace as a spray booth, all the fumes and odors are carried off up the chimney by the draft. Also, when the painting is done, all the paint spots will burn off the bricks. Of course, I only do this when the fireplace is clean, as the spray could stir up soot and ruin a paint job."

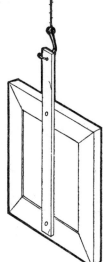

"After having to throw away a couple of partly-used cans of spray paint because they were clogged up with dried paint, I learned a trick. When you're through painting, turn the can upside down and spray. This clears out the tube inside, and there's no more clogging."

"Here's a trick I used in spray painting a bunch of picture frames. I tacked a stick on the back of each frame, which allowed me to pick them up and spray them from all angles and yet not spray my hand or have to handle any part I had sprayed. For drying, I had drilled a hole in the end of the sticks, and I hung them from the clothesline on shower curtain hooks."

"Ever try to spray-paint drawer pulls? I have thunk up an easier way. All you need are a few empty, throw-away soft drink bottles. Insert the screws part way into the pulls and put the screw down into the neck of the bottle. The bottle turns around, so you can spray all around the knob, and you can leave it as is until the paint dries. Then instead of throwing the bottles away, figure out a solution to aid in recycling them."

Weight

"I have a sprayer attachment for my garden hose. I noticed that, as it got low on liquid, it sometimes didn't pick up all that was left. The reason was that the little hose didn't stay down in the bottom of the container. I remedied this very simply, by adding enough extra weight to the hose so it hung down into the lowest level of the jar, no matter what the hangle it was held at. For weight, I wrapped the end with wire. Now my sprayer is 'good to the last drop.'"

SQUARES "If you don't have a square handy and need to saw a board off at a right angle, your handsaw will help you get a perfectly square cut. Place the back of the saw down on the board. You will see the reflection of the board in the shiny surface of the saw blade. Swing the blade back and forth until the edge of the board and the reflection of the edge on the saw form a straight line. Then you can run a pencil along the saw edge and be assured of a square cut."

STAPLES AND STAPLING   "Round-head staples can be pulled out quite easily with my stunt. I slip a finishing nail into the rounded part of the staple. A claw hammer is then used to extract the staple. The claw straddles the staple and goes under the nail. You can really zip out the staples in a hurry."

Nail

Staple

"I slip a wide rubber band from an old inner tube over the end of the staple machine so it's raised slightly above the surface. Then when I want to convert back to putting the staples all the way in, I just slip the rubber band off."

"We use our stapler for many things, and just recently I added a feature to it that makes it even more serviceable. To find out exactly where the staple came out, and thus where it would enter the work, I always had to look underneath just before stapling. Then I painted a thin red line on each side to indicate where the staple comes out. No guesswork."

← Large staple from link of chain

"If you ever have use for real heavy-duty staples, make your own out of links from an old chain. Just cut the links at an angle so they end up with sharp points to make them easier to drive. If you want added holding power, score the shank of your staple with a file."

STEEL WOOL   "To prevent slivers from getting in my fingers when I'm using steel wool, I keep a small hinge around to use as a holder. Just slap a glob of steel wool into the jaws of the hinge and clamp it tight with your hands. Be sure to leave enough sticking out to work with."

"Steel wool is a must for fine finishing, as well as for other home handyman chores. However, using it bare-handed can result in getting some painful splinters of steel wool. I use half of a hollow rubber ball as a holder for the steel wool. It's flexible enough so I can get a good grip on the steel wool which fits up into the empty rubber shell. Sure saves the hands!"

The other half of that rubber ball had no uses until a reader suggested, "Poke a paint brush handle through it the next time you're going to be painting up over your head. Have the cupped part aimed up, and it will act as a catcher for all the drips."

Once you've used a piece of steel wool with water, it will usually rust before you have another use for it. Not so if you keep it stored in a solution of a cup of water and a teaspoonful of baking soda. Of course, if you use the steel wool every day, as your wife might, you'll probably wear it out before rust can set in.

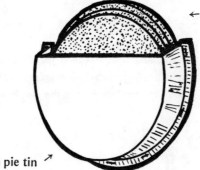

← Sandpaper discs

Aluminum pie tin ↗

STORAGE   "I made a wall rack for my shop, to hold sandpaper discs. It is made from one of those aluminum pie tins that come with the pies you buy at the grocery. They are almost a heavy foil and can be cut with tin snips. The pie tin should be cut in half and then stapled at the desired spot on the wall. A strong staple gun will go through the lip of the pie tin without any trouble. With the cut-out half pointing up and the bottom facing out, you have an excellent disc holder."

Screen door spring

"Maybe this idea will solve a problem for other men as it did for me. A wheelbarrow is about as difficult to store as anything. The best way is flat against the wall. I took a screen door spring, the longest I could find, and attached it to the wall in my garage so that when the wheelbarrow is standing on end, the spring is about half way down on the handles. The spring is stretched so that it's a little longer than the distance between the handles. To store the wheelbarrow, I merely put the handles under the spring—which holds the wheelbarrow flat against the wall."

"If the studs are exposed at your workbench, here is an excellent tool-storage idea. Drill various-sized holes in these studs, slanting down into the stud at about a 45-degree angle. Screwdrivers, awls, drill bits, and all sorts of hand tools will fit down into these holes that you have sized just for them. They are always easy to get to, and it will always be a snap to get them back in the proper place."

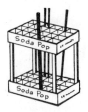

"How do you like my storage rack for rods, pipes, and long dowels? It was made from two wooden soft-drink cases. I removed the bottom from the top case, attached it to the bottom case by four strips of 1" x 4" lumber about a yard long. The rods fit down into the sections for the bottles in the top case and rest in the sections in the bottom case below. This keeps them separated by size and holds them upright."

"I thought you and your readers might like my storage bin for molding and doweling. It is made from two coffee cans. One has both ends cut out of it. This one is mounted on the garage wall, about three feet off the floor. The other can is attached to the wall on the floor and is directly below the first can. The material to be stored is then poked through the top can and rests in the other."

Coffee cans

"I keep a supply of various-sized dowels in my workshop. To store these all in one place and out of the way, I improvised a holder. I cut both ends out of three coffee cans and left one end on a fourth. By placing these end-to-end and taping them together, I made a metal tube. The one with the end still in it is the bottom, of course. I used inch-wide masking tape to hold them together. Then I nailed the top of the tube to the shop wall in a corner so it won't fall."

Rubber band

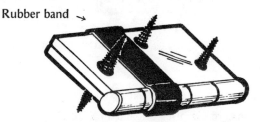

"When storing hinges, here's a trick that will insure the right screws being with the hinges when you want to use them later on. Put the screws in place in the holes in the hinges. Then fold the two leaves back against each other so that the screws point out on either side with their heads on the inside. Now take tape of some sort and wrap it around the entire hinge. The screws will be held in place and can't stray, since their heads are too big to come through the holes."

"My idea for storing hinges also keeps the metal protected against rust. I store the hinges and screws inside a plastic sandwich bag. But before I put them in the bag, I coat them with petroleum jelly. The lubricant can easily be wiped off when you are ready to use them."

"A saber saw takes up much less storage space if you bore a hole in the shelf for the blade to go through."

(And you can protect the blade by cutting a piece of ¼" rubber tubing to slip over it.)

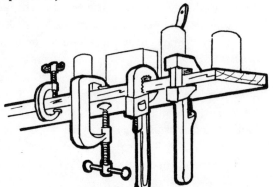

"The best place to store adjustable wrenches and C-clamps is on the edges of the shelves in your workshop. They tighten onto the shelf and will stay put. They're always in sight, so you don't have to go digging for them."

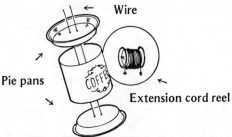

Wire

Pie pans

Extension cord reel

"Here's how to make a handy reel on which to wind and store that electric extension cord. A coffee can and a pair of old pie pans form the reel. The pie pans go at either end of the can. Punch holes in each of the pie plates, about an inch apart. Loop a length of wire through one pan, and bring the ends out of the other. Then twist the ends together to pull the pans tight against the can."

"Here's a shop idea that I've used for quite a long time. Empty adhesive-bandage boxes make ideal containers for small shop items—screws, brads, tacks, rivets, small bolts, and the like. By cementing or soldering a sample of the item on the lid of each box, you can easily identify the contents. And if you make a wooden box to hold several bandage boxes, you can take the whole carton to the work and use the items as needed. Quite a step-saver."

"I made permanent racks on my garage ceiling to hold lumber. They are quite sturdy and will hold great weight, yet are very simple to construct and install. The racks consist of two U-shaped pieces suspended from the ceiling with the lumber resting between the two. Each 'U' is made of two floor flanges connected to two short lengths of pipe. Right-angle elbows are attached on the other end of these short pipes. A long section of pipe is attached to the elbows connecting the two parts and completing the 'U.' The floor flanges are then attached to beams in the ceiling with lag screws. The width can be varied with the length of connecting pipe, while the length of the lumber to be stored will determine the distance apart for the two U's."

Safety recommends retiring ladders that begin to show any structural weakness. Here's a way to semi-retire a straight ladder. Suspend it from your shop or garage ceiling and use it as a rack for storing molding and light but long lumber.

"After our last youngster outgrew the diaper stage, we still had one of those great big laundry-type safety pins. Rather than throw it away, I found that by slipping the opened pin through the ends of my box wrenches, they can all be kept together. Often I can use one of the wrenches while it is still on the safety pin if I need the end of the wrench that is not threaded on the pin."

After a while, the cases that tools come in have a way of disappearing. Finding new storage methods has long been a Super Handyman pastime. Here's how one reader stored his taps so the threads are protected: He runs appropriately sized nuts onto the taps so that the threads are completely covered up. This not only acts as a protector, but also cleans out any particles that might be in the threads.

"I have a unique way to store hacksaw blades. I got some scraps of tubular aluminum, a shade longer than the blades to be stored. I found corks to fit in each end, and presto, a container for storing hack- and coping-saw blades. I put a coating of oil on the blades before putting them in the tubes. They keep as long as need be, and I never have to worry about their getting nicked."

"Here's a way to use a pair of old towel racks to solve a storage problem in the shop. Attach the racks to the wall several feet apart, but in a vertical position instead of the normal horizontal way. Now they will serve as wall holders for lightweight pieces such as molding. The distance between them can, of course, be determined by the length of the material to be stored."

End view of beam

Section of pipe . . . . inserted in hole

"Here is a lumber storage idea for those who have exposed ceiling beams in their garage or shop. I drilled holes in the sides of the beams. They were drilled at a slight angle and are big enough to accomodate a length of ½" pipe. The angle of the hole is such that when the pipe is inserted, it points upward slightly. The pipes I used are about 10" long. By putting two of these on one side of a beam, a good supply of lumber can be stacked on the pipes. Extra-long lumber may need a pipe in the middle to keep it from sagging."

"My method for storing my sanding belts is quite easy to devise and keeps them from getting damaged. I drilled holes in my shop wall and inserted lengths of dowelling that were slit down the middle with a saw. Each of the dowels projects out from the wall a bit more than the width of the sanding belts. The slits are deep enough to receive the belts. To store, the belts are slipped into the slits and are hung on the wall out of the way."

"There are many screwdriver racks that you can buy, but I've never seen one that holds as many as I own. So I made one that extends the full width of the bench. I drilled various-sized holes in a length of angle iron and screwed it to the side of the workbench. It holds 27 different tools, and they're right at hand, too. It's tailor-made for my bench and my tools and took only minutes and a piece of scrap metal to make."

"Sometimes when you store a metal object away, you'd rather not coat it with grease, oil, or rust-preventive paint. Here's another method: Coat the metal with rubber cement after it's been cleaned. When you're ready to take it out of storage, the rubber cement peels right off, and the metal is as shiny as when you put it away."

(Note: Silver is tarnished by rubber, but iron, steel, and other metals are unaffected.)

"When I need to store various metal items for some time, I first coat them with oil and then put them in plastic bags. So many things come in plastic bags that there is no problem in getting one to fit almost any object. I then close the bags by using a pipe cleaner as a twist tie. It closes them up tight, is easy to work with, and can be used over again."

"Each year when I put up screens, I'm faced with a problem of the best way to store the storm windows. This year I've tried something new: I cut a section of corrugated metal roofing to the same width as the windows. (The corrugations run across the piece.) I then counted the 'valleys' and cut a section with the same number of valleys as I had windows. This piece I nailed to the attic floor up close to a wall. The windows are stored in a leaning position, with each one in its own valley. The valleys prevent them from sliding out, and with the windows upright instead of flat as they have been in the past, there's less likelihood of their getting broken."

"Here is another hint for storing storm windows. I slip them inside those big plastic suit bags that we get from the dry cleaners, seal up the ends with cellophane tape, and have dust-free storm windows when it is time to put them back up next fall. Then I take down the screens and store them the same way."

"When it's time to take down screens and put up storm windows, they should be marked to be sure they get back into the same window. I make Roman numerals with a staple gun on the edge of the wooden frames, and corresponding numbers in the windows. This is very easy to do, and you don't have to worry about the numbers coming off as you do if they're painted on."

(The reason for the Roman numerals—if you haven't already figured it out—is that only straight lines are involved, and the staples form only straight lines. Just make sure you know which end is up, or you'll try fitting window IX where XI ought to be.)

"Here is another aid in storing storm windows that will allow you to get them all back in the same windows they came out of. As you take each window off, smear it with window cleaner of the type that dries chalky. When it is dry, identify the location by printing right on the glass with your finger. When it is time to put them back in, you will know where each goes, and they can then be wiped clean and sparkling."

"We've had an old bed stored in our basement for years. The springs leaned against one wall, the slats were in a pile, and the ends were against another wall. Recently I decided there must be a better way: I assembled the bed as it would be for use. On the springs I placed some sheets of plywood that weren't to be used right away. I then stored all my storm windows flat on the springs. There was still room for many other things that I wanted to keep away from the moisture on the basement floor. Most of all, I don't have to worry about those springs poised against the wall, ready to fall down on me the next time I bump into them."

"Most of us use corrugated boxes to store away out-of-season clothes—as well as all sorts of other things. If these are to be stored in the garage, attic, or basement where there may be some exposure to moisture, here is a way to protect the contents: Give the boxes a coat of thinned shellac. This makes them much more moisture-resistant and is added protection against rodents, too. Do your shellacking before you pack the boxes, of course."

"Last year we converted a garage into a rec room. I installed one of those suspended ceilings that have panels fitting into frames that hang from the old ceiling. Recently we needed extra storage space, and it suddenly occurred to me that there was quite a bit of dead space between our new ceiling and the old one. The panels are easy to put in and take out, so I removed some of them and attached shelves between a number of the joists. This took care of our storage needs and still leaves room for more shelves if the need arises. The shelves are easy to get to, and yet are completely out of sight."

(Be sure you have clean, dry hands when removing the panels, or they are liable to show the wear.)

STRAIGHTEDGES   "You can keep from nicking a wooden or plastic straightedge, even though you're cutting along it with a razor blade. Just tape a coin to one side of the blade, leaving the cutting edge exposed below the coin. Either masking or cellophane tape will do. Now, let the coin be a 'buffer zone' between blade and straight edge. If measurement is a critical factor, be sure to take into consideration the extra width added to the blade by the coin."

Wire

STRING "The metal spool from an expired roll of adhesive tape makes a dandy reel for winding up string or wire. After it is wound, the spool can be snapped back in place in the cover, and there is never any worry about its unraveling. The spool is converted to a reel by the addition of a small drawer knob on the side. To wind it up, stick the spool over a finger of one hand and crank away with the other hand."

Tiny drawer knob

"Another way to keep a ball of twine handy is to use a mesh bag such as the type used by markets for oranges, onions, and potatoes. Place the ball in the bag with the loose end of twine sticking through the mesh, and hang it on the wall over the workbench. The bag prevents the ball from unraveling."

"My twine holder is a plastic strawberry box stapled up on my shop wall. The ball of string goes in the basket, and the end sticks out through one of the holes and hangs down within easy reach."

String

"In the shipping department of a local store I ran into a tricky idea for hanging up a ball of twine. The ball was hung from a wire coathanger that had been bent and elongated so the ball of twine fitted down over it. There was a base of hanger for the ball to rest on to keep it from sliding off. I have adapted the idea for my workshop; the hanger keeps the string out of the way, and yet is a handy dispenser."

"I keep a ball of twine stored in a coffee can attached to the wall up above my workbench. A hole is punched in the bottom part of the side of the can for the string to feed through. . . . I also added a string cutter that works well—a single-edge razor blade taped to the can above the string feed hole. The blade has to be single-edged to bend around the curve of the can. Under the blade, I place a few thicknesses of rubber so the blade sticks out a little from the can. To cut the string, I just pull it up against the blade. Since the blade is out a little way from the can, there is still a bit of string sticking out when I need to use it again."

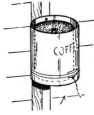

Razor blade

STRING SNAPPING DIAGRAM

For practice purposes, let's assume you need to tie a package for mailing. You have wrapped the string around the package and now you need to break it so you can tie the knot.

Lay string over left hand. The palm-side of the string will be "A," and the back-side "B." Sec. "A" is coming from the package, and sec. "B" from ball of twine. Grasp "B" with thumb and forefinger of the right hand and bring it toward you so it is 4" or 5" in front of the left hand, as shown. Keep points "X" and "Y." in mind for next step. . . .

. . . Which is a tricky maneuver with the left hand. The left hand is brought down completely under both sec. "A" and "B." Point "X" on the left hand loops under point "Y" of the string. Now "A" is to the back of the hand, as above. The left hand is now returned to its original position. The tricky maneuver has caused "A" to form a "V" in the palm of the left hand, with "B" coming out to the right hand from the point at bottom of "V." All this time, the right hand has not moved and is still in front of the left hand.

Now twist the fore- and middle-fingers around sec. "A," forming loops as above for extra leverage. If the string doesn't look as above, start over.

Gently pull the string tight and adjust the "V" up to the middle or upper part of the palm. Now give a quick outward and downward snap with the right hand. If you have done everything right, the string should break

An added twist for greater snapping power: Before the snap, hold sec. B with the right thumb and forefinger, and with the string around the outside of the forefinger, bring it down on the inside of the other three fingers. Close the fingers so the string comes from the inside of the palm at the little finger and then leads to the "V." This gives a better grip and makes the quick snap more effective.

4 *Super Hint:* Start out with a light-weight string until you have mastered the technique—because if you get the string twisted around wrong, it can be really painful when you give it the snap.

"I've added a keen string cutter to the back of my workbench, and at no cost. I took an old window shade guide and sharpened the part where the shade used to fit. Then I attached it to the bench. It's always handy, but not in a place where I could easily get injured on it."

Window shade guide sharpened here

STUD FINDERS   "I have discovered a great way to 'see through' wall board to find the studs that the carpenters hid every 16″ or so. Just tie a magnet to a string and sweep it back and forth on the wall. The lath nails will stop the magnet."

"I take a flashlight and place it flat against the wall, with the light shining parallel to the wall. Then I move the flashlight along the wall. The patching fill over the nails shows up, and I've found the stud."

Here is another way: Turn on your electric razor and run the non-business end along the wall. There is a subtle but distinct difference in the sound when you reach a stud. It will help if you can test this out ahead of time—go to where you know there is a stud, place the razor against the wall at this point, and move it away along the wall to hear the change in sound.

Head of nail driven into wood

STUDS   "When nailing studs in place, you always have a problem of holding them in position while driving a nail on the other side. I take the head of a large-size nail and put it flat against the stud. Then I drive the head down into the wood. This acts as a stop and holds the stud in place while I drive another nail into the stud on the other side. The stop is easily extracted when the other nailing is finished."

SWIMMING   "With summertime upon us, the inflatable swim toys and floats are not far behind. Rather than having to use lung power, did you know that a tank-type vacuum cleaner can do the chore for you? Move the hose to the back or blower end of the tank. Make a stopper from something like the plastic lid of a coffee can, with a hole punched in it for the stem of the float to fit into. Hold this tight over the end of the hose and turn on the cleaner. Sure saves the lungs."

And another reader improved on this: "That idea will work even better if you use a funnel to fit over the end of the hose. The wide mouth will completely cover the opening, and the small spout will usually fit into the stem on the float."

"Between trips to the old swimming hole, what do you do with your rubber floats? It is best to leave them inflated while in limbo. This prevents folding, which causes creases, which causes cracks. Even though it takes up a little more room, it's worth it."

"When we've been out to the old swimming hole, I put 'box seats' in the car—cut-out sections of corrugated boxes that protect the seat and back of the car from wet bathing suits. I just stick a few in the trunk on the way out, and it sure saves the interior of the car on the way back."

"If you have a family full of swimmers, save those large plastic bags that come back from the cleaners. Then the next time you come back from the old swimming hole or the beach, they can be spread out on the car seats and will protect the seats from wet suits and sand. When you get home, they can be shaken out and hung over the clothesline to dry. Saves the upholstery and keeps the blood pressure down."

"I want to pass along a super lifesaving idea that might keep someone from drowning. Even with the heavy wheel, the spare tire you have in your trunk will float and support a person, if it is properly inflated. It can be taken out of the trunk quickly and be tossed to a person in the water. Just be sure not to hit the person when tossing the tire out. If you are going to visit a body of water, check to be sure your spare is properly inflated."

"Yesterday we were down at the beach when a car pulled up, and a family got out. They had their regular street clothes on, but apparently had decided this would be a good spot to swim. Since there were no dressing rooms around, I thought their solution was very handy. The father took out some glass cleaner that is opaque when applied to glass. With this, he covered all the car windows. Then the individual nembers got into the car and changed into swimwear without anyone's being able to see in. When the swim was over and they had changed back, the family wiped off the window cleaner and drove off."

"A word of warning for pool owners. As you clean up and prepare for summer, don't make my mistake of using steel wool to clean the tile or coping. Little slivers of steel that get into the pool form thousands of little rust spots that are almost impossible to remove."

Best way to remove the rust at the bottom of your pool is to take an old hone that's rounded on the end. Attach this to a stick that's long enough to reach the bottom, and gently hone the rust away.

"For those lucky enough to go to the beach, here is my way of bringing back a lot less sand in the car. We gather up all the sand buckets and playthings just before we leave and put them in the kind of mesh bag that produce comes in. This is then dunked in the water, and all the sand is washed off. By the time we get to the car, all the water has drained off, and we take home a clean batch of toys. It sure helps make cleaning the car an easier job."

How about mesh bags for the kids too?

T
.

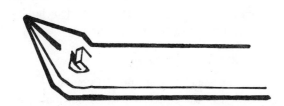

TACK PULLER   'With so many canned drinks coming in those ring-top cans, the old V-pointed beer openers don't get much of a workout. Here's what I did with one to make it especially useful. First I cut a slit starting at the 'V' and going back about ½". Then I filed the bottom of the 'V' so it tapers off to become very thin. This taper allows the tool to slip under tacks, and it becomes a great tack puller."

TAPE MEASURES   "I added a feature that's been quite handy on the side of the case of my retractable steel tape measure. It's a metal pencil pocket clip stuck on with epoxy. I inserted a short stub of a pencil, so the tape still fits easily into my pocket. After all, most of the time when I measure something, I want to mark it, and now there's always a pencil at hand."

Saw-toothed cutter

TAPES   "Usually, the economy-size rolls of the various tapes used in workshops don't have a dispenser included. So to each roll I add a dispenser made from a section of the saw-toothed cutter blade taken from an empty wax paper or aluminum foil carton from the kitchen. Just cut off enough of the blade to go through the spindle and around the roll of tape. Bend it around so it forms a loose square around the tape. Now, when you peel off the amount of tape you need, you can hold the blade firmly against the roll and tear the tape off. When the tape is gone, move the cutter to the new roll."

"While industry has developed many new and useful pressure-sensitive tapes, it has done very little to help you get a free end when you're ready to use the roll. I have, however, by the simple use of a paper clip. Each time I'm through using the tape, I press the end over a wire paper clip that I lay down across the edge of the roll. The tape holds the clip in place. Next time I need to use the tape, the paper clip serves as a handle."

End of tape over string

Or try this to get the end of the tape up: "If you tie a loop of string around the roll, the end of the tape can be stuck down over the string. Then when you need more tape, a slight tug on the string will lift up the end. This makes it more practical to buy the large economy-size rolls of cellophane and masking tape that don't have their own dispenser."

"I discovered a way to revive a roll of masking tape after it had apparently lost its zip. Hold a hot iron up close to the roll. Very soon, the tape can be peeled away from the roll and will have regained its adhesive qualities. If there are spots that don't stick, apply the iron to these spots. No sense in throwing away a roll of tape without trying this first."

When tape has been allowed to stay stuck in place too long in the sunlight, the sun—or any other heat source for that matter—can cause the tape to become a gummy glob that's next to impossible to remove. One of the manufacturers of masking tape has some good advice. First, apply additional heat in the form of warm water or a hot iron wrapped in aluminum foil to loosen up the paper backing of the tape. When the backing is removed, a rag soaked with lighter fluid will take off the remaining adhesive residue. (Lighter fluid is highly flammable, so use caution.)

"Here's a real step saver. I always keep a small supply of electrical tape wrapped around the nonworking parts of various hand tools. It's positively amazing how many times you'll find need for a small piece of tape when you're doing a chore away from your workbench."

"Sometimes tape has wrapped around a wire or some other object in such a tight place that only one hand can get in to do the job. It may help to unroll the desired length of tape and reroll it, but with the sticky side out. Make this as compact a roll as possible. You'll be able to put this type of roll in place and wrap it around and around with just the thumb and forefinger of one hand."

TAPS AND TAPPING   "Back when I was a pipe smoker, I used to keep pipe cleaners out in my workshop. I found lots of uses for them in the shop, and now, even though I've given up my pipe, I still keep a packet of pipe cleaners as part of my tool inventory. One of the many uses for pipe cleaners is in the storing of my taps. I wrap a pipe cleaner around each tap, completely covering the threads. This protects them from getting damaged from contact. Then I take a can of machine oil and dampen the pipe cleaner well. This holds oil for a long time and distributes the oil all over the tap threads."

"After tapping a blind hole in metal, the problem arises of removing the tiny metal shavings. Everyone has a magnetic-tipped screwdriver, and this will pick up all the filings. It may not be a sensational idea, but I just caught my neighbor trying to blow the particles out, and they could easily end up in his eye."

Or try this one. "Cut a few slivers off a bar of soap and put them into the hole. Then, as your tap goes in, the soap will be forced out and will carry most of the metal shavings out too."

TARPS   "Tying down the corners of a tarpaulin not fitted with grommets can be a hit-and-miss proposition. You can take the miss out if you double the corner back over a smooth round object such as a marble or small rubber ball. Then tie the rope around the corner just inside the round object. The knot can't slip over this, and so your tarp will stay tied down. This'll work on either a canvas or plastic cover."

THEFT AND BURGLAR PROOFING   Theft of hand tools goes on at an alarming rate. When I discussed this problem with a policeman, he came up with some guidelines to follow. First, of course, keep your tools under lock and key at all times. Also jot down serial numbers, model numbers, make, and description of all your tools. And, if you can't stamp or engrave your name on the tools, spray an unusual color on various parts of the tools. (Makes 'em easier to see and find, too.) A thief will often pass over tools with these paint jobs, as he knows they're too easily identifiable.

"Since we live in a friendly neighborhood, there's a lot of borrowing of tools. To make sure which are mine, I put my 'brand' on them. I paint my initials on all the wooden handles with some of my wife's nail polish. While the polish is still wet, I light a match to it, and it burns a nice set of initials into the wood."

Or: "Use a hand paper puncher and punch out initials on a strip of aluminum foil. Tape the foil on the handle of the tool in an appropriate place. Then, with a propane torch, run over the punched-out dots until the wood is burned. When the foil is removed, the brand is there, and it really looks good."

"My mini-wall-safe is such a good idea I have to share it and just hope there are no burglars as readers. I cut a hole in the wall the size of an ordinary electric outlet and down at the height where one would be. Inside, I mounted a box made of sheet metal. Then I covered over the opening with a dummy wall-outlet plate that looks as normal as any. All I have to do to get in my mini-safe is remove one screw."

"I have a unique safe in our house, for small items that I don't feel would ever be found. I chiseled out a space in the top of one of our doors. Even with the door open, only a basketball player would be tall enough to see the top of the door."

(If you have a hollow-core door, make sure you don't cut far enough down in the top rail to go through. If you do, not even you will be able to get the loot out.)

Many folks use a flashlight as a hiding place for a spare car key or house key, or even mad money. This idea can be bad, because too many flashlights disappear from the car. If you have something hidden in your auto flashlight, think it over.

Loose hinge plate

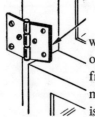

"Anyone who has double-hung windows with a fixed top pane may wish to install these extra locks that allow the window to be propped open an inch or so for ventilation, but will not allow it to be opened from the outside any more than that. This lock is a small butt hinge mounted at the right height next to the window. One plate of the hinge is left free and is swung over so that when the window is raised, it runs into the edge of this hinge plate and can go no farther. If it needs to be opened from the inside, the hinge is closed, allowing the window to go on up."

"We like fresh air at night, and leave our double-hung windows open a couple of inches. I fixed it so we can do this and yet the windows will still be burglarproof. With the window raised about 2″, I drilled through the stile of the bottom window and into the stile of the top window about halfway. The hole is big enough to accomodate a ¼″ metal rod and is at a slight downward angle. A similar hole was drilled on the other side of the window. The two rods act as bolts, and the window can't be opened from the outside."

"When we locked our door keys in the house, a neighbor showed me how easy it was to break in through our sliding glass patio doors. He also showed me how to make them burglarproof by putting a length of pipe down into the track where the door slides to open. The pipe should be the same length as the track. When it's in place, it prevents the door from sliding open."

(However, after you've done this, don't be dumb enough to lock your keys inside again.)

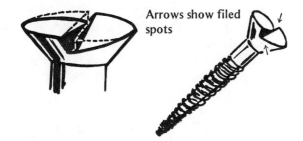

Arrows show filed spots

"Some screws never need to be taken off. In such cases, I always make the screws 'one way' with the help of a file. Establish the edges on the screw slot that the screwdriver would push against in unscrewing, and file these off. Just be sure you leave enough edge on each side for the screwdriver to bite into in the tightening-down process. In effect, these 'one-way' screws render whatever you've used them on theftproof."

THIRD HANDS　　It seems that the Good Lord should have given the handyman a third hand. There's almost no chore he tackles that wouldn't be easier to do with that extra assist. Here are some helpers!

When it comes to soldering two or more wires together, you really need extra hands. A paper cup can provide the help you need. Make slits in the rim of the cup to accommodate the wires. Slip each wire into a slit, and the cup will hold them in place while you work. Also, the cup catches any drops of solder. If the cup needs extra weight for stability, pour in sand or water.

"There have been times in soldering when an extra hand would been 'handy.' One trick is to lock the trigger of your soldering gun to the 'On' position and prop it up in place to use. This will leave both hands free to hold other things. The easiest way to lock the trigger is by placing a strong rubber band around the trigger and the handle. I keep a rubber band around the handle of my gun just for that purpose."

"There are lots of times when you're working in a tight place and hate to let go of the grip you have on a pair of pliers to change positions or something. If you add a strong rubber band around the handles, you can let go without the pliers letting go."

(This trick can also turn your pliers into a small vise. The rubber band will keep the plier jaws clamped tight on the work, leaving hands free to do other things.)

"If you need to get a metal bolt started in a tight place, insert the head of the bolt in a length of plastic or rubber tube. With the end of the bolt pointed down, it can be twisted into its threaded hole by twisting the tubing. After it's started in the hole, a tug will pull the tube up and off, as the threads will hold the bolt. The job can be finished with a socket wrench."

"I decided I wanted to start cutting firewood, but didn't have anyone to help with my two-man saw. Since all you need on one stroke of the saw is a return, I devised an automatic return stroke from an inner tube. With one end of the inner tube around one of the saw handles and the other around a post, the elasticity of the rubber pulls the saw back just as another person would. This enabled me to do the job by myself."

"This is for the home handyman who has to drive nails up higher than he can reach. The hammer will, of course, add 8″ to 10″ reach to your nailing arm, but that won't help unless you have extra reach with the other hand to hold the nails. If you don't want to be hauling a ladder around, make a slit in the end of a yardstick, using a saw that will leave a kerf a little smaller than the shank of the nails you're using. Slip the nail in the slit. The yardstick will give you the extra reach and hold the nail in place. When the nail is started, the yardstick can be pulled down, leaving the nail to be driven home."

"When getting a nail started, use a bar magnet to hold the nail. This leaves one hand free to do something else, and also, you can't smash a finger this way."

"I put a small rubber suction cup on the end of my flexible metal measuring tape. It will stick to walls, floors, and any smooth surface. Just be sure the suction cup is far enough from the end so the tape measure can be butted up against walls if need be."

A proud father tells us: "My nine-year-old got tired of holding the flashlight for me while I worked under the car. He left, and returned in a few minutes with a glass fruit jar. When the flashlight was put into the jar, the jar held it straight upright, and the light beamed up where I wanted it."

C-clamp and wood scrap

"When you don't have a helper to hold up one end of a heavy joist while you nail up the other end, you'll find this idea a real help. Tighten down a scrap of wood to the top of the joist by means of a large C-clamp on the end, and allow it to stick out a couple of inches past the end. This will become a support which will lie on top of the cross member and hold that end in position while you go to work on the other end."

"If you need to work on the edge of a door before installing it, your biggest problem will probably be in holding it up. No problem. Get a couple of apple crates and two C-clamps, and you're in business. Clamp the door flat against the crates on both ends. It will be very steady while you work."

"I've made a handy addition to my tool kit by magnetizing a bunch of alligator clips. When I get ready to climb up on the ladder to do some task, I clip these to my belt. Nails, screws, and small parts and tools that would ordinarily be falling off on the floor can be held on my belt by the magnets."

Wire hanger taped to box

"Most dry shop ingredients come in boxes, and boxes don't come with handles. When I need a handle for a box, I just bend a wire coat hanger to fit and attach it to the box with masking tape. I sometimes use the hanger hook to hang the box on something when I need both hands. When I'm finished with the box, I untape the handle and put the box back on the shelf."

"Long, heavy objects such as posts or pipes are unwieldy for one man to move around. Not so if you place one end of the object in an old pan or bucket and slide it to the place it's needed. The pan will slide on almost any surface."

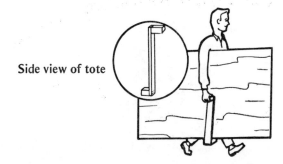

Side view of tote

"When I paneled our den I got tired of wrestling with those 4' x 8' sheets of plywood and came up with a sort of crude 'tote stick.' I took a 3'-long 1" x 4" and nailed 2" x 4" blocks on either end—one facing in, and the other out. The one facing in hooks under the plywood, while the one facing out is a handle. Center it and pick it up. The plywood fits neatly under your arm." (A spare metal towel rack will also help with this task.)

2" x 4"s

"Cutting across a 4' x 8' sheet of plywood with a handsaw is not a big muscle job, but because of the size of the sheet, it's downright unhandy to get at unless your arms are four or five feet long. Solve this by leaning a pair of 6'-long 2 x 4's up against a wall, and then leaning the sheet of plywood against them. Adjust the angle to suit you, and then start sawing. You'll find it's quite easy to saw this way, because you can position yourself as close as need be to the work, and sawing from a standing position is easier. By the time you've sawed down far enough to have to bend over too much, you can transfer the sheet to sawhorses, and the cut will be far enough through to allow you to reach with normal arms."

Paint roller in vise

"One person trying to handle long stock while ripping can run into all sorts of trouble. However, I solved this by putting a paint roller in my vise and adjusting the roller so it's the same height as the saw table. This supports one end of the stock and allows me to push it through. The roller rolls so that the stock moves easily."

THREADS "A nut and bolt that has developed just a little play because the threads may have worn down a bit needn't always be replaced. One layer of cellophane tape around the threads of the bolt will often take up the slack. The tape should be pressed into the threads carefully. The bolt will finish the pressing, and the tape will have made the two fit tight once again. This won't always work, but then, nobody's perfect."

"Many times you really need to grip a bolt or other object by its threads. This can be touchy, since the vise, pliers, or whatever you use to grip with can ruin the threads. Make a protector by wrapping soft wire around and in the threads. Just be sure the wire is big enough around to stick up above the threads. The wire then takes the beating—not the threads."

"As a temporary—and maybe even permanent—means when a screw hole in wood or plaster is stripped of threads, take a small piece of steel wool and put it on the end of the screw. Reinsert the screw and turn it down tightly. This will probably cure the problem."

"Here is a quick trick that may restore the botched-up threads on a screw so it can still be used. Grip the screw up close to the head with a pair of cutting pliers. Make sure the cutting edges of the pliers are down in between the threads. Apply enough pressure so the pliers cut into the screw. Then turn the screw just as if you were unscrewing, so it comes out all the way through the pliers. The cutting pliers will reestablish the threads as the screw is turned through. You'll probably want to do this several times to make sure that the threads are cut deep enough."

THUMBTACKS   "Most handymen need thumbtacks from time to time, and usually need them in a hurry. I keep mine handy stuck in a cork that hangs on a string from the ceiling of my workshop. The cork hangs out of the way but within easy reach, and holds lots of thumbtacks.

TINY PARTS   "I try to keep all the different sizes of screws, bolts, and nuts in separate containers in my workshop. The best holders I've found for very tiny items are deodorant jars. Those curved bottoms inside enable me to pick up the tiny things much easier."

"Since we got a new refrigerator with an ice maker, I ended up with several of those plastic ice trays. They make great storage drawers for all sorts of small items—nuts, bolts, screws, and parts."

"In the normal home workshop, there seems to be no end to the hundreds of small screws, bolts, and parts you accumulate. I've made some handy trays in which to keep these tiny items, using the bottoms of those molded paper-fiber egg cartons. I gave them a coat of shellac to make them have a tough finish. They fit in the workbench drawer and hold lots of little things, and so far they haven't shown any signs of wear. And, as you've said before, the price is right!"

"Here's a good step to include any time you're disassembling a small object that has a lot of small parts. Before you start the job, stick a strip of double-faced pressure-sensitive tape down on your work table. Then, as you take out each part, stick it down on the tape. Keep the parts in the order in which they've been removed. This, of course, makes reassembly a lot easier, and the tape prevents any of the tiny parts from rolling away and getting lost."

"A flat gallon can with a handle on top makes an admirable washing container for small parts. Just cut a section out on one side, starting the cut at the top of the can and going down about 3″ or 4″. Put in the solvent almost up to where the cut stops. For the parts cleaning, the container is laid down flat and acts like a tray. However, when you're through, the tray has a handle for carrying and is its own container."

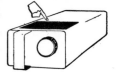
Cut out section here

"If you've ever had to dig around in your tool box for several different small items, you'll agree that my idea is a good one. I've stuck several small magnets inside the lid of my tool box. They just stay there out of the way until I start rummaging around. Then, as I come across an item I'm looking for, I let a magnet hold it until I've found all of them. It's been very handy for me."

Who among you hasn't wasted time crawling around on the floor looking for some tiny part that was accidentally dropped? Here's a tip that will cut down on that floor time. Lay a flashlight down on the floor and turn it on. As you move it around on the floor, even the tiniest missing part will cast a pretty good-sized shadow that will be easy to see. Try it next time you get clumsy.

"You and your readers have come up with many ideas for holding tiny nails so you don't bang up your fingers with the hammer. Probably the easiest is just to use a pair of needle-nose pliers to hold the nails. Every tool box has a pair, and some of the other ideas require you to use something you don't necessarily find with your tools."

"Before throwing away the old coffee pot, I latched on to the metal basket that holds the coffee grounds. It makes an ideal basket for cleaning small parts in the shop. I put a wire handle through the hole in the center so the basket can be put down into the cleaning solvent, sloshed about, and lifted out without getting my hands in the liquid. The holes in the basket allow for the solvent to get in to clean the parts."

TOENAILING   "As you know, when you're toenailing a stud in place, the force of the hammer can knock the stud out of position if there's not something on the other side to hold it there. One of the best old carpenter's tricks is to use an ice pick. Place it up against the stud and push the point down into the sill on the side opposite to where the nail goes. This will hold it while you hammer the nail down."

TOOLS–PROTECTION, CARE, REPAIR, ETC.   The craftsman or the home handyman is only as good as his tools. Proper care will make those tools last longer and perform better. Here are some tool protection hints.

"Many home handymen keep a cone of carpenter's chalk in the tool box to absorb the moisture and thereby protect the tools. I've found that a few mothballs will do the same thing. I've done this over a period of several years, and my tools show no evidence of moisture damage."

(Bet they haven't been attacked by moths or silverfish either!)

"I only get the urge to start some shop project every so often, and so I have to make sure my tools are well protected during a sometimes long period of idleness. The best way I've found is to wrap them tightly in aluminum foil. This keeps out all air and moisture. The tools that should be kept lubricated are sprayed with silicone lube before being wrapped. Some articles that I haven't used in a year look brand new when unwrapped."

"I keep a bucket of drained motor oil around and find many uses for it. One I would like to pass along certainly makes digging post holes a lot easier. I coat the post hole digger with the oil, and it keeps mud from sticking to the tool. This also works on shovels or forks. After I'm through using one of these tools, I put it away with a light coat of this oil on it to protect it from rust."

"I've discovered that using toothpaste to clean hand tools really gets the job done. Unlike some cleaning methods, this one never scratches a delicate cutting edge. I apply it with a damp rag."

"Maybe you would like to pass along to your readers my method of protecting a plane from damage when not in use. I cut a rubber band about 3″ wide from a bicycle inner tube. This slips over the plane, holds itself tight in place, and keeps the plane iron (cutting blade) from getting nicked."

"When a saw blade gets a layer of gum on it, you may want to borrow your wife's spray-on oven cleaner from the kitchen and give the blade a blast. It will tell you on the container how long to wait before wiping off. It sure cuts tough deposits."

"I've come up with a good way to keep from banging up the blades for my table saw. It also protects my hands from getting nicked when the blades are stored in the drawer. I cut a bunch of rubber bands about an inch wide from an old inner tube and stretch these around the outside edge of the blade. They make great protectors."

Wide rubber band

"No matter how carefully you put away cutting tools, they seem to get nicks from time to time. I put a tab of masking tape over the cutting edges of chisels, planes, and the like. This is good protection."

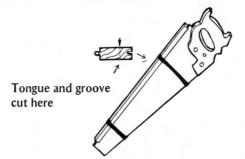

Tongue and groove
cut here

"I've made a blade protector for my handsaw from the grooved edge
of a piece of tongue-and-groove flooring. I cut a strip about an inch
wide and the length of the blade. The blade fits into the groove and is
held in place with rubber bands."

"The hand power tool I use most of all is my ¼″ drill. I decided to
put it in my tool box so that I'd have it along at all times. Knowing
how important it is to protect the chuck, I found a rubber crutch-tip
that exactly fit over the end of the chuck."

"I made a cover for my files out of rubber bands cut from old inner
tubes. The rubber bands should be cut just a little wider than the widest
part of the file. Then cut a hole about ¼″ in diameter. Insert the tang
(pointed handle) of the file through this hole. Then pull the band down
over the other end, and it's completely covered and protected."

"Rub a thin layer of clear paste wax over the table of your power
saw. This makes wood glide over the surface more easily, and the paste
wax doesn't stain. Protects the table and the work."

Not all tool storage ideas are for protection. Some are just cleverly
convenient:

"Our teen-age daughter has outgrown her 45-rpm records and discarded a wire record rack. It's the kind that has inverted U-shaped wires
in a long row; the records were stored upright between the U's. I found
that there's enough give between these partitions to store about a dozen
small hand tools. Just push them down in, and they stay in place. The
rack sits on top of the workbench or can be used as a caddy for
carrying these tools to some other place."

"A screen door spring attached horizontally to a wall becomes a useful holder for all sorts of small hand tools. After attaching it at both ends, hammer in large staples every 6". The tools are then held flat against the wall." (Attached inside a kitchen cabinet door, this same type of spring will hold all those empty grocery bags for your wife.)

Rubber band

"A free holder for all sorts of small screwdrivers can be made from a section of corrugated cardboard that's rolled tightly and held together with a rubber band. The tools go point down into the corrugations. This type of holder can be made big or small to handle as many tools as you have. It's good as a bench top holder or can be tossed in the tool box."

"I made a neat holder for all my smaller drill bits. It consists of a flip-top cigarette box and a piece of corrugated cardboard. Cut the corrugated board so it fits into the cigarette box. The bits are kept down in between the corrugations. Before putting them in, however, pour melted paraffin down into the corrugations to fill them up. This keeps the drill bits in tight and also automatically lubricates them after each use."

Corrugated cardboard

"I carry all of my tiny drill bits in the empty barrel of an old ball-point pen. The pen fits nicely in my tool chest when not in use, or in my pocket when I get ready to use the bits. I poured paraffin in the bottom to seal up the hole where the point used to go. I put in a few drops of oil every so often, and this keeps the bits lubricated."

"Here's my tool holder idea. My shop walls have exposed studs. I cut 1" x 4" pieces to fit exactly between the studs. Holes are then drilled in these boards especially for each tool. When the board is put in place between the studs, nails can be driven through the studs and into the ends of the holder boards to keep them in place. These look good and are easy to fix, and they're made exactly for each of your tools."

String & spool

"I devised a gadget that acts as a holder for my putty knife and other such small hand tools. The wall in my garage which backs up my shop equipment has exposed studs. I bored a hole through the stud, and then put a string through this hole. I threaded the string through the hole in a wooden spool and tied it so the spool hangs against the exposed side of the stud. When I want to put the knife away, I lift up the spool and insert the putty knife between the spool and the stud. When the spool is allowed to rest on the stud, it holds the knife in place flat against the stud. This will also work for screwdrivers, chisels, and other such tools."

"I think my homemade hangers for garden tools are worthy of your fine column. They're made from empty wooden spools attached to my garage wall by nails driven through the holes in the spools. Spaced the right distance apart, each pair of spools becomes a tailor-made hanger for a particular tool. Be sure the nail is longer than the spool, or it won't go far enough into the wall to hold. Also, use a nail with a head bigger than the spool hole. These hangers work well, look neat, and cost nothing."

Spools on nails in wall

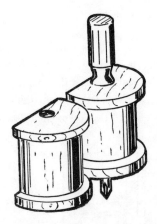

"Here's my spool trick. I saw off a portion of wooden spools to give them a flat side. Then I glue them to my shop wall and use them as wall holders for screwdrivers. They're easy to make and look good."

"Here's how I made some handy holders for screwdrivers, files, and chisels. I cut bamboo sections from an old fishing pole. The cut at the top of each section was made just below the joint, and at the bottom it was made just below a joint. This left a hollow section all the way from the top except for the solid section at the bottom. I then drilled a hole up near the top of each section to hang the holder on the shop wall. They could even hang nicely on hooks in pegboard walls, too."

"My yardstick doesn't stray away from my workbench since I installed my free holder. It's a cardboard tube from a roll of kitchen paper towels, taped to the leg of my workbench. The yardstick is stored upright in the tube and resting on the floor. It's always within easy reach."

"I ran across a chunk of Styrofoam left over from some project of my kids and found it a great bench-top holder for small, sharp tools. The ends of the tools go right down into the Styrofoam, which holds them upright until needed again. When the tools are stuck back in, it doesn't make any difference if you hit the same hole or not. I use this holder for all my screwdrivers, chisels, and other such equipment. After several months, it has had no apparent effect on the cutting edges of the tools."

"To keep my power drill out of the way, I hang it on the wall. The hanger is a screw eye on which the chuck tightens to hold the drill."

"I've mounted a cost-free holster for my electric drill on my shop wall. It was made from a plastic bleach bottle. All I did was cut the bottom of the bottle out and screw the bottle to the wall with the spout pointing down. The cap was left off to provide a place for the drill bit to stick out. The bottle is big enough to house both the drill and the electric cord. Now I've hung the chuck key on a string tied to the handle of the bottle so that it's always nearby."

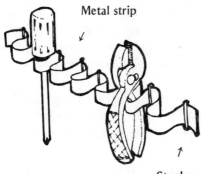

Metal strip

Staples

"The thin metal strips from sardine and coffee cans that are opened with keys need not be thrown away. By unrolling the strip, it can be stapled to the wall at intervals so that loops are formed, and small tools can be inserted into the loops. If the strips are painted the same color as the wall, these free holders even look good."

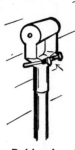

"When I broke our old grass rake, I found a good use for the rake head. I attached it to my shop wall by clenching nails over the frame, and presto, it became a tool hanger. The tools are held by screw eyes in the ends of the tool handles."

"With two large nails and a wide rubber band, you can custom a tool holder for your garage wall. Drive a nail in to fit on either side of the handle of the tool. When the tool is in place, put the rubber band over the heads of the nails so the tool cannot fall or be knocked down."

Rubber band
over nails

"Since stands for large power tools sometimes cost almost as much as the tools they hold, your economy-minded readers will like my brain-child. I use discarded 55-gallon drums as tool stands. I fill them part of the way up with sand to give them good stability and paint them to match the metal legs on my workbench, so they are not only very functional but good looking too. And they cost me nothing."

"For the various socket attachments for my socket wrench I made a holder that keeps the sockets and handle always together. I cut a strip from an old inner tube, about 8" long and 1" wide and cut a pair of 'X' slits in each end. I slipped the slits on one end over the wrench handle, then threaded the sockets on the strip. When all were on the strip, I slipped the slits on the other end over the end of the handle. The sockets are held there until I'm ready to remove them for use."

"In my tool box, all the pointed tools like awls and screwdrivers have guards on them to protect the points (as well as my hands, when I'm scratching around for something). I made these guards from sections of corrugated board cut just a shade longer than the shank of the tool. The points fit down into the corrugations. Although it's not necessary, I seal off the edges of these holsters with masking tape."

"Rather than throw away a worn set of floor mats from the car, I've covered the bottom of my tool chest with a piece cut to fit. This cuts down on my tools' banging around. I also did the same thing to a drawer in my workbench and had enough left to put down in front of the workbench to stand on. Beats standing on the cement floor."

"Here's an addition to the home handyman tool chest. Buy a small purse mirror from the dime store and glue a small magnet to the back of it. Then the next time you've work to do on the furnace, the auto engine, or a motor that's hard to see into, your mirror can attach itself to something metal and be positioned so that you can see those parts of the work that you wouldn't be able to otherwise. Mine has come in handy many times."

(This certainly will come in handy—unless you fail to wrap the mirror for protection. In which case, it will never survive the tool box, and you'll end up having seven years' bad luck.)

"When a pair of my socks wear out, I save them for my workshop. A sock makes a great protective holder for a plane. Socks are also good for keeping other tools so they won't rattle around. And they're excellent mittens for applying lubricants or for wiping tools off."

"Some of the hand tools at my workbench are duplicates of ones I have in my portable tool box, so there's no need for them to ever leave the bench. I worked it out so they'll always stay there, and yet are always neatly hung on the wall when not in use—I made them retractable. I have pegboard walls in my shop, and each tool is attached to a string long enough to reach any part of the bench. The string is threaded through one of the pegboard holes and attached to a weight on the back of the pegboard. When the tool is not in use, the weight falls back down, draws the string back, and holds the tool tight against the wall."

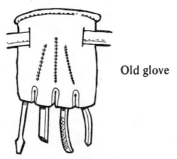

Old glove

"I made a tool holster from an old work glove. All I did was cut the ends of the fingers out and then cut the two slits for the belt to go through. The finger holes allow screwdrivers and other long tools to stick through."

"A tool carrier that's easy to make and easy to carry and will hold quite a number of items can be made from a pair of flat two-gallon oil cans. One of the large flat sides is cut from each can. A piece of hardboard with a cut-out area to form a handle is placed between the

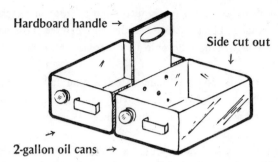

Hardboard handle →

Side cut out
↓

2-gallon oil cans →

two cans, and the three pieces are bolted together. It's handy and handsome."

"Somewhere in the north woods, I walked off and left a nice leather sheath that used to belong on my hand axe. When I couldn't retrace my steps to find it, I made one from an old tin can that at least got us back to civilization without anyone's getting cut. If you ever need to do this, select a can that's not quite as wide as the blade of your hatchet or axe. Cut both ends out of the can, and flatten it with your foot. It will then be wide enough for the blade. If it's the right size can, the blade will wedge in and the sheath will stay in place."

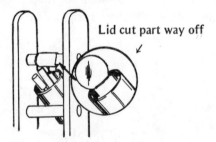

Lid cut part way off
↙

"Here's my super-tricky tool holder for working on a ladder. I took a large juice can and cut the lid only partially off, running the can opener all the way around except for aoout the last inch or so. This lid now bends around the rung of my ladder and hangs right in front of me. It makes a convenient holder for the hand tools I need for the job."

Open-end wrenches
↓   ↓

Most home handymen are not satisfied with tools as they come from the hardware store. Here are some improvements, as well as some creations:

"I have a super tool that no one else in the world has—because I made it myself. On the handles of my regular pliers I welded two different sizes of open-end wrenches that I use the most. This three-in-one tool fits nicely into a pocket, whereas all three of the tools carried separately would weigh me down. The wrenches are welded to the outside of the handles, of course, so that the pliers can still be closed."

"I saw an ad in the paper for a chrome-plated tool that was a combination hammer, pliers, screwdriver, and heaven knows what else. While it was a little too fancy for me, it gave me a good idea. I took an ordinary pair of pliers and filed one handle so that it was shaped like the end of a screwdriver. It's really a handy tool, and I can't tell you how many times I've been able to save steps by having this two-in-one gadget."

"Here's an idea my father passed on to me 20 years ago. Did you know you can make regular pliers into vise-grip pliers with a turnbuckle? The turnbuckle must be big enough so the stationary center piece will fit over the handles of the pliers. When the pliers are gripping whatever you want them to hold, slip the turnbuckle over the handles. Then tighten the screw eyes down against the handles firmly, and the pliers can't be opened. This trick is a big help when you need both your hands for other things."

Hacksaw blade
← section

"I've created a tool that I call my 'hack-driver'—a small section of old hacksaw blade welded to the shank of a medium-sized screwdriver. I did this so I would have a tool to reslot damaged screws, but I've found that it also comes in handy when I need a tiny saw in a tight place."

Section of saw blade

"Every home handyman will find many uses for a rough scraper of some sort. I made one that's on the end of a wire brush I have in my tool box. All it took was a small section of an old hacksaw blade with a pair of holes drilled in it, which I screwed in place on the end of the brush handle. The teeth stick up over the handle, and I turn the brush upside down to use the scraper."

(Another handyman suggested the blade could be put in the top of your hammerhead or the end of any other wooden-handled tool.)

Another reader did just the opposite, though, and came up with the same handy tool: "I glued an old suede shoebrush to the back of my scraper handle. This fine wire brush certainly comes in handy when the scraping area needs brushing off."

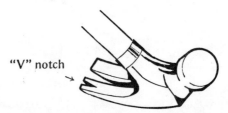

"V" notch

"The ordinary claw hammer is almost useless for pulling out tacks and small nails. I altered my hammer to make it a tack extractor too. All it took was to file a 'V' notch only about 1/8" deep in the end of one of the claws. Then I dressed down this claw with a grinding wheel so it was thin enough to get under the tacks. A simple change, but very effective!"

"Hammers and nails are natural go-togethers, so I made a nail gauge on my hammer. I used a scribe and marked of '2d' on up through '60d' on the hammer handle."

Eraser acts as fulcrum

"Here's an alteration to my nail set that makes it a double tool. I had an old hard-rubber eraser about an inch thick. I drilled a hole through it lengthwise and forced the handle of the nail set through it. I did this to give me a better grip, but soon found that it made an excellent fulcrum to use under the hammer when pulling nails."

"Why don't they make adjustable wrenches with gauges to show the size of their openings? I've marked all of mine in 1/8" graduations so that when I get ready to use one, it's no longer a guessing proposition. I did mine with an electric etching tool, but it could be done with a file or scriber. I did this on my monkey wrenches, too."

"If your child replaces the handlebar grips on his bicycle, don't throw the old grips away. They will come in very handy as grips for a number of tools such as torque wrenches and pipe cutters. This grip will make the tool a lot more comfortable to your hands and in most cases will allow you to get a better hold."

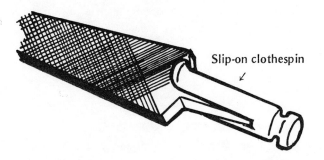

Slip-on clothespin

"Maybe some other home handymen will want to add a handle to a file. If so, I can tell them the quickest way to do it. Just take a slip-on type wooden clothespin and slip this over the tang of the file. Then tape it on tight, and you'll have a comfortable handle to make filing a lot easier on the hand."

Drawer knob

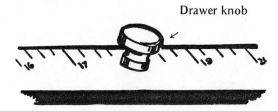

"Although many companies give away free yardsticks, I think many people would pay for one if they made them with my addition. I added a handle to mine by attaching an old drawer knob to the center of the yardstick. It's held on by a flat-head stove bolt that can be countersunk on the bottom side so that the yardstick lies flat. I find it much easier to use."

"Some time ago, I picked up a screwdriver lying in the street. It was beat-up and not usable, but the idea struck me that I had no tack puller, and so I made one from the screwdriver. Placing the screwdriver horizontally in the vise, I took a triangular file and filed a groove in the center of the blade until the opening was about ¼″ deep. Next I filed both points chisel-sharp. Then I put an inch of the blade into the vise, with the groove toward me, and bent the handle toward me about 30 degrees. Now I have a tack puller and small pry-bar."

"I've made a simple addition to all of my screwdrivers that works great for me. I welded a nut around the shank about halfway up. This doesn't get in the way for any of the normal uses, but when I need additional pressure I can use a wrench on the nut, and this gives me tremendous extra turning power."

"Since a little paraffin on screws aids in their installation, why not keep some handy? The most logical place is in a hole drilled in the end of the screwdriver handle. Drill the hole large enough to accommodate fairly large-sized screws, but not so large as to weaken the handle. Pour melted paraffin into the hole and dip the end of the screws into this wax-well as needed."

"I noticed my fishing tackle box has a ruler on the top for measuring fish. While I've never used this (because I'm a lousy fisherman), it gave me an idea for a very useful addition to my tool chest. I took an old broken retractable tape rule and cut off a section the same length as the top of my tool box. Then I attached it to the top. There are lots of times when I need to measure something, and it's easier to lay it down on the tool box than to search out a measure."

"Since I have a roll-away workshop in my garage, all of my power tools are on casters and are rolled out for use. Some didn't have brakes, though, and would end up creeping. I solved this by simply drilling an off-center hole in a pair of the wheels and their mounts. When the hole in a wheel is lined up with the hole in its mount, a nail can be inserted, and the wheel can't roll until the nail is removed."

(This will also work on any piece of furniture on casters that creeps around the house.)

"The toggle switch on my power saw was hard to reach, so I put an extension arm on it, made from the barrel of an old ball-point pen. The plastic barrel was flexible enough to allow it to be forced over the lever, yet stiff enough to flip the switch."

If your tool care has been less than super, here are a few repair hints.

When the plastic- or rubber-tipped head of a mallet goes, the mallet suddenly becomes about as effective as a sledge hammer on finishes. Before you throw it away, however, why not reface it? One excellent material to use for facing is that silicone adhesive sealant that comes in a tube. Make a form around the head of the mallet with masking tape. Let the tape extend up about ¼" above the head of the mallet. Put the mallet in a vise and make sure the top is level. Then put on a fine layer of the silicone. If the head is level, the silicone will flow out level. When it sets up hard, take the tape off, flip the mallet over, and reface the other end. This will give an excellent rubber-like face that will not mar.

"Because I broke my Allen wrench off at the place where it's bent to form the 'L,' I adapted the remainder and came up with a better tool. I ground off the rough edges and slipped this in my Yankee drill. This new tool now tightens up Allen screws quicker and easier than the original tool."

Cracked or broken handles on any sort of tool are a menace and should be either replaced or repaired. If you decide on replacement, here's one method that will help you get rid of the old handle. First, saw it off right down next to the metal part of the tool. Then select a drill of the right size and start drilling through the wood left on the tool. Be careful not to hit any metal wedges that are present. Usually a few holes will make it easy to drive the remainder of the handle out with a punch. There are other ways, but this one will usually work.

Here's another and even trickier way of removing a stubborn worn wooden handle. Pack it in wet sand with just the wooden handle sticking out. Take a blowtorch and burn the old handle away. The wet sand will protect the working part of the tool from the heat which could effect its temper, and will also hold the tool in place at the desired angle.

If you've an axe to grind and no grinder, then you must sharpen it by hand. You know that the best position is to have the blade flat. However, holding it in that position is not always easy. A C-clamp will probably allow you to clamp the axe to your bench at just the right position.

"If your wooden-handled hammer turns up with a loosening head, and you don't have any metal wedges, here's a way to keep it from loosing its head. Insert a screw into the handle where the wedge would have gone. This will spread the wood and tighten the head. To tighten it further, put the hammerhead into a bucket of water and let it soak for a while. This will cause the wood to swell, resulting in more tightening. More permanent than water is soaking the hammer overnight in a bucket of linseed oil. When you take the hammer out, wipe off the excess. The oil won't evaporate as the water will."

Cut out here

TOTES   "I made a very useful tool tote out of one of those rectangular gallon cans, and maybe some of your readers would like to do the same. I cut out about half of the top, leaving the part with the handle intact. I then rolled under about ½″ of the edge I had cut, so there wouldn't be any danger of cutting my hands. It's a very handy gadget and carries a good number of tools."

"People who've seen me carry plywood sheets and large screens with my simple rope trick are always impressed. Here's hoping you'll be too. For a 4′ x 8′ sheet of plywood, you'll need a piece of rope about 18′

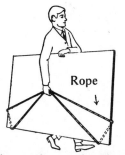

Rope ↓

long. Tie the two ends together so that the rope forms a circle. Now grasp the rope at two points opposite each other on the circle. This will leave a loop of rope coming from each side of your fist. With the sheet of plywood standing up, put the loops around the two corners next to the ground. The section you were gripping now becomes a handle, and by lifting the sheet up under your arm, it'll be quite easy to carry."

COFFEE COFFEE

"Here's a nail caddy that takes less than an hour to make and is a super addition for any handyman to have. I used eight coffee cans, a 1″ x 4″ scrap of wood, and a screen door handle. I bolted the coffee cans to the board, four on each side. I then put the handle in the middle of the board so the tote could be carried easily. The coffee cans are large enough for you to reach into to get nails out and also to carry a good quantity. The board should be about ¼″ from the top of the cans so the plastic tops can be put on the cans when not in use, thus protecting the nails from the moisture in the air. With compartments for eight different sizes of nails, you're all set for most chores. When not being carried, the tote rests on the bases of the cans."

(Spray-paint it, and it will look so good your wife will liberate it for toting her cleaning supplies.)

TOWING   "Faced with the problem of towing our second car to a garage, I had no tow bar or towing hooks. But by using a pair of C-clamps and a short length of chain, I solved my problem. I put the clamps through the end links of the chain, and then clamped them to the bumpers of the two autos. My neighbor steered the rear car. This got me there and saved a towing charge."

(Make sure you take it easy when towing, and that you work out signals ahead of time. Also, check to see if there are any local ordinances against a tow-it-yourself project.)

TRAILER HITCHES "Here's a way to protect your trailer hitch ball from rust and corrosion. Coat it with heavy grease, and then slip a plastic sandwich bag over the ball and hold it in place with a rubber band. This completely seals out the elements and protects the ball."

"I have a trailer hitch on the back of my car, which I use to haul my boat to and from the lake. Since I don't use it very often, I found a way to protect it from rust and corrosion when not being used. I slit an old tennis ball so it fits over the ball on the trailer hitch. Just before I slip it on, I coat the ball with a good layer of petroleum jelly. The tennis ball keeps the lubrication in place on the ball and also protects it from the elements."

TREES "If you've ever planted a new little tree only to find that Peter Cottontail had stripped the bark off for food during the winter, you'll appreciate my precautionary idea. I tie burlap to the trunk from the ground up for about 3'. This takes only a few moments and yet will insure a live tree next spring. I don't mind feeding our furry friends, but would just as soon leave a few carrots out instead of my saplings."

(Unless you've got West Texas jackrabbits. They'll pull up small trees and eat roots and all! And never staple or nail anything to a tree—the breaks in the bark merely invite decay and disease.)

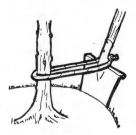

"Tree wells look good and help water and air get to the roots. If you need to dig a tree well around your trees, you'll want the edge to be as near a perfect circle as possible. Loop a heavy cord around the tree trunk and your shovel. Size the loop so that when it's pulled tight, the shovel will be as far away as you want the edge of your tree well. As you go around the tree, the shovel stays the same distance from the tree. Your well will be a perfect circle with the tree in the very center."

TROUBLE LIGHT "If you don't have a trouble light and decide to tinker around under the hood of your auto, this idea will save the day. Use an extension cord and a medium-sized 'U' magnet. Make a loop in the cord about 3″ from the light socket. Put the magnet in the loop, and then let the magnet attach itself to some metal part under the hood. The light will hang down, and you'll have a dandy trouble light (if you remembered to plug in the cord). It can be moved around and adjusted with more flexibility than a regular light."

"U" magnet

"I've lined the shield of my trouble light with aluminum foil. It acts as a reflector and gives off a better light. Also, as you know, those things throw off quite a bit of heat, and this keeps the back of the shield from getting so hot and saves me from burned spots on my hands."

"I created a trouble light for a recent trip under our house. I put a point on one end of a stick about 18″ long, and attached a light socket with an extension cord to the other. When I got to the spot where I needed to work, I poked the point into the ground, leaving both hands free."

"I think my 'clamp-lamp' is a great idea. I needed a trouble light for some work in the attic, so I took an extension cord and a large C-clamp. I taped the socket to the clamp. It's an easy light to carry, and can be clamped to rafters so you have both hands free to work."

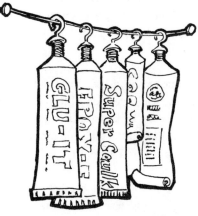

TUBES "Whenever I open a tube of glue or something for shop use, I use a cup hook to recap the tube. This not only seals the tube up tight, but acts as a hanger. I have a wire tacked to my shop wall, on which I hang these tubes by the cup hook."

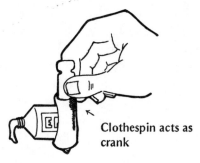

Clothespin acts as
crank

"Most of the adhesives and other compounds that come in tubes are expensive enough that it pays to get all out of the tube that you can. Therefore, my simple homemade crank will save you money. It's an old-fashioned slip-on clothespin that goes on the end of the partly used tube. By turning this crank to roll up the tube, you can squeeze out much more of the contents. And after the tube is empty, the crank pulls right off for use again."

(Another good tube squeezing crank can be made from a large cotter pin.)

Next time you open a tube of glue or something else that tends to ooze out under the cap and stick it to the threads when you've stored the tube away, take a bar of soap and coat the threads well. This retards and usually eliminates such a sticky problem.

"Too many tubes of things get stuck after the first time you use them, because of the glue, paint, paste, or such that gets on the top. I always apply a little petroleum jelly to the threads, and the cap won't stick. Gives you a tight seal too."

TUBING "For some reason, I have hung onto several assorted steel ball bearings. Suddenly, while working with some metal tubing, I found a use for them. When I got a kink in a section of the tubing, I selected a bearing that would just fit into the tube and dropped it in. It stopped at the kink, and I then put a rod in and tapped the ball on through. It removed the kink and left no lumps. Later, when I needed to flare out the end of the tube, I selected a bearing slightly larger than the diameter of the pipe, and by placing it in the opening and tapping it with a hammer, the pipe was easily flared."

TV One Sunday afternoon, we had a group over watching one of the many football games, and the set required some minor knob-twisting from the back. In making the adjustments, I employed an old, old trick I've used since the beginning of television ... that of holding a mirror in front of the set to see the changes I'm making on the screen while twisting the knobs on the back of the set. I was amazed that some of the viewers thougnt this was some new stunt some of my readers had thought up and sent in. In case there are others who don't know about this one, I wanted to include it. It's the only way to adjust the back and see the front at the same time unless you have extra-long arms.

"If your TV set requires adjusting quite a bit, as mine does, you'll know how aggravating it is to have to reach around in back of the set and fiddle with those little knobs that are recessed and can't be reached. I've made my life a lot easier by putting extension arms on the adjustment knobs so they now stick out an inch or so from the set. The extension arms are made from sections cut from the plastic barrels of old ball-point pens. Since the pen tapers down at the point, you can find a section that will fit almost any size control shaft. Warming the plastic will make it more pliable so it can be slipped on. Now, you can reach behind the set and make the adjustments without any trouble."

Installing an outside antenna for your TV is a fairly easy task for most home handymen. One point to keep in mind will make it a safer installation. Make sure the antenna isn't situated so that it would fall across a power line should it ever topple over. In most communities, there is a regulation against this, but I find it's one that's often overlooked. Even if you decide to have the antenna installed, make sure the serviceman remembers this.

U.

UNDERGROUND PIPE   "I had to replace a section of pipe under my lawn, and rather than dig up the entire length of pipe, I dug down to each end of the pipe to be replaced. I then slanted a trench leading into and out of this section of pipe. I attached a flange at one end and the section of new pipe to the other. The flange enabled me to attach a chain from a heavy-duty winch which was fastened to a big tree. The winch then pulled the old pipe out of the ground, and at the same time pulled the new pipe into place. This saved some work and was much easier on my lawn."

UNDERWRITERS' KNOT   The underwriters' knot is a special method of attaching a cord to a plug so that the wires will not be pulled out of the plug if suddenly subjected to a yank. It's quite simple to do . . . just follow the sketches.

STEP 1

Pull out about 3" of wire.

STEP 2

Form knot as shown. Pull the knot tight and then pull the cord down into the plug. In most cases it will fit down into the space in the plug. Twist the bare wire so there are no loose strands.

STEP 3

Bring each wire around a prong. Hook the wire around the screw in the same direction as the screw turns. Tighten down, and it should look like this when looking down on the knot and plug. You will note it forms a sort of "S" if properly tied . . . this "S" stands for super.

UNREACHABLES "The radio antenna from our car broke off, and I converted it into a useful tool. By taping a small magnet to the end of it, I made a telescoping rod for picking up metal objects in hard-to-reach places. It has come in handy many times."

"I keep a 2″ length of small flexible rubber tubing on the shank of my screwdriver for tight places where I can't reach in to hold a screw in position. With the screwdriver in the screw slot, I pull the rubber tube down to hold the screw in place. When not being used, the screw holder can be pushed back up on the shank."

(With this and all the following screw holder ideas, a predrilled hole will take much pressure off the holder.)

"To turn a screw down in a hard-to-reach spot, I punch the screw through the sticky side of masking tape and bring the tape back up to the shank of the screwdriver. After the screw is started, the tape pulls off."

"Glue the screw in place on the screwdriver with rubber cement. It dries quickly, and when it's dry, the screw can be put in place and turned down. When the screw is in, a tug on the screwdriver will break loose the rubber cement."

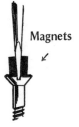

Magnets

"A pair of small magnets will adhere to the shank of a screwdriver and can be pushed down to be flush with the head of the screw when it's in place on the screwdriver. I like this method better than magnetized screwdrivers, which can sometimes be a bother."

"I wrap a 3″ piece of soldering wire around the head of the screw. Then I put the screwdriver into the slot and wrap the solder wire around the tip and on up the blade of the screwdriver. This holds these two together until I can get the screw started. Then, because of the flexibility of the solder, an upward tug will pull it away from the screw."

Soldering wire →

"For a nut that has to be installed in one of those hard-to-reach places, get a socket wrench the next size larger than the nut and line the walls with a piece of double-faced pressure-sensitive tape. Put the nut inside the socket, and it will be held in place. However, once the nut is started, the tape will let go of it and stay in the wrench socket. Then the correct-size wrench can be used to finish the job."

You can hold the nut inside a socket wrench with very heavy grease. Just put a blob of the grease into the socket. After the nut is tightened down, the excess grease can be removed with a rag on the end of a screwdriver or any long tool. In some instances, you may just want to leave the grease on as a protective coating. In the absence of heavy grease, get some shortening from the kitchen.

When there isn't enough room to reach in and hold a nail in place, it can be held against the hammerhead with a scrap of that clear plastic, self-adhering food wrap. Just poke the nail through the center of the scrap and put the nail head flat against the hammerhead. Pulling the plastic wrap back around the hammer will hold the nail in place.

"To drill a hole in a tight place where there isn't enough room for the drill above, use the proper-size bit with square tang and a box wrench that will fit over and grip the square tang. This means your turning is done from the side instead of from the top."

As an aid to reaching those hard-to-get-at spots for oiling, slip a flexible drinking straw over the spout of your oil can. You will be able to bend it to reach almost anywhere.

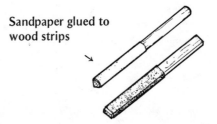

Sandpaper glued to
wood strips

"For sanding in places hard to reach, I've prepared a variety of hardwood strips about a foot long, to which I've glued strips of sandpaper of various grits. I can use these 'sanding sticks' somewhat like using a file. For sanding curved surfaces, attach sandpaper strips to quarter-round molding. If you need to sand in a 90-degree corner, attach the paper around the square side."

"Here's a good fishing tool for getting those dropped screws and other small metal parts that fall into inaccessible spots. Tape a small bar magnet on the end of your retractable metal measuring tape. Soon as you've caught the missing part, just reel it in."

UPHOLSTERING "For upholstering, I put a simple wooden frame around a 6" square of wire mesh. I pour tacks on the wire and jiggle until all the points go down into the holes in the screen. This leaves only the tack heads sticking up, and the magnetic tack hammer can pick them up the right way—head first. This sure saves time."

"That foam rubber upholstery padding is easy to cut if you have a paper cutter. Use a flat board to compress the foam down as flat as possible against the paper cutter, and the blade will cut through on a very even line."

"When I reupholstered our dining room chairs two years ago, I noticed that the seats were worn and dirty but the fabric on the backs was still in good shape. However, that particular kind of fabric was no longer available, so I had to recover both backs and seats. But this time I put two layers of fabric on the seats. Sure enough—recently when I decided the seats needed to be replaced, the backs were still good. All I had to do was remove the top layer, and they were almost like brand new again."

VACATIONS "The plastic coat hooks over the back seat windows of my car broke off. My improvised hooks worked just as well and took only seconds to install. Each hook is made from a piece of heavy venetian blind cord about 6″ long. Hold the two ends together, and tie

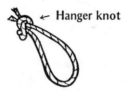

← Hanger knot

a knot forming a loop of the rest of the cord. With the back window rolled down just enough for the knot to go through, push it through so it's outside the car and the loop is on the inside. With the window back up tight against the cord, the hook stays in place to hold hanging clothes."

"Those side hooks for hanging suit bags will only hold so many, and for a vacation trip we often need more hanging space. What I've done is install eye hooks on the rear window deck, which is upholstered plywood. The hangers hook through the eyes, and the suits lie down flat across the back seat. Even though the eye hooks are small enough that they don't show, I wrapped them with thread to match the car's interior."

"Here's an accessory I added to the car for our vacation trips. As we drive along, the children are always wanting a soft drink, and this brings on a search for the bottle opener. Before we left this summer, I installed a wall-type opener right on the dash. It's down low, and isn't conspicuous—but even so, it's chrome and doesn't look bad. It was an easy matter to drill through the metal dash, and two screws hold the opener firmly in place."

"House plants still need water while you're away on vacation. Unless you plan to be gone more than two weeks, you can probably get by with this maneuver. Water them well, and then wrap a large plastic bag completely around each pot and tie it up around the plant. Since the moisture recirculates, this will hold enough in to keep most plants going for the two weeks. If you're able to take a longer vacation, you can probably also afford to have someone come in and water them for you."

When company comes to call, somehow it falls to the man of the house to show the slides of last year's vacation—probably because we men really don't feel that a wife can handle such a tricky electronic gadget as a slide projector. Actually, though, we usually put the slides back in the tray wrong, and the picture appears on the screen upside down. There's a simple way to make sure all the slides are put back in place properly. As soon as they're in right, take the tray out and mark a line with a felt marker all along the top of the slides. To get the slide back in place, all you have to do is see that the mark is on top. Now you can come on like a pro.

VACUUM CLEANERS "Although a shop vacuum cleaner has a strong bag, I don't like the idea of subjecting mine to nails and other sharp metal objects. Therefore, I put a ring of tiny magnets around the nozzle entrance to pick up light metal slivers and save wear and tear on the bag."

VARNISHING "Freshly varnished items actually seem to attract dust particles. After varnishing, hang small articles upside down until dry, and they'll end up almost 100 percent free of any lint and dust. It's a very little task to get a much better finish."

VENEER "To reglue blistered veneer, drill two or three holes in under the blister from the *back* side of the wood. Care should be taken to drill only as far as the air space and not through the finish. Then force glue into the blister through the holes you've drilled. Clamping pressure should be applied on a gradual basis. Mop up the glue as it's forced back out by the pressure. After the finished side is flat again, allow the proper drying time for the glue."

VENETIAN BLINDS The most vulnerable spot on venetian blinds is at the tiny cross tapes that hold up the slats between the wider vertical tapes. To replace one of these, use iron-on mending tape cut to fit. Without even taking the blinds down, you can iron the replacement tape on. Back it with something solid while you apply the hot iron.

"Learning the hard way seems to be the story of my life. I cleaned our venetian blinds, and when I got ready to put them back up, I found the tapes had shrunk so they couldn't be fastened down on the hooks. The right way is to put them back in place while the tape is still damp and hook them down. Then they will be the right length when dry."

"The plastic pulls on our venetian blind cords were beginning to crack, so I had my wife start saving the plastic caps off a particular kind of toothpaste. When we had enough, I drilled holes in the ends, and we had a free matching set of brand new pulls."

VIBRATION "The best thing I've found to keep screws in a vibrating tool from coming loose is to coat them with rubber cement and put them back in place while the cement is still wet. If you ever need to remove the screws, the rubber cement will release with ordinary pressure from a screwdriver."

Either a nut or a screw subjected to vibration can be coated with clear shellac to keep it in place.

VINES "Although there are special nails for holding vines against brick walls, I made holders that work just as well and cost a lot less. I stuck little blobs of putty formed around 6″ lengths of wire in place between the bricks on the wall, and as soon as the putty set up, I wrapped the wires around the vines. Should we decide we don't want vines along this wall, the putty can easily be chipped off and won't leave holes in the mortar as the nails would."

VISES Every workbench should have a vise, and almost every home handyman has left unwanted vise jaw marks on a finished piece of work. There are many ways to guard against this:

"I glued carpet scraps to the jaws of my vise with rubber cement. I even use that vise on intricate pieces I've turned on my lathe without it's leaving a scratch."

"Plastic coffee can lids are good pads for a vise. Just stick them in between the work and the jaws and clamp away."

"A good way to keep vise jaws from chewing up work is to use a sponge between the jaws and the wood. One kitchen sponge cut in half will do the job."

"To avoid damage to threaded parts, I crumple scraps of aluminum foil and put these between the vise and the threads. This allows the vise to get a good grip, but the foil prevents it from chewing up the threads."

"A vise with the jaws worn away can cause a whale of a lot of trouble. I renewed mine by welding a piece of an old file to each side. With these file grips, the vise works better than when it was new."

"To drill into a steel ball, I put a pair of regular square nuts in the vise. With one of these nuts against each vise jaw, the openings for the bolts hold the steel ball firmly in place when the vise is tightened."

A pipe vise is mighty handy to have when you need to do any work on pipes, but most handymen don't need one often enough to warrant buying one. Fashion your own with your regular vise and a pair of combination pliers. Grip the pipe with the coarse teeth of the curved middle part of the plier jaws and place the plier jaws pointed down into the vise, making sure the face of the pliers is at right angles to the vise jaws. Tighten the vise down on the pliers, and the pipe will be held firmly.

"Here's a way to convert your vise into a pipe vise. Dig out four fairly good-sized bolts that are threaded all the way up on the shank and place two bolts on each side of a pipe. Put pipe and bolts into your vise and tighten down against the bolts. As the threads are tightened against the pipe, they'll act as teeth and grip the pipe so it won't slip."

"A leather strap made from a discarded belt will usually hold pipe or dowelling in a vise. Wrap the strap tightly around the object and put the ends into the vise. As the vise is tightened against the ends of the strap, it will be tightened around the object."

"Don't toss away an old section of bike chain. When looped around a piece of pipe you're working on, it can be put in a vise, and when the vise is tightened down, it will act as an excellent pipe vise. Just pull the pipe and chain down as close to the jaws of the vise as possible before tightening."

"Here are two quick methods that usually solve the problem of holding round objects in a vise. One method is to take two pieces of steel wool and place the round object to be clamped between them.

Another is to take a pair of thick kitchen sponges. Unless the round work is to be subjected to some sort of extreme force, either of these methods will hold when your vise is clamped down."

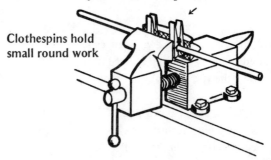

Clothespins hold
small round work

"To hold dowelling in a vise, I clamp a pair of spring-type wooden clothespins on the piece of dowel. This gives a flat surface for the vise jaws to close against. The wood-against-wood doesn't score the work. This will also work on small pipe or tubing up to about ½"."

Sometimes a full-sized vise is just too big. Here are some mini-vise ideas.

Hinge + wing nut

"If you have a small hinge lying around, get a wing nut and bolt that will fit one of the holes in the hinge. This will allow you to tighten the two leaves of the hinge down to hold those small pieces. This entire unit—hinge and work—can then be put in your regular vise for more convenience and to hold it in place."

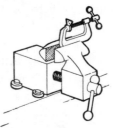

'Take a small C-clamp and put it in your regular workbench vise, leaving the clamp part out. You can tighten the clamp just as you would a vise for small parts."

"Make a portable mini-vise from a spring-type paper clip and a small suction cup that has a threaded hole in the end. Attach the clip to the suction cup by means of a screw through the hole in one of its **handles**. The suction cup allows you to set up the vise on any smooth surface and remove it when the job is done. This is great for electrical soldering where the small wires and parts need a small vise."

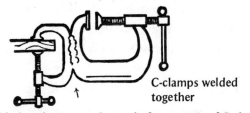

C-clamps welded
together

"A portable bench vise can be made from a pair of C-clamps welded together. One clamp attaches to the workbench or any table and the other acts as the vise. In welding, the two clamps may be back to back or so their clamp mouths are at right angles (as shown). Since C-clamps are inexpensive, you can have several in different sizes."

"There are times when you need steady extra pressure to spread something made of metal. I adapted my vise to take care of this by drilling a ¼" hole in each jaw of the vise, about ½" deep. I then cut a pair of 3" steel rods to fit in these holes. Whatever needs spreading apart is put on the two rods, and the vise is then turned open to apply spreading pressure."

Wall Anchors • Wall Paneling • Wallpaper • Wall Switch-
plates • Washers • Water Hammer • Weeds • Weighing
• Welding • Wheelbarrow • Wife Pleasers • Windows •
Winter Hints • Wire • Wire Brushes • Wives' Tricks •
Women Drivers • Workbench • Work Clothes • Wrenches

W
●

WALL ANCHORS   "When it comes to hanging things on a masonry
wall, every home handyman knows to use some sort of special wall
anchor. But what if you don't have a Molly or toggle bolt? I improvised by cutting a section from the plastic barrel of an old ball-point
pen. By using a screw a shade larger than the barrel, the plastic
expanded in the hole in the wall and became quite secure. I wouldn't
try this homemade expansion anchor with a heavy mirror or the like,
but it will work nicely for an object of moderate weight."

"Although they make anchors and toggle bolts for use on plaster and
sheetrock walls, there are times when you don't have one of these
gadgets available. A good substitute is to put in a pilot hole and then
wrap a screw with steel wool. You'll be pleasantly surprised at how well
this will hold."

Or maybe you will want to "take an empty toothpaste tube and cut
a section from it. Roll it up very tight. Drill a hole in the wall a shade
smaller than the roll. Tap the roll into the hole. When a screw is turned
into the center of the roll, the soft metal will be forced out against the
sides of the hole and will work just like a lead anchor."

Another improvised wall anchor is a strip of aluminum foil rolled
very tight. It will hold just like a lead anchor.

"In an emergency, I have improvised a wall anchor from plastic wire
insulation. Just remove the wire and cut a section of the housing a trifle
longer than the screw. Insert the screw, and then put both screw and
plastic into a predrilled hole. Leave enough of the screw unturned so
that after it has been tapped in, you can turn the screw down,
tightening the anchor in the wall."
Incidentally, that insulation is called *spaghetti.*

WALL PANELING   "Here's a trick that might come in handy in
nailing those big sheets of plywood in place on walls. I just paneled our
den, and to be flush against our ceiling, the paneling needed to be about

¼" off the floor. I held the sheets in place by myself with the aid of a flat shovel. I inserted the shovel under the sheet of paneling while it was flat against the wall, then raised it by applying pressure to the handle with my foot. This made the shovel act as a lever and held the sheet of plywood against the ceiling until I could nail it in place."

"If you have ever installed paneling, you know that making the proper cut-outs for electrical wall outlets is a tricky part of the operation. To take the guesswork out of this step, paint a line around the outlets, and, while the paint is still wet, hold the piece of paneling in place against the wall. The paint will then outline on the back of the paneling the exact spot to be cut out."

WALLPAPER   The old ambiguous question "How long is a piece of string?" is like what you run into when you order wallpaper. Although you figure how much you need in "rolls," you will usually buy in what they refer to as "double rolls." The length of a roll will vary with the width, but most will have a standard number of square feet . . . 36. So if the roll is 18" wide, it should be 24' long. But since it will probably be in a double roll, it will be 48' long. Most dealers will suggest you use 30 square feet as the yield per roll when figuring how much you need, since you will have waste. These tips from readers will help make the job a lot easier:

"The last time my husband papered all of our walls, I got smart and made a record of exactly how much paper we used for each wall. This way we will not have to figure, and then buy too much, as we have done in the past. We keep this record in each room, written on the wall behind a picture or mirror."

"In wallpaper hanging, one key to a super job is to start by completely covering the paper with paste. That clear paste, however, is often difficult to see. If you'll drop just the smallest amount of food coloring in as you mix it, you'll be able to spot at a glance any places you've skipped. Be sure not to put in enough for the color to bleed through . . . a pale tint is all you need."

"Have you ever used a paint roller to put paste on wallpaper? I was forced to ad-lib not long ago, since I didn't want to buy a regular wallpaper paste brush for one small job. I poured the paste into the regular paint tray and found that the roller actually worked better than the regular brush would have."

"To get a good wallpapering job, the first width has to be hung in a straight-up-and-down line. The best way to be sure is to use a plumb bob. Hang it from the top of the wall, almost down to the floor. If the first width is straight, the others can be lined up from it. However, it won't take much time to move the plumb bob and use it for a better job on each width."

"If you've put wall anchors in a wall to hold mirrors and other heavy objects, you'll probably want to continue to use them even after you've wallpapered over them. Usually, you can locate them again by trial and error, but why not avoid having to search? Before you start the papering job, stick a piece of toothpick into each anchor hole so that the point sticks out ½" or so. If the hole is too big to hold the toothpick in place, wedge other pieces in to hold the point in tight. Now, as you paper over the holes, the toothpick points will come through the paper. When the papering chore is finished, the toothpicks can be either pulled out or poked on through the hole into the wall."

"Here's another use for a plastic squeeze bottle. When you've finished a wallpapering job, fill up one of these spare containers with leftover wallpaper paste. Chances are, after a week or so your wife will find several spots where the seams are sticking up a little. The repair job can be done in minutes, because you already have the paste mixed and the spout on the plastic bottle will slip right under the edges of the paper. Tightly sealed, the bottle of paste will last until your wife gets tired of looking for flaws."

"Here is my method of having wallpaper patch pieces that will almost match. Everyone has a couch somewhere that backs up to the wall. Pin the patch pieces to the back of the couch where they will never be seen. Almost any couch will be big enough for all the patch pieces you would ever need for every room in the house. They will weather the same way the paper on the wall does, and, therefore, will be a nearly perfect match at patch time."

Or: "Store the scraps by stapling them facing out on the walls in your attic or storeroom so the air and light can be working on them too."

"Patching wallpaper that has a small flaw can be done in such a way that it will hardly be noticeable. Tear the patch rather than cutting it, and make it more or less circular. Then turn the patch face down and taper the edges with a very fine sandpaper. If the wallpaper is patterned, care must be used in matching up the pattern. If this is done right, you will be amazed at how the patch gets lost."

"You may laugh, but did you know you can clean lightly soiled places from your wallpaper by rubbing the spots with a slice of rye bread? Other bread won't work. If you don't believe it, try it and see."
(Of course, the sandwiches don't taste the same afterwards.)

For those of you who don't want to use rye bread, dry borax powder will do an excellent job. Wipe it on the wallpaper with a clean dry cloth, and then remove any powder left with another clean cloth. (Incidentally, I got a letter from a baker who said that the reason rye worked and other bread didn't was because rye has gluten in it. At any rate, borax works without gluten.)

WALL SWITCHPLATES   To dress up wall switchplates, cut out pictures you like from magazines, or take old playing cards, pieces of wallpaper—anything at all. Using a sharp knife, remove a section for the switch to fit through, and attach the decoration to the plate with clear plastic spray. Another layer of spray plastic will keep the plate from being begrimed and frayed. Keeping a number of "extra" switchplates on hand assures you a variety of different designs. If this idea "turns you on," you may want to make a simple frame out of cardboard, with an opening just the size of the switchplate, to help you prospect for good prospects. And if you want to be really professional, cover your frame with clear plastic and paste in the center a square of paper to show you how the picture will look when that hole is punched to let the switch through."

← When slot is closed, nut is locked on

WASHERS   "If I don't have a lock washer, I take my hacksaw and cut a slot on one side of the nut, at right angles to the bolt. It is cut just deep enough to reach the hole in the nut. After the nut is put on, it is tapped above and below the slot, closing it up. Now the nut cannot be turned until the slot is reopened with the prying action of a screwdriver. This is particularly good, too, when there is not enough room on the end of the bolt for both the nut and a lock washer."

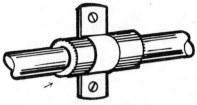

Section of hose
around pipe

WATER HAMMER   "We experienced a slight hammering of our water pipes, and I found that the pipe straps were a little larger than the diameter of the pipe. This, of course, allowed the pipes to move. I solved the problem by placing slit sections of old garden hose around the pipe and reinstalling the pipe straps over these sections. This gives a very tight grip, and there is no more water hammer."

(I would also recommend this trick when you're first installing pipe straps. Quite often they will leave a little play, and this allows the pipes to play a tune on your eardrums.)

WEEDS   "Here is a tip to save on the use of liquid weed killer, and at the same time concentrate it where it needs to be instead of spraying it over a broad area. Fill up a plastic squeeze bottle with the weed killer, and squirt it right on the weed and nowhere else."

"We let our lawn get taken over by a plant called stinging nettle. If you touch it, you itch for an hour or so. I pulled it all up without one itch, and then threw my itchy gloves away. The 'gloves' were plastic sandwich bags."

"We still use an old-fashioned ice cream freezer. As you know, rock salt is poured on the ice to help with the freezing process. After the ice cream is gone and the ice all melted, the salt-water solution is the best weed killer I have ever seen. It is great for any weeds or grass growing between the cracks in the walks and drives. It will also sterilize any plot of ground where you don't want any vegetation."

WEIGHING   "If you have a hanging scale and want to weigh something too heavy for it, don't give up. You can double its capacity by tieing one end of a string on the scale hook and the other end to the wall. With this rig, the wall now supports part of the weight. To find out at just what point on the string the wall takes half the load off the scale, use an object of known weight and suspend it from the string. If the scale shows it to weigh only half as much as you know it to weigh,

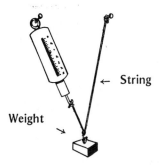

Weight ← String

mark this point on the string. Anything hung from that point will weigh twice as much as shows on the scale."

WELDING   Need a quick small clamp for a small welding or soldering job? Why not use a spring-type clothespin? "But wait," you say. "The wooden clothespin might catch fire." Not if you wrap the two clamping ends with aluminum foil. How's that for foiling the fire!

"Even though I reside in an apartment, I have a small welding rig. Since my workshop space is at a minimum, I don't have room for a welding table and a workbench. I solve this by putting a welding surface on my bench. It consists of bricks that are laid out in a square over a large piece of aluminum foil. This prevents my burning my workbench top. It also has the advantage of being flexible as to size. If I need more surface, all I do is add more bricks."

"I've always heard that finding a horseshoe brings good luck. I found one and stuck it in my garage and forgot it until I was doing a welding chore last week. I used the horseshoe plus a pair of C-clamps for holding together the two pieces to be welded. With a clamp holding one piece of the work to each prong of the horseshoe, I was able to station the two pieces to be welded right against each other in the open center space of the horseshoe. It brought me luck as well as acting like a third hand."

WHEELBARROW   "I was faced with hauling 6 cubic yards of gravel and negotiating two curbs with each load. You would have been proud of the way I changed my wheelbarrow so it could hop up over the curb. I took a pair of old casters off a piece of furniture and welded them to the legs. Now when I approach the curb, I merely push down on the

Casters on wheelbarrow legs

handle and the front wheel raises up. The back casters then allow the wheelbarrow to be pushed forward until the front wheel is up on the curb."

"With my new welding set, I added a rack under my wheelbarrow which allows me to carry all the tools I need to the spot where I need them. It is a simple affair and could be done any number of ways, depending on how the wheelbarrow is made. Mine took only two crosspieces plus a shelf I added to take care of small tools. I'm surprised wheelbarrows aren't made that way to begin with."

"I made an addition to my wheelbarrow that has been a big help—a hand brake taken from an old bicycle. This is great for slowing down the wheelbarrow when on an incline with a heavy load."

"When our son got his first bicycle, we bought a set of those training wheels so he could learn to ride. After a couple of weeks, he wanted the training wheels off. Since they were still good, I kept them in the garage until I found a use for them. I installed them on the front of my wheelbarrow as outrigger wheels. This makes my wheelbarrow next to impossible to tip over, and yet these wheels in no way interfere with the regular use of the wheelbarrow."

"There is nothing more frustrating than to sweep up a wheelbarrowful of those beautiful autumn leaves and then lose half of them before you get them hauled away. I improvised a cover for my wheelbarrow that prevents this. I use one of those plastic suit bags from the cleaners to cover the top of the heap. To hold this in place, I slip a piece of old garden hose that has been slit from one end to the other over the rim all the way around the wheelbarrow. It was easy to make and just as easy to put on or take off."

WIFE PLEASERS A husband may not become a real honest-to-goodness Super Handyman, but he can become a Super Husband by keeping some of these hints in mind . . . and using one at the right time. Many of them were even passed on to us by the Pleased Wife. . . .

"Recently, I asked my husband for a tool kit of my own for making minor daily repairs. He has a large workshop separate from the house but so crammed full of equipment and tools I never could find the exact one I needed.

"He attached a plastic container to my pantry door and filled it with a variety of tools, all marked with bright red tape. Now the whole family uses it, but I recognize mine and see that they are returned to my tool kit."

"If you want to surprise your wife sometime, why not clean those stains off her kitchen cutting board as my husband did. My board had become rather dark, and my cleaning aids would not remove the stain. I came home from the market last weekend to find it white as new. My husband sprinkled salt on the board, and then rubbed this in with a juicy lemon half. Then he rinsed the board off with water, and it came out super clean."

"My husband should get the Wife Pleaser award for this idea. We have a large serving platter that I had always stored by leaning it up against the back of the cabinet. At best, it seemed to want to slide down. My husband took two strips of what he called the groove part of a tongue-and-groove board. He screwed these to the bottom of a kitchen shelf and positioned them with the grooves facing each other. They were spaced so they were as far apart as the platter is wide. The platter is now slipped into the grooves and is held out of the way against the bottom of the shelf, yet is easy to get out when needed."

Kitchen shelf

Platter

Strips from piece of tongue and groove

Twist with screwdriver to form wire hoop

"Here is a way to make points with your wife, and save money at the same time. Those hanging baskets that are so popular actually don't look as good as hanging pots, and yet both cost more than they should. Here is how to take ordinary clay pots and make them into hanging ones:

"Make a wire hoop whose diameter is about three or four times that of the clay pot. Next take a pair of pliers and make four loops equidistant from each other around the hoop. Now put the hoop around the pot, just below the rim at the top. Insert a screwdriver into each loop and twist. Do this to all four until they close the hoop to where it fits tight against the pot. Now these four loops can be bent upward and wires or strings attached to each to hang the pot. When planted, these look great, and are guaranteed to make a wife happy."

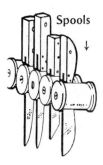

Spools

"A home handyman can install these knife holders for his wife. All he needs is a few empty spools from her sewing basket. Put screws through the holes in the spools and attach them inside a cabinet door. Use screws about ¼" longer than the spools and put a touch of glue on the bottom of each spool for a better hold. Place them in a row, butted right up next to each other. The gaps between the spools will receive the blades, with the handles resting on the spools. Paint 'em up to match the kitchen decor, because your wife will be showing them off to all her friends."

"When we added a utility room to our house, my wife stopped using the old built-in ironing board in the kitchen. It was too much trouble to take it out of the wall, and there wasn't enough space behind it to store much of anything in, so it just stayed there in the wall for about two years. Then I came up with a great idea and removed the board and made the space into a spice cabinet. It is just the right depth and has room for lots of shelves."

"With so many food items coming in envelopes these days, it occurred to me that there was really no way to store these packages except to leave them lying around on shelves or in drawers. At the grocery store, however, these envelopes hang from display racks. I installed a series of L-shaped drapery hooks into the wall inside our pantry, and these envelopes can now hang in an orderly manner, out of the way."

"Women seem to go around making a habit of straightening pictures 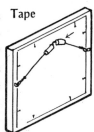 which never want to stay that way. I fixed every picture in our house so it has to stay straight. After picking out the center point on the hanger wire, I wrapped a few rounds of masking tape on either side of this point, leaving only enough exposed wire for the hook to hold onto. The taped sections keep the wire from slipping, and this easy trick got me lots of praise and an apple pie."

"After getting hit in the face with a falling ironing board every time I opened our utility closet, I finally came up with an innovation that has saved my nose—and at the same time showed my wife what a handy husband she has. I took an old towel bar we had all but discarded, and installed it on the closet wall at a height that allows the board to be slipped under the bar. This holds the ironing board in an upright position but will not let it fall out."

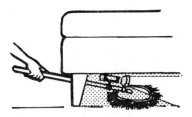

"My husband is the type who thinks he's done something nice for me when he buys a power mower to make it easier for me to cut the lawn. Not long ago he did do something for me that I thought was a little weird, but it turned out to be a pretty helpful thing. He took an old bicycle flashlight holder and attached it to the end of my dust mop. He then put in a flashlight and explained that now I would be able to see under furniture while using the dust mop. Oddly enough, it has really been a big help."

"By attaching a screen door coil spring across the length of the inside of a kitchen cabinet door, you will create a dandy paper sack holder for your wife. The spring will hold the bags flat against the inside of the door, and they will be completely out of the way."

"During the winter, I ended up doing small sanding jobs in the house and had to do something about the sawdust. I solved the problem by doing the whole operation inside a plastic bag from the cleaners. This type of bag is big enough to get your hands in and clear enough to see what you're doing. When you're finished, throw both bag and dust away. This may have saved my marriage."

"Since many jars with screw-on tops are hard to open, I made a gripper pad out of a piece of old inner tube. I cut a circle about 6" across, then gave it a good roughing-up with a file for less slippage. In most cases, my wife can now get the top of a jar off without pulling me away from something I'd rather be doing. And for the really tough lids, it is sure a help for me."

Hinge folds up when not used . . . screen door hook holds it

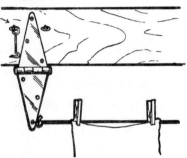

"Since there isn't much head room in our basement, I put up a rainy-day clothesline that folds down to use, and then back up and out of the way. All I did was install a pair of large strap hinges at either end of a beam. One side of each hinge was fastened down with screws, leaving the other free to hang, point down. The line was then tied to the bottom hole in the free-hanging part of the hinge. I installed a screen door hook to hold the hinges and line up when not in use."

(If you don't have a basement, this may be an idea for your attic or garage.)

"My husband is really a Super Handyman. When I hung out drip-dry clothes on hangers, he noticed that the wind was liable to blow them off the clothesline or bunch them all up together at the end of the line. He cut out a section from one line and put a length of light chain back in its place. Coat hangers go through the links of chain and can't blow off or slide."

"In your utility room, paint lines on the inside of your sinks to indicate pints and quarts up to 2 gallons. This enables your wife to mix all of her soaks, detergents, starches, and other washing compounds right in the sink. Mine says it has been a real help. Since no one but her and me sees it, the fact that I am not an artist made no difference. I did this right before I told her about the new set of golf clubs I bought. It helped!"

"When I took down our old wire-bound picket fence in favor of one that afforded more privacy, I used part of it to make a walkway under my wife's clothesline so that when the ground is muddy she can still hang out clothes without sinking to her knees in mud. The fence was just put down flat on the ground. Another section was used to make a walk from the house to our garage. It's wide enough that it doesn't sink into the ground, and isn't bad-looking, either."

WINDOWS   "Our windows rattled like crazy when the wind blew. To stop this, I put strips of masking tape inside the window casing. The sash was then pressed against this, and the rattling was stopped. On some, I had to put several layers, but it is barely noticeable and sure did the job."

"One of our double-hung windows was stuck. Rather than strain myself, I let the windows unstick themselves. I pulled the ropes holding the sash weights all the way out and then let go. The weights fell and jarred the stuck window loose."

(Don't do this if the ropes are old. One reader tried it, and the rope broke. He had a few choice names both for me and for the guy who sent in this idea.)

"Some neighborhood vandal apparently got a new air rifle and managed to put several holes in our windows. While I intend to replace each damaged pane, I don't have time or money to do it right now. So I came up with a temporary repair that will at least stop dust and insects and keep the air conditioning from having to fight any extra hot air. I applied clear fingernail polish to the holes. The first coat will close a portion of the hole. Let it dry and apply another. After this has been done several times, the holes are filled in. It is a temporary seal, but very unobtrusive."

WINTER HINTS   If it happens to be a summer day as you read this, skip over it, but go make a note on your calendar to pick up the book again on the first day of winter. Before you do, though, at least read the first hint.

A sudden freeze sent one of our neighbors out to shut off the water to his outside faucets. One of the valves was so corroded he couldn't turn it without a real wrestling match. It is one of those things that never needs to happen. All outside valves should be turned a couple of times each year to make sure they don't get locked tight with rust or corrosion. This is also a good idea for any valves that are not used very often, whether they are inside or out. Any that seem to be hard to turn can be lubricated. It is sure easier to do this at your leisure on a nice day than to find out they won't work on some cold night.

Inner tube

"There is nothing more frustrating than to try to unlock a padlock that got wet and then froze up. To keep the moisture away from my locks, I use rectangular pieces of an old inner tube with two holes punched to accommodate the shackle of the lock. The remainder of the rubber acts as flaps and hangs down over either side of the lock. The flaps lift up when you want to unlock. In cutting the protector, just make sure that it is sufficiently large to more than cover the lock."

"Another good way to protect an outside padlock from moisture is to keep it inside a plastic sandwich bag. To seal it up, put a rubber band tight around the top, and you'll never have to worry about a lock frozen because the moisture got to it. In summertime, this retards rust and corrosion by keeping the lock sealed away from the elements. Yet the lock is still easy to get to."

"When I put away all of my garden tools for the winter, I put a winter coat on them—a thin coat of linseed oil. Rub the oil into the wood and also coat the metal parts. The wood is then protected from drying out, and the metal is protected against rust or corrosion. Also, when they are put back in use next spring, the wooden handles on garden tools and the like are smooth and much easier on the hands."

"Since so many workshops are relegated to the garage or basement, cold weather is a problem for many a handyman. If your shop light has a socket-type bulb, why not replace it with a heat lamp for the winter? This will give off a good light and focus a lot of warmth on you from fairly close range. Even if you have another heat source in your shop, this can be a welcome addition."

"Winter outdoor handyman chores are much less painful if you can keep warm. Maybe my homemade heater will come in handy for some of your readers who have to face frostbite in order to keep the house running. All you need is a 2-pound coffee can, a roll of toilet paper, and some wood alcohol. First punch a few holes around the side of the can.

Put the roll of paper into the can and soak it with the fluid. When lit, the paper will burn very slowly but steadily and will throw off a good amount of heat. It won't be as cozy as being in the house, but it will sure help to keep warm."

"At the very best, shoveling snow is not one of life's big pleasures. However, this maneuver will make it a lot easier. Get your snowshovel out and put a good coat of wax on it. The best way is to heat the shovel and rub it with a candle or a block of paraffin. This will prevent snow from building up on the shovel, and the shovel will go into the snow with more ease. It may even make it so easy that your wife will go out and shovel off your walks."

"Here's an even easier way to coat your snow shovel. Use that spray wax made for use on furniture. What could be easier? Also, use this to spray in the chute of your snow blower to keep snow from sticking to it."

"Your regular snowshovel isn't very handy when it comes to scooping snow off window ledges, planter boxes, and other off-the-ground objects. However, your wife will probably loan you her dustpan, and this works great. It is much easier to use, and since the short handle brings you closer to the work, it allows you to scoop snow out of tight places."

Wire mesh tied to shoes by strings

"After slipping on ice and snow for half the winter, I made some shoe treads that have helped a lot. I took 3″ strips of expanded metal and cut them to the width of my shoe. Then, with a length of cord at the four corners, I tie one to each shoe right at the ball of the foot. I keep a set at each door and in the car so they will always be handy."

"Here is a quick way to put an anti-slip edging on wooden steps. Take a staple gun and shoot a row of staples along the edge of each step. If your gun can be set so that the staples won't go all the way in, the edges will be even more effective, and the staples will be much easier to pull out next spring."

Here's another remedy for icy steps. "Cut out strips from burlap bags, the size of your steps. When the freeze comes, lay these down on the steps and pour hot water over each one. They refreeze quickly and each step keeps the traction of the burlap. When additional moisture builds up an icy coat, all you need to do is pour some hot water on the steps, and this removes the extra ice down to the burlap."

"Here's a way to make outside and basement steps a little less slippery. When you've finished painting them the next time, sprinkle a layer of sand over the surface while the paint is still wet. When it dries, enough of the sand will be stuck to the step to give it a rough surface that won't get slick from moisture. However, there won't be enough sand to make the paint job look bad."

(Two things on this idea: It won't help with a thick layer of ice, so if the step looks glazed, don't trust it. Secondly, don't use it where appearance is important. Even though it doesn't show up a lot, the sand makes the surface look like it needs scrubbing all the time. It's great for those basement steps and others that only you will see—also concrete steps can be given this treatment by coating them with a clear-varnish-and-sand mixture.)

"In the dead of winter I use my lawn fertilizer-spreader to spread sand on the icy walks and drives. It does an even and super-quick job."

"My sand sprinkler is made from one of those square gallon-sized turpentine cans. I punched holes in the bottom of the can with an ice pick. Then I put masking tape over the holes before filling up the can with sand. (A funnel helps here.) When you are ready to spread the sand, peel off the masking tape, and the sand will sprinkle out as you walk along the area to be sanded. This works particularly well when there is a big wind blowing, as my sprinkler can be held down to within ½" or so of the surface to keep the sand from being blown away."

"Long before the time of the frozen sidewalk slips up on us, handymen should save all the sawdust they can. This is the best stuff I have found to sprinkle over frozen walks to prevent slipping. The nicest part about using sawdust will be apparent next spring—the sawdust will just blow away instead of having to be swept, like sand."

"Here's a tip I learned the hard way about thawing frozen water pipes. I started in the middle, and the pipe burst. The plumber who replaced the pipe told me you should always start the thawing process at the section of pipe that is *away* from the water supply—and with a tap open. Then work back with the heat toward the water supply."

"If you need to thaw pipes in the basement with a heat lamp, here is a trick that cuts the time in half. Make a curved reflector out of aluminum foil wrapped over a curled piece of cardboard. Put this on the opposite side of the pipe from the heat lamp, and you will reflect heat on the frozen pipe from all sides."

"This may prove helpful to a home handyman who is unfortunate enough to have a frozen pipe between the walls of his house. It happened to me, and I was able to thaw the pipe by using a super idea . . . I removed the wall flange where the pipe entered the wall from the sink. There was enough room around the pipe to get one of the attachments from my wife's vacuum cleaner in beside the pipe. It was the flat one called a crevice tool. I then attached the hose to the blower end of the unit. When turned on, it forced the warm air down along the pipe and thawed it out."

Snows and freezing can often wreck the shape of a tree that has taken you and Mother Nature years to grow. As soon as possible after a snowfall, gently shake the tree to remove the loose snow. This will prevent the weight from damaging the branches. However, if the branches are frozen over, don't try to remove the ice. Prop the branches up and wait until the ice melts.

"Yesterday morning, I went to get into my car, only to find it covered with a sheet of ice. Even the door lock was frozen, so I could not get in to get the defroster going. However, after holding the key over the flame of my cigarette lighter a few seconds, I was able to get the key into the lock. By repeating this a couple of times, I got the door open."

Another way for those who do not carry lighters is to roll up a piece of newspaper. Hold one end over the lock and breathe into the other. Your hot breath (98.6 degrees) will soon thaw out the lock. Or try a preventive handyman trick. The night before, stick a piece of masking tape over the lock, leaving an ample pull tab sticking out. No moisture gets in, so no problem. Better still . . . build a garage.

"In the wintertime, when the car windows are always shut, a leaky exhaust system can be very dangerous. There is an easy way to check for any leaks. Merely remove the air filter and, with the engine running, squirt machine oil into the air intake. This will cause very visible smoke to come out the tail pipe, and by looking down under the car, you can easily spot smoke coming out of any leaks in the system."

Or, if you have someone cover up the end of the exhaust pipe for a few seconds, you will force smoke out from even the tiniest leak.

"My car windows were iced over recently, and I was caught without an ice scraper, but not without a bright idea. I took the plastic plate off one of our light switches, and it worked as well as any ready-made scraper. After I put that one back in place, I rummaged around in my shop and found a spare to go into my glove compartment."

"We came out of a movie the other night to find a sheet of ice over the windshield of the car. There wasn't a scraper in the car. I found that my pocket comb was an excellent substitute."

"I always keep an expired credit card in my wallet, as I have found it to be the best yet for scraping snow and ice off my auto windshield. In an emergency, you can use an unexpired one, as the scraping really won't hurt it."

"Another good windshield ice scraper is one of those ever-present plastic lids from coffee cans. Use the top edge and bend it slightly, and you will find it does an excellent job."

"When snow has arrived, here's a keen idea for getting the night's accumulation of cold white stuff off the old jalopy. Use one of those plastic dust pans (a metal one will scratch the paint) as a short-handled snow shovel. With one in each hand, you can clear off a Detroit-sized car in a couple of minutes, and it scrapes ice crust off the windshield too! Also, it's easier to carry in the car than a regular shovel or broom."

"If you have ever needed to get into the trunk of your car, only to find that moisture has gotten between the rubber gasket and the trunk lid and frozen there, you will really like my tip. I found that by brushing a thin coat of olive oil over the gasket, freezing will be prevented."

(Silicone spray will also help prevent this, but it won't give your car that great Italian restaurant smell.)

"Gallon-size plastic milk cartons make ideal holders for sand to be carried in the trunk of the car for ice and snow emergencies. They are easy to fill, store, and handle. When they're filled, the top crimps closed, and they're heavy enough to ride in the trunk without tipping over. Each carton is about the right size for the sand needed under two tires. We also keep a few cartons handy on the back porch for use on the walks and drives."

"I solve the problem of sand for ice, snow, and mud emergencies with plastic produce bags saved from the kitchen. We keep several bags full of sand in the trunk of the car. The wire ties twisted around the top of the bags keep the sand in. If you don't have ties, use pipe cleaners."

"Carry a few pieces of composition roofing material, 2' to 3' long, in the trunk of the car. Should the car end up on a slick icy spot or in a snowy dip, a piece of this roofing under the rear tires will provide great traction. The pieces lie flat in the trunk of the car and take up practically no room."

Another good thing to carry in the trunk of your car in case you get stuck in the snow is a couple of pieces of chicken wire about 4' long.

"Remembering last winter, I've made sure I don't have to freeze my hands off on a cold metal tire tool in case I have a flat tire. I slit sections of garden hose to slip on the lug wrench and jack handle, so that they now have insulated grips. After taking this much trouble, I bet I won't have a flat tire."

"With no garage in which to park my car, I had to come up with something to keep my outside rear-view mirror from freezing over at night. My solution was to put a plastic sandwich bag over the mirror. A rubber band holds the bag on, and each morning when I remove the bag, the mirror is in perfect shape."

WIRE   Here are some neat twists to keep in mind:

Kinked-up wire is of no use, but it can be a simple task to straighten it out. One of the best tricks to use is to put one end of the wire into the chuck of your hand drill. Then put the other end of the wire in your vise. With the wire pulled taut, start turning the drill. A few turns will tell you if you are turning the right way. If the snarls start getting tighter, then you know to reverse the drill. This is also a good way to twist wires together.

"Getting the kinks out of wire is a lot easier if you draw the wire around a pipe. This will straighten it out in no time."

WIRE BRUSHES   "A wire brush used in the home workshop will usually wear out on the ends first because this is where it gets the most punishment. Before sending it to the junk pile, try sawing off the worn row of bristles, including the wooden back. This will leave a new front line of bristles that should be in pretty good shape."

"After much use, steel brushes begin to get droopy and lose their bizaz. Did you know they can usually be rejuvenated by grinding off the bent, out-of-shape ends? I wrap masking tape all around the outside of the bristles to keep them together, and let the tape extend down to the point where the grinding should stop. The tape will act as a guide, and at the same time keep the grinding wheel from flaring out the bristles on the edge. Done properly, this will make the brush as good as new and can be done several times before the brush has to be retired."

"I needed a wire brush, and rather than go buy one, I made a very good one from a scrap of screen wire. I cut a strip of the mesh about 3″ wide. From along the newly cut side, I peeled off several of the wires that run along the full length of the strip. They are easy to grab hold of with a pair of pliers, and when pulled down they will unravel. When you have unraveled about a ½″ or so, roll the strip into a tight roll. Then wrap the roll with masking tape down to where the frayed section begins. This will do the same things a store-bought wire brush will do."

WIVES' TRICKS   "Here is a super hint for wives who cannot get their husbands to repair that leaky faucet. Mine kept putting it off, saying a few drops of water didn't matter that much. I got a friend who is a math teacher to figure out that one drop of water per second will amount to 700 gallons of water in the course of a year. When I presented this fact to my dear husband, along with how much it cost, he couldn't get the drip fixed quick enough."

"You are always suggesting to husbands that they borrow things from their wife's kitchen to use in the workshop. I have turned the tables by appropriating a C-clamp from my husband's shop to use as a nutcracker. It is the best I have found—and when I went out to get it, I discovered and retrieved some of my kitchen gadgets he had converted to shop use."

WOMEN DRIVERS   "My workshop is in the space formerly occupied by a storage cabinet in the rear of the garage. This means if my wife drives the car too far into the garage, I cannot get up to my workbench without moving the car. In fact, once she even hit the bench. I solved this problem very simply by hanging a string with a rubber ball on the end from a rafter in the garage ceiling. It is hung head-high on the driver's side, so as she pulls the car in, she drives up until the ball and windshield almost meet. She knows she is far enough in to close the garage, and yet not too close to my workbench. As a matter of fact, I use it myself when I park the car."

"My wife knows she has our car far enough into the garage when it hits the wall. I soon realized this was not doing either the car or the wall any good. Rather than try to change her, I added my 'bumper-thumper.' I took sections from an old tire and nailed them around three sides of a 2″ x 4″ that is the same length as my car bumper. I attached this to the wall of the garage at the exact height of the bumper. Now, all the shock is absorbed by the 'bumper-thumper,' and my wife doesn't even get her feelings hurt."

Removable pin →

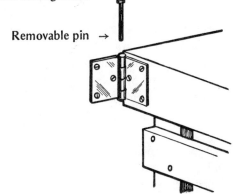

WORKBENCH   "I was a victim of 'wandering workbench.' Since it was not attached to my garage wall, it 'walked' around from the vibration of tools. I wanted to keep the bench so it could be moved out, but I cured the 'walking' with a hinge at each end of the bench. The hinges have removable pins. One leaf is attached to the bench, the other to the wall. When I need to move the bench, I knock out the pins."

This tip prompted another solution to the same problem:

"I use a screen door hook on the bench and an eye on the wall, and this works just fine. It is much easier to hook and unhook than to remove and replace a hinge pin. I use this device on both sides of the bench."

"Many times a handyman will store and use a tool properly, but damage it when it is out on the workbench. Provide a pad for the cutting tools by keeping a large thin piece of foam rubber on your bench. A large kitchen sponge works well for this. As a matter of fact, some men attach this pad to the bench with rubber cement. Not only does this pad protect your tools, but it makes the tools easy to see, so they won't be left out."

"I modified my workbench with a piece of angle iron all along the edge. I had a piece cut and drilled, and attached it. First of all, it protects the edge, which gets quite a beating. Secondly, it acts as a lip for the working surface, preventing things from rolling off. Also, it acts as a small anvil, which I have used dozens of times."

"I file or cut a flat spot on all the round wooden handles of hand tools. This keeps them from rolling off the workbench, and they still fit my hand comfortably."

"Because of the baseboard, I had a space between my workbench and the shop wall. This meant I was always dropping small hand tools behind the bench. However, I turned this space into an asset by installing a strip of expanded metal between the bench and the wall. Now I store all my screwdrivers, chisels, and other such tools by inserting the blades between the mesh holes in the expanded metal."

"The best workbench pencil holder is a 3"- or 4"-deep hole in the edge of the bench. Drill it on the side and make it slant down just a fraction. Your shop pencil will rest in the hole and always be handy!"

"My workbench has a built-in cutter blade that sticks up over to one side. It is a cold chisel that has been inserted into a hole drilled in the top of the bench for that purpose. A block was installed under the bench for the handle of the chisel to rest upon. Only the point of the blade sticks out, and objects to be cut are set on the point to be hit—and thus cut. If I need to use the chisel away from the bench, it can be lifted out of the hole, as it is not fastened down."

(If you try this idea, it's my suggestion that you use a wood block between the hammer and the work to save the chisel point.)

WORK CLOTHES   "Last year I discovered that I had several perfectly good canvas work gloves for my left hand, but that all the right-handed gloves had holes in them. I promptly threw them all away and went out and bought a new pair of gloves. Then I realized how dumb that was. By merely turning the left-handed gloves wrong side out, I would have had right-handed gloves. At least this gave me a good idea about how to get twice the wear out of my new pair. Every so often, I turn them inside out, and this means they both share the wear that used to go all to the right glove."

"As the wife of a professional handyman (my hubby is a carpenter), I can pass along a tip that will prolong the life of work clothes. I have learned that when the edges of pockets are coated with clear nail polish, they will resist wear. The protective coating lasts through many washings, and when it starts to go, I just add another coat. I feel this trick adds 50 percent more life to work clothes."

"As the wife of a handy husband, I solved a problem that results from all the nails, screws, and sharp tools that men carry in the pockets of their work clothes. Before anything ever pokes a hole in one of my husband's pockets, I get some of those iron-on denim knee patches at the dime store. I fold one of these around the bottom of each pocket and press them on. With that extra thickness, most of my husband's pockets last longer than the rest of the pants."

"Many do-it-yourselfers will buy work clothes that fit everywhere but in the length. The extra length—2″ or 3″—is then folded up to form what is known as a Carpenter's Cuff. This comes in very handy for carrying nails when working in a crouching position, like when nailing down flooring. It puts the nails very close to the work, and they are a lot easier to get to than if they are in an apron or pocket."

Push here

WRENCHES   "If you do not have just the right-sized wrench, why not take a C-clamp and tighten it to the nut? It will work about as well."

"If you find the wrench you're using is just a fraction too large to give you the sure grip you'd like, you might try this trick. Slip a layer of plastic bag (like you get from the cleaners) over the work and see if that doesn't make the wrench take a better hold. Sometimes a double layer is needed."

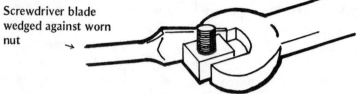

Screwdriver blade wedged against worn nut ⟶

"Sometimes when your open-end wrench won't grab hold of a worn nut, get the next size larger wrench and insert the blade of a screwdriver in to fill up the gap. The flat screwdriver blade will give the wrench a lot more biting area and will often make the difference. Give it a try!"

"Yesterday, while working on a project over at a friend's house, I noticed he had some thin lead strips in his tool box. He explained that he has used these for two purposes. Any time he has to apply a metal wrench to a finished metal part, he wraps the lead around the part to protect the finish. The lead can easily be bent to conform to any shape, and the grip of the wrench is not diminished as it might be with another material. The lead is still soft enough not to mar the finished metal. Also, the lead takes up any slack when using a wrench that doesn't fit tight enough against the item it is used on."

"You can make a very serviceable adjustable wrench with nothing more than a pair of square nuts and a bolt they will fit on. The nuts can be tightened down against the work to be turned, no matter what odd size it may be. Use a bolt long enough to give you plenty of leverage when you start turning."

Nuts adjust to fit

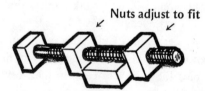

A neighbor was complaining about the quality of an adjustable wrench he had. I suspect he was guilty of not using this tool in the best manner. Naturally, the fixed jaw will be stronger than the side that adjusts. Therefore, it makes sense to apply the force so it works mainly against the stronger jaw. This will make the wrench last longer and be safer to use.

X-RAY VISION "Since we're not blessed with X-ray vision, all those who keep fuel oil (or any liquid) in metal drums may find the level of the liquid inside the drum by attaching a hose to the faucet. Hold the loose end of the hose up above the top of the drum. Open the faucet and slowly lower the loose end of the hose. Because liquids seek their own level, when you lower the end to the level in the drum, the liquid will reach the open end of the hose."

(So you don't waste the liquid in the hose, drain it into a container and pour it back into the drum.)

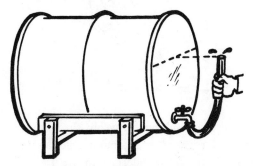

"I really needed to be able to see through the floor in order to know where to put screws to stop squeaks. That's when I learned about this trick from one of my neighbors. While I was under the house, he went along and held a strong magnet at each squeak point. I would come along underneath with a small magnetic compass, and it would tell me exactly where the magnet was. As soon as I marked the place, I tapped a signal on the floor, and he would move on to the next squeak."

(Don't vacuum your floors so much if you've used talcum powder to stop squeaks.)

Y

YARD   "Since we've given up playing croquet, I've put the wickets to great use. I put one in the ground at the corner of each flower bed. Now, with the wicket standing guard when I'm watering, I can pull the hose around corners without its getting into the flower beds and ruining plants."

← Croquet wicket

"If chemical fertilizer isn't put on evenly, the result is a zebra-striped lawn. The type of fertilizer I use is drab in color and doesn't show up too well against the ground, so I decided to give it a little help. I mixed flour with the fertilizer granules to show the exact path of my spreader. A handful of flour mixed in each time the spreader is filled does the trick for me, and I never miss a spot."

(Flour is not that expensive, but why not pick up some damaged sacks the grocery store is going to throw away?)

"Rather than throw away those empty chemical fertilizer sacks, save them. Next time you need to put mulch around a plant or tree, put these down instead. Cover them with a thin layer of dirt, and then punch a few holes to make sure enough air and water gets through. The bag will not only do the job as mulch, but there's always enough fertilizer left in the bag to enrich the soil."

"I use coffee grounds and egg shells as a mulch in my flower beds, and it must have some magical powers, because I have the best-looking flowers in town."

(There are two schools of thought about coffee grounds on plants. Some folks swear by them and have great results, and some folks believe they're bad—and also get beautiful results.)

"When digging to plant trees and shrubs, spread out one of those large plastic suit bags from the dry cleaners As you dig, place the dirt on the plastic sheet. The hole can be refilled by just picking up the edge of the plastic sheet and dumping the dirt back into the hole. This also keeps dirt from being scattered all over the lawn. Any leftover dirt can be picked up in the plastic and carted away."

(Burlap works well for this, too—and is better for heavy duty.)

"For tieing vines, small trees, and other plants to stakes, use strips from the plastic bags from the cleaners. Just cut off a section and twist until it becomes a sort of rope. These ties will hold the plant tight, but still have enough give not to cut into the trunk. They're unobtrusive, as they can hardly be seen."

"If you had been in our neighborhood last weekend, you might have agreed with my neighbors that I'd gone daffy. After all, it's not often you see someone going over his yard with a vacuum cleaner. However, the weeds had taken over, and I noticed that as I started to mow them, the blooms and seeds were being scattered all over. This meant even more weeds in the future, so I stopped cutting and vacuumed up the tops of the weeds. This picked up all the seeds before they could be broadcast all over the lawn, so it wasn't such a crazy idea."

YARD TOOLS "I made a portable carryall for my long-handled yard tools like hoes, rakes, and forks. It's made from an old metal garbage can to which I added some old furniture casters. It sure makes carrying these tools to the job a lot easier. I even sprayed a coat of paint on it, so it looks good too."

"I keep a pail of sand in our toolshed for cleaning my shovel, hoe, and other such yard tools. I poured about a pint of old crankcase oil I had drained from the car into the sand, and by working the tools around in the sand, they're cleaned. At the same time, the tools are given a protective oily coating."

"How many times have you leaned the handle of a rake or hoe up against a wall only to have it slide off and fall to the ground? It only has to hit your foot once to make you appreciate my idea. I put rubber crutch-tips on the ends of all the long-handled yard tools, so when they're leaned against even a smooth wall, they'll stay there."

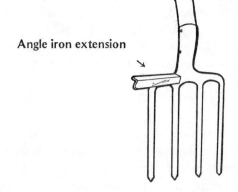

Angle iron extension

"Here's a way to add more foot power to a garden fork or shovel. Weld an extra length of angle iron on the place where your foot goes, and you'll be amazed at how much easier it goes into the ground. The extra room for your foot makes the difference—just be sure you weld it on the side where your digging foot goes."

"I saw a neighbor rubbing dirt over the handle of a brand new hoe he had just bought. After he had it looking like it was 20 years old, he wrapped part of it with friction tape. He wouldn't tell me why at first—just took me into his garage and showed me his other yard tools. They all looked as if they were on their last legs too. He explained that after he lost several new tools to thieves, he came upon this disguise to make them look as if they weren't worth stealing. Since then nobody has ever bothered to take any of them.

"He also puts a couple of taped places on his garden hoses to make them look like they're leaky. This may sound ridiculous, but it works."

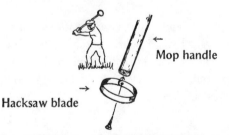

Mop handle

Hacksaw blade

"We needed to clear out a weed patch, and rather than buy a long-handled weed cutter that would be used just once, I made one. All it took was an old hacksaw blade and a mop handle. I bent the blade into a circle, and brought together the holes at either end. Then I inserted a wood screw into the holes and into the end of the mop handle. This made a great swinging weed cutter, and also allowed me to practice my golf swing as I cleared the weeds."

(By sharpening the back of the blade, you would have a cutting edge on both forward *and* backward strokes.)

"To prevent my lawnmower from taking nicks out of trees each time I mowed around them, I made bumpers to go around them from sections of old garden hose. I put a strip of rubber from an old inner tube through the hose to tie it around the tree. This is better than wire or rope because as the tree grows, the bumper will expand and not choke the tree."

(Or, just plant ground cover—pachysandra is best—around the tree in a circle a foot in diameter. It's easier to cut, looks better, and keeps weeds down, too.)

"The makers of power mowers and edgers are very skillful at getting the oil intake hole in such a position that it's impossible to pour oil from a can without a funnel. Rather than have to look for a funnel (which I can never find anyway), I've transferred the oil into a plastic bottle that formerly contained dishwashing liquid. It has a pull-up top that allows the liquid to squirt out, and I enlarged the hole so the oil comes out faster. With this, I can get the pouring spout right down to the hole and never spill a drop. And I don't have to worry about finding the funnel."

(That's great—if you don't lose the plastic bottle.)

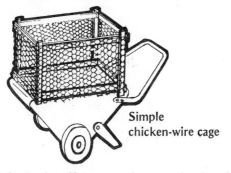

Simple
chicken-wire cage

"One of the blades broke off my grass shears, and rather than throw them away, I repointed the broken blade and ground off the other blade to the same length. They're a little bit stubby-looking, but they still clip grass."

"For hauling cut grass or leaves in the fall, I use my garden cart. But here's how I cut my hauling trips in half. I built a lightweight wooden frame about 2' high that fits on top of the car. The four sides are covered with chicken wire. When I'm using the cart for other purposes, the wire top lifts off."

"I made a traveling yard litter bag by attaching a clothespin bag to my power mower. The wire hook is bent easily over the mower handle, and the bottom of the bag ties to the handle shaft. As I mow, I pick up any debris, such as rocks, sticks, and wires, and deposit it in the bag. These objects, if left, are potential accidents."

Dowel screw in broom handle

"With my slipped disc, I don't bend over much anymore. However, the litter bugs in our neighborhood don't seem to care about my back, so I rigged up a paper-picker-upper like the ones park clean-up men use. It's a long stick with a sharp stabber on the end. All I did was take an old broom handle cut to the right length and install a dowel screw in the end."

(A dowel screw is one of those gadgets that has a threaded screw point on both ends, with a smooth center.)

ZIG-ZAG RULES "I'm a carpenter and always carry my zigzag rule in my coveralls. A long time ago, I found that the exposed sides of the rule wore out from going in and out of my pocket so often. With the numbers gone on two sections of the rule, it certainly wasn't as efficient as it was meant to be. When I bought a new one, I put a coat of clear shellac over all the exposed parts, and it's constantly fresh and easy to read."

(Clear plastic spray will also protect this tool.)

ZIPPERS "Canvas camping equipment usually has metal zippers, and these are often exposed to the elements. I run the end of a candle along each side of the track before each outing. The wax protects the zipper and keeps it working easier."

INDEX

Abrasives, 1-5
  grades and uses for, 2, 3
  selecting, 1
  See also Sandpaper
Accident prevention, 5-10
  acid and, 10
  for children, 59, 60, 61
  fire and, 9, 63
  hand tools and, 6-10
  heating devices and, 9
  luminous paint for, 6
  poisons and, 238-39
  power tools and, 6-7, 9
  safety locks for, 8
  scaffolding and, 6
  for stalled automobiles, 25
  See also Safety
Acid, safety hints for, 10
Acres, conversion table for, 72
Adhesives, 10-13
  bonding hints for, 11-12
  chewing gum as, 31
  removal of, 10-11
  as safety devices, 9-10
  spreading, 11
  storing, 11
  for vinyl squares, 113
  wall poster, 62
  See also Glue; *and names of specific*
    adhesives
Aerosol spray cans, *see* Spray cans
Air conditioning units, protection of, 13
Alarm clocks, repairing, 68
Allen screws, 13, 315
Allen wrenches, 13
Alligator clips, 13, 298
Aluminum, filing, 104
Aluminum foil
  as tool protectors, 303
  for vise supports, 329
Aluminum oxide abrasives, 2
Ammonia
  for dissolving corks, 79
  for removing decals, 83
Anchor bolts, 71
Anchors
  for boats, 110

Anchors (*cont.*)
  for posts, 13
Angles, calculating, 49-50
Antenna rods
  for garden stakes, 124
  radio, 19, 323
  television, 140, 321
  visible guy wire, 140
Antifreeze for storing brushes, 43
Antiseptics for campers, 55-56
Anvils, 13-14
Apartment dwellers, shop substitutes for,
  14
Appliances
  instruction booklets for, 15
  lubricating, 179
  See also specific appliances
Area units, conversion table for, 72, 74, 77,
  78
Aromas, cedar closet, 57
  See also Odors
Asbestos for soldering vise, 270-71
Ash removal, 107
Asphalt squares, 113
Attics, lighting for, 175
Automobiles, 15-31
  battery hints for, 26-27
  carburetor protection for, 29
  checking exhaust leaks in, 347-48
  chewing gum as adhesive for, 31
  cleaning and washing, 15-18
  convertible top maintenance for, 19
  easing dipstick into, 30
  emergency flares for, 25
  foiled goggles for repairing, 29
  garages and, *see* Garages
  gas memory-jogger for, 30
  gas siphoning hose for, 30
  glove compartments in, 24-25
  hauling by, 146-47
  headlight cleaning for, 18
  hose care for, 28
  hub caps as water carriers for, 31
  ice-control for, 348
  jack hints for, 20-21
  license plates for, 173
  luggage racks for, 180
  mat-coating in, 16-17
  painted radiator caps for, 30
  parts' receptacles for, 29
  personal cleanliness and, 66-67
  preventive maintenance for, 18
  protecting, 117
  reflective tapes for, 25-26

Broken glass, cleaning, 39
Brooms, worn-out, 39-40
Brushes
    bottle, 223
    paint, *see* Paintbrushes
    shoeshine, 254
    wire, 350
Btu, conversion table for, 72
Buckets
    auto hubs as, 31
    hand savers for, 144
    hoisting, 149
    paint, 46, 149
Building
    accommodations for window drapes, 47
    bricks and bricklaying in, 38-39
    cement in, 57-58
    concrete in, *see* Concrete; Concrete
        blocks
    electrical problems in, *see* Electrical
        problems
    glueing in, 129-30
    plumbing access plates in, 46-47
    stack-sack, 247-48
    woodwork in, *see* Woodworking
Building paper, unrolling, 100
Buoys, marker, 37
Burglary, prevention of, 294-95
    See also Theft
Bushels (unit), conversion table for, 72
BX cable
    cutting, 94
    as plumber's snake, 237

Cabinet doors, noise-reduction of, 48
Cabinets, abrasives for finishing, 1
Cables, electrical, 93
    BX, 94, 237
    cutting, 94
Calculations, 48-52
    for center of circle, 48
    for change made by pulleys, 50-51
    for distance, 49
    for ellipses, 50
    for height, 48-49
    for 90-degree angle, 49-50
    for solution concentrations, 50
    for temperature-conversion scales, 52
    for volume, 51
Calibrations
    improving visibility of, 52, 184
    shellacking, 361
Calipers, 52-53

Camp fires, starters for, 106-7
Camp stools, coffee cans as, 69
Campers, 53-56
    antiseptics for, 55-56
    axe guards for, 310
    cooking for, 54-55, 200-201
    luggage for, 180
    outdoor fires for, 53-54
    tent hints for, 55
    trailer hints for, 55
Canvas goods, 56
Capping liquids, 176-77
Carburetors, protection for, 29
Carpentry, *see* Woodworking
Carpet scraps, 56-57, 328
Carrying, grippers for, 153, 316-17
    See also Moving
Casters, 57, 315
Caulking, 57
Cedar closets, aromas of, 57
Ceiling, painting, 209, 213
Cellophane tape as straightedge, 284
Cement
    defined, 57-58
    as garage floor cleansing agent, 117
    stack-sack building with, 247-48
    See also Concrete
Center of circles, calculating, 48
Centimeters, conversion tables, for, 72, 73,
    77
Chains
    installing tire, 21
    making and repairing, 58
Chains (surveyor's), conversion table for, 73
Chairs
    painting, 215
    repairing, 58
Chalk
    as moisture absorbers, 301-2
    protecting, 58
Chamois, restoring, 15
Charcoal cooking for campers, 54
Charts and plans, protecting, 58-59
Children, 59-63
    items made for, 61-63
    safety for, 59
        outdoor swings, 60-61, 152
        poison controls, 238-39
        power tools, 60
        sliding doors, 61-62
Chimneys, cleaning, 107
Chipping of concrete, 183
Chisels
    holders for, 151, 306

Chisels (*cont.*)
protecting, 303-4
Christmas stockings, 63
Christmas trees, 63
Chrome
abrasives for cleaning, 4
rust-prevention for, 18-19
Chucks, drill
keys for, 63-64
protecting, 304
Clamps, 64-66
band, 65
bar, 65
big, 66
earrings as, 149
for frame corners, 64
for glueing, 11, 65-66
pads for, 64
radial saw arm as, 66
as safety devices, 9
Cleaning, 66-69
of automobiles, 15-18
of bricks, 39
of broken glass slivers, 39
broom wear in, 39-40
of brushes, 44, 45-46
of chimneys, 107-8
of clocks, 68
of copper, 186
of decals, 83
efflorescence, 93
of files, 104
of fireplaces, 107
of furnace filters, 105
of garage floors, 117
of golf-cart wheels, 131
in good shop practice, 66, 67, 137, 138
of grease, 66-67
of grinding wheel particles, 139
of heating systems, 148
kitchen ware, 4, 339
with magnets, 181
of metal shavings, 293
of odious chemicals, 198
of paint rollers, 211
of plastic bleach bottles, 231
of rain-gutters, 140
in rust-removal, 61, 250-51
of sawdust, 67
of soldering irons, 274
of swimming pools, 290
of tiny parts, 301
of tools, 303
of venetian blinds, 328

Cleaning (*cont.*)
of wallpaper, 335
in washing up, 22
of yard tools, 357
Cleaning agents
for automobile washes, 17
for glue spots, 10-11
for windshield wiper units, 19-20
Cleanliness
for grease work, 66-67
in puttying, 240
swimming and, 290
Clips, alligator, 13, 298
Clocks
cleaning, 68
reassembling, 246
Closed-coat abrasives, 1
Closets, cedar, 57
Clotheslines
basement, 342
removing clothing creases from, 153
Clothespins
for holding wires, 134
as reminders, 30
Clothing, *see* Garments
Coat hooks, 68
Coated abrasives, 1, 3
Coffee can lids as funnels, 115
Coffee cans
as barbecue grills, 54
for barbells, 33
as brush soakers, 42
for camp stools, 69
for fishing bait, 109
as garden hose hangers, 126
as hand tool holders, 397
rust rings on, 69
as tool holders, 26, 57
Coffee pots for cleaning small parts, 302
Color-coding, reassembly with, 247
Combs, hair
as compasses, 70
as nail holders, 195
as snow removers, 348
Comfort in installing floors, 113-14
Compasses
large, 69
pocket comb, 70
Composition boards, abrasives for finishing, 2
Concrete, 70-72
depth gauges for, 84
drilling, 88, 183
efflorescence removal from, 93

Concrete (*cont.*)
for fence support, 102
finishing trowels for, 71
metal reinforcements for, 70
patching cracks in, 71-72
for patio work, 71
safety in chipping, 183
stack-sack building with, 247-48
for steps, 70-71
writing in, 71
Concrete blocks
hand savers for, 144
spacers for, 39
Concrete forms, 71
Connections, solderless electrical, 94-95
See also Wires; Wiring
Construction, *see* Building
Containers
capping, 176-77
for oil, 179
See also specific containers
Contour gauges, 72
Conversion table, 72-78
Convertible tops, maintaining, 19
Cooking, outdoor, 54, 200-201
Cooking fat as lubricating medium, 179
Cooking hints for campers, 54-55
Cookware, 338-40
cleaning, 4, 339
holders for, 340
shelves for, 268
Copper, cleansing agent for, 186
Cork, 7
for broken light-bulb removal, 174
for gasket repairs, 124
Cork boards, abrasives for finishing, 2
Corkscrews, 79
Corncobs
as camp fire, 53
as depth gauges, 83
Corrosion
abrasives for removing, 2
of dry cell batteries, 33
of toilet floats, 237
Cots for campers, 55
Cotter pins, 79-80
Countersinking, 80
Credit cards
identification plates from, 155
as snow removers, 348
Crocus abrasives, grades and uses for, 2
Cubic units, conversion table for, 73
Cups (unit), conversion table for, 73
Curtain rods, 80-81
Curtain rods (*cont.*)
as compasses, 69
as guard rails, 81
installing, 81
as measuring rods, 80
Curved areas, sanding of, 253, 254-55
painting, 219
sanding, 253, 254-55
Curving wood, 82
Cutting
of foam rubber, 114
of glass, 125-26
heated blade, 147
of metal, 185, 187
of pipe, 14, 185, 313
of plywood, 238

De-burring
pipe, 236
sheet metal, 186
Decals, removing, 83
Decorating aids for Christmas trees, 63
Depth, conversion table for, 73
Depth gauges, 83-84
Dipsticks
automobile, 30
paint, 220
Disassembling, parts sequence in, 246-47, 301
Distances
calculating, 49
conversion table for, 72, 73, 75
See also Measuring instruments
Dogs, 228-29
Door hinges, lubricating, 179-80
Door knobs
as grip for boring holes, 89
tightening, 86
Door mats, 87
Door screens, painting, 218-19
See also Screens
Doorbells for children, 61
Doors, 84-87
child safety and, 61-62
hasps for, 146
lubricating hinges on, 86
noise-reduction for, 84, 86
opening and closing, 86
painting, 211, 220
removing, 86-87
stops for, 87, 153
supports for installing, 298
warped, 85

Doors *(cont.)*
    weatherstripping, 152
Dowels
    drying, 87
    glueing, 12, 87, 129-30
    jigs for cutting, 156
    for pipe cutting, 185
    as polishing attachments, 186
    shaping, 87-88
    storage of, 279
    strengthening, 157
Downspouts
    controlling gushing water in, 140
    leafproofing, 140
Drains
    clogged, 236
    dry wells for, 91-92
    See also Plumbing
Drams (unit), conversion table for, 73
Drawer pulls
    painting, 217, 276
    repairing, 88
Drawers
    childproofing, 59
    moisture reduction for, 154
Drill bits, 89
    holders for, 305
    storage for, 90, 278
Drill chucks
    key holders for, 63-64
    protecting, 304
Drill shafts, renewing sizes on, 52
Drilling, 88-90
    attachments for, 186, 307
    depth gauges for, 83
    in inaccessible areas, 324
    jigs for, 156
    for masonry, 88, 183
    overhead, 90
    plaster wall, 90
    for woodwork, 88
Drinking cups, holsters for, 150
Driveways, 90
Driving stakes, 90-91
Drums, metal, liquid levels in, 355
Dry cell batteries, 33-34
Dry ingredients, 91
Dry wells, 91-92
Duplicate cuts, 92
Dust proofing, 327

Earrings as clamps, 149
Easels, 93

Efflorescence, 93
Electric cords, 97-98
    hanging, 133
    storage of, 280
    underwriters' knot for, 322
    See also Wiring
Electric fans, lubricating, 179
Electric plugs
    epoxy glues for, 94
    fingernail polish for, 95
    magnets for holding, 181
Electric razors as stud finders, 288
Electric switches, plates for, 335
Electrical problems, 93-96
    connections as, 94-95
    insulation as, 95
    outlets as, 96
    plugs as, 94
    wiring as, 93-94
Electrical units, conversion table for, 78
Ellipses, calculating, 50
Emery abrasives, 1-2
Engines, brushes for cleaning, 16
Epoxy glues
    avoiding hardening of, 96
    for electrical plugs, 94
    mixing receptacles for, 130
Epoxy paint, storing, 221
Erasers for rust removal, 250-51
Exercise, barbells improvised for, 33
Expansion bolts, covering, 96
Extension cords, *see* Electric cords
Extra muscle, 98-100
    for furniture, 98-99
    for removing nails, 99
    for unrolling building paper, 100
    for unscrewing caps, 99
Eye hooks, 100

Farm, 101
    See also Gardening
Fathoms, conversion table for, 73
Feet (unit), conversion table for, 73-74, 78
Fences
    driving, 102
    farm, 101
    gate latches for, 102-3
    painting, 103-4, 216
    for pets, 229
    postholes for, 101-2
Fertilizers, garden, 356
Files, 104-5
    cleaning, 104

Good shop practices (*cont.*)
    shelves for, 267
    storage in, 9, 132-33, 135-36, 150-51,
        278, 280-82
    work area arrangements in, 131, 132,
        133
    workbenches in, 13-14, 136-37
Grains (unit), conversion table for, 74
Grams, conversion table for, 74
Graphite grease, 180
Grass shears, repairing, 359
Grease
    cleaning, 66, 67
    dispensers for, 139
    See also Lubricating; Oil
Grease guns, mechanical pencils as, 149
Grease removal, personal, 66-67
Grinding wheels, 139
Grit, 3
Grommets
    electrical, 96
    holes for, 56
Grooves, sanding, 252
Grout, cleaning, 139
Guard rails, curtain rods as, 81
Guides
    cellophane tape as, 181
    magnets as, 181
    masking tape as, 284
    See also Rules
Gum erasers for cleaning car tops, 18
Gutters, roof, *see* Roof gutters
Guy wires, 140

Hacksaw blades
    in close work, 141
    for dressing grinding wheels, 139
    easing metal cuttings with, 186, 187
    heated, 147
    protecting, 304
    as rasps, 244
    as scrapers, 312
    as screwdrivers, 311
    storage of, 141, 281-82
    wider slots with, 141
Hair combs
    as compasses, 70
    as nail holders, 195
    as snow removers, 318
Hammering in apartments, 14
Hammers, 141-43
    hand savers for, 143

Hammers (*cont.*)
    holsters for, 150
    improving, 142, 194
    nail-pulling with, 142-43
    protecting walls from, 143
    as tack extractors, 312
    tightening handles on, 141-42, 316
Hand axes
    grinding techniques for, 316
    protecting, 151, 310
Hand savers, 143-44
Hand tools, 302-17
    carriers for, 309-10
    cleaning, 303
    holders for, 29, 150, 226, 232, 296
        305-10, 313, 316
    improving, 310-15
    mini-, 187-88, 330-31
    multi-purpose, 310-11
    protection of, 302-4, 308-9
    removing handles from, 315-16
    repairing, 315-16
    safety hints for, 6-10
    storing, 132, 204, 278-79, 280, 281-82,
        304
    theft proofing, 293-94
    tightening handles on, 141-42, 316
    See also specific hand tools
Handles
    for boxes, 298
    for flat measuring, 184
    for hydrants, 154
    loose, 141-42
    removing, 315-16
    suitcase, 145
    from thread spools, 144
    tightening, 141-42, 316
    for yardsticks, 313
Handrails, holes in concrete for, 70
Handsaw blades, *see* Hacksaw blades; Saws
Hang-ups, wall, 145
Hard wood, abrasives for finishing, 1
    See also Woodworking
Hardboard as tool carriers, 309-10
Hasps, 146
Hauling, 146-47
    in car trunks, 146-47
    of dirt, 147
    of furniture, 98-99
    of refrigerators, 98
    wood, 146
Hay forks, easing steps of, 151
Headlights, cleaning, 18

Heated blade cutting, 147
Heating systems, 147-48
    filter replacement for, 147
    radiator reflector in, 148
    safety hints for, 9
    soot removal in, 148
    thermostat irregularities in, 148
    for workshops, 344
    See also Fireplaces; Fires; Fuel
Hectares, conversion table for, 74
Hedges, straightening, 148
Height
    calculating, 48-49
    conversion table for, 72, 73, 75
    See also Measuring instruments
Hi-fi speakers, 274
Hinges
    lubricating, 179-80
    rust-prevention for, 280
    storage of, 279-80
Hobbies, tools for, 148-49
Hoes
    cleaning, 357
    garden-hose holders for, 151
    grips for, 357
    theft-proofing, 358
Hoisting, 149-50
Hold-downs, 150
Holders
    for doors, 298
    for hand tools, 29, 150, 226, 232, 296,
        305-10, 313, 316
    for joists, 297
    for kitchen knives, 340
    for measuring tapes, 297
    for nails, 297, 302
    for paintbrushes, 41-43, 44
    for plywood, 299
    for power drills, 307
    for soldering, 296
    for vines, 238
    for yard tools, 357
Holes
    fence, 101-2
    patching wall nail, 223, 224-25
    repairing screen, 260
Holsters, belt, 150, 309
Home accidents, prevention of, 5-10
    See also Safety
Home construction, *see* Building
Home remodeling, 247
Hooking of furniture, 115-16
Hooks
    coat, 68

Hooks (*cont.*)
    eye, 100
Horsepower, conversion table for, 74
Horseshoe pitching sets, 62
Hoses, *see* Automobile hoses; Garden hoses
House numbers, visibility for, 153, 154
Houses
    cleaning, *see* Cleaning
    construction of, *see* Building
    painting, 211, 213-14
Hub caps
    removal of, 22
    as water carriers, 31
Humidity, reducing, 154, 302-3
Hydrants, substitute handles for, 154
Hypodermic needles for glueing, 12

Ice, controlling, 345-48
Ice pick for pre-drilling starter holes, 90
Identification plates, 155
Inches, conversion table for, 73, 74-75, 78
Indoor plants, 155
Insects, control of, 227
Instruction booklets, appliance, 15
Insulation
    electrical, 95, 155
    weather, 57, 152
Insulator connections, 32
Iodine as penetrating oil substitute, 226

Jacks, automobile, 20-21
Jars
    for storage of small parts, 135
    unscrewing caps of, 99
Jigs, 156
    See also Guides; Shields; Templates
Joints, 156-57
    See also Dowels; Glue
Joists, supports for holding, 297
Jumper cables, taping, 26-27

Kerosene
    as campfire starter, 53
    odor from, 198
    for oilstones, 199
    as rust inhibitor, 68
Key holders, floating, 36
Keys, chuck, 63-64
Keys, door
    color-coded, 159
    spare, 158

Motors (*cont.*)
   See also Power machinery
Moving day, 191-92
   See also Hauling
Mulch
   garden, 356
   tree, 56

Nail caddy, 317
Nail holes
   filling, 241
   patching, 223, 224-25
Nails, 192-96
   clinching, 194
   driving, 193
   extraction of, 99, 142-43, 195-96
   hiding, 193
   holders for, 150, 195, 297, 302
   in inaccessible areas, 324
   increasing hammering reach for, 296-97
   magnets for collecting, 181
   safety in using, 194
   soap as lubricating agent for, 179
   types of, 192, 194
Narrow seam soldering, 273
Noise reduction
   in boating, 37
   of cabinet doors, 48
   of doors, 84, 86
   of floors, 112, 355
   of patio furniture, 152
Nozzles
   aerosol spray can, 12-13
   for car washing, 15-16
   garden hose, 121
Nut threads, 300
Nuts, 196-97
   adapting oversized, 196
   containers for, 301
   for inaccessible areas, 323-24
   locking, 197
   storage for, 135, 281

Oarlocks, noise reduction of, 37
Odors
   from cedar closets, 57
   from fireplaces, 198
   from painting, 198
Oil, 178-80
   for appliances, 179
   cleaning, 66-67
   for hinges, 86, 179-80

Oil (*cont.*)
   for locks, 170
   penetrating, 226
   for saws, 257
   for speedometers, 180
   substitutes for, 179
   for tight spots, 178, 324
Oil cans, 198-99
Oilstones, 199-200
Open-coat abrasives, 1
Ornaments, Christmas, 63
Ounces, conversion table for, 76
Outboard boat motors, testing, 38
Outdoor cooking, 54, 200-201
Outdoor fires for campers, 53-54
Outdoor furniture, 201-2
Outdoor lights, 202
Outdoor painting, 211, 213-14
Outdoor swings, safety measures for, 152
Outlets, electrical, 96

Packages
   string for, 285-88
   tying, 203
Padding
   for automobiles, 16-17
   for clamps, 64
   for tool boxes, 308
Padlocks, 344
   See also Locks
Paint, 204-23
   abrasives for finishing, 3, 4
   abrasives for removing, 2, 3
   for accident prevention, 6
   as caulking thinner, 57
   choosing, 204
   drip-catching, 206, 213, 216
   ladder supports for, 165
   luminous, 6
   mixing, 190
   pouring, 205
   recording use of, 219
   small cans of, 207, 208-9
   stabilizing cans of, 207-8
   stirring, 204-5
   storing, 221
   straining, 205-6
   tinting, 213
   trays for, 208
   See also Paintbrushes; Paint buckets;
       Painting
Paint aerosol spray cans, 12-13
Paintbrushes, 40-46

Rouge abrasives, 1, 4
Router bits, 249
Rubber, traction for, 20
Rubber bands
    as plane protectors, 303
    from rubber gloves, 249
    for tool supports on ladders, 163
Rubber cement
    for masonry templates, 88
    in painting, 206, 219
    for rug stiffening, 250
    for rust prevention, 282-83
    sheet metal polishing and, 187
    thinning, 249
    for wall posters, 62
Rubber heels as finish protectors, 106
Rubber tubes
    for pipe patches, 235-36
    for reaching inaccessible items, 323
    See also Garden hoses
Rugs, uncurling, 250
Rules
    magnets for marking metal, 184
    money as, 185
    renewing calibrations on, 52
    visibility improvement for, 184
    zig-zag, 361
    See also Measuring instruments
Runoff water, dry wells for, 91-92
Rust, abrasives for removing, 2, 3
Rust prevention
    for auto chrome, 18-19
    for coffee cans, 69
    for hinges, 280
    of metals, 282-83
    of pipe valves, 344-45
    of steel wool, 278
    storage and, 251, 282-83
    of trailer hitches, 318
Rust removal, 61, 250-51

Saber saws, 257, 280
Safes, 294
Safety
    accident prevention and, 5-10
    adhesives and, 9-10
    in automobile repairs, 29
    broken lights and, 174
    in broken windowpane removal, 128
    with chemicals, 10
    for children, 59
        outdoor swings, 60-61, 152
        poison controls, 238-39

Safety (*cont.*)
    power tools, 60
    sliding doors, 61-62
    in chipping concrete, 183
    Christmas tree, 63
    in drilling metals, 186
    electric lawn mowers and, 169
    electric switches and, 96
    with hand tools, 6-10
    with heating devices, 9
    hose use for, 151
    with ladders, 6, 160-62, 210, 281
    lighting for, 175
    luminous paint for, 6
    in nail driving, 194
    in painting, 210, 213
    for pets, 238-39
    in poison control, 238-39
    safety locks for, 8
    scaffolding and, 6, 259
    stalled automobiles and, 25
    steel wool and, 277
    for swimmers, 289
    in woodworking, 9
Safety chains for swing sets, 60-61
Safety locks, 8
Safety pins
    as box wrench links, 281
    as cotter pins, 79
Safety razors, *see* Razor blades
Salvaging
    of brushes, 46
    of drill bits, 89
    of garbage cans, 119
    in shop work, 56
Sand
    for cleaning yard tools, 357
    for ice control, 346, 349
    removing lumps in, 252
Sand containers for automobiles, 25
Sand sprinklers, 346
Sandboxes, hints for, 62
Sanding
    abrasives for, 1-5
    of curved surfaces, 253, 254-55
    of grooves, 252
    in inaccessible areas, 324
    narrow slit, 4-5
    of small objects, 252
    See also Abrasives; Sandpaper
Sanding belts, storage of, 282
Sanding blocks, 5, 252-55
Sandpaper, 1
    fine grade, 255